A.T.I.'S Nursing Q&A

A.T.I.'S NURSING Q&A
Critical-Thinking Exercises

Sally Lambert Lagerquist, RN, MS

President and Course Coordinator, Review for Nurses, Inc. and RN Tapes Company; Former Instructor of Undergraduate, Graduate, and Continuing Education, School of Nursing, University of California, San Francisco

Assessment Technologies Institute™ LLC

ATI Technologies Institute™, LLC
Overland Park, Kansas

Library of Congress Cataloging-in-Publication Data

Lagerquist, Sally L.

   A.T.I.'s nursing Q&A: critical-thinking exercises / Sally Lambert Lagerquist.

   p. cm. — (RN NCLEX® review series)

Includes bibliographical references and index.
   ISBN 0976006308

   1. Nursing—Examinations, questions, etc. I. Title. II. Series.

   RT55.L34 2004-2005

610.73'076—dc2O   96-10793 CIP

Notice. The indications for and dosages of all drugs in this book have been recommended in the medical literature and conform to the practices of the general medical community. The medications described do not necessarily have specific approval by the Food and Drug Administration for use in the diseases and dosages for which they are recommended. The package insert for each drug should be consulted for use and dosage as approved by the FDA. Because standards for usage change, it is advisable to keep abreast of revised recommendations, particularly those concerning new drugs.

Printed in the United States of America

MV-NY

Author/Editor: Sally Lagerquist
Production Editor: Sally Volkoff
Art Direction: Hara Allison
Design Production: Element Media Productions
Illustrator: Allen Croswhite
Programmer: Trevor Gunter
Proofreaders: Angie Rothrock and Molly Obetz
Acquisiton Editor: Bob Cole

Dedication

This book is dedicated to...

My *husband* - This book is my tribute to you for all that you are, all that you've done all these years for me, for us, for our family, and for Review for Nurses.

Together always (22/7), through seasons of joys and days of trials.
Over 39 years of blazing new trails (both professionally and personally.)
Making memories for us to cherish, meeting challenges all along the way.

Our *daughter* - We are the grateful recipients of your...

Enthusiastic, energetic, "I'll handle it" approach as you take on many of your own professional responsibilities as well as continuing to care for us, your extended family.
Loving kindness, even when we seem not to "hear" your guidance.
Acceptance of us for the way we are (most of the time) as we put on years.
Nurturing ways as your envelope us still as an important part of your life.
Artistic talents - to be admired in awe!

Our *son-in-law* - "Appreciation" is an understatement for your "gifts" to us of your...

Determination to master technology and enter into a new healthcare field with us as our webmaster and then some!
Acumen and amazing instinct for what to do, when to do it, and how to make our new ventures such a success.
Non-verbal expressions of your sensitivity to our cares and concerns. You have been there for us many times!

Our *first granddaughter*...

Kisses to Kaya Marina, who loves to laugh and say "skunk", to sing and dance to any music with a beat (especially to "Big Island Guys.")
Always inquisitive, always verbal, as well as highly imaginative in "pretend play"
You bring smiles and joyfulness to our lives, as we share in your growing up (from infancy and ongoing.)
Amazing in your innate ability to learn, retain and apply whatever you see and hear all around you.

continued on next page

Our *son* - Through 31+ years you have been our "svenska pojke". You have...

Kind-spirited ways when special family needs call for an extra "dose" (e.g. when caring for your 92 year old grandmother.)

Amazing aptitude, intellect, and memory to learn whatever you need to do, want to do.

Loving ways, especially when connecting your past and present, and responding to your own multicultural heritage.

Energy and enthusiasm to do more in a day than most people can even conceive of!

Never-ending passion for new experiences and adding new interests to an already admirable list.

Contents

Preface

An open letter to all nursing students and graduate nurses who want a practical study guide for hands-on review of nursing knowledge, and who want to apply critical-thinking and diagnostic reasoning skills to real-life clinical situations...

Every nursing student needs to be familiar with the most important content in each major clinical area: medical, surgical, obstetric, pediatric, and psychiatric care. *A.T.I.'s Nursing Q&A: Critical-Thinking Exercises* is designed to effectively provide the essential content you need in order to master all exams throughout nursing school, as well as achievement tests, and re-entry and challenge exams. This highly practical and concise study guide provides you with important means for developing competency in taking nursing exams while in school, and focuses on *nursing behaviors* (nursing process) applied to *integrated* health care management situations throughout the *life cycle* (childhood and adolescent years, young adulthood, adult years, older adult years).

You'll study 75 cases representing situations that are encountered in all areas of nursing. You'll be able to think through major considerations for each case and review management of client care in each of the major clinical areas. You'll be able to work with nursing diagnoses (nursing problems) and look for desired client outcome.

Features of this book:

1. The exam preparation guide (**Part I**) offers tips and strategies for optimum performance.

2. Detailed *case management scenarios*, covering all stages of the life cycle, precede nursing process–oriented critical-thinking exercises (**Part II**). Behavioral and physical components of health care are *integrated*; client needs and nursing problems are selected from the major health care areas and combined within a *life cycle* framework. The detailed case management scenarios are presented for practice and self-evaluation of your ability to *apply the steps of the nursing process*.

3. Reference codes are provided in **Part III** for all questions in this book. The codes represent *four* areas—*nursing process, client needs and subneeds, cognitive level,* and *human function,* to help you determine which areas you need to concentrate on for further study.

4. The book also includes two additional study aids: an *Index to Nursing Problems/Diagnosis* and an *Index to Medical Diagnosis/Case*

Management Scenarios. For each case, questions that cover *nursing problems/diagnosis* are cataloged in the nursing problems/diagnosis index and *medical problems* are cataloged in the case management scenario index. These indexes are indispensable tools for determining which practice questions test similar problems; they focus your review by identifying related content areas.

We compiled this book in direct response to the requests from our students who want a study guide with practice questions and answers to use during nursing school. These requests came from more than 300,000 students who have attended our Review for Nurses courses held nationwide since 1976, and from subscribers to our online and taped review series. The enrollees find that the practice tests from our review lectures on each clinical topic, combined with our online and taped review series, are the most effective and successful ways to review for the nursing exams. We are pleased to offer this edition of the book along with the other NCLEX-RN® review study aids available through A.T.I.; Review for Nurses, Inc.*; and Review for Nurses Tapes Company** to help you in your review of nursing.

This study aid is companion to and is coordinated with the following nursing review resources:

- *A.T.I.'s NurseNotes Series* (Medical-Surgical, Pediatrics, Maternal-Newborn, and Psychiatric-Mental Health).

- *Davis's NCLEX-RN® Success.*

- The NCLEX-RN® Review classroom courses offered nationwide and sponsored by *Review for Nurses, Inc.*

- The nursing process–oriented NCLEX-RN® Review lecture series on DVD/CD-ROM, audiocassette and videotape, produced by *Review for Nurses Tapes Company.*

- *P.A.S.S.™ Online Test* on *reviewfornurses.com* website.

- The special Relaxation Approaches for Nurses, also produced by *Review for Nurses Tapes Company*, on audiocassette.

- *Effective Test-taking Techniques*, on audiocassette, produced by *Review for Nurses Tapes Company.*

- *Review of Diets and Review of Drugs for NCLEX-RN®*, on CD and audiocassettes, produced by *Review for Nurses Tapes Company.*

The questions included in *A.T.I.'s Nursing Q&A: Critical-Thinking Exercises* are field-tested to include relevant trends, latest knowledge, and current practice, and are directly geared to the main clinical nursing content and behaviors currently covered on the NCLEX-RN®. Complete answers with detailed rationale are included to help you understand the reasons behind the best choice and to explain why the other choices can be eliminated.

We believe that a question-answer book such as this one should serve several purposes:

*Review for Nurses, Inc. is an organization that conducts nationwide review courses.
**Review for Nurses Tapes Company publishes nursing lectures on video disks, and printed study guides.

1. The primary purpose is to serve as a *tool for evaluation* of knowledge in specific subject areas and application of the nursing process to acute and chronic health problems in children and adults.

Practice questions in this book can be used for self-evaluation of *baseline content knowledge* and application of nursing process, and to *pinpoint* where further study, review, and practice are needed in any step of the nursing process or subject areas. By taking these practice tests, you will be able to assess your *patterns of difficulties* by determining the types of questions—related to nursing process and human function areas—that pose difficulties for you. Do the questions you answer incorrectly deal with knowledge of nutrition?, elimination?, growth and development?, the process of assessment?, the process of determining priorities of nursing action?, interpersonal relationships?, your own speed and accuracy in reading the case description and the stem and options? The test questions in **Part II** of this book reflect the type of nursing process–oriented questions that are typical on nursing exams with integrated case scenarios covering the life cycle.

2. The book should also serve as a *learning tool*.

We include detailed answers, with explanations, to *reinforce* what you know, to *fill in gaps* of information, and to *clarify* points as you go through each clinical area in nursing school. Our questions-answers are designed to emphasize how to *apply nursing process* and *transfer your knowledge* of essential concepts and principles to a test question.

The answer sections, with rationale for all the options, help you to look at *reasons* for the correct and incorrect answers and discourage rote memorization of a correct response.

In addition to fulfilling the two main purposes for a study guide in a question-and-answer format, this book includes *special* features that are essential to the process of doing well on exams; namely, **how to study effectively** (how to take notes from lectures and textbooks), **how to prepare yourself emotionally**, **how to cope with exam anxiety**, and **how to take tests**. We believe that all too often the student is blocked from exceptional performance in exams, not only by lack of basic knowledge, but also by not knowing how to study and not having the test-taking know-how, as well as by a high level of anxiety.

The experience of fear, anxiety, and apprehension about exams is a common pitfall. These feelings can affect how you think, what you remember, and your critical judgment in analyzing questions. Special sections in this book are devoted to test-taking approaches and to anxiety reduction. These sections are aimed at helping you to overcome the feelings of dread and inadequacy, and to gain confidence in what you know, your ability to apply what you know to an unfamiliar situation, and your ability to take tests and handle exam-related anxiety.

This study guide is a tool designed to test nursing students for competency in providing safe nursing care in any health situation in all clinical areas. It is crucial for you to be proficient in taking objective tests. *A.T.I.'s Nursing*

Q&A: Critical-Thinking Exercises contains critical-thinking exercises with more than 1,000 objective questions. They will provide you with the opportunity to *master test-taking techniques* and to *apply classroom content* to a test-taking situation, as well as to *evaluate your knowledge* base and identify areas where you may need further study.

Theoretical content has been omitted from this book, as this material is completely reviewed in A.T.I.'s *NurseNotes* series and *Davis's NCLEX-RN® Success*, which is co-authored by some of the contributors to this book.

The special experience of our contributing authors in successfully conducting our nationally held NCLEX-RN® review courses, plus their expertise in teaching major clinical nursing subjects at leading US schools of nursing, has enabled us to prepare these practice questions and answers for you with a key goal in mind—to assist you in reviewing nursing content thoroughly and effectively, with minimum stress and maximum success and confidence.

We are pleased to offer *A.T.I.'s Nursing Q&A: Critical-Thinking Exercises* as a study guide and nursing exam review aid for you. We welcome your comments so that we can continue in our collaborative effort to respond to your needs and to continue to offer effective review study guides that increase your confidence and skills as a nursing practitioner, as well as in test-taking situations. Here's to a successful performance on the exams!

S.L.L.

Acknowledgments

To *Sally Volkoff*...
We share the same first name, but you are *one-of-a-kind*! This book wouldn't have happened without your....

Singular devotion to getting this book done, despite a number of "pulls" on your energy and time, and stops and starts.
Attention to a myriad of complex details.
Labor-intensive coordination involving five different authors and their variable timeframes.
Learning as you went along to avoid pitfalls with a "can-do" attitude at all times.
Yardstick of excellence by which to measure this project.

To *Don Walde*...
Your contagious enthusiasm and super responsiveness to our many calls was the beacon that steered us through from start to crossing the finish line. You are a significant part of this successful venture.

To *John Hemmingson*...
You had a vision of our mutual efforts being a success...we met...we joined forces...this book happened! You are more to me than the collection of the many "hats" that you wear - you are my friend!

Book Reviewers

Item Writers for the Disk in This Edition

Janet Baatz Darrow, MS, RN, CPN
Lecturer
San Jose State University
San Jose, California
(Pediatrics)

Christine Hooper, RN EdD
Associate Professor
San Jose State University
San Jose, California
(Medical-Surgical)

Janice McMillin, BSN, MSN, EdD
Instructor of Maternal-Child
    Nursing
Sacramento State University
Clinical Coordinator of Family
    Birth Center
Methodist Hospital
Sacramento, California
(Maternal-Newborn)

Mary St. John Seed, RN, PhD
Associate Professor
Department of Community Mental
Health
School of Nursing
University of San Francisco
San Francisco, California
(Psychiatric-Mental Health)

Kathleen E. Snider, RN, MSN, CNS
Professor of Nursing
Los Angeles Valley College
Valley Glen, California
(Pediatrics)

Christine Hooper, RN, EdD
Associate Professor
San Jose State University
San Jose, California
(Medical-Surgical)

Janice McMillin, BSN, MSN, EdD
Instructor of Maternal-Child
    Nursing
Sacramento State University
Clinical Coordinator of Family
    Birth Center Methodist Hospital
Sacramento, California
(Maternal-Newborn)

Mary St. John Seed, RN, PhD
Associate Professor
Department of Community Mental
    Health
School of Nursing
University of San Francisco
San Francisco, California
(Psychiatric-Mental Health)

Kathleen E. Snider, RN, MSN, CNS
Professor of Nursing
Los Angeles Valley College
Valley Glen, California
(Pediatrics)

Contributing Authors to Previous Editions

Judith E. Barrett, RN, MSN, MNP
Former Associate Professor, University of San Francisco, School of Nursing, San Francisco

Irene M. Bobak, RN, PhD, FAAN
Professor Emerita, Women's Health and Maternity Nursing, San Francisco State University, San Francisco

Geraldine C. Colombraro, RN, MA, PhD
Assistant Dean, Center for Continuing Education in Nursing and Health Care, Lienhard School of Nursing, Pace University, Pleasantville, New York

Jane Corbett, RN, MS, PhD
Professor Emerita, University of San Francisco, School of Nursing, San Francisco

Marlene Farrell, RN, MA
Former Professor of Nursing, California State University, Los Angeles

Sandra Faux, RN, MN
Former Faculty, University of Illinois College of Nursing, Chicago

Lois A. Fenner Giles, RN, MS
Former Faculty, University of Maryland, School of Nursing, Baltimore, Maryland

Marilyn Brolin Hopkins, RN, MS, DNSc
Professor of Nursing, California State University, Sacramento, California

Sister Mary Brian Kelber, RN, DNSc
Associate Professor, University of San Francisco, School of Nursing, San Francisco

Sally Lambert Lagerquist, RN, MS
President and Course Coordinator, Review for Nurses, Inc. and RN Tapes Company; Former Instructor of Undergraduate, Graduate, and Continuing Education in Nursing, University of California, San Francisco, School of Nursing, San Francisco

Diane R. Lapkin, RN, MS, EdD
Former Dean, School of Nursing, Salem State College, Salem, Massachusetts

Sister Mary Peter McKusker, RN, MS, MA
Former Instructor, Puno, Peru

Janice Majewski Rhoades, RN, MS, DNSc
Former Clinical Research Nurse, Cardiac Rehabilitation, Sequoia Hospital District, Redwood City, California

Karen L. Miller, RN, MSN
Wilmette, Illinois

Robyn M. Nelson, RN, DNSc
Department Chair and Professor of Nursing, California State University, Sacramento, California

Agnes F. Padernal, RN, MS
Former Assistant Clinical Professor, University of California, Los Angeles, School of Nursing, Los Angeles

Kathy Rose, RN, MS
Former Assistant Professor, University of Illinois School of Nursing, Chicago

Williamina Rose, RN, MS
Former Education Director and Associate Professor, Montana State University, Butte Extended Campus, Butte, Montana

Patricia Sparacino, RN, MS
Vice Chairperson, Family Health Care Nursing, University of California School of Nursing, San Francisco

Janice Horman Stecchi, RN, EdD
Dean Emerita, College of Health Professions, University of Massachusetts Lowell, Lowell, Massachusetts

Janet Jordan Veatch, RN, MN
Clinical Nurse Specialist, Pediatric Oncology, University of California, San Francisco, Department of Nursing, San Francisco

Kathleen Hickel Viger, RN, MS
Director of Nursing, River Ridge Brain Injury Rehabilitation Center, Kennebunk, Maine

How to Use This Book

Student's Use of Case Scenarios

- Read **Part I** first, focusing on the test-preparation guidelines (intellectual, emotional, and physical preparation).

- Read and practice the suggested approaches for anxiety reduction in order to experience self-mastery over anxiety.

- Familiarize yourself with the chapter on *how to take tests*.

- Test your ability to *apply nursing process* to integrated health care situations by answering the questions in **Part II**.

- Set a 1-minute time limit per question.

- Read the case situations and the stems of the questions carefully, paying attention to key words. Be sure not to "read into" the stem.

- Select the *best* answer from the presented options. Circle the letter of the best choice.

- After you have completed a particular exam section (or at the end of the time limit), look up the correct answers.

- Study the rationale given to help you to *understand* the *process* of selecting the best answer and the reasons *why* the *other* options are incorrect. Do not memorize the correct answer, because it is not likely to appear in exactly the same form on any other test you might take; instead, use the reasoning process to help you on other test questions.

- Using the reference codes explained on page 427-428, see if there is a pattern to the type of questions you answered incorrectly: Did you have trouble with questions that deal with sensory-perceptual functions?, fluid and gas? Or did you incorrectly answer questions that require you to analyze presented data, select goals, and intervene with priority measures? If you identify patterns, focus your content review on those areas.

- For more detailed review of specific content areas, refer to *A.T.I.'s NurseNotes Series* and *Davis's NCLEX-RN® Success*, the references given at the end of this book, and your own class notes or textbooks.

Before you can do well on the nursing *process-oriented questions*, you need to know *nursing content*.

- If you answer 80% to 85% of the questions in this book correctly, you can feel confident in your ability to do well on nursing exams.

Instructor's Use of Case Scenarios

Teaching/Learning Objectives that Can Be Met by Using the Case Scenarios

Focus

To separate major nursing problems from secondary ones
To clarify major nursing care problem(s)
To seek a clear statement of the nursing care problem(s)

Language

To define key terms
To practice clear and precise charting

Assumptions

To recognize values, frame of reference, and stereotypes held by client, family, health professionals, health agency, and society

Assessment/Data Gathering

To determine relevance of assessment data to clinical situation
To take into account the total situation
To categorize data

Analysis

To note patterns and relationships in the case study data
To make appropriate inferences based on assessment data

Evaluation

To develop criteria for expected outcome and unexpected consequences

Overall Benefits

1. Discussing ideas in an organized way, to exchange and explore thoughts and ideas with others

2. Viewing a situation from different perspectives in order to develop in-depth comprehension

Suggestions for Instructor's Use of Case Scenarios

This book has 75 case situations that cover each of the major clinical nursing areas of Pediatrics, Maternity and the Childbearing Family, Acute and Chronic Care of the Adult, Geriatrics, and Mental Health Throughout the Lifespan.

The instructor can select the number of cases that fit his or her class schedule (6-, 12-, or 16-week course). From the 75 cases, the instructor can even select some cases to use one year and then use a completely different set the next year. If problem-based learning and critical thinking is the core component of the nursing program, instructors in *each* clinical rotation and theory class can use all of the cases as part of team teaching during the academic year.

Instructors can use these cases for varying purposes. *One* use is as a substitute for lectures. *Another* is to add them to clinical seminars, with the goal of expanding or reemphasizing aspects of the case that are being discussed in lecture or encountered in the clinical experience at that time.

A *third* possible use of the case scenarios is as supplements in a program that is reduced in scope. A *fourth* possibility is for the instructor to use the cases as a review at the end of each clinical area, or for self-assessment by the students.

The following formats for use in the classroom have proved successful.

A case scenario is assigned for reading; the students meet in small groups to share information based on previous knowledge, and to decide on the answers. They are asked to provide rationale for their choices.

The instructor can then point out relevant data in the vignette, add what further assessment is needed, and introduce new questions related to other conditions.

A "What if…" approach can stimulate lively discussions. "If… then… on the other hand" are useful beginnings for discussions that center on critical thinking; these discussions can have the learning impact of first-hand experience.

Exploration of stereotypes can also come from these cases. Ask the students to discuss their mental picture of a homeless person, an elderly person living alone, a person with a lifestyle dissimilar from their own. The instructor can then propose alternative frames of reference through which students can view a particular situation or set of facts.

This allows for an intensive analysis of the selected case and associated conditions. The students can achieve a depth of knowledge that is useful not only for the short-term (one course), but also for long-term use in their clinical years after graduation.

Sample Study Questions that Can Be Used as Additional Critical–Thinking Exercises

Adult

1. Was the condition related to lifestyle choices?, genetic factors?, environmental factors?

2. Discuss a controversial issue. For example, should CPR be attempted on someone over 85 years of age? Ask students to support their position with reasons.

3. How would your concerns be different if you were seeing the client for home health care?

Peds

1. Should all children be immunized? Ask the students to support their position.

2. A preschool child is to have a T&A tomorrow morning. What will you do to prepare the child so the child is cooperative? How will you present the information if the child does not speak English?, can't hear?, can't see?

3. What is it about the situation that will bring you feelings of satisfaction?, frustration?

Maternity

1. How would your nursing care plan be different if there were complications like diabetes or an infectious disease?

2. What is the significance of the findings?

3. What are your assumptions about bonding?

Mental Health

1. How would you use your senses (sight, hearing, smell, touch) to collect additional data? For example, what visual observations would you make?

2. What are your assumptions about appropriate behaviors?, individual rights?, beliefs?, values?

3. What would you do to validate your initial assumptions about the client's expectations?

I. How to Prepare for Examinations

Introduction

You do not need an inborn gift or a magic secret to do well on tests. You do need to prepare yourself intellectually, emotionally, and physically. This is something you can learn. The person who just whizzes through exams not only has mastered the material, but also has developed a certain test-taking know-how and an effective approach to coping with anxiety.

1. Preparing Yourself Intellectually

The learning process relates and mingles information from many sources. It is impossible to be intellectually prepared without studying the information contained in your textbooks and that conveyed in classroom lectures. This section segregates the components of intellectual preparedness, for simplicity, but all are interrelated.

How to Study

Study necessitates committing certain facts and concepts to memory. If you have had trouble memorizing in the past, or if it has seemed unimportant, we offer some approaches that can increase your success. Give them a try. There is no getting around the fact that training your memory requires effort. But it is an essential step toward your goals—graduation, and your RN License.

Preparation for nursing exams involves memorizing some facts. Some questions directly test your knowledge base. The majority of the questions usually emphasize logical reasoning, interpersonal relationships, and your application of nursing process (i.e., assessing needs, setting priorities, implementing goals, evaluating results).

13 Ways to Aid Your Memory

1.   To remember anything, you must believe it is worthwhile. That is the first step. If you do not feel the subject matter itself is worth memorizing, it is hard to feel involved with the content. Make it *important to your self-concept* (e.g., as a nurse, you need to know CPR) that you know the material. Also, recognize that your goal (passing nursing exams) demands this knowledge. If you want to achieve your goal, you will accept the need to memorize certain facts (such as growth and development milestones, lab values, dosages, drug side effects) as an unpleasant but necessary adjunct.

2.   In addition, you must begin your study with the intention of remembering the material.

3.   Have confidence in yourself and your ability to remember the best answer.   Set aside negatives, such as "I didn't study enough." Forget past experiences of not doing well on objective exams. We will talk more about attitude in the chapter on emotional preparation, but you must take a positive approach if you want to study effectively.

4.   Be flexible in your learning and study patterns. If you are comfortable with the approaches you use and they are effective for you, continue with what is successful. But if you have a mental block against studying or feel you have been unsuccessful in the past, try some new methods. Do not immediately discard an idea because it sounds silly. Give it a chance. If your methods are not meeting the challenge, what is the harm of trying something new?

5. *Schedule time to study* and find out what time frame is effective for you. Perhaps you learn best when you set aside 3 or 4 hours of uninterrupted time and focus totally on study. On the other hand, you may have trouble maintaining your attention for a long period. For you, intense 1-hour periods throughout the day may be more effective.

Many people find it worthwhile to use otherwise wasted time (waiting for and riding public transit, waiting for appointments) to review notes or textbooks. This spreads "study" through the day and makes it less tedious. It takes some planning, but discipline is a necessity regardless of your study method.

Some authorities recommend scheduling study periods in such a way that you will learn material close to the time you intend to use it. If, for example, you have decided to learn yoga and you intend to practice it in the early morning and before dinner, try to find a yoga class that meets at those times.

6. *Eliminate interruptions.* Memory requires your full attention. The mental assimilation process is disrupted by jangling telephones and the competition of television.

7. *Explain and rephrase* the process or concept aloud, first to yourself and then to a friend or classmate. It is impossible to remember something you do not understand. Role-playing can be useful. Deliver a mini-lecture to a classmate on some aspect of nursing. Ask your classmate for criticisms and questions. Then switch roles. If you cannot explain something, you may not really know it.

8. *Associate what you want to memorize with something you already know.* If what you are trying to learn disagrees with what you already know, so much the better. Trying to figure out which is right and where the disagreement lies will fix the new information in your mind more quickly.

9. *Assign priorities and establish orders of importance.* Organizing the material so that you can file it in your memory bank requires you to act on the material. This makes remembering easier because you have created a mental outline of what is important, what is subsidiary, and how the whole fits together. If you can remember part of it, often you can then remember the rest. Physically jotting down an outline (add it to your notes) will help fix the material in your mind.

10. *Organize by dividing and grouping.* Associate like or related points. Then place them in the appropriate contexts. Information is best taken in as "little packets."

11. *"Use a word three times and it is yours."* This adage may work for you—not only for words, but for concepts as well. If your task is to learn a number of unfamiliar medical terms, begin *using them in your conversations*—particularly with other nursing students, and even with roommates and friends. Nonnursing students may enjoy the game. Encourage them to participate by occasionally asking you to spell terms or questioning you on their meaning. Substitute appropriate medical terminology for lay language at every chance.

12. *Make your mistakes work for you.* Review test results and any comments from the instructor. Why was your answer incorrect? And what is the correct response? Do some research and find out. You clearly remember embarrassing moments in your life. Apply the same principle to test mistakes—learn from them. It is easy to remember your mistakes. You can then work to eliminate them.

13. *Finally, use devices and gimmicks as aids.* Mechanical memory aids are called *mnemonic devices.* You create them yourself. Establish some pattern for remembering otherwise tedious or easily forgotten material (such as the cranial nerves). Such devices are best applied to rote memorization of terms: parts of the body or its systems, for example. Usually the first letter, letters, or syllable of a group of related items are combined to form words—the more bizarre sounding, the better, if it helps jog your memory.

Or perhaps you can identify an existing pattern among the things you must memorize that is reflected in an actual word. For example, the first letters of the terms for the parts of a certain system may spell "carrot." Remember that system as the carrot system; this will jog your memory when you need the specific names.

Mnemonic devices must be kept simple. Creating a more complex system than the one you are attempting to remember is self-defeating.

Individuals who must remember the names of a number of people they meet only briefly often use the association approach. Salesmen employ it in their work, businesswomen make use of it at cocktail parties, and many people apply it to daily situations. When you are introduced to Mr. John Harrington, repeat his name and look for something striking about the man. If you can associate his name with something he is wearing or a physical characteristic, so much the better. John Harrington in the herringbone jacket. If not, focus on the most memorable, preferably outrageous, element of the person's appearance. Long, tall Mr. McFadden. Use rhymes if possible. Electric blue, Lyla LaRue.

This approach can be expanded to facts and ideas. Associate the idea or fact with an illustration—a diagram, a drawing, a map. Visualize that illustration and mentally tack, staple, or glue the fact to it. Picture your class lecturer conveying a certain important piece of information. Visualize his or her actions: noting the number or word on the blackboard, gesturing to indicate it was important, raising the voice to emphasize it.

These are general hints to help you remember more effectively. Let us look now at methods for mastering the lecture and the textbook.

How to Listen and Take Lecture Notes

Knowing how to listen effectively is the key to learning from lectures. You cannot take useful notes until you have developed your listening skills. Listening is not instinctive, nor is effective listening a passive process. You can learn to listen effectively and improve your listening skills with practice.

10 Steps to Effective Listening

1. The first step is the appropriate mind-set. Figure out why what the lecturer is saying is important to you. You need to have a *reason for listening.* The subject may interest you, or the topic may be important to you only because it will help you to score well on a test. Whatever your reason, motivate yourself to focus on it.

2. Set up a conducive physical environment for learning. Eliminate distractions. Choose your seat in the lecture room carefully. The center front section is usually best. Position yourself so that you can see and hear the speaker without glare or craning your neck or shifting constantly in your seat. Avoid sources of noise—fans, open doors, students who are talking. If you find what is going on outside more interesting than what is happening in the lecture, do not sit next to the window. If heat makes you drowsy, avoid the heater or the direct sun.

3. Get your note-taking supplies together. A loose-leaf notebook that lies flat works best for most people. You can reorganize and add material later. Wide-lined paper helps keep things in order and will make review easier. Try a nonglare paper—light green or light gray. Have plenty of blank paper in reserve so you do not run out during the lecture.

A pen requires less pressure than a pencil, so it saves energy. Your notes will also be easier to read. Carry two pens; if one runs out of ink, you will have a backup.

Label what you are recording with the name of the course, the date, and the subject matter. Use one large notebook, with dividers for each course, or a series of smaller notebooks, one for each subject.

You have prepared your mind and your materials. You are ready to begin listening.

4. Do not let the speaker's appearance or mannerisms distract you from the content. If you disagree with what is being said, pay more attention. We tend to tune out what we do not agree with, but opposing ideas are one of the best sources of new information.

5. Identify the speaker's organization. Focus your listening to look for the main ideas. Recognize digressions and figure out what is being supported or explained by them.

6. Taking notes helps you to pay attention. Write down all important points, even those you think you know. These notes will remind you of the lecture content later, in your review.

A handy device for improving your listening and concentration abilities is the *TQLR* approach: *Tune in, Question, Listen,* and *Review.* It summarizes what we have been talking about.

7. Tune your mind to the lecture about to begin. Block out distractions. Consolidate and focus your energy on this one task. *Look* at the lecturer to help focus your attention.

8. Formulate questions as you focus your mind. "What's the lecturer going to talk about today?" "What should I get out of it?" "I wonder if the lecturer will explain the material that I was having trouble with yesterday?" You are becoming interested.

9. Listen carefully. Keep your eyes on the speaker and your mind on what is being said. Focus on *main points* and important details, look for the speaker's *organization*, and *relate* one point to another. Be alert to tone, gestures, repetition, illustrations, and useful words such as "remember," "but," "most important," "however," and "rarely."

10. Review constantly during the lecture. Think back and see if a pattern is emerging. Clarify anything you are unsure of by asking questions at the end of the lecture. Look for implications beyond what is being said. Relate the content to your other classes and life experiences.

Ways to *practice your listening skills* include jotting down one identifying word for each item in a news broadcast. After the broadcast, fill in as much detail as you can remember for each item.

Another *practice suggestion* is: For 1 minute of each hour of 1 day, give your full listening attention to the person talking. If no one is talking, focus on a sound.

9 Guidelines to Taking Effective Lecture Notes

Taking notes is part of effective listening. Try the following general guidelines if you want to improve your note-taking skills. Many of them are identical with the principles of effective listening.

1. Understanding something does not guarantee remembering it. Write it down to *reinforce* it in your mind.

2. Sort and filter information. Note only the *main points*. Think before you write. You want only information that will be of value later, not a verbatim transcript.

3. Use *key* words or *short* sentences. During digressions, go back and fill in sketchy notations.

4. Develop your own system of *abbreviations, underlining,* and *starring.* Try a skeleton outline format. Show importance by *indenting.* Leave plenty of space for later additions.

5. Use your own words, but be accurate. *Condense* and *rephrase.* This active involvement helps you understand what is being said.

6. Do not worry about missing a point. *Leave space* and fill it in later.

7. Keep your notes in a *notebook.* Do not use scraps of paper or the backs of envelopes.

8. Set aside time to *rework*, not just recopy, your notes as soon after taking them as possible. Add points. Spell out unclear items. Fill in any gaps. Try summarizing the important points and making up some test questions on the material. Jot them down at the end of your notes. They will be valuable when you are reviewing before exams. Arrange to compare notes with other students.

9. Try to *review* your notes periodically during the course. Do not let this go until the week before exams.

5 R Method

In summary, if the notes you take now do not seem to be of much use, try the **5 R method** - *Record, Reduce, Recite, Reflect,* and *Review.*

Make two columns, a 6-inch column at the right and a 2-inch column at the left. This immediately limits the quantity of notes you can *record*, because the lecture notes go in the 6-inch column. Use the 2-inch column to *reduce* your lecture notes. Use "flags"—words such as "important," "memorize," or two- or three-word summaries of the material in the 6-inch column.

Now cover the 6-inch column and *recite*, using the 2-inch column to jog your memory. If you cannot do this, reread your notes and try again.

Reflect on the relationship of one idea to another, the important points, and the interconnections.

And finally, *review* your notes at intervals throughout the course.

How to Use a Textbook

Mastering a textbook requires the same active involvement as learning from a lecture. Think as you read. You may read a novel or a magazine as a diversion from the pressures and anxieties of the day. It is fine to let your mind wander when you are reading for pleasure or to escape. But using your "novel" approach on the textbook will be a disaster.

Remember that *attending the lectures* will make your reading easier and more effective. Often the content of the lecture will parallel the material in the textbook and you will have a better idea of what to look for during your reading. Also, the repetition will help fix the information in your mind.

When you buy a new text, first *look the whole book over*. Read the *table of contents* to find out what is in the book and how it is organized. Do you know anything about the author—interests, orientation—that will help you understand the material? You may find some of this information in the preface or the introduction. Is the author your lecturer?

Look in the *back of the book*. Find out what is there so you can use it in your study. Does the book have a *glossary*? Take a look at the words in it. Tape a tab or glue a piece of cardboard to the edge of the first page of the glossary to help you find it easily as you study.

Skim through the *index*. See what percentage of the words you recognize. It will help you determine how hard the material will be for you. And remember to use the index to help you review for exams.

See if the book contains an *overview* or a *summary*. If your time is limited, that may be all you read.

Look at a chapter. See how it is constructed. (They will all be organized in the same way.) Is there a summary at the beginning . . . or at the end? Has the author provided *study questions* at the end of each chapter or section or at the back of the book? Know what is there so you can make use of it.

O K 4 R Method

When there is a choice between "quick and effective" and "slow and effective," it makes sense to choose "quick." There is a quick, effective way to master the textbook. It is simply a matter of focusing your energy. Why spread the process out by plodding along, when with a little more effort you can successfully learn what you need to know in much less time? Use the **OK4R** method: *Overview, Key ideas, Read, Recall, Reflect,* and *Review.*

When you open the textbook to begin an assignment, do not start to read immediately. First orient yourself. Establish a direction for your mind. Set it on a track.

Overview

To get an *overview*, look at the first and last paragraphs of the material. Read the headings and examine the illustrations. With this approach, you discover the organization and give yourself a basis for selecting and rejecting, to speed your reading. The overview also prods your mind to remember related knowledge, and it arouses your interest, as well as giving you a double exposure.

The point of the overview is to focus your reading. Now you are ready to begin.

Key Ideas

What you are looking for in each paragraph is the *key idea*. You will usually find it in the first sentence. Sort it out from the examples. All these do is repeat the key idea in a variety of ways, so read them quickly. When you come to the key idea, slow down and read carefully.

A good way to remember key ideas is to *turn them into questions*. This helps you to keep in touch with what you are reading. If you think the key idea is that the dynamics of schizophrenia are interrelated, ask yourself, "How are they interrelated?" Then look for the answers to your question as you read the paragraph or section.

You now have a general idea of the assignment and you are looking for key ideas.

Read

As you *read*, ask yourself, "What main point is being made in this section?" Look at everything you read and relate it to that point. Keep in mind that recognition and learning is not the same thing. You do not necessarily *understand* something simply because it is familiar.

Recall

When you finish a section, look away from the page. You are ready for the second **R**. Say to yourself, "The main point of this section is _____ ___." If you can repeat the main point, you have successfully completed the *recall* step. If you cannot remember it, repeat the overview and key idea steps. When you are sure you understand and remember the main point—and *not* before—make notes and mark the textbook.

Jot down your notes from memory, using your own words. Use cue words and short phrases. Making notes from memory minimizes self-deception. Either you can write down the main points or you cannot.

There are many *ways to mark a textbook*. Use whatever works best for you—or a combination of the methods we suggest.

1. Circle (key words) or phrases.

2. Underline <u>major points</u>.

3. Fold corners of pages containing important information or tables and charts to which you refer repeatedly.

4. Use vertical lines in the margin to emphasize important items you have underlined.

5. Place some symbol—an asterisk (*), an X, or something of your own design—in the margin to emphasize the book's key points. Keep these to a minimum. You might have only 10 or 20 marks in an entire book.

6. Note questions, outline major points, summarize complex arguments, or briefly identify important points. Use the top and bottom margins as well as the side ones.

7. Put page numbers in the margins so you can skip explanations and flip quickly from important point to important point when reviewing.

8. If color helps or you enjoy it, use it: yellow highlighter for important words, red lines in the margin, blue for summarizing important points. But do not make your system so complicated that it distracts you from the material.

Reflect

You have read the material and marked the important items in the book. Now *reflect*. This simply means to think. Ask yourself, "How does what I've read relate to what I already know?" Try to link the *new with the familiar,* to give it more meaning. Then think of *examples* from your own experience. The best way to remember something is to personalize it.

Review

Finally, *review* the sequence of the main ideas to see how one flows into the next, and the next. Help yourself by scanning the text.

What can you do when you do not have time to read the entire assignment? What you should *not do* is start reading word by word on the first page and see how far you get. Instead, skim. Use the overview and key idea parts of the OK4R approach. Read the first sentence of each paragraph. (They usually contain the main ideas.) Read the headings and look at the illustrations.

What if you work through all the material and still do not understand it? Try to get a simpler book on the same subject and study it first.

If your trouble is vocabulary, sign up for a vocabulary-building course or buy a good vocabulary book and use it.

Remember, the responsibility for learning—mastering the lecture and the textbook material—is yours. Do whatever is necessary to help yourself.

2. Preparing Yourself Emotionally

Demystifying Exam Taking

A key to preparing yourself emotionally is *eliminating* as many *potential sources of anxiety* as possible about the test environment. Corrective and adequate information may take care of many of these. This chapter is intended to demystify exam taking and to provide answers to many of your questions.

Identify Your Test-Taking Strengths and Weaknesses

By the time you are ready to graduate from a nursing program, you have been in school for at least 15 years. You have already established a track record for studying and taking exams and have formed certain patterns. Now is the time to assess the patterns you use in test-taking situations. Identify your strengths and your weaknesses. What is your reading speed? What is your reading accuracy? How well do you do with factual questions? with those requiring quantitative analysis? or in application or judgment types of questions? If you have weaknesses in any of these areas, you need to practice and drill to improve them before you take the exams. You cannot prepare yourself emotionally if you are worried about problems in test-taking skills.

Look Forward to the Exam

A positive mental set is essential to emotional preparation. You are your own worst enemy if your attitude is "Oh no, another exam!" Taking a test can be fun—and a challenge. An important step in the challenge is to discern what the writers of the questions had in mind when they prepared the test. Approach it with a *flexible* attitude. You defeat yourself when you think, "This exam better cover what I studied," and you set yourself up for disappointment if it does not cover all those areas. The important thing is not what you think should be there, but what the test writers *have put* there. How can you learn about what the test is like? Focus on the test writers.

Identify with the Test Writers

Who writes your nursing exams, and what is their *perspective*? The test must be broad enough to reflect a consensus by all item writers from all clinical areas as to the solutions to certain nursing problems.

Think "Average"

A highly specialized health science background can be both a blessing and a problem to you. You may know too much detail and specialized content. Remember that the perspective of most nursing exams is basic, general, and noncontroversial. If one of the choices offered in an exam question is a new approach, still under debate, that is not the best answer—even though it may be true in some areas of practice and you may have been exposed to it. *It is best to choose the safest, most conservative answer.*

The thrust of most nursing school exams will be on basic, safe care. What is everyone expected to know?

For example, do not expect too many questions on nursing research and clinical specialization. These areas may be a part of your curriculum in a generic 2-year program, as well as in a 3-year or a 4-year program, but the mandate of most nursing school exams is to test for minimum competency of entry-level practitioners, not researchers and educators. Therefore, exam questions are not meant to test for responses appropriate for specialists in the major clinical areas.

You Can Be "In Charge" Not a Victim

We have answered the first and most important question: Who wrote the exam and what are they looking for? Now let us tackle a common myth about an exam being tricky.

Most nursing exams have no hidden tricks nor a scheme afoot to trap you. If you find yourself wondering "What are they going to pull on us?" change your mental set from passive victim to active strategist. Decide to attack the questions, not to be "done in" by them. Envision yourself a general with a successful confrontational strategy. An attitude of that type provides a tremendous mental uplift.

Allow Yourself to Be "Average"

Do not expect to get a perfect score. That may sound counterproductive, but it is an approach termed *paradoxical intention*. Set as your goal a passing score. Forget that you are at the top of your class or want to be Phi Beta Kappa. This is not a competition for grades. Your goal is to pass each nursing exam and become an RN.

The key is to give yourself permission to score "average." When you permit your mind or body to do what it fears or is resisting, it appears to no longer need to fight it. For example, have you ever tried to fall asleep and the more you tried to sleep, the harder it was? What happened when you opened up a textbook you *had* to read while in bed? How soon before you fell asleep *then*? In the same light, allow yourself to score average. You may find you *will* score much higher when you remove the pressure from yourself and stop thinking you *must* score high.

Know the Purpose of the Test in Order to Make Relevant Choices

Making the wrong choice between two close options is another major reason some students do poorly on exams. They may have mastered the material, they may be excellent clinicians, but they do not select the best answers on a test. They may successfully narrow the four choices down to two, but then they panic and go off on side issues and lose track of what the test is all about. This is where mental preparedness is important: determining the purpose of a test.

Remember that most nursing exams test for essential nursing behaviors to demonstrate competence. The focus is on *basic, common*, and *general* knowledge. You are being tested to find out if you are a safe practitioner, not a clinical specialist. Look for the answer that will let the exam writers know the client is in safe hands.

Questions on nursing exams usually test for one or more of the following areas: (1) *skills*, (2) *knowledge*, (3) *interpersonal relationships*, and (4) *nursing process*.

Skills

There are *"how to"* questions: How do you irrigate a catheter? How do you apply a sterile dressing?

Knowledge

There are questions on specific facts and knowledge related to categories of human function, pathophysiology, and certain health care trends or statistics.

Certain "pet" subjects appear repeatedly on nursing exams. You might hear about topics from past examinees. These topics, throughout the years, may emerge as patterns of examining, where certain concepts, principles, and procedures are most likely to be tested and thus may be anticipated.

Perhaps on one exam there may have been 40 questions on Addison's disease, 10 on arthritis, and 10 on tetanus. "What kind of an exam is that?" you ask. "I thought the exam would be on common disorders, but I've never even seen a client with Addison's."

Do not panic. Ask yourself, "What are the basic pathophysiologic principles of Addison's disease?" Acid-base? Corticosteroids? Electrolytes?

In the same light, you may not find one question on commonly seen diabetes, but an uncommon condition that manifests a similar pathophysiology as diabetes, which you *have* studied and clinically observed, may be tested. Apply that same knowledge of underlying pathophysiologic concepts and principles to these unfamiliar situations.

Why have 10 questions on arthritis been included? The key underlying concerns here may be range-of-motion exercises, chronic illness concepts, rehabilitation process, and medication (the corticoids) common to a number of other related disorders.

Why ask about tetanus? Because it is a communicable disease. The examiners want to find out if you know what to report and what not to report, how to prevent it, and how to treat it. Again, it could be representative of a broad spectrum of other diseases.

In a question related to children, you might be asked, "Which of the following diets would you give a child with PKU?" You say to yourself, "The only thing we learned was low phenylalanine, but Lo-Fenolac is not among the choices." Of what is PKU a disturbance or imbalance? Protein metabolism. Knowing that one fact, you choose the diet that is low in protein.

In a question related to a client on phenothiazines, you see the question "During which client activity is it important for the nurse to make sure that precautions are taken with the clients?" The choices are (A) going to church on Sunday, (B) going to the museum, (C) going to a concert, and (D) going on a picnic. Let us suppose that you have no idea what answer is wanted. Look for patterns. Church, concert, museum—all indoor activities. Picnic—outdoor activity. Explore the choice that differs from the others (picnic) further. What are some other characteristics of a picnic? It is usually held outdoors . . . in the afternoon . . . in the sun. Clients taking phenothiazines sunburn easily. The answer is "picnic." You could not have memorized the answer to that question. It requires that you reason it out. Do not be immobilized by such questions. Look for patterns and similarities throughout the exam.

Interpersonal Relationships

Questions based on interpersonal relationships constitute another portion of all nursing exams. A caution: In the questions focusing on acute or chronic health problems of children or adults, do not overlook the possibility that the best answer may be an "emotional coping behavior" type of answer. You may think the answer is too obvious, but if your first hunch is "it seems to be a therapeutic communication type of answer," follow that feeling.

The same principle applies to the questions focusing on emotional disorders. You may find a choice that seems correct, but is oriented to physical care. Do not ignore that answer if you think it is correct. That test item could call for a "physical care–oriented" answer.

Nursing Process

Nursing process questions may place heavy emphasis on assessment of priorities. "What do you do *first*?" "Which is the *most* important?" "What is the *long-range* goal . . . or the *short-range* goal?" When all the choices are true, look for the key word—"first," "last," "most," "least."

Aspects of nursing process commonly tested on exams include the following five nursing behaviors, with definitions and examples*:

I. Assessment

A. *Definition*: Ability to establish a database about the client.

B. *Examples*:

1. Can gather objective and subjective data about the client.

   a. Gathers data from verbal contact with client, family, and/or significant resource persons.

   b. Gathers data from chart, lab reports, progress notes, and nursing care plans.

   c. Recognizes signs and symptoms.

   d. Assesses client's ability to perform activities of daily living.

   e. Assesses client's environment.

   f. Identifies reactions (own, staff) to client and family.

2. Can verify information.

   a. Questions information.

   b. Confirms observations.

3. Can communicate information based on assessment.

II. Analysis

A. *Definition*: Ability to identify actual, potential specific health care needs and problems based on assessment.

B. *Examples*:

1. Interprets data.

2. Collects additional data as indicated.

3. Identifies and communicates client's nursing diagnoses.

4. Determines congruency between client's needs/problems and health team member's ability to meet client's needs.

III. Planning

A. *Definition*: Ability to develop a nursing care plan with *goals* for meeting client's needs, and designing strategies to achieve these goals.

B. *Examples*:

1. Includes needs based on comfort and priorities.

2. Includes factors such as age, sex, culture, and ethnicity.

3. Utilizes resources in the community.

4. Collaborates and coordinates care with other personnel for delivery of client's care.

5. Formulates expected outcomes of nursing interventions.

*Adapted from mimeographed sheets distributed at state Nursing Students Association conventions and to all schools of nursing. Source: State Boards of Nursing.

IV. Implementation

A. *Definition*: Ability to begin and complete *specific actions* to meet the set goals.

B. *Examples*:

1. Organizes and manages client's care.

2. Performs or assists in performing activities of daily living.

3. Teaches and counsels client and family and/or health team members.

4. Provides care and therapeutic measures to achieve established client goals.

   a. Provides preventive care.

   b. Provides life-saving care.

   c. Prepares for surgery and other procedures.

   d. Uses correct techniques.

5. Provides care to optimize achievement of client's health care goals; stimulates growth and maintains optimum health.

   a. Encourages self-care and independence.

   b. Adjusts care to meet needs.

   c. Motivates client.

   d. Encourages client to accept treatment.

6. Supervises, coordinates, and evaluates the delivery of the client's care provided by other staff.

7. Records and exchanges information about actions taken.

V. Evaluation

A. *Definition*: Ability to determine the extent to which goals have been met.

B. *Examples*:

1. Determines extent to which goals were appropriate.

2. Compares actual outcomes with expected outcomes of therapy.

3. Changes goals and reorders priorities as necessary.

4. Recognizes effects of measures on client, family, and staff.

5. Investigates if measures taken are appropriate.

6. Evaluates compliance with prescribed and/or proscribed therapy.

7. Records response to care and/or treatment.

Eliminate Anxiety about the "Unknown"

We have given you general information on the kinds of questions you can expect. Let us look at some specifics that will help decrease anxiety about the "unknowns" and eliminate other reasons for anxiety.

- Find out how long the exam will be.
- Ask how many questions will be on the exam.
- Learn the format of the exam (e.g., multiple choice).
- If multiple choice, check how many options will be offered, and whether there is only one correct answer to each question.
- Note the location of the test and the room in which it will be given.

If you have any doubts about the location of the exam site, or if you are upsetting your mental equilibrium by worrying about what the room will be like, we suggest you make a "*test run.*" If you are concerned about the room, look at it. Is it light, dark, cold, overheated?

How the Test Is Scored

You should also know how an exam is scored. Will you receive a pass/fail determination, a letter grade, or a percentage score? Is there a penalty for guessing? Will it be scored "on a curve" or criterion referenced?

Helpful Emotional Attitudes

Forget Anger

Another emotional attitude to work on is a decrease in your level of anger or hostility before you enter the testing room. People who enter an exam furious—with a spouse, friend, parent, child, traffic, or the nursing profession—put themselves at a disadvantage. Anger and hostility distract thought processes, slanting them and upsetting balance. Immediately before an exam, avoid people who incite your anger. You may find this difficult if these people are part of your household, but there are doors and locks, and you can set time limits. As a last resort, consider a "retreat" away, such as a motel room the night before the examination.

Last, Not First

A few final thoughts on emotional preparedness. Decide that you will be the last person to leave the exam room, not the first. This will immediately eliminate another area of anxiety, when you notice some people leaving while you are still answering questions. You begin to think, "There must be something wrong. It must be easier than I thought it was." Forget about everyone else and concentrate on using all the time allotted.

Have Tunnel Vision

Prepare yourself, on entering the examination room, to block out everything except the task ahead of you. The psychiatric term for this is *selective inattention*; it is more commonly called *tunnel vision*. Focus only on the test. Block out your worries about sick relatives or the argument you had with a friend. Eliminate from your awareness the person chewing gum next to you, the sneezes and coughs, or the children laughing and the screeching tires outside.

The Test: A "Game" of Skills and Confrontation

In conclusion, we encourage you to "play with" the test. It is a challenge. Walk into the test with an aggressive, confident attitude. Prepare to analyze and dissect and attack and confront the questions. This gives you power. Do not take the passive approach. The correct answer will not magically leap out at you. It is your job to find it. You can put to use your mastery of content, your practical experiences, your memory, your test-taking strategies, and your confidence that it *will* all come together. Why shouldn't it?

3. Preparing Yourself Physically

---

6 Suggestions

Sleep Versus Cramming

Following all the tips provided earlier on intellectual and emotional preparedness will do little good if you arrive at a nursing exam exhausted. The first principle of being physically prepared is to get adequate sleep. Many people stay up late or all night 2 or 3 days before exams, to cram. We will not say, "Don't do it," because it is your choice. But ask yourself whether the gain in information is worth the sacrifice in effective thinking.

If your nursing exams were simply testing recall of facts, there might be some merit in cramming. Without an adequate background of facts, you have no chance at all in such a situation. But usually only 10-15% of most nursing exam questions test for the recall of facts. The remaining 85% usually test for nursing action and interpersonal relationships, with emphasis on *application* of nursing process. Questions such as these require analysis, critical thought, reasoning, application, and figuring things out. Your brain cells must be rested to allow you to think clearly. So weigh the losses against the gains.

Stress and Medications

Let us also talk about drugs—in lay terms, "uppers" and "downers." You may feel you are so nervous that you cannot think properly. "Perhaps," you think, "medication would calm me down. I think I'll ask my doctor for some." Again, carefully weigh the losses against the gains: the loss of alertness versus the gain in decreased tension. And if you have never before taken tranquilizers, do not take other people's advice in this area—drugs have different effects on different people.

Also consider that there are other effective ways to reduce anxiety and tension without drugs. We will look at some of these in the chapter on anxiety reduction. Give these approaches a try.

Perhaps your problem is depression or lack of energy. You think, "I need something for energy and to keep me awake." Again, weigh the losses against the gains: potential loss of clear, rational thought and powers of concentration versus increased "alertness." You have probably heard many stories about what "uppers" have done for others—how good, alert, and on top of things they can make you feel. But they can have other effects detrimental to successful performance on exams.

So weigh *all* the effects before you make a decision.

Stress and the Gastrointestinal Tract

What you eat before exams is also important. Prepare your body for stress. Gastrointestinal (GI) distress is a normal effect of stress and tension. Treat yourself with care. If you are unaccustomed to spicy foods, do not eat them in the 3 or 4 days preceding the exam. Someone may suggest relaxing at a wonderful Indian restaurant with calming music and great curry. If you do not normally eat curry, have some yogurt or some milk or something bland. Do not increase your chances of GI distress by adding unusual or spicy foods to your diet at this time.

Prepare your GI tract with a diet high in carbohydrates and avoid hypoglycemia. You may want to limit your general food intake. Eating great quantities of food may make you sluggish; you may want to keep the blood supply going to your brain where you need it, not to your digestive tract. These are very simple principles, but things we often overlook when our concentration is elsewhere.

Stress and the Urinary Tract

A normal sign of anxiety is the need for frequent urination. At this time you will be under stress to do well—as you should be. Expect urinary frequency. You can control it somewhat by avoiding dietary sources that act like diuretics—coffee, tea, beer. Be aware of your own body and its reactions to various products.

Stress and Temperature Control

Hot and cold flashes are also signs of anxiety. Prepare for them. Plan to dress in layers. If you are cold, you can keep all your clothing on. As you warm, a natural result of the speeded metabolism caused by anxiety, shed the clothing items one by one. It is terribly frustrating to find yourself in the exam room wearing a wool turtleneck sweater (which was appropriate for the outside temperature) and discover that you are sweltering. You have no alternative but to sit there and feel physically miserable. Plan what you wear.

When choosing your layers, select them from your oldest, most comfortable, most familiar clothing. No one will care what you are wearing. Be comfortable. Pinching, binding clothing is a distraction.

Remember also the effects of stress on hormones. Women need to be prepared for any contingency—regardless of the date. Arm yourself with supplies.

Psychosomatic Distress

Expect that psychosomatic distress will strike! Sometime before an important exam, you may catch cold or develop a sore throat or an earache. You may also find yourself losing your car keys or your wallet, or being forgetful. You may sprain an extremity. What may be happening is a "normal" response to anxiety. It is not uncommon to develop psychosomatic disorders before a major exam. Often, they too will pass once you pass this time of stress.

4. Coping with Exam-Related Anxiety

---

7 Techniques

In the earlier discussion on preparing emotionally for exams, we considered ways of eliminating many of the causes of anxiety. This chapter focuses on mental and physical techniques for coping with and dissipating the natural anxiety associated with the test-taking process.

We highly recommend that you read C. Eugene Walker's book *Learn to Relax: Thirteen Ways to Reduce Tension*. Most of the techniques mentioned below are described in detail by Walker, as are others you may find more effective. You can also find detailed, step-by-step self-mastery exercises on the special audiocassette tape *Relaxation Approaches for Nurses*, available from this editor.

Cognitive Restructuring, or Turn-Around Thinking

The first approach is borrowed from Albert Ellis's rational-emotive therapy. It is termed *straight thinking*. Ellis claims that we carry with us into certain situations a mental script designed for failure.

A part of the straight-thinking concept is the premise that people think in irrational ways. Read the statements below. If you recognize any of these thoughts, now is the time to begin changing them.

- **Perfectionism:** "Making a mistake is terrible. I've got to get a perfect score."

  Instead, say to yourself, "I don't need or want a perfect score."

- **Powerlessness:** "My emotions can't be controlled." Or, "Self-discipline is too difficult. I'll never be able to crack a book for these exams. And there is no way in the world I'll be able to sit through a four-day review session."

  Turn it around and say, "Of course I can and will when I make small, realistic goals, such as to review one subject at a time."

- **Comparisons:** "I have to do better than my mother... or my sister ... or my roommate did." Or, "I've got to do better than I did on the last test."

  Restructure that to say, "I just want to do OK, not the best."

- **Putdowns**: "Healthy people don't get upset. I must be crazy." Or, "I'm inferior. I never do well on exams. In fact, nothing ever works out well for me." "Giving up is the best policy. If I don't know the answer right away, I'll just forget about it. If I don't know the first three or four, I'll just 'shut down' and leave. Why torture myself?"

  New script to try out: "Test-taking anxiety is normal, not crazy." "I've passed tests before. This is not that different."

- **Magic cures**: "I'll put a tape recorder under my pillow; when I wake up, I'll know all the answers."

  Tell yourself: "Not knowledge by magic, but by knowing *how to figure out* the best answers."

- **Evading responsibility**: "If I don't pass this exam, it's the fault of my nursing school instructors. They didn't teach me the right things."

  Instead, you go back to the books to fill in *your* gaps of knowledge for *yourself.*

- **Punishment**: "If I can't pass this test, I'll show them... I'm going to give up nursing."

  Better to view taking each exam as a quiz, not *the* test to end all tests... It's an *episode* in your life, not your whole existence.

- **Unrealistic thinking**: "I'm going to smile and act like I'm happy and carefree, even though I'm scared half out of my mind. I'm not going to yell at my children, or my spouse, or my roommates and let them know how I'm feeling." Or, "Anxiety is always dangerous. I'd better not let anyone know how anxious I feel."

  Instead, let it out!

What should you do if you recognize any of these irrational thought patterns? Begin by accepting responsibility for yourself and your actions. Practice turning around some of your "lines."

Assertive Rights—for Success

Ellis's straight-thinking approach is based on the assumption that each human being possesses 10 assertive rights. These are the attitudes you must begin to develop within yourself to rewrite a mental script that fosters "success" instead of failure. A few of these rights, as they relate to examinations, are:

1. The right to offer no reasons or excuses to justify your behavior. If doing cartwheels on the sidewalk makes you feel better and releases your anxiety, there is no need to justify it—to yourself or to anyone else. Your first commitment is to make yourself feel good so you can focus your attention on where you want it to be.

2. The right to change your mind. Go back and change answers if it feels right to do so before you click-on to the next question.

3. The right to make mistakes and to be responsible for them. You have the right *not* to get the "right" answer.

4. The right to say "I don't know why this is the correct answer, but it is," rather than "This is the right answer, and I should know why."

5. The right to go with what feels correct to you, even if you did not select it in a logical manner. You have the right to be illogical in making decisions.

6. The right to say, "I don't understand."

7. The right to say, "I don't care."

That is a capsule summary of Albert Ellis's straight thinking.

Life Structuring

Another approach that may help you to prepare for exams and cope with the accompanying anxiety is *life structuring* or *engineering*. This involves using "games" or rewards to help you get what you want.

For example, you might say, "I'll go home now and review schizophrenia, and when I'm finished, I'll go out with some friends." You are structuring your life around what you want to do and the reward you are going to give yourself for doing it. It is a little game and it is OK. People need rewards.

But be careful how you structure yourself. Do not decide to cover 50 pages or study for an hour. You set yourself up to waste that hour or to learn little from those 50 pages. *Give yourself a specific goal*—something you intend to master. If you complete the task quickly, you can go out earlier. If it takes you a long time, you go out later. In either case you *do* go out—and you *can* enjoy yourself because you know you have accomplished something. You need not feel guilty because you worked for an hour or read the 50 pages but did not learn anything.

Be sure your goals are realistic. You are courting failure if you try to do in 3 hours something you know will take you 6.

There are a number of rewards you can employ between now and the date of the exam to structure your life. Begin to think of some.

Progressive Relaxation

Jacobsen's progressive relaxation approach is also effective in alleviating anxiety. In essence, it involves relaxing the parts of your body one at a time. Close your eyes, focus on a muscle, and relax it. Move on to the next body part, and the next, until your entire body is relaxed. To help yourself learn this technique, record the material that appears in the orientation chapter of *Davis's NCLEX-RN® Success* by Sally Lagerquist. Get into a comfortable position in a darkened room, close your eyes, and listen to yourself on the tape. It takes practice. Saying, "That's simple. When I get tense during exams, I'll do it" will not work. Practice the technique until it becomes second nature; then you can call on it automatically when you feel yourself becoming tense.

All the techniques described in this section work for a limited time and for a specific goal. We are not talking about therapy; these are self-help techniques.

Tension and Relaxation

Tightening and letting go is a very simple method of releasing tension. It is fun, it is easy, and it works. If your neck and shoulders are tense, increase and exaggerate that tension, hold it, and suddenly let go. You might say, "I can't do that in the examination room. I'll look ridiculous." Who cares? Give yourself permission to do whatever works for you.

Psychiatric nurses used to ask clients, "Why do you bang your head?" The nonjoking response was, "It feels good when I stop."

Perhaps when you are nervous your hands shake. Exaggerate the shakiness. Shake them as hard as possible for 10 seconds, and suddenly let them go limp. If you do not want to do that in public, find an unobtrusive part of your body to which you can apply the same approach.

Imagine that you are about to have an attack of explosive diarrhea. Tighten your gluteus muscles as hard as you can and stop that attack. Or clench your fists as hard as you can and hold them. Then let go. No one will notice. If you are really self-conscious, wear closed-toed shoes and contract your toes. Focusing this tension-relaxing technique on another part of your body distracts you from the tension you are feeling elsewhere.

Desensitization

Desensitization is a more specialized approach that normally involves a therapist. The principle is the same as that of allergy shots. The noxious stimulus is increased until the unwanted response no longer occurs in reaction to it. If, for example, you are afraid of dogs, you begin your conditioning by looking at pictures of very small, very friendly dogs. If you do not break out in hives or begin to perspire, you move on to pictures of larger, more ferocious dogs. Soon you will be able to walk down the opposite side of the street from a small, friendly dog with no negative results—and later, down the opposite side of the street from a large, ferocious dog. Finally, you will be able to pet a dog without experiencing any of the previous symptoms.

The same approach can work with tests. As a self-control approach, begin with an insignificant, "who cares" test, and keep taking practice tests until you are able to do it without panic and anxiety. When you are faced with a test that really matters, it will be just "another test." You may have already been through this process without really being aware of it. By this point, you have taken hundreds of tests, so you should be able to say, "So what? It's just another test. I've taken plenty of tests and passed them all or I wouldn't be here." Act out a positive script in your mind.

Breathing Exercises

Breathing awareness can reduce anxiety. Close your eyes and focus on your breathing. Say to yourself, "My chest is moving in and out." How fast is it moving? Track that speed. Is it shallow? Concentrate on that. Is it deep? This distracts your mind from the anxiety you are feeling and focuses it elsewhere. It is similar to the principles of Lamaze childbirth. For specific exercises, refer to *Davis's NCLEX-RN® Success.*

Yoga or Zen meditation can also help focus your attention.

Guided Imagery

Guided imagery is an easy and enjoyable method of reducing anxiety. When you find yourself daydreaming during a stressful situation, "go" with that feeling. You are probably daydreaming because you want to escape from something unpleasant in your immediate environment. Fighting the feeling will increase your anxiety. Follow your thoughts and let yourself float. Let the pleasurable experience in. See examples also in the review book mentioned above.

We suggest that during the preexam period you think of peak experiences, the "highs," in your life. It might be the birth of your first child, the day you were accepted into nursing school, or the way you felt when you accomplished something you had worked hard for and very much wanted. Get in touch with that feeling and remember it. When your anxiety level begins to climb, blank out the pain and relive the peak experience. Pleasure and pain are usually mutually exclusive. If you are in great pain, substitute thoughts of pleasure.

To reiterate: These are self-help techniques. They must be practiced to be effective. Find out if they work for you by experimenting with them. Then when you need them, they will have become almost second nature.

5. *How to Take Tests*

Before getting into the mechanics of answering questions, let us talk about the things you can do immediately before a test to simplify the process for yourself. We have already gone into some of these points in the chapter on being emotionally prepared, but they are important enough to be repeated here.

About a week before a nursing exam, ask where the exam will be given, how many questions will be on the test, what the time limits will be, and what you can bring with you. Knowing what to expect frees your mind to tackle the major concern—answering the test questions—so find out early.

You may need a watch during the exams. Plan to wear or carry a watch and expect to use it.

Be prepared for monitoring. Each school has a different system, but there are similarities. You may not be allowed to bring anything except pencils with you into the testing room—especially no books or notes. Many people feel insulted when asked to open their satchels before entering the testing room. Do not take it personally. Make it easy for yourself by removing all nonessentials before the exam. There is no point in complicating things for yourself by being asked to empty the contents of your backpack for a monitor to examine.

If you lean down to get a tissue from your coat during the exam, a monitor may come over to see what you are doing. Do not be offended. The monitors are simply doing their job, and they treat everyone in the same way.

Use the Question/Answer Booklet Correctly

Some schools still use an electronically scored question/answer booklet for exams. You will need to use a special No. 2 pencil to mark your answers. If you do not use this pencil, your answers may not be clearly marked for the machine scoring. You will be instructed to fill in the circle that corresponds with the correct answer. Do not use check marks, vertical marks, or cross-outs. A shaded circle is the only acceptable mark.

Follow Directions

Perhaps the most important aspect of test taking is reading directions. "That's old stuff," you say. "Of course I read the directions." The point is to read the directions in front of you *for this exam*, and to read them thoroughly and carefully. Take nothing for granted. Assume nothing. It may be a tired point, but it is the No. 1 source of trouble on all nursing exams.

Before you begin the test, the proctor will generally explain the directions and instruct you how the answer is to be marked. This is not the time to tune out.

If the proctor gives you a sample question to try out, take it seriously. It will offer an invaluable opportunity to figure out the test approach early in the test. Study the reasons given for the correct answer. It may be an obvious, easy answer, but try to pinpoint what makes it correct. What kind of thinking is behind the question? This may help you identify the "set" of the examination.

Ask for clarification of the directions if you have any doubts. Do not be concerned with appearing stupid. Find out what is expected of you.

Structure Your Time

You are now ready to begin your nursing test. Before you even look at the first question, examine the entire exam (unless, of course, it is administered by computer and does not allow for looking ahead). Note the number of questions and the type of questions. Are they long-winded, situational case descriptions, or are they short and to the point?

Take the number of questions and divide it into the length of time you will have to complete the exam. The answer will tell you about the speed you must maintain to complete the examination in the time allotted. Then set a schedule for yourself. For example, if you have 1½ hours for a 90-question test, plan to complete one question per minute to finish; note what questions you should be beginning at the end of 30 and 60 minutes.

These checkpoints help, particularly when you begin to tire. They offer reinforcement when you reach each one, and they jog you if you fall behind. If you miss a checkpoint, do not become discouraged. Recognize that you must speed up a bit. Work quickly, but not at the expense of accuracy.

Go Fast on the "Easy" Ones

It is time to begin question 1. Your strategy should be to accumulate the greatest number of points in the shortest amount of time. The goal is to get as many questions correct as possible.

Answer Each Question

Answer each question. If the question is long, break it down into its basic elements and tackle each part one by one. Do not give up immediately if you encounter an unfamiliar word. It may not be important.

Anticipate the Answer

Try this approach. After you have read the question, but before looking at the choices, anticipate the answer. Then check the choices to see if your answer is among them.

If you do not find the answer you anticipated, give that answer up. Do not cling tenaciously to your answer as if it were a prized possession. This should act as a warning beacon that something is wrong. Perhaps you did not read the question correctly. Do not alter words in an option to make it agree with your anticipated answer.

Relate Each Option to the Stem

Test each actual option against the actual question. Grammatically place the answer in the same sentence with the question. "Blank (insert choice A, B, C, and D to see how each fits) is the most important element of treatment...."

Do Not Get Stuck on the More Difficult Questions

Do not get bogged down with one question. If you have no idea what the answer is, give it a serious try, then *move on.*

Focus Your Reading

In reading the questions and the choices, skim past the "frills." Read the situation quickly, looking for the key words. Read the choices quickly, with the same focus. Drill yourself and put yourself in the mind-set to ignore unimportant words and to zero in on the key words.

Identify Key Words

What are these key words? Which one is *incorrect*? Which one is *correct*? Which one is *most important*? Which one is *least important*? Which *is*? Which *is not*? All of the following *except*? Are they asking for ounces or pounds? Hours or minutes?

Do Not Overthink

It is vital that you read the questions as *they are written.* Do not read anything into them. And do not misinterpret them. If the question is simple and obvious, pick a simple, obvious answer. Forget any subtleties you may know about the subject. Choose the answer intended. Recognize the level of sophistication of the question.

Answer the Condition in the Stem

Be sure you know what is being asked. If the question asks, "Which is true *only sometimes?*" the answer will be different than if the question asks, "Which is *never* true?"

Or perhaps the test writer is not looking for what is "true," but for what is "important." All the choices may be true, but *only one will be the most important.* Do not put down the first answer you read as correct, simply because it is true. It may not be true for the specific situation described, or it may be true but not of major importance to that situation.

If the question asks for a reason, the choice you make should be phrased in such a way that it *provides a reason.* If the question asks for an explanation, the answer should "explain." Ask yourself, "Is the answer to this question likely to be phrased in a positive or a negative manner?" Then look for a choice that meets that criterion.

Look first for a simple, straightforward, conservative, "garden variety" answer. It will save you time.

Give special attention to questions in which each word counts.

Client-Focused Approach Is Important

A very important aid, and one too often overlooked, is to focus on the client. What appears to be a correct answer can be wrong if it ignores the concerns and feelings of the client.

"Feelings"-Oriented Answers May Be Emphasized

Keep the word *feelings* uppermost in your mind. Often the best choice may be the one that focuses on "feelings."

Watch for Negatives

Note that *incorrect* statements can be *correct* answers. If the question asks, "Which is an *incorrect* treatment?" the incorrect statement is the right answer.

All of the preceding suggestions assume that you know something about the questions being asked. What do you do about difficult or totally unfamiliar questions? Try educated guessing.

Educated Guessing

General Versus Specific Answer

When you do not know the specific facts called for in a question, immediately turn to your powers of reasoning and search your related experience. Ask yourself, "Is the question asking for a general or a specific answer?" There will be a clue. Tests are generally not tricky. For example, "Which *one* is… " gives you the clue that the question requires a *specific*, not a general, answer.

Rephrase and Think of Clinical Examples

Paraphrasing the question may help. Change it into simple language. Reduce intellectual or abstract situations to the concrete. Substitute actual examples for concepts.

Use Process of Elimination: Wrong and Irrelevant

Narrow multiple-choice options (usually four per question) to two choices, if possible. First eliminate the answers you suspect are wrong. Then eliminate any choices you suspect are *true, but not relevant* to the question. If you know enough to eliminate two of the four choices, there is a 50-50 chance you will guess correctly.

Guess Between Two Choices

Should you guess? If the odds are 50-50, yes.

If all four answers seem to be correct, then go through a process of elimination.

What process can you use to help you make a guess or to check your guess to see if it might be correct? Read the following six suggestions.

Look for Patterns Among the Given Options

Compare the choices with each other. If several options look good, or if none of the options look good, try to examine patterns. If three of the four choices are similar, focus on the one that is different. It may well be the best choice.

Look for the Most Comprehensive Answer

Another method of elimination is to look for "telescoping" or "*umbrella*" answers. Eliminate the options that are contained in another option. If choice "C" takes in "A," "B," and "D," then it is likely that choice "C" is the best answer.

Avoid Global Terms: All, Always, Never, None, etc.

For example, if the words "it is always" are contained in an option, 9 times out of 10, it is the wrong answer. This is not a hard-and-fast rule, but if you are guessing, it is worth eliminating such an option.

Find the Plausible Distractors

Often the best answer may appear in the "B" or "C" position. This is certainly not true 100% of the time, but it is based on the premise that test writers are human. They are not infallible. The most attractive distractors are often placed first or last in the series of options. The best answer may then be more readily placed in the middle. Again, if you are guessing, take a second look at the middle options.

Choose an Answer That Makes Sense

And—all things being equal—if you are guessing, select the response you best understand. If you are leaning toward an answer you do not understand, discard it and choose one you do understand.

We have said this before, but *use all the time allotted*. You have already decided to be the last, rather than the first, to leave.

Last Hunch May Be Better Than First Hunch

When checking your answers (before going on to the next question, or at the end of the test if that is possible), do not hesitate to change an answer if it seems appropriate to you on review. This is contrary to past popular belief, which was to keep your first-hunch answer. But current thinking on the subject says: If after you have answered a question, you think you have marked an incorrect choice, change it to what you now believe to be correct. If you are still unsure, then keep your original answer. Remember that you are not breaking an ironclad rule by changing your answers. What you do depends on information you may have remembered and its effect on your previous decisions.

Application of these test-taking guidelines and reminders can make taking nursing exams a less stressful process. It can also improve your scores. But there are no magic formulas. The responsibility for preparing yourself intellectually, emotionally, and physically for this challenge rests with you—the nursing student. And you *can* meet the challenge with confidence, skill, and success!

II. Case Management Scenarios with Critical-Thinking Exercises: Questions and Answers

11 Behavioral and Emotional Problems 363

Introduction

The National Council of State Boards of Nursing has identified measurable abilities that it believes a nurse must demonstrate in order to give competent care as a safe practitioner. These critical-thinking exercises are prepared to test for these abilities.

The practice questions and answers in this section are presented with detailed case management scenarios for practice and self-evaluation in applying the *nursing process*. The scenarios involve *integrated* health problems, and are organized within a *life-cycle* framework.

When you are ready to take the practice questions, set a time limit of 1 minute per question. The number of questions varies from case to case. You may choose to take a certain number of them at a time, check your answers, then take another segment. Use these questions as a "test run" for your nursing exams. *Do* set time limits for yourself.

Make full use of the answer and rationale sections provided. In addition to indicating the correct answer to each question, these sections give explanations of *why* the answer is *correct* and why the other choices are *incorrect*. Use these practice questions to identify areas in which you need more study or review—and then refer to your textbooks, classroom notes, or the references listed at the end of this book.

In Section III, you will find coding tables, summary grids, and the index to nursing problems/diagnosis. Use these study aids to identify areas with which you are having difficulty, and then focus your study on those areas.

6. Typical Test Designs for Critical–Thinking Exams in Clinical Nursing Areas

The following seven sections summarize the general structure and content focus of many exams that you may encounter in nursing school.

I. *Exam questions are designed to test for safe, effective nursing practice.* The following outline of categories of safe, effective practice is adapted from a classic study entitled *Critical Requirements for Safe/Effective Nursing Practice.* Nursing curricula are often designed to prepare students for nursing practice as identified in critical incidents periodically collected and analyzed, as well as activities identified in the job analysis of what an entry-level nurse does. Nursing behaviors tested in school exams are often derived from these ongoing studies, which identify behaviors relevant to current nursing practice (*critical requirements*) in each of the five clinical specialties.*

   A. Exercises professional prerogatives based on clinical judgment.

      1. Adapts care to individual client needs.

      2. Fulfills responsibility to client and others despite difficulty.

      3. Challenges *inappropriate* orders and decisions by medical and other professional staff.

      4. Acts as client advocate in obtaining appropriate medical, psychiatric, or other help.

      5. Recognizes own limitations and errors.

      6. Analyzes and adjusts own or *staff reactions* in order to maintain therapeutic relationship with client.

   B. Promotes client's ability to cope with *immediate, long-range, or potential health-related change.*

*Sources: (1) Literature from National Council of State Boards of Nursing. (2) Adapted from *A Study of Nursing Practice and Role Delineation of Entry Level Performance of Registered Nurses* by the American College Testing Program for the National Council of State Boards of Nursing, Inc., Chicago (1986 and **reviewed regularly since then**).

1. Provides *health care instruction* or information to client, family, or significant others.

2. Encourages client or family to make decisions about accepting care or adhering to treatment regime.

3. Helps client recognize and deal with *psychological stress.*

4. Avoids creating or increasing anxiety or stress.

5. Conveys and invites *acceptance, respect,* and *trust.*

6. Facilitates relationship of family, staff, or significant others with client.

7. Stimulates and remotivates client, or enables client to achieve *self-care* and *independence.*

C. Helps maintain client comfort and *normal body functions.*

   1. Keeps client clean and comfortable.

   2. Helps client maintain or regain normal body functions.

D. Takes precautionary and *preventive* measures in giving client care.

   1. Prevents infection.

   2. Protects skin and mucous membranes from injurious materials.

   3. Uses *positioning* or exercise to prevent injury or the *complications of immobility.*

   4. Avoids using injurious technique in administering and managing intrusive or other potentially traumatic treatments.

   5. Protects client from falls or other contact injuries.

   6. Maintains surveillance of client's activities.

   7. Reduces or removes *environmental hazards.*

E. Checks, compares, verifies, monitors, and follows up medication and treatment processes.

   1. Checks correctness, condition, and safety of medication being prepared.

   2. Ensures that correct medication or care is given to the right client and that client takes or receives it.

   3. Adheres to schedule in giving medication, treatment, or test.

   4. Administers medication by correct route, rate, or mode.

   5. Checks client's readiness for medication, treatment, surgery, or other care.

   6. Checks to ensure that tests or measurements are done correctly.

      7. Monitors ongoing infusions and inhalations.

      8. Checks for and *interprets effect of medication, treatment,* or *care,* and *takes corrective action* if necessary.

F. Interprets symptom complex and intervenes appropriately.

      1. Checks client's condition or status.

      2. Remains objective, further investigates, or verifies client's complaint or problem.

      3. *Uses alarms and signals on automatic equipment as adjunct to personal assessment.*

      4. Observes and correctly *assesses signs of anxiety or behavioral stress.*

      5. Observes and correctly *assesses physical signs, symptoms, or findings,* and intervenes appropriately.

      6. Correctly *assesses* severity or *priority* of client's condition, and gives or obtains necessary care.

G. Responds to emergencies.

      1. Anticipates need for *crisis care.*

      2. Takes instant, correct action in emergency situations.

      3. Maintains calm and efficient approach under pressure.

      4. Assumes leadership role in crisis situation when necessary.

H. Obtains, records, and exchanges information on behalf of the client.

      1. Checks data sources for orders and other information about client.

      2. Obtains information from client and family.

      3. Transcribes or records information on chart, or other information system.

      4. Exchanges information with nursing staff and other departments.

      5. Exchanges information with medical staff.

I. Utilizes client *care planning.*

      1. Develops and modifies client care plan.

      2. Implements client care plan.

J. *Teaches* and supervises other staff.

      1. Teaches correct principles, procedures, and techniques of client care.

      2. Supervises and checks the work of staff for whom she or he is responsible.

II. *Nursing exam questions mainly reflect two levels of cognitive knowledge* as described by Benjamin Bloom: *application* and *analysis*. *Recall* and *comprehension* levels (understanding) are usually *not* emphasized. About 80% of the test items tend to be:

A. ***Application: The use of abstractions in particular or concrete situations. They may be in the form of general ideas, rules, procedures, or general methods. The abstractions may also be technical principles, ideas, and theories that need to be remembered and applied, using a concept or principle in a new situation.***

B. ***Analysis: The breakdown of the whole into constituent parts or elements so that a rank priority of ideas can emerge and relationships between ideas can be made clear.***

C. *Recall/Knowledge:* Rote remembering of significant facts or terms; to define, to name and to list.

D. *Comprehension:* To understand; to restate; to reorganize; to translate; to find an illustration or example; to interpret by explanation or summary; to determine implications, consequences and effects.

E. *Synthesis:* Putting ideas together to form a new whole.

F. *Evaluation:* Judging material using criteria.

III. *Categories of general nursing knowledge* included across clinical areas are:

A. Normal growth and development throughout the life cycle.

1. *Recommendation:* Review theories of growth and development by Duvall, Sullivan, Piaget, Freud, and Erikson.

B. Basic human needs.

1. *Recommendation:* Review Maslow and Havighurst.

C. Coping mechanisms used by individuals.

1. *Recommendation:* Review most common adaptive behaviors, for example, blocking, compensation, denial, displacement, fixation, identification, introjection, projection, rationalization, reaction formation, regression, repression, sublimation, substitution, suppression, undoing.

D. Common health problems (actual or potential) in the major health areas and based on current morbidity studies.

1. *Recommendation:* Review the 10 most common diseases, disorders, and causes of death.

E. Variations in health needs as affected by age, sex, culture, ethnicity, and religion.

1. *Recommendation:* Be aware of *food* preferences and dietary restrictions; *belief systems* about causes of illness, methods

of treatment, concept of death, concept of time; kinship structure and role of the men, women, and extended family; *ethnic variations in susceptibility* to certain diseases.

F. Nursing goals and interventions to assist individuals in maintaining life and health, coping with health problems, and recovering from the effects of injury or disease.

1. *Recommendation*: Review nursing priorities for clients in *life-threatening* situations, *health teaching* and health maintenance situations, and *rehabilitation* situations.

IV. Concepts relevant to general nursing practice are integrated throughout nursing exams:

A. Management.

1. *Recommendation*: Know the scope of RN functions, and what can be delegated to an LVN/LPN or UAP (unlicensed assistive personnel).

B. Accountability.

1. *Recommendation*: Review major legal and ethical issues, areas of nursing responsibilities, and standards of nursing practice.

C. Life cycle.

1. *Recommendation*: Review major health concerns, problems, and nursing care during birth, childhood, school age, adolescence, young adult and reproductive years, middle age, and older adult and geriatric years.

D. Client environment.

1. *Recommendation*: Review measures to protect from harm against airborne irritants, cold, and heat; review approaches to eliminate environmental discomforts, such as odors, noise, poor ventilation, dust; know *safety hazards*; review measures to maintain environmental order and cleanliness.

V. Test items may emphasize four categories of client needs and six client needs with activities designed to meet these needs (as on the RN licensure exam, NCLEX-RN®).

A. You can expect that the most emphasis will be on meeting the client's physical needs (*physiological integrity*) in actual or potential life-threatening, chronic, recurring *physiological* conditions and with clients who are at risk for complications or untoward effects of treatment. Subcategories include:

1. *Basic care and comfort:* performing routine nursing activities of daily living.

2. *Pharmacological and parenteral therapies:* expected and unexpected effects, chemotherapy; blood products; pain management; calculations; TPN, IV; central venous access devices.

   3. *Reduction of risk potential:* monitoring and reducing likelihood of complications related to existing conditions, treatments or procedures.

   4. *Physiological adaptation:* meeting acute, chronic or life-threatening physical health conditions.

B.   *Safe, effective care environment* subcategories include:

   1. *Management of care:* staff development, collaboration, supervision of multidisciplinary health team; delegation; client rights; prioritization; ethical and legal responsibilities; referrals.

   2. *Safety and infection control:* protecting clients, family/significant others and health care personnel from health and environmental hazards; e.g., disaster planning, home safety, medical and surgical asepsis, use of restraints/safety devices, safe use of equipment; standard precautions.

C.   *Health promotion and maintenance* includes these topics: *growth and development throughout the life span*: meeting client needs through normal expected stages from conception to advanced old age; principles of teaching/learning; *self-care and integrity of support systems*: assisting clients with self-care and supporting client's family; *prevention and early detection of disease:* immunizing/screening; physical assessment.

D.   *Psychosocial integrity*, with a focus on stress and crisis-related situations throughout the life cycle, as well as providing and directing nursing care of clients with acute or chronic mental illness; includes these topics: *psychosocial adaptation*: meeting acute or chronic emotional, social, and behavioral needs; cultural diversity; support systems; helping clients to cope with stress (e.g., end-of-life, family dynamics, situational role changes, sensory/perceptual alterations, abuse/neglect).

VI. A critical component of most nursing exams is nursing process (i.e., five steps) applied to *client situations*, in all stages of the *life cycle.*

A.   The following are five specific behaviors in all of the client situations listed in item **V.**

   1. Ability to assess (*assessment*).

   2. Ability to analyze data and identify specific needs (*analysis*).

   3. Ability to plan and set goals (*planning*).

   4. Ability to implement specific actions (*implementation*).

   5. Ability to evaluate outcome (*evaluation*).

B.   Examples of questions focusing on specific nursing behaviors (i.e., aspects or steps of the nursing process) are given below.

   1. *Assessment type.*

A multigravida in labor is admitted to the maternity unit. What information does the nurse need to evaluate the status of her labor?

A. Blood pressure.

B. FHR.

C. Contour of abdomen.

D. Duration, frequency, and intervals of contractions.

Comment: The nurse needs to know the relative importance of the signs and symptoms of labor to assess the status of labor when all the signs are correct. In this case, *D* is the most important. There is a need for interaction between the nurse and client to assess the client's progress in labor.

2. *Analysis type.*

A 30-year-old client with diabetes, who has previously been stabilized on insulin, calls the emergency department to relate that although the urine is negative for sugar and acetone, the client feels as if about to pass out. The client reports eating three regular meals a day and taking insulin as directed. What would be a valid interpretation of this current condition?

A. The client is not physically active enough.

B. The client needs to change the insulin dose.

C. The client has low blood sugar.

D. The client's insulin level is high.

Comment: In order to select *C* as the best answer, the nurse needs not only to understand diabetes, but also to assess the symptoms and to interpret them correctly.

3. *Planning type.*

A client who is comatose is admitted to the hospital. Which nursing goal would be of prime importance at the outset?

A. Establish a flexible visiting schedule so that relatives can watch the client closely.

B. Include the family in the immediate physical care.

C. Provide consistency of care by assigning the same nursing personnel to the client.

D. Place the client in a room where the nurse can closely monitor the condition from the nursing station.

Comment: To choose the best response, *D*, the nurse needs to analyze the situation correctly and apply that knowledge in planning a strategy to achieve the goal of providing close observation of the client's condition.

4. *Implementation type.*

A client who is emaciated-looking with anorexia nervosa is admitted to the mental health unit. The client refuses to eat lunch when it is served, just as the client has refused most meals at home. What can the nurse say that would be most effective in encouraging the client to eat?

A. "You will have to eat if you do not want us to tube-feed you."

B. "Here is a small sandwich. I will sit with you to keep you company while you eat."

C. "It is important that you eat your meals, as it is part of your therapy to help you gain weight."

D. "Aren't you hungry? It is a long time before you can eat dinner if you don't eat your lunch."

Comment: ***B*** is the best nursing action, to provide the basic need for nutrition when the psychological condition prevents the client from taking care of own physiologic need for food.

5. *Evaluation type.*

A person who is obese began a weight loss program after Christmas. The plan was to lose a minimum of 10 pounds a month. By February 1, the client had lost 15 pounds. What action should the nurse take at this time?

A. Praise the client for the results and ask if the client would like to set the next goal at 15 pounds.

B. Refer to the dietitian to regulate the weight loss.

C. Encourage to lose even more weight since the client is doing so well.

D. Ask why more weight was lost than planned.

Comment: The weight loss is controlled by the client, with the nurse providing needed support and encouragement. Here, the best answer is ***A*** because it measures the results (15 pounds) against the goal (10 pounds) and works with the client to change the goal appropriately.

VII. Exam questions focus on client care situations and nursing measures that can be categorized into eight areas of human functioning:

A. *Protective functions:* The client's capacity or ability to maintain defenses and prevent physical and chemical trauma, injury, infection, and threats to health status. *Examples* include:

1. Communicable diseases (including sexually transmitted diseases).

2. Immunity.

3. Physical trauma and abuse.

4. Asepsis.

5. Safety hazards.

6. Poisoning.

7. Skin disorders.

8. Preoperative care and postoperative complications.

B. *Sensory-perceptual functions:* The client's capacity or ability to perceive, interpret, and respond to sensory and cognitive stimuli (visual, auditory, tactile, taste, and smell). *Examples* include:

1. Auditory, visual, and verbal impairments.

2. Sensory deprivation and sensory overload.

3. Aphasia.

4. Brain tumors.

5. Laryngectomy.

6. Delirium, dementia, and other amnestic disorders.

7. Body image.

8. Reality orientation.

9. Learning disabilities.

10. Seizure disorders.

C. *Comfort, rest, activity, and mobility:* The client's capacity or ability to maintain mobility; desired level of activity; and adequate sleep, rest, and comfort. *Examples* include:

1. Joint impairment.

2. Body alignment.

3. Pain.

4. Sleep disturbances.

5. Activities of daily living.

6. Neuromuscular and musculoskeletal impairment.

7. Endocrine disorders that affect activity.

D. *Nutrition:* The client's capacity or ability to maintain the intake and processing of the essential nutrients. *Examples* include:

1. Normal nutrition.

2. Diet in pregnancy and lactation.

3. Obesity.

4. Conditions such as diabetes, gastric disorders, and metabolic disorders that primarily affect the nutritional status.

E. *Growth and development:* The client's capacity or ability to maintain maturational processes throughout the life span. *Examples* include:

   1. Childbearing and child rearing.

   2. Conditions that interfere with the maturation process.

   3. Maturational crises.

   4. Changes in aging.

   5. Psychosocial development.

   6. Sterility.

   7. Conditions of the reproductive system.

F. *Fluid-gas transport:* The client's capacity or ability to maintain fluid-gas transport. *Examples* include:

   1. Fluid volume deficit and overload.

   2. Cardiopulmonary diseases.

   3. Acid-base balance.

   4. Cardiopulmonary resuscitation.

   5. Anemias.

   6. Hemorrhagic disorders.

   7. Leukemias.

   8. Infectious pulmonary diseases.

G. *Psychosocial-cultural functions:* The client's capacity or ability to function in intrapersonal, interpersonal, intergroup, and sociocultural relationships. *Examples* include:

   1. Grieving; end-of-life.

   2. Psychotic and anxiety behaviors.

   3. Self-concept.

   4. Therapeutic communication.

   5. Group dynamics.

   6. Ethical-legal aspects.

   7. Community resources.

   8. Spiritual needs.

   9. Situational crises.

   10. Substance abuse.

H. *Elimination:* The client's capacity or ability to maintain functions related to relieving the body of waste products. *Examples* include:

   1. Conditions of the gastrointestinal system (vomiting, diarrhea, constipation, ulcers, neoplasms, colostomy, hernia).

2. Conditions of the urinary system (kidney stones, transplants, renal failure, prostatic hypertrophy).

7. Children and Adolescents

Case Management Scenarios and Critical-Thinking Exercises

Medical Diagnosis: Cleft lip and palate.

- *Nursing Problems/Diagnosis:*

  Risk for caregiver role strain.

  Risk for impaired home maintenance management.

  Risk for infection.

  Risk for injury.

  Knowledge deficit: feeding, medication administration.

  Altered nutrition requirements.

  Risk for altered parent—infant attachment.

  Parental role deficit.

- *Chief Complaint:*

  Anne Jones is a newborn with unilateral cleft lip and palate.

- *Past History:*

  Anne was born 3 days ago to Mr. and Mrs. Jones. She is their first child. Both are in their early 30s and are college educated. The paternal grandparents have told the mother that it is her fault: "There has never been a person with a hare lip in our family before." Mrs. Jones is very disturbed and very anxious about handling the infant; she has refused to see the child for the past day.

- *Symptoms:*

  Inability to suck appropriately.

  Liquid taken into the mouth tends to escape via the cleft palate through the nose.

- *Physical Exam:*

  Newborn infant with visible cleft of lip and cleft palate.

  Birth weight: 7 pounds, 6 ounces. No other defects noted.

Heart: No murmurs. Pulse: 152 and regular.

Lungs: Clear to auscultation.

Skin: Pink, warm, and intact except for cleft; slightly jaundiced.

Vitamin K given in the nursery on day 1. Child now taking formula via a syringe.

- *Laboratory Data:*

Hct: 56%. Hgb: 17 g. Bilirubin: 6.

- *Plan:*

Infant to go home with parents when parents can feed her well. She is to return at 3 months of age for cleft lip repair.

Parents to meet with multidisciplinary health care team (general pediatrics, plastic surgery, otolaryngology, orthodontics, speech, audiology, nursing, dietary and social work) prior to discharge.

---

1. Immediately after Anne's birth, what should be included in planning nursing care of Mrs. Jones?

    A. Place her in a room with a woman who has had a set of twins.

    B. Restrict her visitors to allow her more rest.

    C. Have her watch the nurse feed the baby.

    D. Do not discuss the baby unless she brings the subject up herself.

2. In teaching Mrs. Jones to feed her daughter, Anne, which is inappropriate to include in nursing care?

    A. Place the tip of the syringe at the front of Anne's mouth so she can suck.

    B. Rinse the mouth with sterile water after each feeding to minimize infections.

    C. Feed Anne in an upright position and burp frequently to reduce air swallowing.

    D. Apply sterile lubricant to the lips to reduce dryness associated with mouth breathing.

3. Part of the discharge teaching should be the signs and symptoms of a common complication for infants with cleft lip and palate. This is:

    A. Ear infections.

    B. Meningitis.

    C. Anemia.

    D. Seizures.

4. Mrs. Jones calls the clinic 2 months after taking Anne home. She tells the nurse that the baby has a temperature of 102°F, has been turning her head from side to side, and has been eating poorly. The nurse would advise her to:

    A. Cleanse Anne's ears with warm water.

    B. Give Anne acetaminophen, 0.3 mL of infant drops, and call back in 4 hours with her temperature.

    C. Bring Anne into the clinic for evaluation.

    D. Give Anne 4 oz. of water and retake her temperature in 1 hour.

5. Mrs. Jones brought Anne to the clinic, where otitis media on the left side was found on examination. Ear drops were prescribed. The nurse teaches Mrs. Jones to instill the ear drops by instructing her to:

    A. Pull the earlobe down and backward.

    B. Pull the earlobe up and backward.

    C. Pull the earlobe down and forward.

    D. Pull the earlobe up and forward.

6. At 3 months of age Anne returns to the hospital for repair of her cleft lip. On admission, the nurse assesses Anne's developmental status as appropriate. What would the nurse not expect to see?

    A. Smiling in response to her mother's face.

    B. Reaching for shiny objects but missing them.

    C. Holding her head erect and steady.

    D. Sitting with slight support.

7. Anne undergoes repair of her cleft lip. She is awake and beginning to whimper. Her color is pink and pulse is 120 with respirations of 38. IV solution is infusing in her right hand at a rate of 15 mL/hour; the fluid is infusing sluggishly and the hand is edematous. The elbow restraint has loosened and one arm has partially come out. The nursing priority should be to:

    A. Recheck vital signs.

    B. Check the IV site for infiltration.

    C. Check to see if she has voided.

    D. Replace the restraints securely.

8. Following surgery, it is important to prevent Anne from crying excessively. To accomplish this, the nurse should:

    A. Give her a pacifier, to soothe her sucking needs.

  B. Place her on her abdomen, which is the position in which she normally sleeps.

  C. Ask Mrs. Jones to stay and hold her.

  D. Request a special nurse to hold Anne because the staff does not have the time to comfort her.

9. Anne is doing well and eating her normal formula via a syringe. The nurse wants to provide her with appropriate stimulation. The best toy for the nurse to give her is:

  A. A colorful rattle.

  B. A string of large beads.

  C. A mobile with a music box.

  D. A teddy bear with button eyes.

10. Anne is receiving ampicillin, 75 mg PO every 6 hours. Which is the appropriate method of administering the medication to her?

  A. Place the medication on a spoon and place it on the back of her tongue.

  B. Mix the medication with her formula to give it to her via syringe.

  C. Place the medication in a nipple and allow her to suck it down.

  D. Give via a syringe to the side of the mouth.

11. While the nurse is instructing Mrs. Jones in Anne's care before the baby's release, which statement by Mrs. Jones should concern the nurse?

  A. "You know, I haven't taken the baby out much because people stare so."

  B. "My mother-in-law blamed me at first for the baby's problem but she's visiting more often now."

  C. "You know, she's so pretty now she will win a beauty contest just as I did."

  D. "My husband and I enjoy her so much and play with her a great deal."

12. In establishing long-term goals for Anne at discharge, the nurse would not include:

  A. Prevention of hearing loss.

  B. Promotion of adequate speech.

  C. Promotion of adequate parent-child relationship.

  D. Prevention of infection of surgical incision.

Medical Diagnosis: Hydrocephalus following myelomeningocele closure.

- *Nursing Problems/Diagnosis:*

  Altered bowel elimination.

  Risk for infection.

  Risk for injury.

  At risk for altered parenting.

  Impaired physical mobility.

  Impaired skin integrity.

  Altered urinary elimination.

- *Chief Complaint:*

  David Stivic is a 2-month-old exhibiting increasing head size.

- *Past History:*

  David was born with a lumbosacral myelomeningocele, which was repaired at 1 week of age. He is the second child; the first child, a girl, is 3 years old and healthy. Mrs. Stivic had multiple problems with the pregnancy. David's birth weight was 6 pounds, 1 ounce.

- *Symptoms:*

  Irritable and difficult to feed. Experiences occasional vomiting.

- *Physical Exam:*

  Listless, irritable infant.

  Heart: No murmurs. Pulse: 126.

  Lungs: Clear to auscultation.

  Skin: Scar in lumbosacral area of back, approximately L1-3. Slightly erythematous area on back of head.

  Extremities: Bilateral clubfeet and dislocated hips.

  Bowels: Two stools per day, hard and dark.

  Bladder: Slightly distended; mother reports that the infant is constantly wet.

  No immunizations. History of frequent colds. Smiles in response to faces. Cannot hold head up.

- *Laboratory Data:*

  Chest x-ray: Clear.

  Hgb: 12 g. Hct: 40%.

  Urinalysis: Cloudy with many WBCs. Specific gravity: 1.015.

  Current weight: 9 pounds, 1 ounce.

  Temperature: 37.8° C/100.0° F (axillary)

■ *Plan:*

Neurological checks q. shift.

Daily head circumference.

---

13. The nurse should emphasize to the families, that the most important goal of long-term care for the child with myelomeningocele is:

    A. Prevention of obesity.

    B. Promotion of skin integrity.

    C. Prevention of urinary tract infections.

    D. Promotion of sensory stimulation.

14. When caring for a child with myelomeningocele the nurse should understand that:

    A. A large percentage of these children also have hydrocephalus.

    B. The child will never be able to walk.

    C. The child is likely to be continent.

    D. It is unlikely that the child will live past the teen years.

15. In the assessment of the infant for hydrocephalus, the *first* sign the nurse would note is:

    A. Widening pulse pressure.

    B. Headache.

    C. Increasing irritability and poor feeding.

    D. Increasing head circumference.

16. An individualized care plan for David would not include:

    A. Daily measurement of head circumference.

    B. Turn frequently and position with hips abducted.

    C. Credé every 2-4 hours.

    D. Feed 6 oz. every 3 hours.

17. While awaiting specific tests and studies in the hospital, David is alert and fairly active. An appropriate toy for him is:

    A. A busy board.

    B. Large, colorful blocks.

    C. A rattle.

    D. A music box.

18. Computed transaxial tomography (CAT) and other tests confirm the diagnosis of hydrocephalus. Surgery is plan-

ned to place a ventriculoperitoneal shunt. In teaching the parents how the shunt works, the nurse should explain that the shunt redirects fluid from the ventricles of the brain to:

A. The right atrium.

B. The peritoneal cavity.

C. The peritoneal membrane.

D. The stomach.

19. David returns from the recovery room after placement of the shunt. The nurse's immediate plan of care would not include:

A. Position off the operative site.

B. Obtain baseline head circumference.

C. Elevate the head 60 degrees to promote cerebrospinal flow.

D. Monitor for signs of increased intracranial pressure.

20. Four days after surgery, the nurse determines that David is progressing well. However, on physical assessment, he or she would not expect him to be able to:

A. Hold head steady in a sitting position.

B. Hold a rattle for a brief time.

C. Smile in response to the human face.

D. Play with hands and fingers.

21. The revised nursing care plan when David leaves the recovery room and for 2 days afterward would emphasize the importance of keeping David flat in bed to:

A. Prevent pain.

B. Avoid fluid overload.

C. Decrease venous return.

D. Prevent subdural hematoma.

22. In discharge teaching with David's parents, the nurse should include:

A. How to measure abdominal circumference.

B. How to check the urine for glucose.

C. The importance of daily weights.

D. How to measure head circumference.

23. When should the nurse instruct the parents that it is not necessary to seek medical advice?

A. When David develops a temperature and a reluctance to turn his head from side to side.

      B. When they note a foul odor to David's urine.

      C. When they note bulging of the anterior fontanelle when David is crying.

      D. When David has persistent, projectile vomiting.

24. David's parents should be aware that the placement of a new shunt may not be required when there is:

      A. Infection.

      B. Pulmonary embolism.

      C. Normal growth and development.

      D. Clogging or disconnection of the shunt.

25. Mrs. Stivic comes to the clinic 2 months after David's discharge. "I'm so tired. I spend all of my time with David. He cries a lot and I can't rest. I just don't know what to do." The nurse notes that David is alert, with normal vital signs and a flat fontanelle. The most helpful comment the nurse could make is:

      A. "Sometimes I bet you wish you hadn't had him."

      B. "Doesn't your husband help at all with the work?"

      C. "Has David been vomiting or eating less than usual?"

      D. "It must be very hard for you. Have you had any time away from the baby?"

26. During this visit the nurse also notes that David has had no immunizations yet. The nurse realizes that he has missed:

      A. 1 dose of DTaP and 1 dose of IPV.

      B. 1 dose of DTaP and 1 dose of MMR.

      C. 2 doses of DTaP and 2 doses of IPV.

      D. 2 doses of DTaP and TB test.

Medical Diagnosis: Diarrhea and dehydration.

■ *Nursing Problems/Diagnosis:*

Altered bowel elimination.

Fluid volume deficit.

Ineffective health maintenance.

Risk for infection.

Risk for injury.

Imbalanced nutrition.

Impaired skin integrity.

Ineffective thermoregulation.

- *Chief Complaint:*

Johnny Jones, 8 months old, has had diarrhea for 2 days.

- *Past History:*

The child had been well until 3 days before admission, when he began having watery stools and his temperature increased. His family lives on a farm with the water supply coming from a well. His mother is healthy and has no health problems; the father has hypertension.

Johnny is one of three children; he has a 3-year-old brother and a 5-year-old sister, both are healthy. Johnny weighed 8 pounds, 2 ounces at birth.

- *Symptoms:*

Poor skin turgor, excoriated diaper area, depressed fontanelle, decreased weight and urine output.

- *Physical Exam:*

Lethargic, pale infant, but irritable and difficult to console.

Heart: No murmurs. Rate: 130.

Lungs: Clear to auscultation. Rate: 44.

Skin: Poor skin turgor. Dry mucous membranes. Fontanelle depressed. Lips dry and cracked. Buttocks erythematous and rash present. Pale, cool, dry skin.

Decreased peripheral perfusion.

No immunizations. No known allergies. Sits well and has begun to drink from a cup according to his mother. On junior foods and some table foods.

- *Laboratory Data:*

Chest x-ray: Clear.

Hgb: 13 g; Hct: 45%.

K: 3.5 mEq/L.

pH: 7.28.

Temperature: 39.0°C/102.2° F (axillary).

Urinalysis: Cloudy and concentrated, with some WBCs. Specific gravity: 1.030.

Current weight: 17 pounds, 5 ounces. Normal weight: 18 pounds, 8 ounces.

- *Plan:*

Strict I & O.

Daily weight.

Rehydrate with IVFs

NPO

27. Which is most useful in assessing the degree of Johnny's dehydration?

    A. Urinary output.

    B. Skin turgor.

    C. Mucous membranes.

    D. Weight.

28. Johnny is placed NPO and IV fluids are started. Which is the immediate goal of care?

    A. Restoration of intravascular volume.

    B. Prevention of further diarrhea.

    C. Promotion of skin integrity.

    D. Maintenance of normal growth and development.

29. 360 mL of D5 0.2 normal saline is ordered to run over 8 hours intravenously.

    At what rate should the nurse run the fluids? (Microdrip = 60 gtt/mL)

    Fill in the blank with the correct calculation:_____gtt/min.

30. Restraints have to be used with Johnny to maintain the IV line. Which statement best explains their use to the parents?

    A. They have to be used to keep Johnny still all the time.

    B. The restraints will prevent him from pushing the needle through his skin.

    C. He will get used to them if you leave him alone.

    D. As soon as he can take fluids again, and the IV is discontinued, the restraints will not be needed.

31. In order to keep an accurate intake and output, the nurse should:

    A. Insert a Foley catheter and weigh diapers.

    B. Weigh the child after each void or stool.

    C. Apply an external 24-hour urine bag and weigh diapers.

    D. Weigh all diapers and estimate stool amount.

32. Johnny has had only two stools in the last 24 hours and has gained 5 ounces. He is more active and alert. His diet has been advanced to clear liquids. Which liquid is the most appropriate for the nurse to offer?

    A. 7-Up and ginger ale.

    B. Half-strength formula.

    C. Tea and clear broth.

    D. Oral electrolyte solution.

33. Johnny is doing well and is alert and cheerful. Which diversion is appropriate for him?

    A. A colorful mobile.

    B. Large blocks to stack.

    C. A rattle and bell.

    D. A game of peek-a-boo.

34. The day before his discharge Johnny's temperature has risen to 39.6°C/103.3°F (axillary). The nurse comes into the room and finds Johnny having a tonic-clonic convulsion. The best *first* action is to:

    A. Stay with the child and protect him from injury during the seizure.

    B. Inform the physician that seizure activity has occurred.

    C. Institute measures to reduce the child's temperature.

    D. Inform the parents that seizures often occur in children when they have elevated temperatures.

35. The seizure has ended and Johnny's vital signs are stable. His parents were in the room when the seizure occurred and are extremely upset. What is the best statement for the nurse to make to them?

    A. "Don't worry. This often occurs with young children and causes them no harm."

    B. "If we can keep his temperature down, this shouldn't happen again."

    C. "Have any of your other children ever had this happen?"

    D. "I know this must worry you. Has anything like this ever happened before?"

36. While assessing Johnny's developmental level, the nurse expects him to be able to:

    A. Stand erect while holding on to his mother's hand.

    B. Crawl and begin to say "Mama" and "Dada."

    C. Still have a Moro reflex.

    D. Sit down from a standing position without help.

37. The nurse's discharge plan with Johnny's mother included the need for immunizations and prevention of infection. Six weeks after discharge Mrs. Jones brings him to the clinic and he still has not been immunized. Which action is indicated?

    A. Repeat the instructions again, more clearly.

    B. Chastise her for not getting the immunizations.

    C. Make an appointment at the clinic to have the immunizations done.

    D. Assess why Mrs. Jones has not had the immunizations done.

Medical Diagnosis: Kawasaki disease (mucocutaneous lymph node syndrome).

- *Nursing Problems/Diagnosis:*

  Altered cardiac output.

  Fluid volume deficit.

  Altered immune response.

  Altered skin integrity.

  Ineffective thermoregulation.

- *Chief Complaint:*

  Jackie Shabata, 8 months old, is admitted to the pediatrics unit with a diagnosis of Kawasaki disease. This is her first hospitalization. She was a full-term infant who had been healthy prior to the onset of this illness. Jackie has received all her immunizations to date; an only child, she lives with both her natural parents. Her parents report she has had a fever and has refused to eat over the past 8 days, taking only sips from her bottle. She has lost almost 16 ounces during this time.

- *Past History:*

  No history of foreign travel.

- **Symptoms**:

  Fever for 5 or more days; erythema, dryness, fissuring of the lips; bilateral conjunctival inflammation; desquamation (peeling) of hands and feet; rash; cervical lymphadenopathy.

- *Physical Exam:*

  Rectal temperature: 40.0°C/104.0°F.

  Apical pulse rate: 148.

  Respiratory rate: 36.

  Blood pressure: 78/50.

- *Laboratory Data:*

  ESR: 58

  Echocardiogram: decreased left ventricular function.

- *Plan:*

  CBC, sedimentation rate, and platelet count.

  Daily weight.

  Acetaminophen (Tylenol) 10 mg/kg/dose PO q4-6h prn for temperature over 38.5°C or 101.3°F.

  IV 5% dextrose in 0.2% normal saline @ 55 mL/hour.

  High dose (3200 mg IV qd x 4 days) IV immune globulin (IVIG) and ASA therapy (160 mg PO q60).

38. Jackie's parents want to know what Kawasaki disease is. The nurse should tell them that it is:

    A. An acute disease characterized by high fever and skin problems that can affect blood vessels.

    B. A forerunner of rheumatic fever found in younger children.

    C. A newly discovered childhood illness that can lead to acute renal failure.

    D. A virally induced cardiomyopathy following motorcycle accidents.

39. In reading through Jackie's chart, the nurse notices the term "mucocutaneous lymph node syndrome" and realizes this is the same as:

    A. Infantile polyarteritis nodosa.

    B. Kawasaki disease.

    C. Nephrotic syndrome.

    D. Still's disease.

40. Since Jackie has received all the immunizations appropriate for an 8-month-old, the nurse checks her record to confirm that she has been immunized against:

    A. Diphtheria, tetanus, pertussis, and polio.

    B. Diphtheria, tetanus, pertussis, and TB.

    C. Diphtheria, TB, polio, and rubella.

    D. Diphtheria, TB, polio, and measles.

41. During the initial nursing assessment, the nurse is unlikely to see:

    A. Bilateral conjunctivitis and strawberry tongue.

    B. Desquamation of fingers and toes.

    C. Petechiae and hematomas.

    D. Macular erythematous rash and lymphadenopathy.

42. Jackie's temperature is 40°C. Her parents ask the nurse what this "really means." The nurse should advise them that:

    A. It is too early to tell for sure.

    B. Jackie is quite sick, and this is most likely a complication.

    C. Jackie's temperature is within normal limits.

    D. Jackie's temperature is 104°F.

43. At 6 P.M., Jackie has a temperature of 102.7°F. The nurse must administer acetaminophen (Tylenol), 80 mg, to Jackie per physician order. The label on the stock bottle reads: 60 mg = 0.6 mL. How many mL should the nurse give?

    Answer: _____mL.

44. The fever associated with Kawasaki disease is often erratic and high spiking. What action by the nurse is most appropriate, in terms of planning care for Jackie related to the fever?

    A. Ask the pediatrician about starting Jackie on antibiotics as soon as possible.

    B. Check Jackie's temperature every 1–2 hours.

    C. Administer antipyretics as ordered by the physician.

    D. Place Jackie on a hypothermia mattress if antipyretics alone prove ineffective.

45. Jackie's platelet count is 790,000/μL. The nurse should:

    A. Immediately notify the physician.

    B. Check for bleeding tendencies in Jackie's gums and rectal mucosa.

    C. Initiate reverse isolation and notify the physician.

    D. Place the lab report in Jackie's chart for the pediatrician to see.

46. The night nurse checks Jackie's IV line at midnight and notes that there is 225 mL left in the bottle that is hanging. At approximately what time does the nurse anticipate having to add a new bottle of IV fluid?

    A. Immediately, so there is enough fluid to last through the night.

    B. Just prior to change of shift, at 6:45 A.M.

    C. Whenever the bottle is nearly empty.

    D. At 3:30 A.M.

47. At 1 A.M., the nurse checks Jackie again and finds her temperature is 104.8°F. Jackie's IV bottle is almost empty. What action is most appropriate for the nurse to take *first*?

    A. Administer acetaminophen (Tylenol), 80 mg, as ordered by the physician.

    B. Add another bottle of IV fluid.

    C. Check the flow rate of Jackie's IV fluid.

    D. Elevate the head of Jackie's bed and check for pulmonary edema.

48. Jackie has received four times the amount of IV fluid that was ordered for her between midnight and 1 A.M. What should the night nurse do in terms of IV fluids for Jackie during the remainder of the shift?

    A. Notify the physician about the increased IV intake.

    B. Slow the flow rate enough so that Jackie will receive the amount ordered for the remainder of the shift.

    C. Discontinue the IV and observe Jackie closely for fluid over-load.

    D. Adjust the flow rate to 55 mL/hour, per physician order.

49. During the night, Jackie's sedimentation rate comes back from the lab; it is 58 mm/hour. The nurse should know that:

    A. This is a normal sedimentation rate for an 8-month-old.

    B. Her sedimentation rate is lower than the norm, because of the extra IV fluid Jackie received during the night.

    C. Her sedimentation rate is elevated, but has nothing to do with her diagnosis.

    D. Her sedimentation rate is elevated and this is a typical lab finding in the child with Kawasaki disease.

50. When the day nurse weighs Jackie the next morning, she finds Jackie has gained 6 ounces since admission. Jackie still seems irritable and restless, diaphoretic, with a cardiac rate of 180 bpm and regular, and a respiratory rate of 44 breaths/min. Her color is pale. The nurse should recognize that Jackie is:

    A. Starting to gain weight due to better intake, but may be anemic.

    B. Showing signs and symptoms of heart failure.

    C. Stable at the moment.

    D. Doing considerably better this morning.

51. Jackie is transferred to PICU for closer monitoring and her parents are very anxious about this sudden transfer. The nurse in PICU should:

    A. Introduce them to the staff and do a thorough orientation to PICU.

    B. Reassure them that the transfer was only routine procedure.

    C. Allow them to discuss their concerns and fears.

    D. Reinforce that Jackie has only a 1–2% chance for survival and then share their grief concerning her very grim prognosis.

52. Jackie is started on digoxin, 65 mcg PO bid. The nurse administering medication to Jackie in PICU should "hold" the 7 P.M. dose of digoxin and notify the pediatrician if:

    A. Jackie has finally fallen asleep for the first time all day.

    B. Jackie's monitor is showing sinus tachycardia.

    C. Jackie appears slightly jaundiced and her liver enzymes are elevated.

    D. Jackie's apical rate is 98 and regular, with normal sinus rhythm on her monitor.

53. In checking Jackie for appropriate response to digoxin therapy, the nurse should look for:

    A. Nausea, vomiting, and diarrhea.

    B. Hypokalemia.

    C. Slowing of the heart rate and increased urinary output.

    D. Bigeminy or trigeminy.

54. While in PICU, nursing care planning for Jackie will not include:

    A. Allowing parents to visit frequently.

    B. Apnea and cardiac monitor.

    C. Play therapy appropriate to Jackie's age and condition.

    D. Restraining Jackie for IV therapy and confining her to her crib.

55. As Jackie's condition improves, she is sent back to the pediatric unit. Doctor's orders for Jackie include continuing digoxin and a sodium-restricted diet. In planning care for Jackie, the nurse must be sure to tell the play therapist that Jackie:

    A. Needs extra rest and cannot go to the playroom at this time.

    B. Is on a special low-sodium formula and should not receive milk.

    C. Has so many toys and dolls in her room that she does not need to go to the playroom at this time.

    D. Is receiving a medication for her heart and needs to remain on the cardiac monitor, although the therapist may play with her in her room.

56. At the discharge planning conference, the nurses are discussing when Jackie will go home. What precludes discharging Jackie?

    A. Axillary temperature = 37.0°C/98.6°F.

    B. Sedimentation rate = 22 mm/hour and platelet count = 319,000/μL.

    C. Stable weight.

    D. Poor appetite with minimal PO intake.

57. Jackie is going home with her parents; she will need to continue taking digoxin at home. Which is inappropriate health instruction to her parents?

    A. Do not mix digoxin with food or fluids; instead, offer digoxin alone.

    B. If one dose of digoxin is missed for more than 4 hours, you need not be concerned or attempt to make up the missed dose.

    C. It is best to give digoxin within 1 hour after feeding your child.

    D. Store the digoxin in a cupboard, preferably locked, out of reach of the child.

Medical Diagnosis: Congenital heart defect.

- *Nursing Problems/Diagnosis:*

Activity intolerance.

Altered cardiac output.

Altered nutrition.

Altered parenting.

- *Chief Complaint:*

Sam Peterson, 18 months old, was diagnosed shortly after birth as having transposition of the great vessels. He is showing increasing frequency of congestive heart failure and failure to thrive.

- *Past History:*

There is maternal history of cardiac anomalies; Sam's mother has a sister with a cardiac problem. Sam is the youngest of three children, with two older sisters 4 and 7 years old. Mother and father are both healthy. Father is employed as a plumber. Crippled Children's Services is helping with the bills. Sam was diagnosed at 2 days of age as having transposition of the great vessels and had a balloon atrial septostomy (Rashkind-Miller) procedure done. He has had an increasing frequency of congestive heart failure, respiratory infections, and failure to thrive. (Height and weight are below the third percentile on the growth charts.) He is not achieving the normal motor tasks for his age. His parents express great concern over the child and are very anxious about his lack of progress.

- *Symptoms:*

Failure to gain weight and increasing cyanosis.

- *Physical Exam:*

Pale, thin, underdeveloped child with cyanotic lips and nailbeds and clubbing of the fingers and toes.

Heart: Harsh systolic murmur. Pulse: 115.

Lungs: Clear to auscultation. Rate: 36.

Skin: Cool, with clubbing of fingers and toes and cyanosis of lips, mucous membranes, and nailbeds. No known allergies.

Currently being treated with digoxin, furosemide (Lasix) and spironolactone (Aldactone).

- *Laboratory Data:*

Hgb: 17 g; Hct: 55%.

WBC: 5700/μL.

K: 3.7 mEq/L.

ECG: Right ventricular hypertrophy.

Chest x-ray: Cardiac enlargement and increased pulmonary vasculature.

- *Plan:*

Continue medication regime.

NAS (no additional salt) diet.

Evaluate for corrective surgery.

---

58. Sam is admitted for a cardiac catheterization. The parents are present at all times in the hospital and do everything for the child—dress him, feed him, even play for him. You want to prepare the child and the parents for the procedure. It would be most appropriate for the nurse to:

    A. Begin preparing Sam well before the procedure.

    B. Talk with the parents to assess their knowledge and how they can help with Sam's care.

    C. Take no specific action because the child and family have been through a cardiac catheterization previously.

    D. Ask the parents to stay away as much as possible because they upset the child.

59. In reviewing the procedure notes, the nurse determines that cardiac catheterization went well but will not yield information about:

    A. The status of the structural abnormalities.

    B. The pressure gradients.

    C. The degree of pulmonary vascularization.

    D. The oxygen levels in the chambers of the heart.

60. Sam is now 6 hours postcatheterization. The nurse would be most concerned if:

    A. Sam complains of his head hurting.

    B. His pulse is 110 and regular.

    C. The skin temperature of his right leg has decreased.

    D. His temperature has risen to 38.0°C/100.4°F.

61. As the nurse administers antibiotics, Sam's parents ask why he needed to be placed on them prior to catheterization. The best answer is based on the nurse's knowledge that the antibiotics will prevent:

    A. Urinary tract infection.

    B. Pneumonia.

    C. Otitis media.

    D. Endocarditis.

62. Sam has had several episodes of congestive heart failure in the past few months. Which is the most useful to the nurse in assessing his current congestive heart failure?

A. The degree of clubbing of his fingers and toes.

B. Amount of fluid and food intake.

C. Recent fluctuations in weight.

D. The degree of sacral edema.

63. Sam's admission laboratory data reveal an elevated hematocrit. The nurse interprets this as being due to:

A. Chronic infection.

B. Recent dehydration.

C. Increased cardiac output.

D. Chronic oxygen deficiency.

64. Sam is given digoxin, 0.035 mg, at 8 A.M. and 8 P.M. each day. Before the 8 A.M. dose, the nurse takes his apical pulse and it is 85 and regular. Which interpretation is the most accurate?

A. He has just awakened and his heart action is slowest in the morning.

B. This is a normal rate for an 18-month-old child.

C. He may be going into heart block due to digoxin toxicity.

D. His potassium level needs to be evaluated.

65. Sam is eating poorly. While all of the following might play a part, which does the nurse consider most significant in planning Sam's care?

A. Delay in developmental milestones.

B. Decreased energy reserve.

C. Separation anxiety.

D. Frustrated autonomy needs.

66. In instructing the aide regarding what to feed Sam, the nurse emphasizes the importance of:

A. Cheese and ice cream.

B. Finger foods such as hot dogs.

C. Apricots and bananas.

D. Four glasses of whole milk per day.

67. Based on the results of the cardiac catheterization, open-heart surgery to do a complete repair is planned. In answering the parents' questions, the nurse bases the explanations on:

A. The knowledge that the repair will include restructuring the heart to a more normal flow by reversing the aorta and the pulmonary artery.

B. The knowledge that the surgery will create a bypass of the right ventricle.

C. The premise that it is the physician's responsibility to explain the surgical procedure.

    D. The importance of directing the parents toward the postoperative recovery period.

68. Prior to surgery, Sam has a hypoxic episode. What should the nurse do *first*?

    A. Administer oxygen and position him in the knee-chest position.

    B. Position him on his side and give the ordered morphine.

    C. Ask the parents to leave and start oxygen.

    D. Give oxygen and notify the physician.

69. In planning postoperative care for Sam, the nurse expects him to be able to:

    A. Button his shirt and tie his shoes.

    B. Feed himself and drink from a cup.

    C. Cut with scissors.

    D. Walk up and down stairs.

70. The nurse discovers that Sam does none of the expected activities well or at all. His mother comments, "I worry constantly about him. I try to feed him myself so he doesn't get so tired." Considering previous data, the nurse would interpret this to mean that:

    A. Sam is physically incapable due to his cardiac defect.

    B. His mother is overprotective and allows Sam few challenges to develop his skills.

    C. Sam is just being stubborn because of his struggle for autonomy.

    D. Sam is regressed due to the effects of hospitalizations.

71. It is now 10 days past Sam's surgery and he is very stable physically. He is alert and fairly active; he is playing well with his parents. Discharge is planned in the next few days. The nurse notes that Sam's parents are still very reluctant to allow him to do anything for himself. The nurse:

    A. Reemphasizes the need for autonomy in toddlers.

    B. Provides opportunities for autonomy when the parents are not present.

    C. Reassesses the parents' needs and concerns.

    D. Discusses the success of the surgery and how well Sam is doing.

Medical Diagnosis: Fracture of Right Arm

- *Nursing Problems/Diagnosis:*

Impaired comfort.

Altered family processes.

Ineffective health maintenance.

Altered parenting.

- *Chief Complaint:*

Larry Walsh, 2½ years old, is admitted with a fracture of the right arm. Child abuse is suspected.

- *Past History:*

Larry is one of five children under the age of 5; his father has been out of work for 6 months and is unable to find a job. His mother has been trying to work part-time as a waitress. Larry has been seen in the emergency room four times in the past 8 months. His immunizations are not current. Larry's mother is being treated for anemia. The other four children are doing well, with no major health problems, although none of them has up-to-date immunizations.

- *Symptoms:*

Pain, edema, and decreased mobility of upper part of right arm.

- *Physical Exam:*

Child appears very quiet and seems afraid of adults.

Clothes are dirty and torn and there is dirt under the nails.

Heart: Normal with no murmurs. Rate: 88.

Lungs: Clear to auscultation. Rate: 26.

Musculoskeletal: Edema of right upperarm, decreased range of motion in right elbow and shoulder. Arm placed in cast in the emergency department.

Skin: Dirty. Several ecchymoses in various stages of resolution found over torso and lower legs.

No known allergies. Received only first and second groups of immunizations. Not yet toilet trained but can feed self. No previous hospitalizations.

- *Laboratory Data:*

Chest x-ray: Clear.

Hgb: 10 g. Hct: 32%.

WBC: 7200/µL.

Urinalysis: Clear.

- *Plan:*

R/O additional "hidden" injuries.

Update immunization status.

Obtain healthcare for other family members.

Evaluate family dynamics.

72. On obtaining an admission history, the nurse notes that Larry's parents give contradictory explanations as to how Larry's fracture occurred. Because of the suspicion of child abuse noted on the ER notes, the nurse plans to prepare Larry for:

    A. Long bone x-rays.

    B. Brain scan.

    C. Repeat CBC.

    D. Placement in foster care.

73. The nurse plans her interactions with Larry's parents taking into account her knowledge that parents who abuse their children are often characterized as:

    A. Having reasonable expectations of their child's developmental skills.

    B. Having been abused or neglected themselves as children.

    C. Able to manage stressful situations appropriately.

    D. Having well developed support systems among family and friends.

74. Larry's parents come to the unit to visit him the next day. The nurse expects:

    A. The parents to express concern about the extent of damage and Larry's current condition.

    B. The parents to appear guilty about the injury and bring Larry presents to compensate for it.

    C. The parents to play with, talk to, and hold Larry, which seems to make him happy.

    D. Excessive crying from Larry when his parents enter the room.

75. The LPN/LVN on the unit has an encounter with Larry's parents and angrily lectures them for hurting such a defenseless little child. The nurse's response to the LPN/LVN should emphasize:

    A. That no legal action has been taken and her comments make her vulnerable to slander charges.

    B. That being completely honest with the parents is the best policy.

    C. That she should not make premature judgments before all the information has been gathered.

    D. Recognition of the LPN's/LVN's feelings.

76. The nurse's plan of care for Larry should include:

    A. Allowing the parents to visit 4 hours every day.

    B. Assigning one person on each shift to care for him.

    C. Encouraging the child to interact with many different people.

D. Placing him in a room with several toddlers and encouraging peer interaction.

77. Child abuse is confirmed by the data and tests. The nurse's notes will assist in preparation of a report to the:

A. Juvenile division of the police department.

B. State attorney's office.

C. Child protective services.

D. Public health agency.

78. The daily nursing observations of Larry and his parents are important because:

A. The nursing notes will be used in court to prove abuse.

B. The notes will provide a database to plan family intervention.

C. Accurate notes are required on all clients by hospital policy.

D. The notes can prevent the parents from removing the child from the hospital.

79. In attempting to present a role model for appropriate parenting behavior for Mr. and Mrs. Walsh, the nurse should provide opportunities for Larry to:

A. Pile seven or eight blocks on top of one another.

B. Obey a set of complex commands.

C. Brush his teeth and count three objects.

D. Walk up and down stairs.

80. Larry is pale, easily fatigued, and has a hemoglobin of 10g. He has been eating poorly in the hospital and is placed on liquid iron. It is not relevant for the nurse to teach the mother to:

A. Prevent staining of teeth.

B. Expect dark stools.

C. Give the iron with orange juice.

D. Look for the appearance of petechiae.

81. In planning the approach of care with Larry's parents, the nurse knows that the preferred treatment for children who have been abused is to:

A. Leave the child in the home and provide counseling for the parents.

B. Remove the child from the home and place him in a foster home.

C. Have the parents undergo psychiatric counseling while the child is hospitalized.

D. Provide the parents with the number of a child abuse hotline so that they can call when they feel angry and are tempted to abuse the child.

82. Larry comes up to the pediatric unit 6 months after discharge home to his parents. He is very talkative, holds on to his mother's hand, and seems more lively than when you saw him last. His mother appears more relaxed and less critical of him. Which action is indicated?

    A. Change the goals of the care plan since they are inappropriate.

    B. Remark on how well the child and his parents are doing.

    C. Say nothing, as things seem to be going very well.

    D. Make an appointment for the family with the social worker.

Medical Diagnosis: Lead poisoning.

- *Nursing Problems/Diagnosis:*

  Delayed growth and development.

  Injury.

  Imbalanced nutrition.

  Altered parenting.

  Poisoning

  Altered tissue perfusion.

  Risk for violence, other-directed.

- *Chief Complaint:*

  Steven Curtis, 3½ years old, is reported by his mother to have become more aggressive in the past month and to fight constantly with his siblings.

- *Past History:*

  Steven is the third of four children; his mother is separated from her husband. The family currently lives in an older apartment building in the poorer section of the city. One other child in the family—a boy, age 2—was seen recently for lead poisoning. The mother also states that Steven seems to eat anything with which he comes in contact—mud, newspaper, and so forth.

- *Symptoms:*

  Pale, constipated and increasingly irritable in the past few weeks.

- *Physical Exam:*

  Pale, irritable child.

  Heart: Murmur present. Rate: 86 and regular.

  Lungs: Clear to auscultation.

  Skin: Intact with no lesions. Teeth: Lead lines visible.

Immunizations are current and there are no known allergies. Mother feels that Steven is developing more slowly than her other children did; he talked later than they did and she is having trouble with toilet training.

- *Laboratory Data:*

  Hct: 27%; Hgb: 9 g; WBC: 6000/μL.

  Lead levels: 82 μg/dL and 86 μg/dL.

  Urinalysis: Clear with specific gravity of 1.010.

  Chest x-ray: Clear.

  Bone x-rays: Long bones reveal lead deposition.

- *Plan:*

  Begin chelation therapy.

  Conduct developmental evaluation.

---

83. Steven is admitted to the pediatric unit for treatment of chronic lead poisoning. The nursing assessment should not focus on:

    A. Mother-child interaction.

    B. Level of consciousness and mental status.

    C. Eating habits.

    D. Peripheral circulation.

84. In building a database for eventual discharge planning, the nurse determines the most likely source of the lead to be:

    A. Drinking from unglazed pottery mugs.

    B. Eating paint chips.

    C. Eating a large amount of fish.

    D. Eating the newspaper.

85. The primary nursing goal is to:

    A. Teach prevention of further lead ingestion.

    B. Improve the child's nutritional status.

    C. Prevent fatigue and discomfort.

    D. Promote excretion of the lead.

86. Steven is pale, easily fatigued, and has a hemoglobin of 9 g. The nurse interprets this as being due to:

    A. Pica.

    B. Blood loss.

    C. Decreased erythropoietin.

    D. Hemoglobin S.

87. A 24-hour urine is ordered. Mrs. Curtis is not being helpful in the collection. The nurse bases the explanation of its importance on knowledge that this is being done to determine:

    A. The presence of corticosteroids.

    B. The effectiveness of the treatment.

    C. Electrolyte balance.

    D. Hematuria.

88. In planning Steven's care, the nurse needs to be aware that the most serious complication of lead poisoning is:

    A. Hematopoietic.

    B. Renal.

    C. Neurologic.

    D. Cardiovascular.

89. When checking on Steven during morning rounds, the nurse enters the room and observes him having a tonic-clonic seizure. The nurse's *initial* action is to:

    A. Prepare an injection of diazepam (Valium).

    B. Suction his nasopharynx.

    C. Maintain a patent airway.

    D. Place a tongue blade between his teeth.

90. CaEDTA (IV) is ordered; BAL is ordered to be given by deep IM injection to Steven. He will be receiving six injections per day. Which is inappropriate to include in the nursing care plan?

    A. Allow the child to play with the needle after the injection.

    B. Push fluids up to 200 mL/hour.

    C. Record accurate intake and output.

    D. Request an order for EMLA to give with the injections to decrease pain.

91. What should the nurse assess daily during Steven's course of therapy?

    A. Glucose and potassium levels.

    B. BUN.

    C. Urinary lead level.

    D. CBC.

92. Which test is the most appropriate for assessing Steven's development?

    A. Stanford-Binet Intelligence Test.

B. Denver II Developmental Screening Test.

C. Peabody Picture Vocabulary Test.

D. Piers-Harris Self-Concept Scale.

93. Just before Steven is to be discharged, Mrs. Curtis says to the nurse, "Steven drives me crazy; he always wants to play out there in the street with his big brothers." Which reply is most helpful to Mrs. Curtis?

A. "Don't worry about it. He will learn safety with experience."

B. "You should never allow him outside unless an adult is with him."

C. "You should keep him in the house with you. At age 3½ he must be protected from what he can't understand."

D. "You should tell him to play in a certain area and enforce the rule with discipline."

94. At 3½ years, it is not expected that Steven is capable of:

A. Nighttime continence.

B. Counting to 3 and dressing himself.

C. Skipping on alternating feet.

D. Having a vocabulary of 2000 words.

95. Which is an appropriate play activity for the nurse to plan for Steven in the hospital?

A. Spinning tops.

B. Finger painting.

C. Dressing up and playing house.

D. Cutting out pictures and pasting them on paper.

96. Which effect of lead poisoning is reversible and therefore does not need to be part of long-term goals for care?

A. Learning disability.

B. Hyperkinesis.

C. Seizure activity.

D. Persistent anemia.

97. Which value indicates that Steven is ready for discharge?

A. Serum lead level of 40 μg.

B. Glucose in the urine.

C. Hemoglobin of 9 g.

D. WBC of 5500/uL.

Medical Diagnosis: Tonsillectomy.

- *Nursing Problems/Diagnosis:*

  Anxiety.

  Impaired comfort.

  Risk for fluid volume deficit.

  Risk for injury.

  Impaired swallowing.

- *Chief Complaint:*

  Mary Hawkins, 4 years old, suffers frequent strep throats and shows decreasing hearing.

- *Past History:*

  Mary has had four strep throats in the past 7 months. She has also had several cases of otitis media, which have led to decreasing hearing in the left ear. Mary is the youngest of three children; neither of the parents has any health problems. The children have had only minor illnesses and none has ever had surgery. Mrs. Hawkins is very concerned about the surgery and has not told her daughter anything about the planned surgery.

- *Symptoms:*

  History of sore throats.

- *Physical Exam:*

  Developmentally appropriate 4-year-old child in no acute distress.

  Heart: Normal with no murmurs. Rate: 90.

  Lungs: Clear to auscultation.

  Ears: Tympanic membranes clear.

  Throat: Tonsils enlarged but not currently inflamed. Adenoids also enlarged. Child has nasal speech and is a mouth breather.

  Mouth: Lips and mucous membranes slightly dry.

  Immunizations current. Has had no previous surgeries. No known allergies.

  Normal growth and development. Will start kindergarten in 3 months.

- *Laboratory Data:*

  Chest x-ray: Clear.

  Hct: 42%; Hgb: 14 g.

  Urinalysis: Clear with no RBCs or WBCs; pH of 7 and specific gravity of 1.015.

  Clotting time: 6.5 minutes. Bleeding time: 3 minutes.

- *Plan:*

  NPO.

  Parent to sign consent for surgery.

  Probable discharge within 23 hours.

---

98. During examination of Mary's throat on admission, which is not indicative of an infection of the tonsils?

    A. Elevated temperature.

    B. Koplik spots on the buccal mucosa.

    C. Cervical lymph node enlargement.

    D. Tonsillar white patches.

99. Mary arrived at the hospital having been told she was going to "the doctor's house for a visit." The mother is emphatic that she does not want the child told about the surgery. Which is the best way for the nurse to manage this situation?

    A. Call the physician and have her or him talk to the mother.

    B. Prepare the child when the parents leave for the evening.

    C. Respect the mother's wishes and do not prepare the child.

    D. Assess the mother's reasons for refusing preparation.

100. Mary becomes very upset and agitated when her parents leave to go home for the night. She refuses to be comforted and is crying and calling out for them. What nursing action is most appropriate?

    A. Tell her that they will be back at 7 A.M.

    B. Bring another child her age to keep her company.

    C. Leave her alone so she will settle down on her own.

    D. Stay in the room and complete the nursing care of her roommate.

101. Prior to surgery, the nurse wants to gather certain data about Mary. It is irrelevant to:

    A. Check her teeth.

    B. Evaluate coagulation studies.

    C. Note the WBC count and urinalysis results.

    D. Check the SGOT and SGPT levels.

102. Just before Mary is to go to surgery, which assessment by the nurse necessitates a call to the surgeon?

    A. Temperature of 38.0°C/100.4°F (axillary).

    B. Mouth breathing.

    C. Urine specific gravity of 1.018.

    D. Bleeding time of 10 minutes.

103. Mary is to receive atropine IM prior to surgery. In explaining the medication to her, which statement is most appropriate?

    A. "All the other boys and girls have shots before surgery. They don't cry."

    B. "The needle will hurt a little bit, but if you don't fight me, I'll give you a balloon."

    C. "The doctor wants you to have this injection so you will go to sleep."

    D. "The needle will hurt like a prick. You choose the leg you want it in and then squeeze your mother's hand when I give it to you."

104. Which is *not* appropriate information about the side effects of atropine for Mary's mother to help alleviate her anxiety about Mary postoperatively? The medication:

    A. Causes a dry mouth.

    B. May produce a flushed face.

    C. Causes increased swallowing.

    D. May cause hallucinations.

105. In assessing Mary for hemorrhage postoperatively, which finding is of least concern?

    A. Frequent swallowing and drooling of serosanguineous mucus.

    B. Increased respiratory rate.

    C. Increased pulse and decreased blood pressure.

    D. Emesis of dark blood.

106. For Mary's postoperative care, which action is appropriate?

    A. Give warm tea and honey to decrease throat pain.

    B. Give aspirin for elevated temperature.

    C. Suction the oropharynx every 2 hours and prn.

    D. Place in side lying position until responsive.

107. Which food item should the nurse offer Mary postoperatively?

    A. Orange juice.

    B. Lemonade.

    C. Vanilla ice cream.

    D. Green Jell-O.

108. Aspirin, 300 mg, PO or rectally, every 4 hours for pain or elevated temperature, has been ordered by the physician. The nurse should:

    A. Check the chart to see if Mary is allergic to aspirin.

    B. Note that this is an overdose and notify the physician that a smaller dose is needed.

    C. Go ahead and give the drug when Mary's temperature reaches 39.0°C/102.2°F (axillary).

    D. Hold the drug and call the physician to question the order.

109. Mary is very angry with her mother after surgery. She tells her, "I hurt. I hurt. Why did you bring me here? I hate you." What is the best advice the nurse can give Mary's mother?

    A. Try to regain Mary's trust by meeting all her needs and bringing extra presents.

    B. Inform the mother that she should have let the nurse prepare the child before surgery, as was recommended.

    C. Ignore Mary's words and allow her more freedom when she re-turns home, to distract her.

    D. Allow Mary to talk about her surgery and play out her anger with her dolls.

110. Mary is to be discharged after a 23-hour hold. Which concern about effects of hospitalization can the nurse omit in discharge teaching with her mother?

    A. Mary's likelihood of following the mother around the house as she does her work.

    B. Nightmares.

    C. Increased independence.

    D. Temper tantrums and bedwetting.

111. The nurse has completed discharge teaching with Mrs. Hawkins. Which signs or symptoms should Mrs. Hawkins report to the physician to indicate that she understood the nurse's teaching?

    A. Temperature elevation of 38.4°C/101.1°F (axillary) and dysphagia.

    B. Minor bleeding between the fifth and tenth postop day, with scab loss.

    C. White patches at the site of the tonsils.

    D. Temperature elevation of 38.4°C/101.1°F (axillary) and pain in the right ear.

Medical Diagnosis: Acute lymphocytic leukemia.

- *Nursing Problems/Diagnosis:*

  Interrupted family process.

  Fear.

  Risk for fluid volume deficit.

  Anticipatory grieving.

  Risk for infection.

  Risk for injury.

  Imbalanced nutrition.

  Impaired oral mucous membrane.

  Impaired skin integrity.

  Ineffective tissue perfusion.

- *Chief Complaint:*

  Amanda Curtis, 7 years old, experienced continued bleeding after having a tooth extracted.

- *Past History:*

  Amanda had been a normal, healthy child previously. She has had increased bruising of the extremities during the past 4 months. Mother reports that she also seems to tire more easily and has not been able to get rid of a cold she has had for 3 weeks. The parents are college educated and both work; the father is a lawyer and the mother works for an advertising firm. They have one other child—a boy, age 11—who is healthy. The maternal grandmother had breast cancer. No other known family health problems. Amanda developed normally and is now just starting second grade and doing well.

- *Symptoms:*

  Pallor, fatigue, and an increase in number and length of infections.

- *Physical Exam:*

  Pale, quiet, white girl, 7 years old. Appears to be slightly underweight.

  Heart: Questionable murmur heard. Rate: 86 and regular.

  Lungs: Minor rhonchi on auscultation.

  Skin: Ecchymoses on legs in various stages of resolution. Petechiae on throat and upper arms. Nailbeds pale.

  Enlarged cervical and inguinal lymph nodes.

  Enlarged liver.

  Has lost 3 pounds in the past month. No known allergies. Has received all required immunizations.

- *Laboratory Data:*

  Chest x-ray: Clear.

  Hct: 26%; Hgb: 8 g.

  WBC: 12,000/µL, with several blast cells seen on peripheral smear. Platelets: 100,000/µL.

  Urinalysis: Clear.

  Cerebrospinal fluid: Clear with no abnormal cells.

  Vital signs: Blood pressure, 110/70. Pulse, 86 and regular. Respirations, 24. Temperature, 100.8°F (orally).

- *Plan:*

  Schedule bone marrow aspiration (BMA).

  Prepare for chemotherapy (induction phase).

  Discuss possibility of bone marrow transplantation (BMT) with parents if first remission fails.

---

112. Amanda is suspected of having acute lymphocytic leukemia; she is admitted to the pediatric unit. The *priority* nursing assessment is:

    A. What Amanda knows about leukemia.

    B. Parents' coping abilities in previous grief situations.

    C. Amanda's previous experiences with illness and hospitalization.

    D. Amanda's cognitive and physical developmental abilities.

113. What is the *priority* nursing goal in selecting an appropriate roommate for Amanda?

    A. Promotion of peer contacts and stimulation.

    B. Prevention of infection.

    C. Provision of privacy.

    D. Promotion of sensory stimulation.

114. To confirm the diagnosis, Amanda is scheduled to have a bone marrow aspiration done. Which approach is not included in the nurse's preparation?

    A. Emphasize that there will be little pain.

    B. Tell Amanda that she can be up and about after she recovers from the premedication.

    C. Explain that the test will be done on her hip and a bandage placed over it afterward.

    D. Tell her that she will receive some medication to make her sleepy before the test is done.

115. In preparing Amanda for the procedure, the nurse positions her with the knowledge that bone marrow aspirations in children are least likely to be done at the following site:

    A. Vertebral.

    B. Tibial.

    C. Sternal.

    D. Iliac crest.

116. During her bone narrow aspiration, Amanda is sedated with midazolam (Versed). Her aspiration was done on the left posterior iliac crest. Which causes the nurse the *greatest* concern 1 hour after the procedure?

    A. Patch of blood about 2 inches in diameter on the pressure dressing.

    B. Responds to her name slowly and pushes the nurse's hand away.

    C. Respirations of 12 and decreased breath sounds.

    D. Blood pressure of 110/72 and pulse of 90.

117. Based on the nurse's analysis of the previous situation, the best action is to:

    A. Call the physician and report a suspicion of hemorrhage.

    B. Elevate the head of the bed to aid respiratory effort.

    C. Prepare an IV line to deliver fluids to expand the intravascular volume.

    D. Provide more covers because she is hypothermic due to shock.

118. The bone marrow aspiration confirms the diagnosis of acute lymphocytic leukemia. Amanda is started on prednisone and vincristine. Which nursing behavior is *not* appropriate?

    A. Increase daily fluid intake.

    B. Provide a footboard for Amanda when she is in bed.

    C. Assess for numbness and tingling in the extremities.

    D. Assess for cardiac arrhythmias.

119. Which laboratory data should the nurse evaluate regularly in the child undergoing chemotherapy?

    A. SGOT and SGPT.

    B. LDH and WBC.

    C. Potassium and pH levels.

    D. CBC.

120. Amanda has nausea and vomiting and has developed stomatitis (mouth ulcers). Her nutritional intake is compromised. In selecting her lunch, the nurse recommends:

    A. Pizza, coke, and cookies.

    B. Tomato soup, toast, and ice cream.

    C. Omelet, Jell-O, and milk shake.

    D. Hot dog, potato chips, and popsicles.

121. Which activity will help a 7-year-old cope with the stress and fear engendered by her hospitalization and treatment?

    A. Demonstrating procedures and treatments on another child her own age.

    B. Explaining all procedures in great detail using a plastic model of the human body to do so.

    C. Using puppets and dolls to explain procedures and permitting the child to handle the hospital equipment.

    D. Diversional activities such as playing house, jigsaw puzzles, and books.

122. Amanda is doing well. It is 3:40 P.M. She has an IV running at 50 mL/hour, of which 75 mL remains, after which it will be discontinued. She has a small, sacral sore, which is healing, and the dressing was to have been changed at 3 P.M. She has IV penicillin due at 4 P.M. However, Amanda is looking forward to seeing her brother in the waiting room. In deciding which action to take first, the most important *priority* is to:

    A. Change the sacral dressing.

    B. Discontinue the IV immediately.

    C. Allow her to visit her brother.

    D. Administer the medication.

123. Amanda's parents are concerned about what they should tell her 11-year-old brother about her illness. The nurse should:

    A. Suggest that the topic be open conversation so that both information and feelings about leukemia can be discussed at home.

    B. Encourage the parents to realize that the brother is not really affected by this event since it is not a hereditary disease.

    C. Suggest that the parents share information about Amanda's condition.

    D. Encourage the parents to act as if everything were completely normal and avoid increasing family stress levels.

124. During her morning care one day, Amanda says to the nurse, "What is going to happen to me when I die?" The nurse's best response is:

    A. "You won't be alone. I'll be here with you."

    B. "I don't know."

    C. "Do you think you're going to die soon?"

    D. "What do you think will happen?"

125. Mrs. Curtis is very critical of the care her daughter is receiving. Every day she has a new complaint. Today she says to you, "Amanda didn't get her bath until 10 o'clock today. I think it's disgraceful, considering the price of a room in this hospital." Before responding, the nurse is least likely to consider:

    A. That anger at the nursing staff is often seen in the grieving process.

    B. That Mrs. Curtis is looking for a reason to sue, particularly since her husband is a lawyer.

    C. That further data are needed about Mrs. Curtis and her current feelings and perceptions of Amanda's situation.

    D. Her own resentment at being criticized for giving poor care to a child who is chronically ill.

126. Amanda is discharged home in remission and on continuing chemotherapy. Her primary nurse phones Mrs. Curtis to discuss her progress 3 weeks after discharge. Her mother reports that she is keeping Amanda out of school to prevent infections. The nurse should:

    A. Explain that Amanda needs her peers and school work.

    B. Recommend further immunizations be done to protect her.

    C. Suggest an appointment with the psychiatrist to discuss why the parents are isolating Amanda.

    D. Agree that this is the best approach for the next year.

Medical Diagnosis: Sickle cell anemia.

- *Nursing Problems/Diagnosis:*

Caregiver role strain.

Interrupted family processes.

Risk for fluid volume deficit.

Delayed growth and development.

Risk for injury.

Acute pain.

Ineffective tissue perfusion.

- *Chief Complaint:*

Ronny Simpson, 8 years old, has been experiencing increased pain in his legs and abdomen after playing a game of tag.

- *Past History:*

Ronny is an African-American child who was diagnosed with sickle cell anemia at 2 years of age when he presented with hand-foot syndrome. He is one of five children; none of his siblings has sickle cell anemia. His mother has hypertension; his father has sickle cell anemia and two cousins also have the problem. Ronny has had several crises over the past 6 years and has missed school frequently. Currently he is one grade behind where he should be in school.

- *Symptoms:*

Pain in legs and abdomen.

- *Physical Exam:*

8-year-old African-American child with complaints of leg and abdominal pain.

Heart: Pulse, 100. Blood pressure, 100/66. Murmur present.

Lungs: Clear to auscultation; good air exchange; rate of 30.

Skin: Intact, with no lesions; slight diaphoresis.

Eyes: Icterus present.

Appears small and underweight for age. No known allergies, and immunizations are up-to-date. Has had three respiratory infections in the past year. Takes folic acid 1 mg q day.

- *Laboratory Data:*

Hct: 20%; Hgb: 6 g.

Urinalysis: Clear, with some RBCs seen; specific gravity of 1.022. Temperature: 37.8°C/100.0°F (orally).

Bilirubin: 25 mg/100 mL.

- *Plan:*

Admit for IVF therapy and pain control.

Refer child and family to comprehensive sickle cell clinic for ongoing care and support.

---

127. Of the following information recited by Mr. and Ms. Simpson in their explanations of sickle cell anemia, the one fact that the nurse needs to correct for them is that:

  A. Sickle cell anemia is due to heterozygous inheritance of a gene responsible for production of abnormal hemoglobin.

  B. Sickle cell anemia is seen in African-American and people of Mediterranean ancestry.

  C. Hemoglobin S sickles in conditions that involve hypoxia.

  D. Sickle cell anemia is associated with a poor prognosis.

128. Ronny has severe abdominal and leg pain. His vital signs are: blood pressure 100/68, pulse 94, and respirations 24. Which is inappropriate to include in the initial care plan?

    A. Oxygen by mask and cold applications to leg to relieve pain.

    B. Morphine for pain and frequent vital signs.

    C. Forcing fluids and strict intake and output.

    D. Bedrest and diversionary activities as tolerated.

129. The best roommate for Ronny is:

    A. An 8-year-old boy 3 days after appendectomy with a temperature of 101°F.

    B. A 7-year-old boy with juvenile rheumatoid arthritis.

    C. An 8-year-old girl with a cardiac defect.

    D. A 9-year-old boy with pneumonia.

130. The nurse wants to assess Ronny's color. It is not helpful to inspect the:

    A. Mucous membranes.

    B. Nailbeds.

    C. Palms of hands.

    D. Earlobes.

131. Ronny normally has a hemoglobin of 7 and a hematocrit of 20. His anemia is due to:

    A. Poor dietary practices and decreased iron inta ke.

    B. Decreased erythropoietin activity.

    C. Blood loss due to the sickle cell crises.

    D. Increased fragility and decreased life span of RBCs.

132. Ronny was placed on folic acid at time of diagnosis (age 2). An order for folic acid, 1 mg once a day, has been continued by the resident in charge of Ronny's case. The nurse should:

    A. Go ahead and give the medication with Ronny's favorite juice.

    B. Question the order because it is too high a dosage for a child.

    C. Give it to Ronny and explain its purpose and side effects in terms Ronny will understand.

    D. Question the order because the nurse knows vitamins are of questionable value in sickle cell anemia.

133. Which activity is best for Ronny while on bed rest?

    A. Television programs most of the day.

    B. Phone calls from his friends at home and at school.

C. Reading books about famous African-American people.

D. Playing checkers and simple card games with his room-mate.

134. Increased fluid intake and fluids that help produce an alkaline environment are recommended. The nurse needs to help Ronny and his parents understand that these fluids will:

   A. Increase his blood volume and prevent sickling.

   B. Promote urinary output and decrease the chance of urinary tract infections.

   C. Promote caloric intake and good nutritional status.

   D. Prevent dehydration, which increases sickling of RBCs.

135. The basis of genetic counseling for the Simpson family stems from the knowledge that Mr. Simpson has sickle cell disease and Ms. Simpson:

   A. Must also have the disease.

   B. Must have the trait.

   C. Is disease free for the rest of her life.

   D. May or may not have the sickle cell trait.

136. There are other children in the family who have never had sickle cell disease. Therefore:

   A. Some of them may be free of the trait.

   B. None of them carries the trait.

   C. Each child carries the trait, but may not have the disease.

   D. Each child will pass the trait on to his or her children.

137. In establishing teaching goals for Ronny's discharge plan, the nurse may want to emphasize that Ronny's current sickle cell crisis was probably due to:

   A. Infection.

   B. Cold weather.

   C. Dehydration.

   D. Increased activity.

Medical Diagnosis: Rheumatic fever.

■ *Nursing Problems/Diagnosis:*

Diversional activity deficit.

Impaired comfort.

Risk for injury.

Ineffective tissue perfusion.

- *Chief Complaint:*

  Kathy Mendez, age 8, is brought to the public health clinic by her mother, who reports that lately the child has not felt like going to school.

- *Past History:*

  Kathy had rubella and chickenpox prior to entering school. In the past 2 years, she has had recurrent sore throats. The most recent complaint of sore throat, according to her mother, was 5 weeks ago. In the past 2 weeks, Kathy has had no energy, has complained of pain, has requested to stay at home, and appears to have lost weight. Other than immunizations required for school, Kathy has had no health care. No major illnesses were reported. Kathy has three brothers, ages 6, 9, and 11. Kathy's parents divorced 3 years ago and she has not seen her father since that time. Her mother works 50–55 hours per week away from home. Kathy and her family live in a three-room apartment in a government housing project.

- *Symptoms:*

  Fatigue and apparent weight loss.

- *Physical Exam:*

  Weight: at 25th percentile.

  Abdomen: Complains of generalized pain on palpation.

  MS: Complains of pain in shoulders, elbows, and wrists during active range of motion.

  Skin: Palpable subcutaneous nodules on knees, scapula, and thoracic spine. Macular rash on anterior trunk. Brown residue in skin creases and under nails.

  Head: Mouth: Brown and yellow plaque lining gums and teeth

  Hair: Oily and matted.

- *Laboratory Data:*

  ASLO: 340 Todd units.

  EKG: prolonged PR interval.

- *Plan:*

  Admit and R/O "Rheumatic Fever".

  Post confirmation of diagnosis, begin Rheumatic Fever Prophylaxis Regime.

---

138. Kathy is admitted to the children's unit of the local hospital. Based on knowledge of rheumatic fever and related current adaptation needs and possible complications, the nurse evaluates which of the following as having *first* priority in Kathy's initial admission assessment?

     A. Reasons for Kathy's apparent lack of hygienic care.

B. Apical pulse rate and coordination of voluntary muscles.

C. Type, intensity, and duration of pain in subcutaneous nodules.

D. Specific foods eaten within the past 24 hours.

139. During the assessment, Kathy's mother states that she thought Kathy's possible rheumatic joint pains were "growing pains." In health teaching regarding differentiation of the two pain types, the nurse replies to Kathy's mother:

A. "During rest or sleep, pains from growth may lessen or disappear, but the joint pains of rheumatic fever do not lessen."

B. "There are no characteristic differences between the two types of pain; therefore, neither one can be specified."

C. "Rheumatic pain consistently occurs bilaterally in joints either above or below the diaphragm, whereas growth pains occur only in joints below the diaphragm."

D. "The 8-year-old child is developmentally incapable of describing pain characteristics; therefore, it is not possible to differentiate between rheumatic joint pain and 'growing pains' based on Kathy's complaints."

140. Based on Kathy's developmental stage, tentative diagnosis, and related health needs, the nurse plans to place Kathy in a room with:

A. Eight-year-old Jolene, who has playroom privileges and was admitted with superficial bruises resulting from an automobile accident.

B. Eight-year-old Alma, who is confined to bed with asthma and pneumonia.

C. Ten-year-old Marta, who is confined to bed with acute systemic lupus erythematosus.

D. Nine-year-old Judy, who is up ad lib and admitted for glucose tolerance tests and insulin therapy regulation.

141. Kathy is diagnosed as having acute rheumatic fever. To destroy any remaining group A beta-hemolytic streptococci, penicillin is ordered for Kathy. Just prior to receiving an intramuscular injection, she cries and says to the nurse, "Will the shot hurt? I'm afraid." The nurse should reply:

A. "You're scared? What would your friends think if they knew you were afraid?"

B. "Yes, there will be a little pain, but it will soon be over."

C. "You may go to the playroom as soon as you have your injection."

D. "I will try not to hurt you. If you cry, it will only make it worse."

142. Polyarthritis migrates to Kathy's knees. Considering physical adaptation needs and appropriate nursing management related to this manifestation, the nurse should:

    A. Apply elastic bandages and leg splints to increase circulation while immobilizing Kathy's knees.

    B. Gently massage Kathy's legs and knees to increase circulation and promote healing.

    C. Perform passive range of motion and encourage Kathy to ambulate frequently to prevent contractures.

    D. Place a bed cradle over Kathy's legs to prevent physical or material contact.

143. In analyzing the school-age child's problems in adapting to hospitalization, the nurse acknowledges which aspect to be the *most* difficult for Kathy to accept?

    A. Separation from her mother and her family.

    B. Separation from her friends and possible alienation from her established group.

    C. Absence from school, possibly falling behind in homework, and failing in her grades.

    D. Restricted mobility, possible bodily injury, and lack of control over self-care.

144. The nurse recognizes Kathy's nervousness, weakness, and emotional instability as indications of Sydenham's chorea, a disorder associated with the rheumatic process. If this condition worsens and clinical manifestations increase and are intensified, nursing actions should include:

    A. Encouraging Kathy to build her strength, vent her emotions, and utilize stored excess energy by scheduling increased playroom time with school-age children.

    B. Preventing complications by providing absolute rest, padded bedding, spoon-feeding, and a diet high in calories, protein, and iron.

    C. Alleviating Kathy's inferiority feelings by providing pencils, paper, and extra study time for keeping up with her schoolwork.

    D. Preventing further psychological damage by removing all visiting restrictions, arranging psychological counseling, and instituting a self-care regimen for Kathy.

145. Kathy is prescribed large-dose acetylsalicylic acid therapy. In observing Kathy for indications of salicylate toxicity, the nurse does not expect to see:

    A. Erythema marginatum, cardiac murmur.

    B. Drowsiness, nausea, and vomiting.

    C. Hyperpnea, purpuric manifestations.

    D. Tinnitus, gastric bleeding.

146. In nursing evaluation of Kathy's progress, which manifestation indicates increasing severity in Kathy's health problem?

    A. Decreasing erythrocyte sedimentation rate.

    B. WBC count of 9000/μL.

    C. Orthopnea and peripheral edema.

    D. Pulse rate 88 and negative C-reactive protein.

147. Kathy is prescribed steroid (cortisone) therapy. Which is not an important nursing action related to long-term steroid administration?

    A. Prevent exposure to infection and check urine for glucose.

    B. Administer with antacid or milk and assess for emotional lability.

    C. Monitor blood pressure, daily weight, and skin for any changes.

    D. Report possible infectious processes suggested by high temperature elevations.

148. Furosemide (Lasix) is added to Kathy's medication regimen. Which is the *most important* nursing action related to simultaneous administration of furosemide and digoxin?

    A. Observe Kathy for headache, nausea, muscular weakness, disordered vision, and changes in apical heart rate and rhythm.

    B. Monitor Kathy for changes in weight, skin turgor, texture of mucous membranes, and radial pulse rate.

    C. Assess Kathy for absent or unequal peripheral pulses, ecchymoses, cyanosis, or numbness/tingling of the lower extremities.

    D. Report elevated temperature, flushed face, anorexia, and bounding radial pulses.

149. Potassium chloride (KC1) is added to Kathy's IV solution. Which does not prevent possible life-threatening complications resulting from IV KC1 administration?

    A. Kathy's urinary output is greater than 30 mL/hour.

    B. Kathy's cardiac status is monitored and recorded.

    C. The solution is infused at a rapid rate.

    D. The KC1 is thoroughly mixed in the IV solution.

150. As Kathy's health status improves, she indicates she is bored and asks the nurse for "something entertaining to do." The nurse requests that Kathy decide on an activity, but omits which option from Kathy's selection?

    A. Finger painting, stringing beads, and making puppets.

    B. Video games, leather crafts, and clay modeling.

      C. Reading, playing catch, and playing guessing games.

      D. Playing checkers, Scrabble, or Monopoly with her roommate.

151. At discharge, Kathy's mother requests information about Kathy's home care. The nurse should reply:

      A. "Kathy *must* have antibiotic therapy indefinitely and exactly as ordered."

      B. "Kathy is now immune to further problems related to rheumatic fever."

      C. "There are no restrictions on Kathy's activities at home or at school."

      D. "Kathy should be provided a diet high in carbohydrates and fats and low in protein."

Medical Diagnosis: Asthma.

- *Nursing Problems/Diagnosis:*

  Activity intolerance.

  Ineffective airway clearance.

  Risk for fluid volume deficit.

  Impaired gas exchange.

  Ineffective individual coping: mother.

  Risk for infection.

- *Chief Complaint:*

  Tom Boyd, 11-years-old, started wheezing during the night.

- *Past History:*

  Tom began having wheezing attacks 5 years ago at age 6 and was subsequently diagnosed as having asthma. He has multiple allergies to house dust; dog and cat dander; cigarette smoke; and some foods, such as chocolate. Father is also known to have respiratory problems and several allergies. His mother is healthy but seems very anxious about Tom and his care. She takes total responsibility for his care, including giving him all his medications; she has concentrated on Tom since his diagnosis. There are two other children, a 7-year-old boy and a 15-year-old girl. The younger boy has been having difficulty in school the past year. Tom has had several upper respiratory infections in the past few months and missed several days of school.

- *Symptoms:*

  Wheezing, increased pulse, and diaphoresis.

- *Physical Exam:*

  11-year-old child in acute respiratory distress.

Heart: Pulse: 96 but regular. No murmurs heard.

Lungs: Audible wheezing. Breath sounds tight, with little air exchange. Coughing frequently. Mucus is thick and clear.

Skin: Intact, with no signs of breakdown; diaphoretic.

Immunizations up-to-date.

Current medications: Salmeterol (*Serevent*) bid and cromolyn sodium 4 times a day.

- **Laboratory Data:**

Chest x-ray: Hyperinflation of the lungs with beginning atelectasis in right middle lobe.

Hgb: 15 g; Hct: 40%.

Urinalysis: Clear, with no cells; specific gravity of 1.020.

Blood gases: Respiratory acidosis. pH 7.30. PCO_2: 45. PO_2: 89. HCO_3: 20.

- **Plan:**

Admit for acute respiratory care.

Enroll in support group and self-management program upon discharge.

---

152. Tom is admitted to the pediatric unit from the emergency room, where he received albuterol without relief. His current vital signs are temperature of 38.2°C/100.8°F (orally), pulse of 110, and respirations of 36. The nurse wants to have which of the following readily available?

    A. Tracheostomy set.

    B. Oxygen.

    C. Morphine sulfate.

    D. ECG monitor.

153. Methylprednisolone is ordered to be given intravenously every 4 hours. Which is the *least* essential to assess?

    A. Phlebitis at the IV site.

    B. GI upset.

    C. Breath sounds.

    D. Urinary output.

154. During his acute attack, in which position will Tom be most comfortable?

    A. Head of bed elevated 15 degrees.

    B. Turned on his side.

    C. Sitting up.

    D. Prone.

155. During morning report, two nurses hear that Tom has been admitted and say, "Oh, no. He's back in. It seems as though he has lived here the past few months." The head nurse's best response is:

    A. "Yes, I agree it is really getting to be monotonous."

    B. "His parents just don't seem to care enough, and they don't give him the care he needs."

    C. "It's discouraging having him come back so often. It seems we aren't doing our discharge teaching right."

    D. "I know it's difficult having him back so frequently. It is upsetting for us and for him and his family."

156. Two days later, Tom's secretions have become thicker and slightly yellow in color. His temperature is 39.0°C/102.2°F (orally) and breath sounds are decreased on the left side. The nurse should *first*:

    A. Increase his fluid intake to mobilize secretions.

    B. Administer acetaminophen (Tylenol) to decrease his temperature.

    C. Increase the frequency of Tom's deep breathing and coughing.

    D. Notify physician of increased temperature and change in mucus.

157. The sputum culture is positive and a chest x-ray confirms pneumonia. Penicillin, 800,000 units IV is ordered. Before the penicillin is given, which nursing action is least relevant?

    A. Assess his medical record for medication allergies.

    B. Explain to him why he will be taking the medication.

    C. Ask the client and family if he has taken penicillin before.

    D. Note his urinary output and BUN.

158. Tom is trying very hard to become more independent and to manage his own care. But his mother says to the nurse, "I just get so scared when he wheezes. I'm afraid he will take too much of his medicine, so I give it to him." The nurse interprets this as an example of:

    A. Overprotection.

    B. Regression.

    C. Hostility.

    D. Normal concern.

159. Tom is being discharged with an albuterol inhaler and cromolyn sodium. What indicates that he has taken too much of either of these medications?

    A. Persistent cough.

B. Prolonged rapid pulse.

C. Diarrhea.

D. Nausea and dizziness.

160. On a return visit to the clinic, which does *not* indicate Tom's increase in independence and responsibility for his own care?

A. Cleans his own room and does his breathing exercises 3 times a day.

B. Demonstrates his ability to take his own pulse and can name his medications and their effects.

C. Has started taking swimming lessons with his friends.

D. Has refused to join the Boy Scouts because being in large crowds of other kids might make him sick.

Medical Diagnosis: Scoliosis.

■ *Nursing Problems/Diagnosis:*

Activity intolerance

Risk for disturbed body image.

Risk for injury.

Noncompliance.

Impaired skin integrity.

■ *Chief Complaint:*

Susan Black, 13-years-old, has one shoulder that appears higher than the other.

■ *Past History:*

Susan is a healthy, well-nourished girl who has been developing normally. One month ago when she went to buy a new dress and could not find one to fit, she noted that one shoulder appeared to be higher than the other. Her mother has a history of multiple allergies; her father is healthy. One other child in the family—a brother, age 9—has allergies. There are no major illnesses; she had an appendectomy at age 10.

■ *Symptoms:*

One shoulder appears higher than the other.

■ *Physical Exam:*

Well-developed adolescent girl.

Heart: Slight shift to the left; no murmurs.

Lungs: Normal to auscultation.

Skin: Intact. Beginning acne on face and shoulders.

GU: Menstruating for 1 year; no pain, but still irregular.

No known allergies. Taking no medications. Does not smoke or drink.

Not sexually active. Attends junior high school, eighth grade, and is doing well.

- **Laboratory Data:**

Hct: 37%; Hgb: 12 g.

Urinalysis: Clear with specific gravity of 1.015.

Spinal X-ray: 35 degree primary lateral curve of spine with compensatory curve above and below the primary curve.

WBC: 6000/uL.

Chest x-ray: Lungs clear; heart displaced slightly to left.

- **Plan:**

Refer to comprehensive scoliosis care clinic for bracing and scoliosis education.

Enroll in Adaptive Physical Education class at school.

Transfer general pediatric care to well adolescent clinic.

---

161. Susan is being followed in the orthopedic clinic following the diagnosis of scoliosis. She is to be treated initially with a Boston brace. Which assessment is *least* likely to suggest scoliosis?

    A. Thoracic asymmetry.

    B. Shoulder height asymmetry.

    C. One hip is higher than the other.

    D. Pain.

162. For evaluation of the extent of secondary problems that could occur, it is least important for the nurse to assess the status of the:

    A. Urinary system.

    B. Stability of the hip.

    C. Social and emotional equilibrium.

    D. Compensatory curvature of the spine.

163. Which point should not be included in the teaching plan for Susan and her parents?

    A. Eating raw fruits and vegetables and chewing sugarless gum.

    B. Use of cotton underclothes and loose-fitting garments.

    C. Daily skin check for redness and pressure points, to avoid breakdown.

    D. Permission to sleep without the brace at night.

164. Taking Erikson's stage of "identity versus role diffusion" into account while planning interventions for Susan, the nurse considers which to be inappropriate for her age group?

    A. Concerns about occupational or job identity.

    B. Psychosexual needs demanding fulfillment.

    C. Peer group interaction should be decreased to avoid embarrassment.

    D. Reevaluation of bodily changes.

165. Susan returns to the clinic 6 weeks later. Her curvature is now 40 degrees. Which is an inappropriate action?

    A. Discussing why she is not wearing the brace as instructed.

    B. Asking her how she feels about having to wear the brace all day.

    C. Evaluating the fit of the brace.

    D. Assessing her cardiac and respiratory status.

166. What point does the nurse want to emphasize in discussing the need for treatment?

    A. Increase in the curvature will cause no pain.

    B. Increase in the degree of curvature will produce paralysis of the legs.

    C. Increase of the curvature will further impair cardio-pulmonary function.

    D. The curvature will not increase further once Susan is past her growth period.

167. After the nurse has finished her teaching, Susan says, "I hate having to wear this. I feel so different from all my friends—like a freak." What is the nurse's best reply?

    A. "You have to wear the brace. The only other way to get better is surgery and you don't want that."

    B. "Have you explained to your friends why you have to wear the brace? I'm sure they will understand."

    C. "You only have to wear it for a few more months. You'll get used to it and then you won't mind it so much."

    D. "I know it's very hard to be different from your friends. Have they said anything to you about the brace?"

168. When Susan visits the clinic a month later, the nurse notes that her acne has become worse. Her hair is long and rather greasy. The nurse should suggest that she:

    A. Go to the doctor for birth control pills to help regulate her hormonal balance.

    B. Reduce her intake of French fries, chocolate, and peanuts.

      C. Cleanse her face several times a day and try a hairstyle off her face.

      D. Evacuate comedones once a day.

169. Mrs. Black is upset with Susan and says that she will not do what she is told, wants to be with her friends all the time, and is even mentioning wanting to go steady with a boy. The nurse's most appropriate response is to:

      A. Assure Mrs. Black that Susan will grow out of it and suggest that she not worry about it.

      B. Agree with her that adolescents are a worry and very difficult to deal with.

      C. Ignore the remarks. The nurse is concerned with Susan, not with her mother's problems.

      D. Discuss what else might be worrying Mrs. Black at the moment.

170. Which behavior indicates that Susan is adapting well to her situation?

      A. She is wearing her brace only at home.

      B. She is attending school regularly.

      C. She has dropped out of her after-school activities in order to stay home with her mother.

      D. She is depending on her mother for all her hygiene needs.

Medical Diagnosis: Insulin dependent diabetes mellitus.

- *Nursing Problems/Diagnosis:*

Knowledge deficit.

Impaired gas exchange.

Risk for injury.

Noncompliance.

Imbalanced nutrition.

Self-esteem disturbance.

- *Chief Complaint:*

Theresa Fox, 16-years-old, has been experiencing frequent episodes of ketoacidosis and poor control of diabetes.

- *Past History:*

Theresa was diagnosed 3 years ago with insulin dependent diabetes mellitus. She presented with ketoacidosis. Her mother has diabetes and is on oral hypoglycemics and a controlled diet. Theresa has been hospitalized three times in the past 8 months with ketoacidosis. She has been treated for a urinary tract infection during the past month. She is also having difficulty with dietary restrictions.

- *Symptoms:*

  Nausea, polyuria, thirst.

- *Physical Exam:*

  Well-developed adolescent girl.

  Heart and lungs: Normal to auscultation. No murmurs.

  Skin: Intact, with no signs of lipodystrophy. No lesions or signs of breakdown.

  GU: Menstruating for 4 years; no problems.

  No known allergies. Has been on NPH and regular insulin once a day, with diet limited in carbohydrates. Attends high school and is doing well in 10th grade; has missed several days due to the flu in the past 6 months.

- *Laboratory Data:*

  Hct: 39%; Hgb: 13 g.

  Glucose: 760 mg/100 mL.

  BUN: 22 mg/100 mL.

  Serum Cl: 100 mEq/L. Na: 130 mEq/L.

  WBC: 18,500/µL.

  Urinalysis: Many WBCs.

  Blood gases: pH: 7.23. PCO_2: 28.

- *Plan:*

  Admit for control of ketoacidosis.

  Nutritional consultation for noncompliance with dietary regime.

  GU consult for repeat urinary tract infection (UTI).

---

171. In working with adolescents with insulin dependent diabetes mellitus, which information is inaccurate?

    A. They need exogenous insulin.

    B. They have sudden onsets of the disease, frequently presenting with ketoacidosis.

    C. Oral hypoglycemics and diet are adequate for control when utilized precisely.

    D. Normal physical growth and development are not hindered with adequate control of the disease.

172. At home, Theresa's mother attempts to wake her daughter for school but finds her difficult to arouse, her skin feels warm, she has an axillary temperature of 38.4°C/101.1°F, and she is breathing deeply. Theresa has had the flu for several days. After Mrs. Fox has called the doctor and asked him to meet them in the emergency room, which action indicates that she has understood the nurse's teaching about diabetes?

    A. Giving Theresa an injection of glucagon to promote gluconeogenesis.

    B. Giving her several glasses of water for hydration.

    C. Giving her an injection of 10 units of regular insulin.

    D. Giving her some orange juice with sugar added to provide a rapid sugar source.

173. The physician decided to admit Theresa to the hospital. In response to Mrs. Fox's questions about what probably precipitated Theresa's current episode of ketoacidosis, the nurse doing the admission history suggests:

    A. Junk food binges.

    B. Infection.

    C. Increased physical activity.

    D. Adolescent growth spurt.

174. During the admitting physical assessment, the nurse is least likely to find:

    A. Increased blood glucose.

    B. Doughy and clammy skin.

    C. Decreased urine specific gravity.

    D. Decreased potassium level.

175. Theresa has been treated for ketoacidosis and is doing well. She is still on sliding-scale insulin according to her fingerstick glucose. She had 5 units of regular insulin at 10 A.M. The nurse enters her room at 11 A.M. and finds her pale, diaphoretic, and tremulous. The *immediate* action is to:

    A. Give her 5 units of regular insulin.

    B. Notify the physician of her condition.

    C. Prepare a syringe with 50 mL of 50% dextrose.

    D. Give her orange juice with extra sugar.

176. Theresa is on a "free diet." Which indicates that she has understood the nurse's teaching with respect to choosing an appropriate diet?

    A. Frankfurter, ice cream bar, apple.

    B. Hamburger, Coke, French fries.

    C. Chicken, fresh banana, brownie.

    D. Pizza slice, milk, fresh fruit.

177. Theresa's glucose is now 150 mg and her urine is negative for ketones. She is alert and up and about. However, she refuses to give her own insulin and check her own blood. She has been responsible for her own care for the past 3 years. She says to the nurse, "I just hate being different from my friends—always sticking needles in myself and not being able to do all the things they can." What is the best way for the nurse to handle this situation?

A. Recognize that it is typical of adolescent rebellion and ignore it.

B. Inform the physician of the situation and suggest that discharge plans be delayed until Theresa assumes responsibility for her own care.

C. Refer Theresa to the diabetic clinical specialist for additional teaching about diabetes.

D. Talk with Theresa about her feelings of exclusion and assess further how she is relating to her friends.

178. The nurse has found from assessment that Theresa has a decreased self-concept and feels less competent than and different from her peers. What would enhance Theresa's self-concept?

A. Mention every day how pretty and attractive she is.

B. Discuss the problem with her mother and father.

C. Encourage her to call her friends every day and keep in touch.

D. Have her help with tasks such as settling the younger children down at bedtime.

179. Theresa has become responsible for her own care again. Which is now the *least* important aspect of the nurse's teaching plan?

A. Eating extra carbohydrate before playing several sets of tennis.

B. Meticulous foot care.

C. Staying away from friends with illnesses.

D. Increasing insulin as indicated with onset of illness.

180. Theresa comes back to the clinic 3 weeks later. She reports that she has been waking up in the middle of the night trembling, diaphoretic, and feeling very nervous and anxious. Which suggestion is most helpful for her?

A. Increase daily insulin.

B. Bedtime snack of cheese.

C. Bedtime snack of cookies and diet soda.

D. Increase in exercise level.

Answers and Rationale

1. C. Have her watch the nurse feed the baby.

C is the best answer in this situation. Seeing the child being fed successfully will help the mother gain confidence in herself. It will also help her begin to accept the child. *A* is an inappropriate choice because Mrs. Jones is grieving the loss of the perfect infant that she anticipated and is trying to accept her "defective" child. This roommate may not necessarily have any effect on helping or hindering that process. *B* is a poor choice because it isolates the mother and increases her concerns and anxieties. *D* is not appropriate because Mrs. Jones will need to start caring for Anne and verbalizing her concerns. She may feel reluctant to talk about the infant; the nurse needs to initiate discussion of the infant, emphasizing her good points.

2. **A. Place the tip of syringe at the front of Anne's mouth so she can suck.**

   A is the inappropriate instruction; the tip of the syringe should be directed to the *side* of the mouth, not into the cleft. Placing it at the front of the mouth will increase the chance of aspiration and nasal regurgitation. *B should* be done to help prevent formula accumulation in the nasopharynx, which can lead to infections. *C is* appropriate; the child will swallow a great deal of air and needs frequent bubbling to prevent vomiting and colic. *D is* also an appropriate action in that mouth care is essential for the child with cleft lip and palate.

3. **A. Ear infections.**

   A is the correct answer; ear infections are common with cleft lip and palate because of ease of access of organisms to the middle ear. *B*, *C*, and *D* are all common problems in infancy but are not specifically associated with this defect.

4. **C. Bring Anne into the clinic for evaluation.**

   C is the best answer. The child's symptoms are those of otitis media and she should be seen and treated immediately. *A* is inappropriate because the parent should never irrigate the ear or put objects into it; this should be done by a professional. *B* and *D* are incorrect because fevers in young infants often indicate an infection, which needs professional treatment.

5. **A. Pull the earlobe down and backward.**

   A is the correct answer for the child under the age of 3. For an older child or an adult, *B* is correct. *C* and *D* are incorrect for any age.

6. **D. Sitting with slight support.**

   D is the correct answer because a 3-month-old cannot sit well with minimal support. Behaviors *A*, *B*, and *C* are typical of a 3-month-old child.

7. **D. Replace the restraints securely.**

   D is the correct answer because protection of the suture line is the highest priority if there are no life-threatening problems. It is not a priority to take Anne's vital signs, *A*, because she is not in respiratory distress, her vital signs are normal, and her color is pink. *B* is the *second* priority, and *C* should be done within an hour of return from the recovery room.

8. **C. Ask Mrs. Jones to stay and hold her.**

   C is the best choice. Anne's mother will be able to comfort her most easily and prevent the crying that will strain the suture line. *A* is incorrect in that sucking causes stress on the suture line. *B* is contraindicated after lip repair because the child can rub her face against the bed and damage the repair. *D* is unrealistic, expensive, and not as beneficial as having Anne's mother do it.

9. **C. A mobile with a music box.**

   C is the most appropriate toy in that it provides visual and auditory stimulation. *A* and *B* are inappropriate because they could be put in the mouth. *D*, a teddy bear with eyes that can come off, is a safety hazard because the eyes could be aspirated.

10. **D. Give via syringe to the side of the mouth.**

    D is the best answer in that the medication is given in the same way as a regular feeding, thus avoiding strain on the suture line. *A* is incorrect because the spoon could damage the suture line. *B* is incorrect for two reasons. First, it is a potentially inaccurate way to administer medication because the child may not drink all the formula; second, such a practice could cause the child to have difficulty eating due to the taste imparted to the food by the medication. *C* is incorrect because the child cannot use a nipple so soon after the repair.

11. **C. "You know, she's so pretty now she will win a beauty contest just as I did."**

    C is the best choice. This response should concern the nurse the most because it indicates potentially unrealistic goals on the part of the mother. *A* is a normal reaction; however, continued isolation of the child will be harmful. After surgery, the child's appearance will be improved and the mother should not isolate her so much. *B* is an indication that the rest of the family is beginning to accept the child. *D* is also a positive indication of the acceptance of the child by the parents.

12. **D. Prevention of infection of surgical incision.**

    D is the correct answer because it is a short-term goal and should no longer be a problem at discharge. *A* and *B* are long-term goals with any cleft lip and palate because ear infections and palate deformity can lead to hearing loss and speech impediments. *C* is always a goal for any child with a congenital deformity where there is a high risk for impaired development of the parent-child relationship.

13. **C. Prevention of urinary tract infections.**

    C is the primary goal because chronic urinary tract infections lead to renal failure, which may cause death. *A*, *B*, and *D* are all important goals with any child who has problems with mobility but they are less important than the urinary problems.

14. ***A. A large percentage of these children also have hydrocephalus.***

    A is the correct answer because up to 95% of children with myelomeningocele also have hydrocephalus. *B* is incorrect because depending on the level of the defect, some children can walk. *C* is incorrect because most children are incontinent. *D* is incorrect because although there can be complications, most children live beyond the teen years.

15. ***D. Increasing head circumference.***

    D is the first sign of hydrocephalus in infants in whom the anterior fontanelle and sutures have not closed. *A* and *C* are later signs. *B* is the first sign in the verbal child, from about 2 years of age and older; the infant may have a headache but cannot tell us.

16. ***D. Feed 6 oz. every 3 hours.***

    D is the inappropriate action. There is no indication of an increased need for calories and fluids; David's weight and hemoglobin are well within normal range. At this age he should be eating every 4–5 hours. In addition, he has been vomiting and this action would increase that likelihood. *A* is an appropriate action in assessing for increasing intracranial pressure. *B* prevents skin breakdown and is the correct position for the child with dislocated hips. *C* is an appropriate action due to the bladder involvement; it helps empty the bladder and prevent urinary stasis and infection.

17. ***C. A rattle.***

    C is the best choice. At 2 months he can grasp and hold a rattle or object. *A*, a busy board, is too advanced and would be appropriate for an older infant. *B*, large blocks, would also be better for the older child. *D* is not a good choice; while a music box provides auditory stimulation, it does not encourage motor development as the rattle does.

18. ***B. The peritoneal cavity.***

    B is correct because the fluid can be slowly absorbed through the peritoneal membrane, with the peritoneal cavity serving as the "holding" area. *A*, *C* and *D* are incorrect locations for a ventriculoperitoneal shunt.

19. ***C. Elevate the head 60 degrees to promote cerebrospinal flow.***

    C would not be included in the plan of care. This is the first shunt and too rapid decompression could lead to a subdural hematoma. The child should be kept flat for a few days after surgery. *A* is appropriate as it will promote functioning of the shunt and prevent skin breakdown. *B* is a correct procedure in that it helps assess for increased intracranial pressure. *D* is appropriate for the same reason, because the shunt occasionally malfunctions.

20. ***A. Hold head steady in a sitting position.***

A is probably the task David cannot do because of the increased weight of the head with hydrocephalus. *B*, *C*, and *D* are three tasks he should be able to do as any normal child can.

21. ***D. Prevent subdural hematoma.***

D is the correct answer because too rapid decompression could lead to subdural hematoma. *A* is not correct because pain can occur in any position. *B* will not occur; the amount of fluid shunted into the circulatory system usually does not cause a problem. *C* is not relevant to hydrocephalus or a ventriculoperitoneal shunt.

22. ***D. How to measure head circumference.***

D is the correct answer because it is one method of evaluating for increasing intracranial pressure. *A* is incorrect because although extra fluid may be absorbed in the abdominal cavity, there is no need to measure abdominal circumference. *B* is incorrect because glucose in the urine is not expected in relation to any of David's problems; it is therefore inappropriate teaching. *C* is unnecessary; David is not in congestive heart failure, nor is he having other fluid problems.

23. ***C. When they note bulging of the anterior fontanelle when David is crying.***

C is the one instance in which the parents should not call the physician, as the fontanelle normally bulges with crying. *A* may indicate signs of meningitis and medical help must be sought. *B* is indicative of a urinary tract infection and *D*, of increasing intracranial pressure.

24. ***B. Pulmonary embolism.***

B does not require placement of a new shunt and it does not interfere with the flow of cerebrospinal fluid. *A*, *C*, and *D* are situations that eventually will require replacement of the shunt.

25. ***D. "It must be very hard for you. Have you had any time away from the baby?"***

D is the best choice in that it reflects the mother's concerns and asks for further data. With the mother receiving no relief from the constant stress of caring for this infant, one aspect the nurse should be concerned about is the potential for abuse. *A* is not therapeutic and may make Mrs. Stivic feel even more guilty. *B* is not the best answer in that it does not reflect the mother's concerns and also makes an assumption without sufficient data. *C* has nothing to do with the mother's concerns.

26. *C. 2 doses of DTaP and 2 doses of IPV.*

    C is the correct answer. David should have received 2 doses of both DTaP and IPV. Recall that he is now about 5 months old. (He was 2 months on admission, plus the hospital stay and this clinic visit 2 months later.) *A* is incorrect in that the first round of immunizations is given at about 2 months of age and the second, at about 4 months of age. *B* is incorrect in that the MMR is given at 15 months of age and *D* is incorrect in that TB is done at about 10 months of age.

27. *D. Weight.*

    D is the correct answer; weight is the most accurate way to determine degree of dehydration. Comparison of his normal weight and his current weight (in the case situation) shows about a 10% weight loss, which is moderate dehydration. *A*, *B*, and *C* are all signs of dehydration but are of little use in determining degree.

28. *A. Restoration of intravascular volume.*

    A is the correct answer. This type of dehydration in infants leads to shock and must be prevented. The goal of care is to restore the lost fluids. *B* is not the primary goal but a *secondary* one; the diarrhea should decrease with the child NPO. *C* is another goal that can be met *later*. *D* is also not primary in that the physiologic stability is of primary importance initially.

29. *Correct answer: 45 gtt/min.*

    The calculation is as follows:

    $360 \div 8 = 45$ mL/hour.

    $(45 \div 60) \times 60 = 45$ gtt/min.

30. *D. As soon as he can take fluids again, the restraints will not be needed.*

    D is the best way to initiate discussion of the restraints. It tells the parents that they are only temporary. *A* is an incorrect statement; the restraints are removed periodically to check for skin breakdown and to move the joints. Also the child can be held with the IV line in place and then the restraints are not needed. *B* is incorrect because explaining the procedure to the parents in this way is frightening and anxiety producing. *C* is false because by limiting the infant's mobility and his way of expressing anxiety, there is little chance he will become used to the restraints. The answer is also incorrect because it indicates that the child should be left totally alone in bed, which is not beneficial for either the child or the parents.

31. *C. Apply an external 24-hour urine bag and weigh diapers.*

   C is the correct answer because it is an accurate and low risk way to measure the urine and stool output separately. *A* is incorrect because a catheter increases the risk for infection. *B* is incorrect because weighing the child after each void or stool is less accurate and impractical. *D* is incorrect because if the child is having frequent loose or liquid stools, it is hard to tell if the output is urine or stool. It is important to monitor urine output to assess hydration, and it is important to assess whether stool quantity is increasing or decreasing.

32. *D. Oral electrolyte solution.*

   D is the best answer. It provides electrolytes and calories in an easily digested form. *A* is incorrect in that the carbonation is irritating to the bowel and the high sugar content will restart the diarrhea. *B* is incorrect because even half-strength formula is not a clear liquid and should not be offered until all the diarrhea has stopped. *C* is incorrect in that few infants will drink the salty broth, and tea is a poor choice because the xanthine in it is a mild diuretic, which could enhance the dehydration.

33. *D. A game of peek-a-boo.*

   D is the best choice. Peek-a-boo is an age-appropriate game for an 8-month-old and also involves personal interaction, which will help social development. *A* is too young for him; he needs something or someone to interact with, not just look at. *B* is too advanced; large blocks are appropriate for a child over 1 year of age. *C* is again rather young for this child and more appropriate to a 4-month-old.

34. *A. Stay with the child and protect him from injury during the seizure.*

   A is the best answer in that it provides for the safety of the child and permits observation of the progression and duration of the seizure. *B* would be an appropriate action after *A*; in fact, the best action would be to have another nurse inform the physician while one nurse stays with the infant. *C* is not correct as the first action; it would be indicated *later*, as this is probably a febrile convulsion. *D* is not the best answer for the child's safety. Again this is an action to take *after* the child's physical safety has been ensured.

35. *D. "I know this must worry you. Has anything like this ever happened before?"*

   D is the best answer; it acknowledges the parents' concerns and asks for further data. *A* is incorrect because seizure activity in children can lead to brain cell hypoxia and cell death. It is true that febrile seizures often stop by age 6; however, there is nothing to indicate that this is the situation here. It is also false reassurance—any parent seeing a seizure is going to worry. *B* is incorrect in that it does not acknowledge the parents' anxieties and gives false information; there is no guarantee that the seizure will not occur again. *C* is incorrect in that it does not address the issue at hand—this infant's seizure.

36. ***B. Crawl and begin to say "Mama" and "Dada."***

B is the correct answer. *A* and *D* are abilities of the infant of about 11–12 months. *C* is incorrect in that the Moro reflex should be gone by now; if it is still present, it indicates neurologic deficit.

37. ***D. Assess why Mrs. Jones has not had the immunizations done.***

D, collecting data as to why the immunizations have not been started, is the best answer. *A* is incorrect in that it assumes that Mrs. Jones did not understand the instructions, an assumption that has no basis in fact. *B* is a poor choice in that it could make the mother angry, defensive, and unlikely to cooperate. *C* is a poor choice in that it takes the locus of care away from the parent, who has primary responsibility for the child's care.

38. ***A. An acute disease characterized by fever and having no known cause.***

A is the correct answer. Kawasaki disease is an acute febrile syndrome of unknown etiology. The disease occurs worldwide and does not seem to be prevalent in any particular geographic, seasonal, socioeconomic, or environmental pattern. Children from 3 months through 14 years old can be affected. *B* is incorrect because there is no known connection with rheumatic fever. *C* and *D* are both incorrect because they have no basis in fact.

39. ***B. Kawasaki disease.***

B is the correct answer. Dr. Kawasaki first identified this syndrome as mucocutaneous lymph node syndrome (MLNS) in 1967, based on the signs and symptoms he identified in children having this disease. *A*, infantile polyarteritis nodosa, is a similar disorder, although characterized by higher fatality rate. *C*, nephrotic syndrome, is a kidney disorder found primarily in toddlers and pre-schoolers. *D*, Still's disease, is also known as juvenile rheumatoid arthritis and is generally a disease of school-age children.

40. ***A. Diphtheria, tetanus, pertussis, and polio.***

A is the correct answer. According to the guidelines of the American Academy of Pediatrics, routine immunizations for an 8-month-old include a primary series of 3 DTP shots for diphtheria, tetanus, and pertussis and 2 or 3 trivalent oral polio vaccines. These are given most commonly at 2, 4, and 6 months of age. Additional immunizations such as HB (hepatitis) and Hib (*Haemophilus influenzae* type B) are also recommended. *B* is incorrect because while children are tested for TB, a vaccine is not given. *C* and *D* are incorrect because the vaccines against German measles and "regular" measles are not given until 15 months; they can be combined with the mumps vaccine in one injection for MMR (measles, mumps, rubella).

41. **C. Petechiae and hematomas.**

C is the correct answer. Kawasaki disease is *not* evidenced by bleeding tendencies; therefore, the nurse will not find petechiae or hematomas on Jackie. *A*, bilateral conjunctivitis, *B*, desquamation of fingers and toes, and *D*, rash and lymphadenopathy, *are* all usually found in the child with Kawasaki disease.

42. **D. Jackie's temperature is 104°F.**

D is the correct answer: 40°C = 104°F. To convert from centigrade to Fahrenheit, use this formula:

$(9/5 \times °C) + 32 = °F.$

$(9/5 \times 40) + 32 = 104°F.$

Option *A* evades the parents' question and is not true. *B* is incorrect because high-spiking fevers are common in Kawasaki disease. *C* is incorrect; a normal temperature on the centigrade scale is 37°C.

43. **The correct answer is: 0.8 mL.**

Dose desired : dose on hand = X : amount on hand
80 mg : 60 mg = X : 0.6 mL
X = 48.0/60
X = 0.8 mL

44. **B. Check Jackie's temperature every 1—2 hours.**

B is the correct answer. The nurse who is conscientious would check Jackie's temperature and document it in the nurse's notes at least every 1-2 hours, knowing that a sudden, sharp rise in temperature might cause a febrile convulsion. *A*, antibiotics, are ineffective as a treatment for Kawasaki disease. *C*, giving antipyretics alone, might not control Jackie's fever, and the pediatrician will have to be notified. *D* is incorrect because an 8-month-old infant should never be placed on a hypothermia mattress without a physician's order.

45. **A. Immediately notify the physician.**

A is the correct answer. The normal platelet count for an infant is 200,000-470,000/μL. Since Jackie's count is quite elevated, Jackie is prone to develop the complication of multiple thromboses and her physician should be promptly notified. Aspirin may be used to help prevent clot formation secondary to the increased platelet count. *B* is incorrect because bleeding tendencies are found with a decreased platelet count. *C* is incorrect because the child with Kawasaki disease does not need reverse isolation. *D* is incorrect because this lab report deviates too far from the norm to simply be placed in the chart.

46. D. At 3:30 A.M.

D is the correct answer; the IV will need changing around 3:30 A.M. If Jackie's IV is adjusted properly, to run at 55 mL/hour as the physician ordered, by 3:30 A.M. there would be about 30-35 mL left in her bottle and this is the best time to hang a new bottle. *A*, hanging a new bottle immediately, not only would waste a modest amount of expensive IV fluid, but also might not encourage the nurse to keep going back hourly to check Jackie's flow rate and IV site. If the bottle were left hanging until 6:45 A.M., *B*, it would probably be empty and Jackie would not have received the amount of IV fluid ordered. *C*, waiting until "whenever" the bottle empties, shows a lack of careful planning by the nurse!

47. C. Check the flow rate of Jackie's 1V fluid.

C is the correct answer. Whenever IV fluid appears to have run in much more quickly than was ordered by the physician, the nurse's first action should be to check the flow rate and adjust it either to the correct rate of flow or to a KVO rate, depending on how much extra fluid has been received by the client. Following this, the physician should be notified, and the client should be checked for signs of fluid overload and placed in semi-Fowler's or high Fowler's position to facilitate breathing, choice *D*. *A* is inappropriate as the *first* nursing measure to be taken at this time; Jackie has been running high-spiking fevers so there is relatively little danger of an immediate febrile convulsion. Valuable time will be lost while the nurse calculates, pours, and administers acetaminophen (Tylenol). *B* is also inappropriate as a first nursing action: Slowing the flow rate will give the nurse adequate time before having to add another bottle of fluid.

48. A. Check with the pediatrician for new IV orders.

A is the correct answer. The physician should be notified and will need to write IV orders for the remainder of the shift. *B* is incorrect since a nurse may not change the prescribed flow rate of IV fluid without a new doctor's order. *C* is incorrect; the IV should never arbitrarily be stopped since Jackie may need to receive emergency drugs through this line. *D* reflects poor nursing judgment because additional fluid may overload Jackie's circulatory system.

49. D. Her sedimentation rate is elevated and this is a typical lab finding in the child with Kawasaki disease.

D is the correct answer. The normal sedimentation rate for an infant is 0-10 mm/hour. Jackie's sedimentation rate is well above normal. One lab finding typical of Kawasaki disease is an elevated sedimentation rate. Therefore, *A*, *B*, and *C* are incorrect.

50. *B. Showing signs and symptoms of heart failure.*

   B is the correct answer. Early signs and symptoms of heart failure in infants include tachycardia, tachypnea, diaphoresis, and a sudden weight gain. Knowing that infants and children with Kawasaki disease are at high risk for cardiac involvement, and given Jackie's signs and symptoms, the nurse is correct in suspecting heart failure. *A* reflects inappropriate nursing judgment related to signs and symptoms. *C* and *D* show lack of nursing knowledge related to heart failure in infants.

51. *C. Allow them to discuss their concerns and fears.*

   C is the correct answer. As with any client demonstrating signs of anxiety, the best nursing intervention is to allow these parents to discuss their fears. This helps the nurse establish herself or himself as a concerned, trustworthy person, which is vital to a therapeutic relationship. *A* is incorrect; when clients have a high anxiety level, "thorough" orientation is inappropriate at that time. *B* is not a true statement, as this was not a routine transfer. *D* is also incorrect; Jackie has a 98-99% chance for survival.

52. *D. Jackie's apical rate is 98 and regular, with normal sinus rhythm on her monitor.*

   D is the correct answer. When giving digoxin to an infant, the apical rate must be checked for 1 full minute. An apical rate of less than 100 may be an early sign of digoxin toxicity. *A* is incorrect because digoxin is an important part of Jackie's treatment and the dose cannot be delayed, even if she is asleep. *B* is incorrect because tachycardia is one sign of congestive heart failure (CHF), for which Jackie needs her digoxin. *C* is also incorrect; in some children with Kawasaki disease, jaundice, elevated bilirubin levels, and elevated liver enzyme levels may be present; however, this will not affect the administration of digoxin.

53. *C. Slowing of the heart rate and increased urinary output.*

   C is the correct answer. Digoxin is a cardiotonic. It should slow the heart rate to normal and it also improves renal perfusion—increasing urinary output. *A*, *B*, and *D* all reflect adverse effects of digoxin therapy and are therefore incorrect choices.

54. *D. Restraining Jackie for IV therapy and confining her to her crib.*

   D is the correct answer because although Jackie might need some restraints during IV therapy, she need *not* be confined to her crib. Her parents and nurses should certainly hold and rock her. *A*, *B*, and *C* *are* appropriate nursing measures for Jackie.

55. ***B. Is on a special low sodium formula and should not receive milk.***

    B is the correct answer. Low salt formulas such as Lonalac and PM 60/40 are often used for infants with congestive heart failure to prevent increased accumulation of fluids. All parties caring for Jackie should be advised of her special dietary needs. ***A*** and ***C*** are incorrect; since Jackie's condition has improved, there is no reason she should not go to the playroom. ***D*** is incorrect; even though she is still on digoxin, there is no need for her to remain on a cardiac monitor unless ordered by the physician.

56. ***D. Poor appetite with minimal PO intake.***

    D is the correct answer. If Jackie were eating and drinking poorly, she would not be ready for discharge. In fact, she might even be showing signs of digoxin toxicity and the dose of this drug would need adjusting. ***A***, 37°C, is a normal 98.6°F temperature and indicates readiness for discharge, as do ***B*** and ***C***.

57. ***C. It is best to give digoxin within 1 hour after feeding your child.***

    C is the best answer because digoxin should not be given within an hour after eating since this decreases its absorption. Digoxin is best given 1 hour *before* or 2 hours after meals for best absorption from the stomach. The nurse would be correct in teaching choices ***A***, ***B***, and ***D***.

58. ***B. Talk with the parents to assess their knowledge and how they can help with Sam's care.***

    B is the best answer. It acknowledges the parents' concern (from the history) and gathers a database to start preparation. ***A*** is incorrect because 18 month olds do not have a concept of time and only benefit from preparation immediately prior. C is not correct because the parents need to know what will happen this time; the previous catheterization was probably performed at a few weeks of age. ***D*** is inappropriate because the child is vulnerable to separation anxiety and the parents have also expressed their need to be present.

59. ***C. The degree of pulmonary vascularization.***

    C is the information *not* revealed by the catheterization. Pulmonary vasculature is usually seen with either a chest x-ray or with an angiogram. Cardiac catheterization yields information about ***A***, ***B***, and ***D***.

60. ***A. Sam complains of his head hurting.***

    A would cause the greatest concern since it might indicate a cerebral infarct, for which the child would be at risk considering that this child is NPO prior to a catheterization. This means a degree of dehydration plus the possibility of an embolus due to the invasive procedure. ***B*** is not a concern as it is within the range of his normal pulse. ***C*** should not concern the nurse because a decreased temperature of the leg in which the catheterization is done is to be expected; it would be of concern if it persisted for an extended time and was accompanied by absent pulses. *D* is not too much of a concern considering the degree of dehydration due to being NPO prior to cardiac catheterization.

61. **D. Endocarditis.**

   D is the correct answer; all children with cardiac defects are prone to infection with invasive procedures. In this case, a cardiac infection is most likely. *A*, *B*, and *C* are not complications commonly seen after cardiac catheterization.

62. **C. Recent fluctuations in weight.**

   C is the correct answer. Systemic edema is best assessed through weight gain, particularly in the child under the age of 2. *A* is a long-term complication of cyanotic heart disease and chronic hypoxemia. *B* is incorrect in that it does not indicate congestive heart failure directly but may add to it indirectly. *D* is incorrect in that peripheral edema is not the best way to assess congestive failure in the toddler.

63. **D. Chronic oxygen deficiency.**

   D is the correct answer, reflecting chronic hypoxia. In children with cardiac anomalies, the bone marrow produces more RBCs, leading to polycythemia and increased problems with clots forming (as noted in question 60). *A* is incorrect in that infection usually is seen with a WBC elevation. *B* is incorrect in that the child did not enter the hospital with symptoms of dehydration and a cyanotic defect is associated with polycythemia. *C* is incorrect in that cardiac output indirectly affects the hematocrit.

64. **C. He may be going into heart block due to digoxin toxicity.**

   C is the correct answer because Sam's pulse is much slower than his admission pulse and bradycardia is a sign of digoxin toxicity. *A* is incorrect because even though the pulse does slow with decreased activity, this pulse rate is more than 20 beats slower than his normal rate. *B* does not apply, since Sam's normal heart rate is different from that of a normal 18-month-old. When digoxin is administered, evaluation of its effects must be individualized. *D* is incorrect in that potassium is more likely to affect rhythmicity than rate.

65. **B. Decreased energy reserve.**

   B, the decreased energy reserve associated with congestive heart failure, is the *most likely* reason Sam is eating poorly. Therefore, the nurse should plan rest periods before meals and smaller and more frequent feedings. Both will provide the necessary oxygen and energy, which must be the nurse's first priority for Sam. *A*, *C*, and *D* are *secondary* considerations.

66. *C. Apricots and bananas.*

    C is the correct answer in that these foods provide potassium. Note from the case situation that Sam's potassium is low; since he is on diuretics, he needs potassium in his diet. *A* is incorrect in that milk products are high in sodium and orders indicate salt and fluid restriction. *B* is also incorrect in that preserved meats, such as hot dogs, are high in sodium. *D* is incorrect because both high sodium content and excess fluids are not appropriate for an 18-month-old on fluid restrictions.

67. *A. The knowledge that the repair will include restructuring the heart to a more normal flow by reversing the aorta and the pulmonary artery.*

    A is the correct answer because it describes in simple terms the repair for a transposition. *B* is incorrect because it describes a repair for a different heart defect. *C* is incorrect because parents often find explanations by the physician confusing and many times hesitate to "take up the doctor's time" with questions. *D* is incorrect because such an approach may ignore real concerns that the parents have for the preoperative and intraoperative stages of Sam's care.

68. *A. Administer oxygen and position him in the knee-chest position.*

    A is the preferred treatment for hypoxic episodes. These episodes are particularly prevalent in children with tetralogy but can occur in any child with a cyanotic cardiac defect. Oxygen and the knee-chest position are most helpful. The position in *B* is incorrect; morphine is given to relieve pain and anxiety while not affecting the blood pressure. *C* is incorrect because asking the parents to leave will probably increase their anxiety; however, the main reason this is a poor choice is because it does not deal with the child exclusively. *D* is not as good a choice as *A* because positioning is omitted. The physician should be notified after the other appropriate actions have been taken.

69. *B. Feed himself and drink from a cup.*

    A, *C*, and *D* are all skills of older children.

70. *B. His mother is overprotective and allows Sam few challenges to develop his skills.*

    B is the best answer. Data from the history and from her comments indicate that the parents have given the child few opportunities to develop normal skills. *A* is incorrect because while the defect may slow down acquisition of skills, Sam will be able to achieve them eventually. *C* is incorrect because there are no data supporting the idea of a struggle for autonomy. *D* is incorrect because Sam's behavior is no different from when he first entered the hospital—note that the case situation indicated developmental lags.

71. **C. Reassess the parents' needs and concerns.**

    C is the best answer. The behavior of the parents indicates they are still overprotecting Sam so the nurse needs to reassess and to plan other goals and interventions. *A* is not the best choice because it is intervention without a basis—there is no indication that the parents do not understand the needs of children. *B* is inappropriate because the child is going home and the parents will have to present the activities and stimulation if Sam is to continue to develop. *D* is also not the best answer because it assumes that the parents do not realize the results of the surgery—this action is included in the correct answer *C*.

72. **A. Long bone x-rays.**

    A is the test done to confirm the other data. Long bone x-rays will reveal old or partially healed bone fractures, which could indicate abuse. *B* is appropriate if the child had neurologic problems, but none are indicated in the history. *C*, a repeat CBC, will not add to the database of suspected child abuse. *D* is incorrect because there is not a diagnosis yet. Removing the child from the home, even for a short period, is not the treatment of choice.

73. **B. Having been abused or neglected themselves as children.**

    B is the correct answer. Many parents who are abusive were abused themselves and this is the only way they know to parent children. *A* is not true; in fact, parents who abuse their children generally have unrealistic development expectations, which leads to abuse when the children cannot meet parental expectations. *C* is incorrect because abuse is associated with multiple stresses, as Larry's history indicates, and parents who are abusive have an inability to deal with stress. *D* is a poor choice because parents who are abusive are frequently isolated from sources of support that will help them cope with stresses.

74. **A. The parents to express concern about the extent of damage and Larry's current condition.**

    A is the correct answer. Once a child who has been abused has been hospitalized and the immediate stresses have been reduced, parents who are abusive may feel quite concerned about the child's welfare. *B* is incorrect because parents who are abusive may not link their actions and the need to compensate for them with a sense of guilt about inflicting injury. *C* is incorrect because children who are abused are often fearful of their parents. *D* is incorrect because children who are abused learn very early that crying often brings punishment or injury from their parents.

75. **D. Recognition of the LVN's/LPN's feelings.**

    D is the best choice. Recognizing the LVN's/LPN's feelings and dealing with them first will aid the nurse in going on to other concerns. *A* is a poor choice in that slander is not really a concern, but it is correct in that legal action has not been initiated. *B* is incorrect because accusing and lecturing the parents will make them angry and defensive and impair further relations between the parents and the nursing staff. *C* is not the best answer in that it does not deal with the LVN's/LPN's primary feelings about the parents. This should be noted prior to any further interaction.

76. *B. Assigning one person on each shift to care for him.*

B is the best answer. This approach provides a consistent set of caretakers and allows trust to develop between the child and the nurse. *A* is inappropriate since it restricts the parents, who have the right to see their child, and also restricts opportunities for the nurse to work with them. *C* is incorrect in that multiple caretakers will increase the child's loneliness and will not meet the need for a consistent person with whom he can identify. *D* is not useful because at this age peer interaction is minimal. Also, the child needs an adult to trust; children would not meet this need.

77. *C. Child protective services.*

C is the correct answer. All 50 states have child abuse laws that provide for reporting such cases, usually to some form of state protective agency. The police, *A*, are not notified routinely unless the child's life is endangered. *B* is incorrect because legal action is not decided on until after the case has been reported. *D* is incorrect in that initial reporting is not done to such agencies although they may be involved in follow-up care.

78. *B. The notes will provide a database to plan family intervention.*

B is the best answer. The interactions will help determine what type of therapy will be effective. *A* would be important if the case was going to court, but there are no data about this therefore it is an unwarranted assumption. *C* is incorrect because it applies to any client; the question asks about the child who is abused and his parents. *D* is not the best answer because preventing the parents from removing the child from the hospital would require some type of legal action.

79. *D. Walk up and down stairs.*

D is the correct answer because it reflects the developmental capabilities of a 2½ year old. *A*, *B*, and *C* are abilities of the 4- or 5-year-old.

80. *D. Look for the appearance of petechiae.*

D is the best answer. Iron is given to build hemoglobin and does not affect coagulation of the blood. *A*, staining of the teeth, and *B*, dark stools, *are* frequent side effects of iron. The vitamin C in the orange juice, *C*, *will* improve absorption of the iron.

81. ***A. Leave the child in the home and provide counseling for the parents.***

A is the primary treatment choice since the child usually does better with his natural parents. The therapy is aimed at helping the parents change their behaviors and learn to cope with their stresses. *B* is not the treatment of choice unless the child is in danger of further physical abuse. *C* may be done, but the child cannot be hospitalized for the entire course of these lengthy treatments. *D* will be included in the treatment plan but it is not the entire plan. *A* is really inclusive of this choice and therefore is the more complete answer.

82. ***B. Remark on how well the child and his parents are doing.***

B is the correct answer. The behaviors are indicative that the treatment plan is working, and reinforcement of the improved behaviors is indicated. Since these behaviors are indicative of an improving relationship, there is no need to change the goals of care and *A* is incorrect. *C* will not be helpful since the family needs all the support it can get; saying nothing is not supportive of any of the observed changes. *D* is incorrect because it is not indicated by the data provided.

83. ***D. Peripheral circulation.***

D is the one area that does not require assessment since there is nothing in the history indicating decreased circulation; and lead poisoning causes anemia, *not* decreased circulation. *A* is an important area to assess because impaired parent-child relationships are often associated with lead poisoning. *B* is important for two reasons—the history reveals changes in mental status and the primary effect of lead on the body is neurologic. *C* is important because the history reveals pica, and data about eating habits will be primary to planning the nursing care.

84. ***B. Eating paint chips.***

B is the correct answer. Most lead poisoning in children is due to old paint from buildings that were built before the 1960's and poorly maintained, and the child's case situation mentions that he lives in such a building. *A* is a very unlikely source of lead poisoning in a child although it may be seen frequently in cases of adult lead poisoning. *C* is incorrect because some fish contain high levels of *mercury*, not lead. *D* is incorrect because there is no lead in the ink or the paper used to print most newspapers. The fact that this is in the case situation is indicative of pica.

85. ***D. Promote excretion of the lead.***

D is the most important nursing goal to help limit permanent damage. *A* is an important goal for discharge planning and follow-up to avoid *continued* poisoning. *B* and *C* are important nursing goals but can be dealt with *later* in the care.

86. **A. Pica.**

    A is the correct answer because ingestion of nonnutritive substances—and therefore a poor diet and lack of iron—lead to iron deficiency anemia. *B* is incorrect because there is no history of blood loss. *C* is not the usual cause of the anemia seen with chronic lead poisoning. *D* is incorrect because the child has no history of, or risk factors for sickle cell anemia.

87. **B. The effectiveness of the treatment.**

    B is the correct answer; 24-hour urine collection is part of the diagnostic studies performed to identify lead poisoning and check for effectiveness of the treatment. *A*, *C*, and *D* have nothing to do with the diagnosis of lead poisoning.

88. **C. Neurologic.**

    C is the correct answer because neurologic damage is the side effect that produces the major serious long-term complications, such as seizure disorders, learning disabilities, hyperkinesis, and other problems. *A* and *B* are also found with lead poisoning, but usually do not lead to death or to other long-term side effects. *D*, the cardiovascular system, is not affected.

89. **C. Maintain a patent airway.**

    C is the correct answer because this will promote respirations. *A* is an action to take once the safety of the child is ensured. *B* also is done once the child is assessed not to be swallowing or to be having difficulty with secretions. *D* is inappropriate in that the child is already convulsing and forcing an object between his teeth could break a tooth and cause other problems.

90. **A. Allow the child to play with the needle after the injection.**

    A is the best answer because it is the action that should *not* be included in the care plan. This child is 3½ years old and playing with the needle could be dangerous. The syringe might be appropriate, but not the needle. *B* is an appropriate action because increased fluids will flush the lead through the kidneys and help prevent kidney damage. *C* is an associated correct action, for the same reason. *D* is a correct action because this medication will help decrease the pain of the many painful injections. EMLA is a cream that is applied over puncture site 2½ hours prior to injection.

91. **B. BUN.**

    B is the most important piece of data to assess on a daily basis due to the toxicity of lead to the kidney. *A* has nothing to do with the lead or the treatment. *C* does not really tell the nurse about ongoing lead levels—a blood lead level would be better. *D* is not appropriate because the anemia will not resolve itself due to the chelation therapy—nutritional and iron intake must be improved.

92. **B. Denver II Developmental Screening Test.**

    B is the correct answer. This test is appropriate for children through the age of 6 and can be easily and quickly given by the nurse on a regular basis. **A** is an IQ test only and does not give the needed developmental information; also, the nurse has neither access to it nor the time to administer it. **C** and **D** are tests that are appropriate for the older, school-age child. Also, the Piers-Harris reflects self-concept only, not the developmental progress that the nurse wants to assess.

93. **D. "You should tell him to play in a certain area and enforce the rule with discipline."**

    D is the best answer because it stresses setting limits and enforcing them consistently to prevent accidents. **A** is inappropriate because the child does not have the ability to learn and formulate rules by himself and he will probably get hurt before he develops that ability. **B** is unrealistic and includes unnecessary and harmful restrictions. **C**, keeping a child in the house at all times, is also unrealistic.

94. **A. Night-time continence.**

    A is the correct answer. Complete night-time dryness is not normally achieved until the child is older. Also, recall from the case situation that the mother spoke of her difficulty in training the child. **B**, **C**, and **D** are all *normal* achievements for a 3-year-old.

95. **B. Finger painting.**

    B is the best choice. It allows Steven to develop motor coordination and is not dangerous. **A** is an activity that is enjoyed more by school-age children. **C** is seen more with the older preschool child of about 5, and **D** is inappropriate because of Steven's neurologic problems and the danger that he might cut himself.

96. **D. Persistent anemia.**

    D is the correct answer because anemia can be reversed. **A**, **B**, and **C** reflect neurologic—and therefore permanent—damage, which requires long-term follow-up.

97. **A. Serum lead level of 40 μg.**

    A is the correct answer because it reflects the downward trend of the lead level. **B** might cause concern but would be followed through the outpatient clinic. **C**, the hemoglobin, will increase with improved nutrition and can also be followed on an outpatient basis. The WBC count in **D** reflects a normal value and shows little change from the admission lab data.

98. **B. Koplik spots on the buccal mucosa.**

    B is the correct answer. Koplik spots are present briefly at the *beginning* of a case of *measles*. **A**, **C**, and **D** may all be indicative of infection of the tonsils.

99.   D. *Assess the mother's reasons for refusing preparation.*

> *D* is the correct approach. Despite the mother's adamant position, the nurse needs to determine the reasons for such a potentially harmful position. *A* is inappropriate because the physician is not in any better position to influence the mother over the phone than the nurse is. Such an approach could lead to tension between the nursing staff and the mother. It will also force the physician to take sides in the situation. *B* is inappropriate because Mary may feel frightened and abandoned by her parents if she is told something different once they leave. *C* is inappropriate without first assessing the reasons for refusal and attempting to support the parents' concerns first.

100.   D. *Stay in the room and complete the nursing care of her roommate.*

> *D* is the best answer. The child is in the phase of protest of separation anxiety and refuses to be comforted; the best approach is to be within the child's sight. *A* is incorrect since the 4-year-old has little concept of time. *B* is not appropriate because she is missing her parents, not children of her own age. *C* is incorrect because the child is anxious and the presence of someone familiar, such as the nurse, will be helpful.

101. D. *Check the SGOT and SGPT levels.*

> *D* is the data the nurse does *not* evaluate since there is no indication of liver dysfunction in the child's history. *A* is evaluated since the 5-year-old child is beginning to lose teeth about this time and a loose tooth could be knocked out during anesthesia and aspirated. *B* is essential because this is Mary's first surgery and hemorrhage is the main complication postoperatively. *C* is evaluated because they are indicators of infection, and surgery would be postponed if infection were indicated.

102. D. *Bleeding time of 10 minutes.*

> *D* necessitates a call to the physician because normal bleeding time is 3-9 minutes. *A* is expected in that the child has been NPO prior to surgery and will be slightly dehydrated. *B* is an expected behavior with enlarged adenoids. *C* is again to be expected with decreased fluids prior to surgery.

103. D. *"The needle will hurt like a prick. You choose the leg you want it in and then squeeze your mother's hand when I give it to you."*

> *D* is the best choice. It informs the child that the injection will hurt and offers her a choice and some control over the situation. *A* is a poor choice because it belittles the child and tells her to suppress her normal reaction to pain. *B* reflects an attempt to bribe the child and is inappropriate. *C* is incorrect because it does not acknowledge the frightening aspect of the injection and also tells the child it will put her

to sleep. Remember that at this age sleep is often confused with death and therefore may make the whole process more frightening.

104. D. May cause hallucinations.

D will certainly increase the mother's anxiety; hallucinations are an infrequent side effect of atropine. *A* and *B* are frequent normal side effects of atropine. *C* will also be a result of the atropine due to decreased secretions.

105. D. Emesis of dark blood.

D does not indicate current hemorrhage; an emesis of old (dark) blood simply reflects a past event. *A* is a classic sign of bleeding after throat surgery. *B* and *C* indicate shock, with the typical signs of increased pulse and respirations and decreased blood pressure.

106. D. Place in side lying position until responsive.

D is the appropriate action because it allows the drainage of pooled secretions caused by decreased swallowing due to pain. *A* is incorrect because warm or hot fluids will increase, rather than decrease, bleeding and pain. *B* is inappropriate since aspirin increases the clotting time, which prolongs any bleeding. *C* is incorrect because suctioning, unless absolutely necessary, is contraindicated because it will traumatize the surgical site and cause further bleeding.

107. D. Green Jell-O.

D is the best answer because gelatin (Jell-O) is chilled, which will help promote clotting and decrease pain. *Green* Jell-O is especially good because if the child vomits, there will be no confusion as to possible bleeding. *A* and *B* are acidic and will increase the child's pain. *C* is not recommended since milk and milk products increase mucus production and lead to more swallowing and pain.

108. D. Hold the drug and call the physician to question the order.

D is the correct answer. Aspirin decreases the ability of the platelets to clot and could lead to bleeding difficulties. Acetaminophen (Tylenol) is preferred for pain and temperature control. *A* is appropriate with any drug and is not the best answer, considering the child's surgery. *B* is not the best choice because 300 mg is an appropriate dosage. *C* is normally an appropriate use of the drug, but not in this situation because of the child and her surgery.

109. D. Allow Mary to talk about her surgery and play-out her anger with dolls.

D is the correct answer because it allows for ventilation of feelings and anxiety. *A* is inappropriate because the nurse is advising the mother to bribe the child to forget, and because it does not deal with the primary problem. *B* is a poor choice because it will increase the mother's anxiety and guilt and does nothing for the child. *C* is a poor choice because it involves ignoring the problem, which is not an appropriate response.

110. *C. Increased independence.*

C is the correct answer since this is the behavior that the mother should not expect. The child has been through a traumatic experience and may regress, showing increased dependency. *A*, *B*, and *D* are all behaviors that may be seen with young children after hospitalizations. The mother should be warned to expect them but told that they are usually self-limiting and will decrease as the child begins to feel safe again.

111. *D. Temperature elevation of 38.4°C/101.1°F (axillary) and pain in the right ear.*

D necessitates a call to the physician because the symptoms indicate an ear infection. *A* is a low-grade temperature, and dysphagia is to be *expected* for several days after a tonsillectomy and adenoidectomy. *B* and *C* are also *normally* seen after surgery as healing progresses and do not necessitate bringing the child to the clinic or to a physician.

112. *C. Amanda's previous experiences with illness and hospitalization.*

C is the correct answer. Assessment of Amanda's situation and her previous experiences is essential; this will be a hospitalization involving several painful diagnostic procedures and treatments. The nurse will have to have data on which to base her approaches. *A* is incorrect because the child is just being admitted; it will be appropriate *later* in her hospitalization. *B* is incorrect because initially the nurse is concerned with Amanda, but this is the *next* priority after assessing Amanda. *D* is incorrect as the immediate nursing priority, but again can be assessed at a *later* date.

113. *B. Prevention of infection.*

B is the correct answer. The data reveal a WBC of 12,000/μL but there is no way to tell how many of these are effective WBCs in the immune process, so prevention of infection is the most important goal. *A*, *C*, and *D* are important to consider, but only *after* the nurse has taken steps to prevent infection.

114. *A. Emphasize that there will be little pain.*

A is the best answer because pain will occur with the procedure and the nurse should always be honest in preparing a child for a procedure. *B*, *C*, and *D* reflect true facts about bone marrow aspiration. Some children do not require premedication as they become more accustomed to the tests, but for the first such test medication is used.

115. C. Sternal.

C is the correct answer. With children, the sternal site is not frequently used, although it can provide the needed tissue. It is not used because there is too great a danger of missing the site and causing a pneumothorax. In addition, it is a very frightening site for the child. *D*, the iliac crest, is the preferred site with *A*, vertebral, and *B*, tibial, used less frequently.

116. C. Respirations of 12 and decreased breath sounds.

C are the manifestations that should cause the greatest concern. Midazolam (Versed) can cause respiratory depression, plus the fact that the child's normal respirations were 24 on admission, should cause concern. *A* indicates bleeding, but not too great an amount; it should be watched, particularly since the platelet count is 100,000/µL. *B* indicates the child is doing well and shows she is beginning to wake up and respond. *D* indicates normal vital signs for the child, based on the admission vitals.

117. B. Elevate the head of the bed to aid respiratory effort.

B is the correct answer. Elevation of the head of the bed aids respiratory effort by providing for maximum expansion. *A* is incorrect because there is presently no indication of hemorrhage. *C* is incorrect for the same reason; there is no evidence of shock. *D* is incorrect for two reasons. There are no data to support shock; second, providing more covers is inappropriate because it will lead to peripheral vasodilation, causing shifting of blood from vital organs to the periphery.

118. D. Assess for cardiac arrhythmias.

D is the incorrect intervention and, therefore, the best answer. Arrhythmias are not common with these two drugs. *A* is appropriate due to the constipation that vincristine causes. *B* and *C* are also seen with vincristine due to peripheral neuropathies seen with the drug.

119. D. CBC.

D is the correct answer due to the fact that chemotherapeutic cancer drugs interfere with rapidly reproducing normal cell activity; the bone marrow is one of the most rapidly reproducing tissues. *A* is incorrect in that it reflects primarily liver activity and the liver will not be affected quickly. *B* is incorrect due to the LDH, which is an enzyme that is usually assessed with cardiac function—that is, after a myocardial infarction. *C* is incorrect because these levels are dependent on many other factors, such as hydration and excretion; the chemotherapy will have an indirect, rather than a direct, effect on them.

120. C. Omelet, Jell-O, and milk shake.

C is the best answer. The eggs and milk shake provide protein and calories, which Amanda needs, and the Jell-O is bland and cold and will not cause increased ulcer pain. *A* is incorrect in that the spices in pizza and the chewing of cookies will increase pain due to the ulcers and therefore lead to less intake and further nutritional deficit. Tomato soup in *B* is hot, and cold liquids are better with stomatitis. In *D*, although the foods would be attractive to a 7-year-old, the hot dog and potato chips would cause increased pain.

121. C. Using puppets and dolls to explain procedures and permitting the child to handle the hospital equipment.

C is the best answer. The objects used in explaining the procedures are non-threatening and appropriate for her age. *A* is incorrect because it is an unethical action, as well as being very threatening and frightening for the child. *B* is inappropriate because the child of 7 has very little knowledge of the body and is unable to think abstractly and to transfer knowledge from the model to herself. *D* is incorrect because the question asked for activities to explain procedures; these activities are age-appropriate but will do little to respond to specific illness stresses.

122. D. Administer the medication.

D is the correct answer. It is important to get the IV antibiotic in before the IV is finished. *A*, *B*, and *C* are all done *later*. Probably the best order is: *D*, give the medication; *B*, discontinue the IV; *C*, let her visit with her brother; and then *A*, change the dressing later when there is time, since the sore is healing well.

123. A. Suggest that the topic be open conversation so that both information and feelings about leukemia can be discussed at home.

A is the best answer since it allows exchange of information and feelings among the family; at 11 years of age, the brother will need information and support, and these actions will help prevent fantasizing. *B* is a poor choice because it says that the brother is only concerned with whether or not he will be affected, which is a very limited and untrue view of the situation. *C* is a poor choice because only information is being shared; *A* is the more inclusive answer. *D* is simply avoiding the situation and does not prepare the brother for illness and the possible death of his sister, which will lead to further problems later.

124. C. "Do you think you are going to die soon?"

C is the best choice because it allows Amanda to express other feelings, and allows the nurse to gather further data. *A* makes an unwarranted assumption that being lonely is what Amanda is concerned with; also, the nurse is guaranteeing something she may be unable to follow through with. *B* completely shuts off the conversation and allows no further discussion. *D* is incorrect because the nurse is indirectly agreeing that she is going to die.

125. B. That Mrs. Curtis is looking for a reason to sue, particularly since her husband is a lawyer.

B is the *exception* and therefore the best answer. Few parents are looking to sue for malpractice. *A* is seen when learning of the diagnosis and not being able to do anything about it; in cases of leukemia, the parents often feel guilty and angry at themselves for not taking the child to the doctor earlier and will project this anger onto the professional staff. *C* is an appropriate consideration because there may be other reasons for her anger. *D* is a normal reaction on the part of staff on being criticized, and this recognition of her own responses should be part of the nurse's considerations.

126. A. Explain that Amanda needs her peers and schoolwork.

A is the best choice; with remission, the child can usually return to school and needs peer contact and normal developmental tasks to continue. *B* is inappropriate because the case situation reveals that all immunizations are up-to-date. In addition, the child is on immunotherapy, which decreases resistance, and immunizations must be done very carefully to prevent complications. *C* reflects jumping to conclusions without data to support them. *D* is incorrect because it is untrue, as noted in the explanation for *A*.

127. A. Sickle cell anemia is due to heterozygous inheritance of a gene responsible for production of abnormal hemoglobin.

A is the statement that is not true and is therefore the best answer. Sickle cell anemia is due to homozygous, not heterozygous, inheritance. *B* is true; sickle cell anemia is primarily seen in African-American and people of Mediterranean ancestry. *C* is true in that conditions of hypoxia, such as increased exercise and high altitudes, cause sickling. *D* is true in that the chronic anemia and multiple infections associated with sickle cell anemia often lead to an early death.

128. A. Oxygen by mask and cold applications to leg to relieve pain.

A is the best answer because cold causes further sickling and increases acidosis, which also increases the sickling process. *B* is an appropriate action in that powerful analgesics (such as morphine, oxycodone, hydromorphone and methadone) are often required with crisis pain. *C* and *D* are appropriate actions because the main treatment of crisis is pain control and fluids to decrease blood viscosity. Bedrest prevents further energy expenditure and more sickling.

129. B. 7-year-old boy with juvenile rheumatoid arthritis.

B is the best choice because it provides a child of like age and sex who also has decreased mobility. *A* is incorrect because the child seems to be developing an infection and Ronny is very susceptible to infections. *C* is incorrect because the client is a girl and modesty is important to the school-age child. School-age children are usually placed in a room with children of the same sex. *D* is incorrect because the child has an active respiratory infection, to which children with sickle cell anemia are particularly susceptible.

130. D. Earlobes.

D is the evaluator that is incorrect. It is impossible to assess an African-American child's color well by checking the earlobes. *A*, *B*, and *C* reflect areas of the body with decreased pigment, which makes it possible to assess Ronny's color. Another place would be the conjunctiva.

131. D. Increased fragility and decreased life span of RBCs.

D is the correct answer. The sickle hemoglobin leads to a shortened life span of about 15–20 days for RBCs; this contrasts with the normal RBC life span of 120 days. *A* is an incorrect choice because diet is the primary cause of iron deficiency anemia and there are no data indicating that Ronny's diet is poor. *B* will lead to decreased RBC production and is not related to RBC life span. *C* is incorrect because there is no blood loss with crises.

132. D. Question the order because the nurse knows vitamins are of questionable value in sickle cell anemia.

D is the correct answer. Vitamins are of use only in circumstances of normal dietary deficiency and there is no indication of this in the case situation. Folic acid in no way halts or alters sickling. *A*, *B*, and *C* indicate poor analysis of the situation and the treatment rationale, and are therefore incorrect.

133. D. Playing checkers and simple card games with his roommate.

D is the best choice because the activities are appropriate developmentally and also involve him in some peer contact. *A* is a very isolating activity, presents the problem of finding appropriate shows, and does not involve peer contact. *B* is incorrect because phone calls are a very transitory activity and do not solve the problem of continued diversion. *C* could be appropriate, but does not involve peer interaction, which might hold his attention longer than reading.

134. D. Prevent dehydration, which increases sickling of RBCs.

D is the correct answer because the fluids help prevent dehydration and the acidosis seen with it, which will increase sickling. *A* is incorrect in that increasing blood volume will not deal with the problem. *B* is incorrect because it is not the primary reason for increasing fluids (the primary reason is the relationship between hydration and sickling), although a side effect of the fluids will be prevention of urinary tract infections. *C* is not the best choice in that it does not address the hydration goal.

135. B. Must have the trait.

B is the correct answer. The genetics of the disease require that the child receive one trait from each parent to express the disease. *A* is incorrect by history and *C* is incorrect physiologically because both parents need not show the disease, although both carry the trait. *D* is incorrect because Ms. Simpson *must* at least have the trait for her child to have the disease.

136. C. Each child carries the trait, but may not have the disease.

C is correct because if Ronny's father has the disease, he will pass the gene to all of his children; they will either carry the trait (if they do not also get the gene from their mother, a carrier) or have the disease (if they do get the gene from their mother). If these children do not have the disease, they at least carry the trait. *A* and *B* are incorrect because *all* the children will at least carry the trait. *D* is incorrect because the children's choices in marital partners will determine whether their children will carry the trait.

137. D. Increased activity.

D is the correct answer. The symptoms were reported after an episode of playing. *A* is incorrect; there is a history of infections but no current data indicating that one is present. *B* and *C* are also incorrect because there is no indication that either of these factors were present.

138. B. Apical pulse rate; coordination of voluntary muscles.

B is correct because tachycardia may indicate carditis, a major manifestation of rheumatic fever. Other signs include heart murmur and cardiomegaly, which result from inflammation, necrosis, scarring, valvular stenosis, and damage to the myocardium. If untreated, congestive heart failure may occur. Chorea, a major CNS (manifestation of) rheumatic fever, affects prepubescent girls more often than boys. Signs include incoordination of small or fine muscles, twitching, weakness, inattention, and emotional lability. The nurse must assess these factors to establish a baseline from which to evaluate progress. Although *A* indicates a teaching need, it is incorrect because this answer relates to a *causal* factor, not current needs or complications of rheumatic fever. Thus, *A* is post hoc in relation to the question. Also, *A* is threatening to the client and the mother. *C* is incorrect because the nodules are painless. *D*, which may indicate a teaching need, is incorrect because a 24-hour diet recall is not specifically related to current manifestations of rheumatic fever. A balanced diet is necessary for healing. Thus, the nurse should include this, as well as hygiene, in planning and intervening.

139. A. *"During rest or sleep, pains from growth may lessen or disappear, but the joint pains of rheumatic fever do not lessen."*

 A is correct since the two pain types may be differentiated by these characteristics. *B* is incorrect for reasons stated in *A*. *C* is incorrect, as neither of the pain types is restricted anatomically. Rheumatic fever joint pains migrate from knees and ankles to the wrists, elbows, and hips. *D* is not correct because the 8-year-old can define intensity of pain on a scale of 1–10; can point to the region of pain; and can, with a limited temporal concept, generally describe when pain does and does not occur.

140. C. *Ten-year-old Marta, who is confined to bed with acute systemic lupus erythematosus.*

 C is the correct answer, as the school-age child (6–12) who has rheumatic fever should be allowed interaction with other school-age children who are the same sex, have similar therapeutic regimens, and have no infectious or communicable conditions. Systemic lupus erythematosus, a long-term noncommunicable inflammatory disease, requires strict bedrest in acute stages, and manifests problems and other management needs similar to rheumatic fever. *A* is incorrect because the child has playroom privileges. The school-age child with rheumatic fever may become depressed because he or she is confined to bed and not allowed activity, which is extremely important at this industrious age. *B* is incorrect. The child with rheumatic fever *must* be kept from persons with respiratory tract infections (e.g., pneumonia) because reinfection with streptococci increases the threat of additional cardiac damage. *D* is incorrect for the same reason as *A*.

141. B. *"Yes, there will be a little pain, but it will soon be over."*

 B is the correct answer. The school-age child fears body injury, needs and can accept honest and specific explanations of procedures and accompanying sensations, and understands the concept of time. Explanation helps the child to maintain control and to cooperate during the procedure. *A* is incorrect. This answer promotes shame and distrust, does not acknowledge the child's needs, is threatening, and intensifies fears. A child of this age is very concerned about peer attitudes and is embarrassed by loss of self-control. *C* is incorrect because this answer does not acknowledge the child's question and is untrue. Clients with acute rheumatic fever are confined to bed for prevention of serious cardiac damage and promotion of comfort. *D* does not answer the child's question, threatens the child, intensifies fear, and inhibits the expression of emotions regarding a natural fear. The child should be offered alternative outlets for pain or fear, such as squeezing a hand or counting. If the child does scream or cry, he or she should not be shamed, but reassured that such expression is normal and accepted.

142. D. Place a bed cradle over Kathy's legs to prevent physical or material contact.

D is correct. The child with rheumatic fever and polyarthritis often self-immobilizes and cannot tolerate movement, manipulation, or anything touching the affected areas. A bed cradle prevents the weight of bedclothes on the extremely painful joints. Nursing care is organized to include only absolutely necessary activities, and pain management includes proper body alignment and support of affected joints with pillows. *A*, *B*, and *C* are incorrect because these actions increase, not relieve, pain.

143. D. Restricted mobility, possible bodily injury, and lack of control over self-care.

D is the correct answer. The school-age child is industrious in nature and desires to be active. Illness and forced immobility may be regarded as a sign of inferiority, failure, or punishment for a misdeed. The nurse must explain the reasons for immobility; reassure about blamelessness; and allow appropriate outlets for anger, anxieties, and energy in order to prevent depression. A child of this age understands the reasons for immobility and should be given the opportunity to express related emotions. The nurse allows maximum possible self-care independence, as this aids in preventing self-image destruction. Honest explanations and involving the child in planning and implementing care will reduce fear of bodily injury. Although an 8-year-old child is not totally free of separation anxiety, he or she can tolerate parental separation because of progressing reality orientation and desires to form relationships outside the family and home. Therefore, *A* is not the *most* difficult to accept and is incorrect. *B* is incorrect because it is not the *most* difficult problem; however, a child of this age does worry about peer group rejection and peers' attitudes and conversations in his or her absence. *C* is incorrect; it is a concern, but not the *most* difficult aspect of hospitalization.

144. B. Preventing complications by providing absolute rest, padded bedding, spoon-feeding, and a diet high in calories, protein, and iron.

B is correct. CNS inflammation results in choreiform movements involving the voluntary muscles. The child may become incontinent, clumsy, and spastic and may demonstrate twitching, facial grimaces, and other involuntary, purposeless, and irregular movements. Constant movement utilizes large amounts of energy (requiring extra calories, protein, vitamins, and minerals) and is abrasive to bony prominences (requiring frequent skin care). Rest is essential to prevent exhaustion or death from cardiac disease. Injury may result from bed frames and sharp eating utensils; therefore, soft toys, padded beds, and spoon-feeding are provided. *A* is incorrect since bedrest is enforced. *C* is incorrect because the lack of voluntary small muscle control, inattention, and activity restrictions prohibit these actions. Writing requires coordination of small, complex muscle structures. Deterioration in penmanship promotes anxiety, frustration, inferiority feelings, and tension—which, in turn, exacerbate choreiform movements. As improvement in condition occurs, short study periods are allowed and utilization of muscle structures gradually progresses from large to small. *D* is incorrect because the child with this manifestation: (1) is incapable of self-care; (2) must have a planned, balanced diet and restricted activity; and (3) needs emotional support for a CNS disorder rather than psychological counseling for an emotional disorder.

145. A. Erythema marginatum and cardiac murmur.

A is the only incorrect indication, so it is the best answer. Erythema marginatum, a major manifestation of rheumatic fever, is a nonpruritic, pink, macular rash appearing on warm body areas. Cardiac murmur signifies carditis, another major manifestation resulting from Aschoff's bodies (inflammatory lesions) on the endocardium, which scar and cause stenosis of heart valves. *B*, *C*, and *D* are common signs of salicylate toxicity. Aspirin should be given with meals to avoid gastric irritation and bleeding. CNS changes indicate neurologic toxicity. Hyperventilation is a respiratory compensation for metabolic acidosis. Bleeding tendencies result from increased prothrombin time.

146. C. Orthopnea and peripheral edema.

C is correct because these are signs of congestive heart failure (CHF), which may occur from inflammation, scarring, and necrosis of the myocardium and consequent inability of the heart to function as a pump. Other signs of CHF include neck vein distention, tachycardia, generalized edema, weight gain, hepatomegaly, dyspnea, and rales. *A* is incorrect, as *increased* ESR indicates increased inflammation and increased severity of rheumatic fever. *B* is incorrect because 9000/μL is within the normal range for the WBC count. *D* is incorrect because the *presence* of C-reactive protein in plasma indicates inflammation. *Increased*, not normal, heart rate indicates increased severity of rheumatic fever.

147. D. Report possible infectious processes suggested by high temperature elevations.

D is the only incorrect action, so it is the best answer. Fever does not usually accompany infection during long-term steroid therapy because the drugs are immunosuppressive, inhibit the inflammatory response, and mask signs and symptoms of infection. The nurse monitors for other indicators, such as lethargy and anorexia. *A* includes important nursing actions. Steroids increase susceptibility to infection by suppressing the immune system and causing a negative nitrogen balance. The urine is checked for glucose because steroids enhance gluconeogenesis and produce insulin antagonism, with subsequent hyperglycemia and spilling of sugar in the urine. *B* is also relevant. Steroids increase secretion of gastric hydrochloric acid, which may aggravate or create an ulcer. The nurse monitors for melena and hematemesis. Extreme mood swings (euphoria, severe depression) may result from CNS effects. *C* is important, because steroids promote sodium and water retention, edema, and weight gain. The nurse must also assess for indications of hypokalemia, because potassium is replaced in the cell by sodium and the K+ moves into the vascular space and is excreted in the urine. Steroid therapy may also cause Cushing's syndrome, with manifestations including skin striae, acne, hirsutism, "moon face," and "buffalo hump." It is important for the nurse to explain to the client and family that these problems disappear when therapy is discontinued.

148. *A. Observe Kathy for headache, nausea, muscular weakness, disordered vision, and changes in apical heart rate and rhythm.*

A is the correct answer. The signs and symptoms listed may indicate life-threatening digitalis toxicity, which may be induced by decreased serum potassium as a result of the potassium-depleting effects of furosemide (Lasix) administration. The nurse assesses for arrhythmias, brady-cardia, tachycardia, or a rapid-weak pulse on arising, as well as for colored or blurred vision, dilated or constricted pupils, and confusion. A resting apical rate (assessed for 1 full minute) less than 60 or greater than 100 bpm, or indications of any other signs or symptoms, warrants immediate notification of the appropriate health team member (prescribing doctor). *B* includes important observations related to furosemide therapy (blood volume and circulation), but is not specific to digitalis toxicity. (Comparison of apical-radial pulses *would* be indicated, but not radial pulse rate alone. An apical pulse rate greater than the radial rate may indicate ineffectual heartbeats and decreased cardiac output.) *C* is incorrect because these signs may indicate peripheral circulatory or neurologic problems, but are not specific to digitalis toxicity. *D* is not correct; although anorexia may accompany signs and symptoms of digitalis toxicity, the other listed signs do not. (In digitalis toxicity the temperature may be decreased, the face pale, and the pulse weak.)

149. C. The solution is infused at a rapid rate.

C is the only *incorrect* activity and is therefore the best answer. Rapid IV administration of potassium may cause cardiac arrhythmias and pain or burning at the infusion site. KCl is infused at a slow to moderate rate in concentrations of not more than 40–60 mEq/L. *A* is a correct action. The nurse ensures adequate urine output prior to IV KCl infusion in order to prevent toxicity. If kidney function is impaired and daily urinary volume is low (less than 500–600 mL), potassium should not be administered. *B* is a correct action. Cardiac arrhythmias may occur with IV KCl infusions; therefore, ECG monitoring and repeated serum potassium levels are indicated. *D* is also a correct action. KCl should not be administered undiluted and must be *thoroughly* mixed in solution to prevent toxic effects of unmixed (or bolus) infusion. Thorough mixing is accomplished by complete inversion (turning upside down) of the KCl in solution at *least* eight rotations.

150. C. Reading, playing catch, and playing guessing games.

C is the answer because it includes an *inappropriate* action, playing catch, which requires physical exertion and the use of small muscles. Reading and playing guessing games *are* appropriate actions. *A*, *B*, and *D* *are* appropriate options, since all of these activities require minimal physical activity. To prevent cardiac complications, children recovering from rheumatic fever are permitted only gradual activity increases as inflammation subsides.

151. A. "Kathy must have antibiotic therapy indefinitely and exactly as ordered."

A is the correct response. Antibiotic administration, either monthly (IM) or daily (PO) is essential for several years (or for a lifetime) after the initial attack to prevent recurrent rheumatic fever attacks and consequent serious cardiac damage or rheumatic heart disease. *B* is incorrect. Recurrent attacks may occur after exposure to group A beta-hemolytic streptococci. *C* is incorrect. The child recovering from rheumatic fever is restricted in physical activities. No physically competitive sports or individually exertive activities are allowed. *D* is incorrect. To prevent complications and promote healing, a balanced diet high in protein, calories, and iron is essential.

152. B. Oxygen.

B is the correct answer. The blood gases reveal respiratory acidosis and oxygen will be needed as part of the therapy. Sodium bicarbonate will probably also be needed to correct the acid-base problem. *A* is incorrect since asthma is a lower respiratory problem, not an upper airway obstruction. Epiglottitis is an example of an upper airway problem where a tracheostomy set should be available. *C* is incorrect because morphine causes respiratory depression and is harmful in this situation. *D* is incorrect because there is no indication of cardiac irregularity.

153. A. Phlebitis at the IV site.

A is the correct answer because IV steroids are not irritating to the vein. *B* and *D* are incorrect because the nurse *would* assess for GI upset and urine output when administering steroids. *C* is incorrect because the nurse *should* assess whether the drug is working to decrease airway inflammation, thus improving breath sounds.

154. C. Sitting up.

C is correct because it is the preferred position for clients with asthma during severe attacks and it allows for maximum expansion of the lungs. *A* is incorrect because the elevation is too little; this position still allows the diaphragm to minimize expansion of the lungs. *B* and *D* are incorrect for the same reasons; they do not allow for maximum expansion of the lungs.

155. D. "I know it's difficult having him back so frequently. It is upsetting for us and for him and his family."

D is the best answer because the head nurse acknowledges the feelings of the staff nurses and also points out the stresses on the family. *A* is incorrect because it agrees with the staff and reinforces their attitudes rather than emphasizing the child's difficulties. *B* is poor because it is an unwarranted assumption and there is nothing in the database to support it. *C* is incorrect for the same reason; it assumes that the teaching has been poor and there is nothing in the database to suggest this.

156. D. Notify physician of increased temperature and change in mucus.

D is the best answer. A respiratory infection appears to have initiated this attack and the data provided in the question indicate that it has become worse. The mucus has changed in consistency and color, which along with the increased temperature suggests a bacterial infection. The best choice is to notify the physician to obtain orders for a chest x-ray, IV antibiotics and possibly a sputum culture. If a culture is ordered, it is best to take it when the temperature is elevated. *A* is incorrect as a *first* action; it is done *after* notifying the physician. *B* is also an action for *later*. Because of his age, Tom is not in danger of a febrile convulsion, so antipyretics could wait for a few minutes. *C* is also appropriate *after* notifying the physician.

157. D. Note his urinary output and BUN.

D is the incorrect action because there is no indication of renal problems in the database. Also, the dosage is not so high that excretion should be a problem. Therefore, it is unnecessary to note urinary output and BUN. *A* and *C* are correct actions because his history and that of his family reveal multiple allergies and make him at high risk for an allergy to penicillin. *B* is a correct action since Tom is 11 years old and of normal mental development; part of his care will always be explaining his therapy and why it is being done.

158. A. Overprotection.

A is the correct answer. Tom is 11 and has had asthma for 5 years. He should be more responsible for his care, and there is nothing in his history to indicate that he could not be. *B* is incorrect because the statement does not indicate regression on either the mother's or Tom's part. *C* is incorrect because the mother is not expressing hostility directly—that is, she has not said she is angry. *D* is incorrect because although the mother is expressing normal concern, the fact that Tom is 11 means that he should have some independence and be involved in the management of his own care.

159. B. Prolonged rapid pulse.

B is the correct answer. Albuterol is a bronchodilator, and a sign of toxicity is prolonged increased pulse. A transient increase in heart rate is expected. *A* is incorrect because although it is a side effect of cromolyn sodium, it is not indicative of toxicity. *C* and *D* are not signs of toxicity with these drugs, although nausea may be seen with any drug taken orally.

160. D. Has refused to join the Boy Scouts because being in large crowds of other kids might make him sick.

D is the correct answer because it shows that Tom is isolating himself from his peers. There is no greater risk of infection in Scout groups than in school. The same precautions should be used in both to minimize respiratory infections. *A*, *B*, and *C* are all positive actions that indicate his involvement in environmental control of allergens, knowledge of medications, and improvement of respiratory capacity.

161. D. Pain.

D is the answer; pain is *not* a common symptom of scoliosis. *A*, *B*, and *C* *are* all reported with lateral curvature of the spine.

162. A. Urinary system.

A is the answer. Susan is going to use a brace, so she will not be totally immobilized. There is nothing in her case situation to indicate that she is at high risk for urinary infections. *B* must be assessed because the hip is often affected by the curvature. *C* is seen with anyone undergoing extended treatment for a problem—particularly an adolescent who is undergoing multiple other bodily and psychological changes. *D* is found with scoliosis and is reported in the physical findings.

163. D. Permission to sleep without the brace at night.

D is the answer. The brace is to be worn at *all* times. *A* is included in the teaching because the brace limits mouth movement, and chewing raw vegetables and fruits will help prevent jaw mobility difficulties; also, dental hygiene may be impaired to some degree so *sugarless* gum is important to protect teeth while providing jaw action. Cotton clothes, *B*, are appropriate because they allow evaporation of moisture. *C* is an important teaching point because any brace can lead to skin breakdown.

164. C. Peer group interaction should be decreased to avoid embarrassment.

C is the answer; in adolescence, it is important to maintain contact with peers. *A*, *B*, and *D* are all characteristic of identity formation.

165. A. Discussing why she is not wearing the brace as instructed.

A is the best answer because it is an *inappropriate* response. The nurse is making an assumption without a database; Susan may not have been wearing the brace but other factors could be operating to increase the curvature. *B* will elicit appropriate data, as it will influence her compliance with the regime. *C* is a correct nursing action because an improperly fitting brace that is not functioning properly could lead to increased curvature. *D* is a necessary action since a main problem with scoliosis is that it causes cardiac shift and compresses the lungs.

166. C. Increase of the curvature will further impair cardio-pulmonary function.

C is a major point; further curvature may lead to Susan being short of breath and fatigued. *A* is incorrect because increasing curvature leads to crowding and nerve impingement on occasion. It is important to note that pain is not an *early* symptom of scoliosis. *B* is incorrect because paralysis is not seen with scoliosis. *D* is incorrect because at 13 Susan is not past her growth period and the curvature can increase even after cessation of the growth spurt.

167. D. "I know it's very hard to be different from your friends. Have they said anything to you about the brace?"

D is the most therapeutic answer because it acknowledges Susan's feelings and also seeks further data before planning any further interventions. *A* is poor in that it contains a threat and scare tactics, which never work for long. *B* is poor because it does not allow Susan to express her feelings further and also assumes that her friends will understand, which they may not do. *C* is false reassurance; there is no guarantee that the treatment will last only a few months. In addition, Susan is an adolescent with many body changes occurring and this is one more change to which she must adapt. Telling her she will get used to it is a very superficial response.

168. C. Cleanse her face several times a day and try a hairstyle off her face.

C is the correct answer. Cleansing of the face and hair will reduce the oil. *A* is incorrect because birth control pills are not used for acne. *B* is not correct because there is no proven association between a diet of fatty foods and acne. *D* is incorrect because it can lead to permanent scarring.

169. D. Discuss what else might be worrying Mrs. Black at the moment.

D is the best approach—assessing what the mother's feelings and concerns are at present may help identify issues that the nurse can help Mrs. Black resolve, along with understanding more about normal adolescent behaviors. *A* is a poor response because it is a superficial statement that cuts off further discussion and is of no help to the mother in dealing with her daughter. *B* is also a poor response since it leaves no opening for discussion and is of no help to the mother, who is asking for help. *C* is incorrect because the nurse must be concerned with the whole family; Mrs. Black's problems will affect her daughter.

170. B. She is attending school regularly.

B is a good indication that Susan is carrying on with her normal activities and is not isolating herself from her friends. *A* does not indicate follow-through in her treatment. *C* indicates poor adaptation because she is isolating herself from her peers and activities; this will be harmful to her psychological health and self-concept. *D* indicates regression, dependence, and poor adaptation. Susan will have to have some help with the brace, but total dependence is unhealthy.

171. C. Oral hypoglycemics and diet for control when utilized precisely.

The answer is *C*. Insulin dependent diabetes mellitus is characterized by a relative lack of insulin, and oral hypoglycemics are of *no* use and may even be harmful. A diet control will be necessary, as with all clients who have diabetes. *A* is true; a person who has insulin dependent diabetes has to rely on injectable insulin. *B* is also true; in contrast to type 2 diabetes, insulin dependent diabetes may have an onset that is very sudden and often occurs with ketoacidosis as the first symptom. *D* is a correct approach in that good control should not hinder the child from growing and developing normally. If the child is in very poor control, he may be smaller and thinner than his peers.

172. B. Giving her several glasses of water for hydration.

B is the correct answer. Theresa is exhibiting signs of ketoacidosis due to hyperglycemia, which has led to dehydration.

The best action after notifying the physician is to begin rehydrating her; note that she is difficult, but not impossible, to arouse and should be able to swallow. *A* and *D* will add further to her hyperglycemia and be of no use; she does not need glucose. *C* is inappropriate until further assessment is done, probably in the hospital where blood glucose levels can be monitored while insulin is being given. In this home situation, hydration is the most appropriate action.

173. B. Infection.

B is the correct answer since infection can precipitate hyperglycemia. Theresa's case situation indicates a recent urinary tract infection plus the history of the flu. *A* could be correct but there are no data to support this inference. *C* is incorrect because increased physical activity leads to hypoglycemia, not hyperglycemia. *D* is a possibility since insulin demands are increased with puberty; however, the data most directly support infection as the cause of Theresa's ketoacidosis.

174. C. Decreased urine specific gravity.

C will not be expected; with dehydration the specific gravity will be increased, not decreased. *A* will be expected since the cause of ketoacidosis is hyperglycemia. *B* is seen with hypertonic dehydration, in contrast to the tenting seen with isotonic dehydration. *D* is seen because the nausea, vomiting, and decreased fluid intake lead to potassium depletion.

175. D. Give her orange juice with extra sugar.

D is the appropriate action since Theresa is exhibiting the classic signs of hypoglycemia. She also had regular insulin an hour previously and onset of action is 30–60 minutes after administration. Glucose is needed. *A* is incorrect; the data indicate hypoglycemia; insulin will exacerbate the condition. *C* provides glucose, but glucose is needed immediately— preferably by the oral route. *B* should be done after giving the glucose and noting its effect so that the physician is aware of the client's status.

176. D. Pizza slice, milk, fresh fruit.

D is the best answer because it provides more protein and less carbohydrate than the other choices. *A*, *B*, and *C* have more carbohydrate than *D* does.

177. D. Talk with Theresa about her feelings of exclusion and assess further how she is relating to her friends.

D is correct because Theresa needs to ventilate her feelings; the nurse also needs to gather more data to aid in planning how to manage her noncompliance. Rebellion and noncompliance are common in adolescents with chronic diseases, particularly since these diseases make them different from their peers at a time in development when similarity to peers is important. *A* is incorrect because the client is expressing her feelings and these need to be explored, not ignored. *B* is indicated, but at a *later* time when further data have been collected and appropriate interventions planned. *C* is not appropriate at this time; no data presented indicate that a lack of knowledge about diabetes is causing the non-compliance.

178. D. Have her help with tasks such as settling the younger children down at bedtime.

D is the correct answer. In this way, the nurse is including her in the activities of the unit and entrusting her with responsibilities, which will enhance her feelings of competence. *A* is helpful but does not address the issue of competence. *B* will be appropriate *later*, in helping her parents understand how she feels about her disease, but is not immediately helpful in promoting her self-concept. *C* is incorrect because although peer contact is important, it is *not immediately* useful in dealing with the feelings of incompetence.

179. B. Meticulous foot care.

The answer that reflects the *least* important aspect of the teaching plan is *B*. Foot care and vascular changes are less important in the child with insulin dependent diabetes than in the adult. The changes will not be seen for several years; remember from the history that Theresa has been diagnosed for only 3 years. *A is* appropriate to include in the teaching plan because sudden increases in physical activity cause hypoglycemia and increasing glucose intake beforehand is appropriate. *C is* useful in preventing hyperglycemia and ketoacidosis, while *D is* also taught to clients to help prevent ketoacidosis. This teaching is done with strict guidelines, but the adolescent can learn to manipulate his or her insulin to some extent.

180. B. Bedtime snack of cheese.

B is the best suggestion. Theresa is experiencing nighttime hypoglycemia due to her peak action time of NPH insulin. A bedtime snack of cheese, a slowly digesting protein, will counterbalance the peak action of the insulin. *A* is incorrect because the symptoms are associated with hypoglycemia. More insulin will compound the problem. *C* is incorrect because the cookies are high in carbohydrate and will not be available at peak action time for insulin. The diet soda has no sugar to combat the hypoglycemia. *D* is incorrect because exercise enhances insulin-induced hypoglycemia.

8. Young Adult and Reproductive Years

Case Management Scenarios and Critical-Thinking Exercises

Medical Situation: Reproductive health maintenance for adolescents.

- *Nursing Problems/Diagnosis:*

  Altered health maintenance.

  Altered immune response.

  Impaired skin integrity.

  The nurse is asked to plan a course about reproductive health maintenance for a group of 14–16-year-old girls. General concepts of anatomy and physiology and the adolescents' level of growth and development help structure the course outline and method of presentation.

1. The nurse can best encourage adolescents' interest and participation in the class by:

   A. Tuning in to own feelings and values about the topic.

   B. Emulating the adolescents' dress and language.

   C. Sharing own experiences as an adolescent.

   D. Explaining how this knowledge will help them later throughout their life span.

2. The nurse instructs the group that during the menstrual cycle, the fertile time occurs:

   A. On day 14 of the cycle.

   B. Just before menstruation.

   C. When the ovum is present.

   D. On day 1 of the menstrual cycle.

3. The cervical mucus of one of the students is clear, copious, like egg white, stretchable to 5 cm, and slippery. The student knows that at this time she:

    A. Is pregnant.

    B. Has a mild leukorrhea.

    C. Is about to menstruate.

    D. Is about to ovulate.

4. Based on the calendar method, the next probable fertile period of a woman whose longest cycle is 35 days and whose shortest cycle is 26 days includes days:

    A. 8 through 24.

    B. 15 through 17.

    C. 12 through 21.

    D. 13 through 17 or 18.

5. The nurse instructs the group that which skin change occurs both during pregnancy and with the use of oral contraceptives, but may not fade after the pill is discontinued?

    A. Chloasma.

    B. Palmar erythema.

    C. Telangiectasia.

    D. Pruritus.

6. Women taking oral contraceptives are cautioned that a hazardous side effect of these contraceptive is:

    A. Ectopic pregnancy.

    B. Cholelithiasis.

    C. Gastroenteritis.

    D. Thromboembolic disease.

7. Jan, one of the students in the group, confides to the nurse that she is pregnant. She is wearing loose clothing and is dieting in an attempt to keep the pregnancy a secret. Jan and her boyfriend, Mike, have decided to "go through with" the pregnancy and then place the baby for adoption. They think they have "lues" and ask the nurse where they can go for treatment. They decide to attend a Teenage Parent clinic. If they have just acquired lues, the clinic nurse expects to obtain the following history:

    A. Appearance of a chancre.

    B. Infection 1 week ago.

    C. A positive test for serology.

    D. Pain in the joints and loss of position sense.

8. Mike and Jan's histories and physical exams reveal that they both have secondary syphilis and that she is 18 weeks pregnant. The nurse knows that:

   A. Lesions of secondary syphilis are not infectious.

   B. Obliterative endarteritis is a possible complication.

   C. Gummas will appear now throughout all body tissues.

   D. The spirochete crosses the placenta after the 16th week of gestation.

9. Which is true about gonorrhea?

   A. It can result in pharyngitis, tonsillitis, perianal pruritus, and burning.

   B. Ophthalmia neonatorum is the only effect of congenital gonorrhea.

   C. Small lesions or blisters occur in the vagina and on the glans penis.

   D. It can be transmitted only by sexual contact.

Medical Situation: Normal pregnancy: health supervision.

- **Nursing Problems/Diagnosis: Anxiety.**

  Altered comfort pattern (discomfort).

  Impaired digestion.

  Impaired family coping.

  Risk for infection.

  Altered nutrition: more than body requirements.

  Altered parenting.

  Impaired physical mobility.

  Sexual dysfunction.

  Ineffective thermoregulation.

- **Chief Complaint:**

  Wendy Wilkes is a 22-year-old married African-American woman who states she is "8 weeks pregnant by dates."

- **Present Status:**

  Wendy has been amenorrheic for two periods. She has had "mild nausea" with no vomiting, mastalgia, urinary frequency, and fatigue for about 5 weeks. This first pregnancy was planned.

- **Past Health History:**

  Wendy states she has always been healthy. She experienced menarche at age 11. Her menstrual cycles have always been regular, occurring every 28-30 days. She disclaims dysmenorrhea. She has never used contraception. She has kept her immunizations current, seldom has colds, and has never been hospitalized.

- *Family History:*

Hypertension has been diagnosed in both sets of grandparents and in Wendy's mother. One grandparent died of a brain attack at age 56. Wendy's youngest brother died in a sickle cell crisis at age 7. Her husband's family denies sickle cell disease. Neither she nor her husband has been tested for the presence of sickle cell trait. Her husband, Ed, is an auto mechanic. The couple plan to attend childbirth classes.

- *Physical Exam:*

Pregnancy test: Positive. Rubella titer: 1:6.

Vital signs: Temperature: 37.1°C, P: 76, R: 18, BP: 134/86. Weight: 140 pounds. Height: 5 feet, 6 inches.

Findings within normal limits for other organ systems.

Pelvic examination reveals uterine enlargement coincident with 8 weeks' gestation; Hegar's and Chadwick's signs positive; gynecoid pelvis; pelvic measurements adequate.

- *Psychological Status:*

Wendy states that she and her husband are pleased and excited about the pregnancy. This will be the first grandchild for both families.

---

10. Wendy's rubella titer is 1:6. In planning Wendy's care, the nurse needs to know that Wendy:

    A. Has had rubella.

    B. Is presently infected with rubella.

    C. Is a candidate for rubella vaccination shortly after birth.

    D. Must wait until she weans the baby before she can get the vaccine.

11. While being prepared for a pelvic examination, Wendy confides in the nurse, "I can't stand this part of the examination. It's so hard to relax." Which nursing action *best* assists Wendy to relax her perineal structures?

    A. Coach her to keep eyes, mouth, and hands open.

    B. Give Wendy a hand or an exam table handle to squeeze.

    C. Provide ongoing explanation during the examination.

    D. Ensure privacy and drape her comfortably.

12. Wendy works as a general surgical scrub technician in the local hospital. The nurse will most likely recommend that for the duration of her pregnancy Wendy take:

    A. Only short surgical cases to avoid long periods of standing.

    B. Frequent walks or rest with legs up between cases.

    C. Only "clean" cases.

D. An assignment on another unit.

13. Wendy states that she and her mother, age 48, are "driving the rest of the family wild." Wendy says that both of them need to change clothes more than once a day because of bouts of perspiration and prefer to keep the home thermostat set on low. Which nurse demonstrates the *best* understanding of the physiologic phenomenon described?

    A. Nurse L: "Mothers tend to identify with their daughters during pregnancy."

    B. Nurse M: "It could be the flu bug. Does anyone else in your household show these symptoms?"

    C. Nurse N: "This is often seen when one is anxious. Let's talk about what is going on with you two."

    D. Nurse 0: "Changes in female hormone levels occur in both pregnancy and menopause."

14. The nurse knows that Wendy has understood anticipatory guidance regarding heartburn when Wendy states that she:

    A. Avoids bending at the waist and does "flying" exercises.

    B. Eats some unsalted, butterless popcorn before getting out of bed in the morning.

    C. Has stopped eating starch or red clay.

    D. Gets plenty of fluids, exercise, and foods containing roughage.

15. Which statement to Wendy *best* demonstrates the nurse's knowledge of placental function?

    A. "Lie on your side to rest or sleep."

    B. "Your baby will obtain all the nutrients he or she needs from your stores."

    C. "Avoid taking any drug unless it is prescribed by your physician."

    D. "Don't worry about your bladder infection. The urinary and reproductive tracts are not connected."

16. When Wendy's husband asks about the best remedy for leg cramps, the nurse instructs him to:

    A. Massage Wendy's leg to relax the calf muscle.

    B. Report the incident to Wendy's physician.

    C. Help Wendy to place her full weight on the affected leg and lean forward on it.

    D. Direct Wendy to point the toes of the affected leg, to stretch the cramped muscle.

17. Wendy is now in her third month of pregnancy. Anticipatory guidance, coincident with the client's readiness for learning, is a significant intervention in the plan of care for the woman

who is pregnant. The choice of which topic demonstrates that the nurse knows the needs of women during the first trimester?

A. Feelings and attitudes toward pregnancy.

B. Preparation for labor.

C. Fetal growth and development.

D. New role as mother, and the new baby.

18. Wendy is given written instructions to notify her physician or mid-wife immediately if she or her family notices any signs and symptoms of complication. Which is not included?

A. Severe, persistent headache.

B. Tight finger rings and puffy eyes.

C. Ptyalism and gums that bleed when teeth are brushed.

D. Dull facial expression or affect.

19. Vitamin C absorption in pregnancy is hindered by the decreased hydrochloric acid in the stomach. The nurse counsels Wendy that the breakfast highest in vitamin C and protein is:

A. Orange juice, Cream of Wheat with milk, toast and margarine, coffee.

B. Grapefruit juice, beef liver with scrambled egg, toast, coffee.

C. Eggs with bacon and fried tomato, toast, coffee.

D. Banana, French toast with syrup, milk.

20. One pregnant friend of Wendy's does not eat meat. Which diet should the nurse recommend to meet Wendy's friend's protein needs?

A. Cottage cheese and tomatoes, peanut butter sandwich, milk.

B. Macaroni and cheddar cheese, an orange, coffee.

C. Dried peas, egg sandwich, skim milk.

D. Dried beans, lettuce and tomato sandwich, milk.

21. During pregnancy, 30-60 mg of supplemental iron is recommended. Wendy, like many mothers, will not eat liver, which is high in iron. The best menu to supply iron is:

A. Pork chops, sweet potatoes, cooked dried beans, raisin pudding.

B. Beef sandwich, spinach salad, dried peaches, milk.

C. Bacon and eggs, toast with butter, milk.

D. Chicken, white potatoes with gravy, green peas, an orange, coffee.

22. In addition to the normal diet, the daily recommended calorie increase for a woman who is pregnant:

    A. 200.

    B. 300.

    C. 800.

    D. 1000.

23. Wendy understands the relationship between good nutrition and its effects on the maternal-fetal unit, so she follows nutritional counseling conscientiously. It is often more difficult for an adolescent to understand and comply. In counseling the teenager who is pregnant about nutrition, the nurse does not need to consider:

    A. Maintenance of a trim figure to promote good body image.

    B. Cultural, economic, and educational background.

    C. Growth needs of the mother and infant.

    D. Individual dietary habits of teenagers.

24. When a woman who is pregnant prefers nonfat to whole milk, the nurse need not worry about replacing the deficient nutrient if the woman's diet contains sufficient quantities of:

    A. Egg yolk.

    B. Wheat germ oil.

    C. Deep-yellow or green vegetables.

    D. Egg yolk and deep-yellow or green vegetables.

25. Wendy has a dislike for milk. The nurse explains to Wendy that to meet her calcium needs during pregnancy, some items can be substituted for 1 cup of milk. Which one is not a good substitute?

    A. 1 cup of yogurt.

    B. 1½ oz. of hard cheese.

    C. ¼ cup of cottage cheese.

    D. 3 cups of vanilla ice cream.

26. On Wendy's next visit to the clinic, the nurse determines that her nutritional needs are being met because Wendy:

    A. Is at her prepregnant weight.

    B. Has increased the amount of meat in her diet.

    C. Is gaining the desired amount of weight.

    D. Does not eat between-meal snacks.

When Wendy is 28 weeks pregnant, she complains of easy fatigability and palpitations. Hematologic evaluation reveals:

Hgb: 9 g/dL.

RBC: 2.5 million/μL; microcytic, hypochromic.

WBC: Normal.

Serum iron: 30 μg/dL (N = 90–150 μg/dL).

Fe-binding capacity: 350–500μg /dL (N = 250–350μg/dL).

Retic/platelets: Normal to high.

Iron deficiency anemia is diagnosed and oral supplementation of iron begun.

---

27. Which foods best ensure Wendy's iron dietary intake?

    A. Oranges, bananas, spinach.

    B. Raw cabbage, brown sugar.

    C. Dried apricots, prune juice, chili con carne.

    D. Enriched milk and milk products.

28. Which instruction is most beneficial to Wendy in regard to her iron supplements?

    A. Take daily in 1 dose before a meal, with milk.

    B. Take divided doses with meals, with water.

    C. Take divided doses after meals, with a glass of fruit juice.

    D. Take daily in 1 dose after a meal, with fruit juice.

29. When discussing prenatal classes with Wendy and Ed, the nurse informs them that the *primary* purpose of these classes is to assist the woman (couple) to:

    A. Minimize the amount of analgesia and/or anesthesia needed.

    B. Experience childbirth without fear or pain.

    C. Prepare for childbirth.

    D. Minimize the possibility of dystocia and medical intervention.

30. The nurse encourages Wendy and Ed to write down any questions they have. Ed says that the childbirth instructor spoke of the "gate control" theory about pain control. The nurse explains that the "gating" theory refers to the mechanism whereby:

    A. Nonpain signals from other parts of the nervous system can greatly alter the degree of transmission of pain signals.

B. In the presence of pain signals, learned responses can override and eliminate the perception of pain, that is, shut the gate.

C. Relaxation of voluntary muscles dulls pain receptors.

D. Pain control is with analgesics.

31. During her seventh month of pregnancy, Wendy tells the nurse about her negative feelings toward motherhood and sex, and her doubts about her husband's qualifications as a father. Wendy is:

A. In need of a psychiatric referral.

B. A candidate to become a parent who is abusive.

C. Trying to resolve previously repressed conflicts.

D. Attempting to shock the nurse.

32. During her eighth month, Wendy says that her "panties are wet." She is concerned that her "water bag broke." To assess for ruptured membranes, the nurse uses the phenaphthazine (Nitrazine) test. To perform the test, the nurse:

A. Puts on a sterile glove and inserts litmus paper into the vagina, placing it near the cervix.

B. Does a finger stick and draws blood into a capillary tube to be centrifuged.

C. Places a drop of urine on a slide and mixes it with anti-serum for 30 seconds.

D. Collects urine for 24 hours, storing it in ice, and sends it to the laboratory.

33. Nursing care for a mother with premature ruptured membranes (PROMs) includes frequent assessment for:

A. Fever.

B. Cervical changes.

C. Coagulopathy.

D. Fetal lung maturity.

34. Wendy arrives on the labor unit. As the nurse is taking Wendy's history and performing an admission examination, Wendy tells the nurse that she is "afraid of the doctor's examinations." Which is the *best* response the nurse could make?

A. "Our clients consider this physician to be one of the best."

B. "Would you like to talk about what you mean when you say you are afraid?"

C. "Don't be afraid. I'll be here with you during the examination."

D. "It's not unusual for new mothers-to-be to be afraid."

35. While Wendy is in labor, the nurse performs Leopold's maneuvers. Leopold's maneuvers refer to palpation of the uterus through the abdominal wall in order to:

    A. Determine fetal presentation, position, lie, and engagement.

    B. Assess frequency, duration, and quality of contractions.

    C. Measure the height of the uterine fundus.

    D. Estimate the fetal weight.

36. The nurse who is responsible for determining priorities for Wendy's care needs to know that the woman who labors unattended or the woman who is discharged from the hospital 12-24 hours after birth without verbalizing understanding of discharge teaching, and then develops a postpartum complication at home, can initiate legal action for:

    A. Abandonment.

    B. Battery.

    C. Ethical dereliction of duty.

    D. Prudent behavior.

37. Wendy gave birth 1½ hours ago. She received no analgesia or anesthesia. She is alert and physically active in bed. She says she needs to urinate. The nurse's *most* therapeutic response is:

    A. "I'll walk you to the bathroom and stay with you."

    B. "You can get up any time you want to now."

    C. "Make sure you wash your hands before and after, and wipe yourself once with each tissue from front to back."

    D. "Lean forward a little as you void. This will keep the urine off your stitches and make you more comfortable."

38. To provide accurate anticipatory guidance, the nurse needs to know that primary breast engorgement results from:

    A. A stasis of milk in the breast.

    B. Increased circulation of blood and lymph in the mammary glands.

    C. Increased fluid intake (oral and parenteral) during the perinatal period.

    D. Increased milk production with each successive pregnancy.

39. The following behavior *best* describes the postpartum behavior of the mother following a normal birth:

    A. Assertive and independent.

    B. Difficulty with hearing, retaining, and making connections.

  C. Eager to make decisions.

  D. Preoccupied with her own needs.

40. The woman who is postpartum is considered to be recovering for the first 2 hours after birth. Her fundus should be:

  A. Firm, three fingerwidths above the umbilicus.

  B. Firm, below the umbilicus in the midline.

  C. Slightly boggy, two fingerwidths above the umbilicus.

  D. Slightly boggy, below the umbilicus in the midline.

41. In the taking-in phase, the nurse expects that the mother is very concerned about:

  A. The normalcy of her infant.

  B. Herself and her needs.

  C. The baby's need for nourishment and touch.

  D. Her husband's response to the baby.

42. What is least relevant in decreasing discomfort of an episiotomy?

  A. Application of an ice pack soon after repair reduces the amount of discomfort experienced later.

  B. Sitting down on and getting up from a chair with the posture straight and the buttocks together decreases discomfort.

  C. Massaging the perineum promotes absorption of the hematoma.

  D. Warm sitz baths ease episiotomy discomfort.

43. In doing health teaching, the nurse usually recommends that parents refrain from sexual intercourse for 4-6 weeks following birth, or until lochia has ceased, because:

  A. Of the possibility of discomfort and infection in the mother.

  B. This is an unsafe time to become pregnant.

  C. It could tear the episiotomy site.

  D. It could delay involution of the uterus.

Medical Situation: Normal pregnancy.

■ *Nursing Problems/Diagnosis:*

Anxiety: related to loss.

Altered bowel and urinary elimination.

Altered cardiac output.

Altered comfort pattern (discomfort, fear).

Impaired digestion.

Impaired skin integrity.

- **■ *Chief Complaint:***

Debby Primings is a 26-year-old Caucasian woman who is 4 months pregnant.

- **■ *Present Status:***

Ms. Primings has been experiencing morning sickness at least 4 times a week since the sixth week of pregnancy. She usually feels nauseated and vomits about 30–40 mL of clear mucus. Remaining in bed and eating a cracker very slowly has helped to alleviate some of her feelings of sickness. She has gained about 5 pounds. Within the last month she has experienced less urinary frequency.

- **■ *Past Health History:***

Ms. Primings has been fairly healthy throughout her life. She started her menstrual periods at age 15. She usually has a period every 30–40 days but has never been on a regular schedule. She was on birth control pills for about 6 months, but she stopped taking them because they made her "feel sick" in the morning. Ms. Primings states that she usually has one or two colds per year. Every once in a while she gets the flu. Other than a slight cold or the flu, she "doesn't remember being really sick." Ms. Primings's husband is "pretty healthy." However, he did have a positive tine test 2 years ago; his chest x-ray was negative. There are no other significant findings regarding his health.

- **■ *Family History:***

Mr. and Ms. Primings have been married 5 years. They lost one baby at 3½ months' gestation 2 years ago. Mr. Primings is employed as a plumber and works 8–10 hours a day, 6 days a week. Ms. Primings is a secretary for a family practice physician. There is no significant history regarding the extended family. However, this will be the first grandchild for both Mr. and Ms. Primings's parents, who are all living.

- **■ *Physical Exam:***

Head: No significant findings.

Neck: No lymph node enlargement, tenderness, or pain. ROM appropriate.

Heart: No murmur noted; pulse strong and regular.

Lungs: Clear to auscultation; respirations unlabored.

Vital signs: Temperature: 98.8°F (37.1°C), BP: 122/80, Pulse: 74, Respirations: 22,

Extremities: ROM appropriate; no pain; tenderness; slight cramping in legs.

Abdomen: Liver and spleen nonpalpable; fundus: slight rise out of pelvis; no pain or tenderness; Ms. Primings complains of anorexia, nausea, and constipation.

- *Elimination System:*

  Urinates 5-6 times daily. During the first 8 weeks of pregnancy, she urinated 8-10 times per day.

  Usually has at least one stool each day. Within the past month has been having only one stool every 2-3 days with slight gas.

  Urine: SG: 1.015. Protein: Negative. Sugar: Negative. Ketones: Negative.

- *Overall Assessment:*

  No spotting or bleeding noted. Can eat very little at one meal without feeling "stuffed and nauseated." There has been a decrease in stool production. Appears somewhat concerned about being able to carry this baby to term due to the loss of her first pregnancy. Husband plans to attend most of the prenatal visits.

---

44. A late objective sign that may cause Ms. Primings to suspect she might be pregnant is:

    A. Mastalgia.

    B. Amenorrhea.

    C. Abdominal enlargement.

    D. Lassitude and easy fatigability.

45. Ms. Primings wonders what she can expect at her initial prenatal visit. Which is not indicated at the first visit and therefore will not be included in the nurse's answer?

    A. Blood tests for Rh, type, hemoglobin, syphilis.

    B. Urine test for pregnancy, protein, sugar, estriol levels.

    C. Blood pressure, pulse, weight, height.

    D. FHR and fundal height.

46. The nurse knows that routine prenatal care for Ms. Primings will not include:

    A. Personal and family history.

    B. Diet counseling to promote appropriate weight gain.

    C. X-ray pelvimetry prior to the onset of labor.

    D. VDRL, gonorrhea cultures, blood type, and Rh factor.

47. Ms. Primings appears quite apprehensive about her pregnancy. She states that this will be her first baby; although she was pregnant before, she lost that baby at about 3½ months' gestation. During this pregnancy, Ms. Primings is:

    A. Gravida 1, para O.

    B. Gravida 1, para 1.

    C. Gravida 2, para O.

    D. Gravida 2, para 1.

48. In planning health teaching to help allay Ms. Primings's anxiety, the nurse needs to explain that in addition to producing hormones, the placenta:

    A. Acts as a barrier to infection and as a shock absorber; it weighs about one-sixth of the fetus's weight at term.

    B. Secretes nutrients for the fetus and removes waste.

    C. Acts as the fetus's organ of respiration, nutrition, and elimination.

    D. Produces the hemoglobin necessary for the fetus during the first trimester.

49. While she is having a pelvic examination, Ms. Primings can best be helped to relax if the assisting nurse:

    A. Coaches her on breathing normally and keeping her hands relaxed.

    B. Assures her that there is really nothing to the pelvic examination.

    C. Distracts her attention from the procedure.

    D. Offers a hand for Ms. Primings to squeeze.

50. In conducting health teaching, the nurse needs to know that increased absorption of phosphorus is thought to be responsible for which pregnancy-associated discomfort?

    A. Leg cramps.

    B. Backache.

    C. Heartburn.

    D. Constipation and hemorrhoids.

51. Ms. Primings asks the nurse how the baby breathes in utero. To explain, the nurse draws a picture showing the cardiovascular structure in fetal circulation that contains the highest concentration of oxygen. The nurse draws the:

    A. Umbilical artery.

    B. Umbilical vein.

    C. Left ventricle.

    D. Arch of the aorta.

52. Which normal physiologic change can the nurse anticipate that Ms. Primings is most likely to notice and bring to the nurse's attention ?

    A. Physiologic anemia.

    B. Palpitation.

    C. Increased blood pressure.

    D. Increase in the anterior-posterior thoracic diameter.

53. Ms. Primings is advised to avoid lying down soon after eating, avoid bending at the waist, to do "flying" exercises (rotating the extended arms at the shoulder in a wide cycle), and to eat frequent, small meals to avoid which discomfort during pregnancy?

    A. Morning sickness.

    B. Heartburn.

    C. Pica.

    D. Backache.

54. The nurse can advise Ms. Primings that she will once again experience urinary frequency and an increased tendency to varicosities, but will be able to breathe easier when what occurs?

    A. Transition.

    B. Quickening.

    C. Effacement.

    D. Lightening.

55. Which emotional change is Ms. Primings likely to experience in the last trimester of pregnancy?

    A. Irritability.

    B. Anxiety about the labor process.

    C. Introspection.

    D. Ambivalence.

Medical Situation: Pregnancy and nutrition.

- *Nursing Problems/Diagnosis:*

  Altered bowel elimination (constipation).

  Altered comfort pattern (discomfort).

  Altered nutrition.

- *Chief Complaint:*

  Bertha London is a 25-year-old Asian woman who is approximately 20 weeks pregnant.

- *Present Status:*

  Bertha suspected that she might be pregnant when she missed two menstrual periods. She became more certain when her breasts became tender and swollen and she began vomiting on arising early each morning. Her physician confirmed that she was 10 weeks pregnant. This pregnancy was unplanned.

- *Past Health History:*

  Bertha has been essentially healthy throughout her life. She had measles as a child, but she is not certain what type she had. She also thinks she had chickenpox when she was about 8 years old. Bertha began menstruating when she was 11 years old. Her cycle has been consistent every 28-30 days. She has never before been pregnant. She usually experiences one or two colds a year. She has had the flu at least once in the past 3 years.

■ *Family History:*

Bertha has been married for 3 years to Chet, a 26-year-old African-American man. Bertha is employed as a high school science teacher and teaches 10th graders. Chet is a social worker for the local department of social services. Bertha is an only child. Both of her parents are living and essentially healthy. Her mother is 46 and her father is 50. They live about 20 minutes from Bertha and Chet. Bertha's parents were unable to conceive any other children. No reasons for this inability were identified because both parents decided not to undergo fertility testing.

Chet's parents live about 4 hours from the couple. Chet is the youngest of three children. He has a brother who is 30 and a sister, age 28. Both of these siblings are healthy. Chet's father is 54 and his mother is 52. Chet's father has had hypertension for the past 7 years; he is currently taking prescribed medications and is adhering to a low-sodium diet. Chet's mother suffered one miscarriage prior to her first successful pregnancy with Chet's brother. The miscarriage occurred at 8 weeks' gestation, and no reason for its occurrence was ever discussed with Chet's parents.

■ *Physical Exam:*

Head and neck: No swelling of lymph nodes; no pain or edema noted; normal ROM. Eyes, nose, and ears clear; no inflammation, edema, or drainage.

Chest: Heart sounds audible; no murmur, splitting, etc. Lungs bilaterally clear to auscultation.

Breasts: Moderately enlarged, tender to touch, and veins engorged. No inflammation or drainage observed.

Abdomen: Spleen and liver nonpalpable; fundus out of the pelvis and palpable. No significant scars noted.

Extremities: ROM within normal limits; no pain or distortions; no edema observed.

Vital signs: Temperature: 98.8°F (37.1°C), P: 78, R: 10, BP = 112/80. Weight: 115 pounds. Height: 5 feet, 1 inch.

Urine tests: Pregnancy: Positive. Sugar: Negative. Protein: Negative. Ketones: Negative.

Hematocrit: 32%.

■ *Significant Complaints:*

Bertha states that she vomits every morning and feels somewhat fatigued throughout the day, especially around 3 P.M. She has been experiencing a need to urinate once or twice per hour. She also has very little, if any, appetite, especially early in the morning. She has tried eating saltines to prevent "this feeling of sickness"; however, nothing seems to work.

56. Before assuming that Bertha may be anemic, what does the nurse need to consider as another possible explanation?

    A. Mothers are supposed to be a little anemic during pregnancy.

    B. The mother's blood volume is decreased during pregnancy, so this is a true anemia.

    C. The mother's blood volume is decreased during pregnancy, so her hematocrit should be higher.

    D. The mother's blood volume is increased during pregnancy, so there might normally be a decrease in hematocrit.

57. It is difficult to maintain the recommended intake of dietary iron during pregnancy. Bertha is given iron pills to meet her pregnancy needs. Which is inaccurate information for the nurse to impart to the client?

    A. Stools will be loose.

    B. Take the pills after food to prevent GI distress.

    C. Stools will be black in color.

    D. Drink fluids and perform moderate exercise.

58. Because of reduced motility of the GI tract during pregnancy, the nurse can expect Bertha to complain of constipation. The nurse recommends to her that she:

    A. Take glycerine suppositories at bedtime.

    B. Increase roughage in the diet.

    C. Drink warm milk at bedtime and on rising.

    D. Decrease walking up stairs.

59. Bertha is complaining of leg cramps during her pregnancy. In discussing her diet, she states that she loves milk shakes, and sometimes drinks 2 quarts of milk a day. The nurse recommends that she:

    A. Decrease her milk intake to 1 quart a day.

    B. Increase her milk intake to include yogurt.

    C. Decrease her ambulations.

    D. Use skim milk for milk shakes.

In her fifth month of pregnancy, Bertha presents with the following hematologic laboratory values:

Hgb: 10 g/dL.

RBC: 2.5 million/μL.

MCV (mean corpuscular volume): 120 (high).

WBC: Hypersegmented with leukocytopenia.

Serum Fe: High normal 150 μg/dL (N = 90-150 μg/dL).

Serum vitamin B12: Normal.

These values, her age, pregnancy, and complaints of lassitude, anorexia, and mental depression suggest folic acid deficiency anemia. She has no history of alcoholism or protracted vomiting.

---

60. In addition to oral or parenteral folic acid, 5-10 mg/day, the nurse suggests that Bertha eat folacin-containing foods. Which foods does the nurse suggest, as they have the most folic acid?

    A. Asparagus and kidney beans.

    B. Chicken and beef.

    C. Bread and bread products.

    D. Milk and milk products.

61. Since Bertha is of normal weight for her age and height, during pregnancy the nurse advises her to gain:

    A. No more than 20 pounds.

    B. 20-24 pounds.

    C. 25-30 pounds.

    D. As little as possible.

Medical Situation: Pregnancy: complications related to diabetes.

- *Nursing Problems/Diagnosis:*

  Anxiety.

  Risk for alteration in endocrine/metabolic processes.

  Altered urinary elimination.

- *Chief Complaint:*

  Leslie Osborne is a 23-year-old Caucasian woman who is 3 months pregnant with her first child.

- *Present Status:*

  Ms. Osborne has had diabetes "all of her life." She has come to the doctor's office for her third prenatal examination. She has been feeling very restless and tired, and continues to complain of nausea and vomiting each morning. In fact, she has been "vomiting sometimes twice a day."

- *Past Health History:*

  Ms. Osborne has been taking insulin since childhood. She states that she cannot remember ever not taking insulin. Her medical records show that she was diagnosed as a diabetic at age 4. Ms. Osborne has never before been pregnant and this is an unplanned pregnancy. However, she has decided to follow through with the pregnancy.

- *Family History:*

  Ms. Osborne is not and has never been married. She has no immediate plans to marry. She is contemplating giving up her baby for adoption, but at this time she is not sure what she will do. Ms. Osborne is employed as a librarian in the university library. She intends to work as long as possible. The father of the baby is unaware that Ms. Osborne is pregnant, and Ms. Osborne has not decided whether she will tell him about the pregnancy.

- *Physical Exam:*

  Head: No complaints of headaches, blurred vision, etc.

  Neck: No swelling of lymph nodes; no pain on palpation.

  Lungs: Clear to auscultation.

  Heart: Heart sounds regular; no splitting or murmurs noted.

  Abdomen: Liver and spleen nonpalpable; uterine size consistent with 3 months' gestation.

  Extremities: ROM appropriate; no edema, pain, or tenderness.

  Urinary system: Complains of urinary frequency. She voids at least 2 or 3 times per hour. SG: 1.006. Hematest: Negative. Protein: Negative. Ketones: Negative. Glucose: Negative.

  Vital signs: Temperature: 98.2°F (36.8°C), P: 72, R: 20, BP: 122/74.

---

62. In assessing Ms. Osborne's overall level of functioning, the nurse is concerned primarily that Ms. Osborne:

    A. Is not married.

    B. Is 23 years old.

    C. Feels tired and restless.

    D. Is experiencing nausea and vomiting.

63. Ms. Osborne asks the nurse what she thinks Ms. Osborne should do in terms of this pregnancy. The *most* appropriate response is to:

    A. Tell Ms. Osborne that she is still within the time limits for obtaining an abortion.

    B. Refer Ms. Osborne for prenatal counseling.

    C. Assess Ms. Osborne's feelings about this pregnancy.

    D. Inform Ms. Osborne that this is essentially her own decision.

64. Ms. Osborne tells the nurse that as a mother who is pregnant and has diabetes, she is concerned about having a healthy baby. She wants to cooperate with the physician in every way, but needs to know what to expect during pregnancy. The nurse informs her that the medical and nursing management will not include the need to:

    A. Monitor her weight closely to ensure appropriate weight gain.

    B. Adjust her insulin dosage as needed to prevent a glucose imbalance.

    C. Attempt to carry the baby to term to ensure adequate fetal lung maturity.

    D. Assess for and treat all infections promptly.

65. Ms. Osborne complains of nausea and vomiting that occur periodically throughout the day. The *most* appropriate nursing intervention is to:

    A. Assess the frequency and amount she vomits each day.

    B. Tell her to relax and try lying down when she feels nauseated.

    C. Suggest that she ask the doctor for an antiemetic medication.

    D. Inform her that the nausea will probably decrease after the first trimester.

66. In developing a plan of care for Ms. Osborne, the nurse incorporates knowledge of the effects of diabetes mellitus on childbearing and the effects of childbearing on diabetes. These effects include:

    A. Insulin requirements are highest during the first trimester and early puerperium.

    B. Fetal macrosomia is due to excessive water retention.

    C. Vaginal birth before 35 weeks is indicated.

    D. Hospitalization may be required to adjust insulin requirements.

67. At her third clinic visit, Ms. Osborne's urinalysis reveals glucosuria. Ms. Osborne can expect:

    A. An increase in insulin dosage.

    B. A decrease in caloric intake.

    C. Frequent glucose monitoring.

    D. Liver function studies.

68. Ms. Osborne is hospitalized for nausea and vomiting during her third month of pregnancy. The most serious nursing concern is:

    A. That the baby will be deprived of nourishment.

    B. That the mother is rejecting her pregnancy.

    C. That the mother may go into ketoacidosis.

    D. Starting an intravenous feeding and preventing it from infiltrating.

69. The nurse knows that Ms. Osborne's expected date of birth is difficult to determine because a mother with uncontrolled diabetes may:

    A. Have infants with congenital problems.

B. Have irregular menstrual cycles.

C. Tend to gain very few pounds.

D. Have small infants.

70. In planning health teaching for Ms. Osborne, the nurse needs to know that although infants of mothers who have diabetes often are large (more than 9 pounds), some infants are small because of:

A. Atherosclerosis of the placenta.

B. Increased blood sugar.

C. Size of the mother.

D. Hypoglycemia in utero.

Medical Situation: High-risk pregnancy: nutrition.

- *Nursing Problems/Diagnosis:*

  Altered cardiac output.

  Fluid volume excess.

  Altered nutrition requirements.

  Altered parenting.

  Self-care deficit: medication administration.

  Self-esteem disturbance.

  Altered urinary elimination.

- *Present Status:*

  Doris Garvey is a 29-year-old married woman, $G_8P_3AB_4$, LC_2. Her expected date of birth is 6/30/05. The father is ambivalent about this pregnancy. He verbalizes that he "doesn't care what happens as long as my wife is OK." He comments that they do not want any more pregnancies. Ms. Garvey's skin is dry, her hair is dull and unkempt, she walks slowly with her head tilted somewhat downward, and she looks as if she has not been sleeping well lately.

- *Past Pregnancy History:*

Year	Weeks Gestation	Weight Gain	Length of Labor	Complications	Sex/Weight
1992	7	—	SAB	None	—
1993	36	40 lb	13 hr	None	Girl 4 lb, 12 oz.
1995	6	—	SAB	None	—
1996	34	45 lb	7 hr	Postpartum hemorrhage	Girl 3 lb, 10 oz.
2000	8	—	SAB	None	—
2002*	32	42 lb	4 hr	PROMs; neonatal	Boy

Year	Weeks Gestation	Weight Gain	Length of Labor	Complications	Sex/Weight
				deaths; postpartum infection	1 Ib, 14 oz.; Boy 2 lb, 2 oz.
2003	6		SAB	Hemorrhage	—
2004	Current pregnancy				

*Note that birth of twins in 2002 is counted as *one* birth in her *para* number.
SAB, spontaneous abortion; PROMs, premature rupture of membranes.

- *Family Health History:*

  Maternal and paternal parents are living and essentially well. Ms. Garvey has six siblings, all living and well. Her older children, 12 and 9 years old, are essentially well. They go to a special school because "the teachers say that they are a little slow."

- *Present Pregnancy Prenatal Record:*

  Pregravid weight: 170 pounds. Height: 5 feet, 4 inches.

Date	Weeks Gestation	Weight	BP	Urine	Hct	Fundal Height	FHR
11/5/04	10	168.5	138/82	Neg	35%	—	—
12/3/04	14	168.5	138/80	Neg	35%	—	—
12/17/04	16	167	140/86	Neg	34%	—	—
1/2/05	18	169	138/82	Neg	33%	16 cm	156
1/16/05	20	169	138/84	Neg	30%	16 cm	154
1/30/05	22	172	138/84	P: +	29%	17 cm	154

P, protein; G, glucose.

71. After plotting Ms. Garvey's weight gain on the graph for desirable prenatal gain in weight, the nurse's assessment of Ms. Garvey's weight gain is that it is:

    A. Consistent with average growth curves.

    B. Adequate in light of her obesity.

    C. Inadequate.

    D. Excessive.

72. Several factors put Ms. Garvey at nutritional risk and therefore increase her risk during this pregnancy. Which does not put Ms. Garvey at nutritional risk?

    A. Weight gain inconsistent with desirable prenatal gain.

    B. Poor reproductive history.

    C. Falling hematocrit (Hct) values.

    D. Age at 29 years.

73. In counseling a woman about nutrition, the nurse has several strategies from which to choose. Which one is the *least* helpful for Ms. Garvey?

    A. Discuss with her how nutrition affected her pregnancies in the past, because she wants a good pregnancy now.

B. Ask her which foods (containing nutrients necessary for forming blood) she would be able to or want to add to the family's diet.

C. Discuss how her physical appearance and feelings now relate to her physiologic and nutritional state.

D. Mutually identify behavioral objectives with emphasis on short-term goals.

74. The simplest and least expensive test that can be employed to identify a person's nutritional status and to evaluate the effectiveness of therapy is the laboratory assessment for serum levels of:

A. Folate.

B. Protein.

C. Mean corpuscular hemoglobin concentration (MCHC).

D. Hematocrit.

75. If tests indicate that Ms. Garvey's nutritional status is compromised by a lack of blood-forming nutrients, the nurse needs to help Ms. Garvey pick out and add to her diet foods that contain blood-forming nutrients. The nurse therefore omits foods high in:

A. Vitamin D.

B. Iron.

C. Folacin.

D. Vitamin B_6.

76. Many nutrients are needed to form blood. However, there is one food group that can be emphasized in Ms. Garvey's nutritional plan. This food group is:

A. Leafy green and yellow vegetables.

B. Fortified or natural breads and cereals.

C. Yellow fruits.

D. Animal proteins such as meat and organs.

77. Ms. Garvey's anemia most likely has been long-standing because of the following facts from her database. Which finding is not a sequela to anemia?

A. Small-for-gestational-age (SGA) neonates.

B. Hemorrhage.

C. Hypertension.

D. Perinatal infection.

78. Ms. Garvey tells you that she would like to lose some weight because "I'm so fat. I'm afraid my husband will start looking at other women." Which statement best demonstrates application of knowledge of pregnancy and the woman's

needs during pregnancy?

   A. "Let's plan a diet that will provide the baby with the food he or she needs and help you trim off some pounds."

   B. "It is important to gain weight with good food to feed the baby and fix your anemia first."

   C. "You sound like you don't like the way you look right now. Do you want to talk about it some more?"

   D. "Would you like me to refer you to the social worker to get food stamps and to talk with you and your husband?"

79. Ms. Garvey tells you that she too wants to have her "tubes tied." When providing counseling in matters such as this, the nurse and physician must keep in mind the client's rights. Which is *not* one of the three elements of a legally effective "informed consent"?

   A. It must be given voluntarily.

   B. Persons must be given information about the procedure and its consequences and any alternative procedures and their consequences.

   C. The person giving consent must be capable of comprehending the information.

   D. The consent form must be written in English, but an interpreter should be used when needed for the person's comprehension.

80. If a procedure that was not clearly specified in the original informed consent is performed, the nurse needs to consider that which of the following legal actions may be initiated?

   A. Abandonment.

   B. Battery.

   C. Ethical dereliction of duty.

   D. Invasion of privacy.

81. Among the data provided for Ms. Garvey's present pregnancy at 20 weeks, which is not associated with increased fetal mortality?

   A. Weight: 169 pounds.

   B. Blood pressure: 138/84.

   C. Fundal height: 16 cm.

   D. FHR: 154.

82. At 36 weeks Ms. Garvey comes to the clinic for her checkup. The nurse suspects she may be developing preeclampsia when the nurse notes:

   A. Decreased systolic blood pressure, ankle edema, 1+ proteinuria.

B. Swollen fingers, increased diastolic blood pressure, 1+ proteinuria.

C. 1 + Proteinuria, 1+ glucose in the urine, hypotension, weight loss.

D. Ankle edema, 2 + glycosuria, increased systolic blood pressure.

83. Ms. Garvey is diagnosed with preeclampsia and admitted to the hospital. What is an inappropriate nursing intervention?

A. Place in a room with mothers to keep her company.

B. Put on bedrest, preferably on left side.

C. Check urine for protein and BP every 4 hours.

D. Place in quiet room and limit visitors.

84. Which equipment should be placed in the room in preparation for an anticipated emergency admission of a woman with severe preeclampsia?

A. Suction apparatus.

B. TV set for distraction.

C. Telephone to maintain contact with her family.

D. Urine collection bottle set in ice bucket for determination of 17-hydroxysteroids.

85. Mothers with preeclampsia often receive an anticonvulsant, magnesium sulfate, which controls cerebral irritability. Which sign indicates that the mother should be carefully assessed for magnesium toxicity?

A. Respirations at 20/min.

B. Decreasing urinary output.

C. Blood pressure of 150/84.

D. Hyperreflexia.

86. The nurse is responsible for planning to have the following antidote for magnesium sulfate close at hand:

A. Calcium gluconate.

B. Naloxone (Narcan).

C. Potassium chloride.

D. Terbutaline.

87. Ms. Garvey has an order for 1000 mL of D5 lactated Ringer's with 10 g of magnesium sulfate to run in over 10 hours. With a macro drop factor of 15 gtt/mL, which number of drops of fluid per minute should Ms. Garvey receive?

A. 14-16.

B. 24-26.

    C. 34-36.

    D. 44-46.

88. A blood pressure reading of 120/80 may be indicative of pre-eclampsia if:

    A. There has been a weight gain of 2 pounds for each of the previous 2 weeks.

    B. The woman is carrying a hydatidiform mole.

    C. The woman has had ankle swelling each evening for the previous 2 weeks.

    D. Her systolic pressure has increased by 30 mm Hg; the diastolic, by 15 mm Hg.

A cesarean birth is planned for Ms. Garvey. A healthy 6-pound, 6-ounce boy is born. Ms. and Mr. Garvey are happy, but Mr. Garvey states that this is definitely the last pregnancy his wife will have. Questions 89 through 95 deal with nursing care of a woman following cesarean birth.

---

89. A check for Homans' sign is performed postpartum, especially on Ms. Garvey, to assess for:

    A. Infection.

    B. Edema.

    C. Phlebitis.

    D. Hemorrhage.

90. Methylergonovine maleate (Methergine), an oxytocic, has a side effect of raising the blood pressure. It is sometimes given to mothers after cesarean birth. The nurse should question giving this medication to Ms. Garvey if she had a history of:

    A. Postpartum hemorrhage.

    B. Preeclampsia.

    C. Diabetes.

    D. Hyperemesis gravidarum.

91. In spite of the recovery process, mothers who have had cesarean birth, are often able to have their newborns with them as early and as much as mothers who have vaginal deliveries. The most important reason for mothers to have their newborns with them at frequent intervals for short periods is:

    A. Mother-infant bonding.

    B. Breastfeeding to prevent engorgement.

C. Breastfeeding for oxytocin stimulation of the uterus.

D. Active involvement in their baby's care.

92. A mother who has had a cesarean birth is given medication for pain. She wishes to start breastfeeding. In analyzing data at hand, the nurse needs to know that:

    A. Mothers who had a cesarean birth should not breastfeed.

    B. Medication should not be given to mothers who are breast-feeding.

    C. Medication should only be given an hour prior to breast-feeding.

    D. Medication should be given at such a time that it will not be in the breast milk when nursing.

93. Due to the incision, mothers who had a cesarean birth, often find it difficult to breastfeed. The nurse encourages:

    A. Bottle feeding until the mother is free of pain and her incision is healed.

    B. The mother to try various breastfeeding positions to find the one that is most comfortable for her.

    C. Pumping the breasts and giving the breast milk to the infant by bottle.

    D. The mother not to bother with breastfeeding since she needs her energy to heal her own body.

94. It is the third postpartum day for a mother who had cesarean birth. She is crying and states, "I feel so abnormal not being able to have my baby the normal way." The nurse would respond:

    A. "I will ask the doctor to explain to you why the cesarean birth was necessary."

    B. "It's normal to feel guilty. You will feel better in a few days."

    C. "You are upset because you did not have a vaginal birth. It must have been hard for you to accept."

    D. "Many of our mothers have cesarean births. I will ask one of them to come and talk to you."

95. The nurse arranges with Ms. Garvey to make a home visit 3 days after her discharge from the hospital. The nurse determines that she has not accomplished her discharge planning goals for Ms. Garvey when the mother states:

    A. "I'm so tired; the baby breastfeeds every hour."

    B. "I'm trying to rest when the baby sleeps."

    C. "I'm enjoying breastfeeding and the baby seems content."

    D. "My lochia is brownish in color and decreasing each day."

96. Ms. and Mr. Garvey decide that he will have a vasectomy. In the plan of care, the nurse prepares Mr. Garvey for vasectomy based on analysis of data that indicate that:

    A. He understands that no change in testosterone levels will result.

    B. Fertility can be restored by reanastomosis.

    C. Recovery may be complicated by balanitis or phimosis.

    D. He will be sterile as soon as the surgery is performed.

Medical Situation: Conception/contraception/hormones.

- *Nursing Problems/Diagnosis:*

Anxiety.

Altered health maintenance.

Health-seeking behaviors: function of estrogen, oral contraceptives, infertility.

- *Chief Complaint:*

John Jackson, 25, and Estelle Jackson, 24, have been trying to conceive a child for the past year without success.

- *Present and Past Health History:*

Mr. Jackson has been relatively healthy throughout his life. His BP normally is 130/78. His vital signs are within normal limits: 98.8°F temperature; pulse 78; respirations 20. He has had no major illnesses or surgery during his life. He is unsure whether he is capable of fathering children and has never been given any tests to screen his fertility. There are no other significant findings at this time.

Ms. Jackson does not remember being seriously ill as a child. She did have chickenpox and mumps as a child. She began menstruating at age 13. She has been regular since her second period, experiencing menstruation every 28–30 days. She has never been pregnant and began taking oral contraceptives when she was 17 years old. She discontinued the oral contraceptives 1 year ago, when she and her husband decided to have a child. Her vital signs are: Temperature: 99°F; P: 72; R: 20; BP: 110/70. Urine analysis was negative for pregnancy. There are no other significant findings.

- *Family History:*

Mr. Jackson is one of two children. He has an identical twin brother, Jason. His mother miscarried several times before she had these boys. Mr. Jackson's family history is essentially unremarkable. Both his parents and grandparents are living and healthy. Mr. Jackson is a high school coach.

Ms. Jackson is an only child; her mother died during her birth. The cause of death was preeclampsia. Her father remarried and has had two other daughters. Ms. Jackson's father has been diagnosed with hypertension. His BP is about 180/90, for which he takes medication daily. Ms. Jackson is employed as a computer programmer.

- *Psychological Evaluation:*

In evaluating Mr. and Ms. Jackson, the infertility clinic nurse found them to be moderately anxious about what to expect. They were concerned about the outcome, the expense of the testing procedures, and the future of their relationship as a couple.

---

97. In planning health teaching with Mr. and Ms. Jackson about the physiologic effects of progesterone, the nurse knows that one of the following is not an effect of progesterone:

    A. Slightly elevated basal body temperature.

    B. Movement of fertilized ovum through the oviduct.

    C. Formation of the corpus luteum.

    D. Inhibition of uterine contractility during pregnancy.

98. Ms. Jackson tells the nurse that she has heard that estrogen is important in facilitating reproduction. The nurse should emphasize that a prominent function of estrogen is not:

    A. Growth of spiral arteries in the endometrium.

    B. Development of the mammary duct system.

    C. Inhibition of uterine contractility during pregnancy.

    D. Augmentation of the quantity of cervical mucus and its receptivity to sperm.

99. In teaching Mr. and Ms. Jackson about conception, the nurse states that conception usually occurs in the presence of high levels of:

    A. Estrogen and luteinizing hormone (LH).

    B. Follicle-stimulating hormone (FSH).

    C. Progesterone.

    D. Human chorionic gonadotropin (HCG).

100. In providing care for Mr. and Ms. Jackson, the clinic nurse realizes that the couple will *primarily* need:

    A. Health teaching regarding conception.

    B. Information about various positions to use during intercourse.

    C. Further physiologic assessment.

    D. Psychotherapy for emotional support.

101. Which factor is the *most* significant in assessing the present inability of the Jacksons to conceive?

    A. The couple's ages.

    B. Ms. Jackson's history of taking oral contraceptives.

    C. Ms. Jackson's father being hypertensive.

    D. Ms. Jackson's being an only child.

102. In planning the infertility tests to be performed, the nurse plans for which test *first*?

    A. Sperm analysis.

    B. Sonogram.

    C. Dilation and curettage.

    D. Basal body temperature evaluation.

103. Ms. Jackson asks the nurse "whether taking oral contraceptives could have made her sterile." The *most* appropriate response includes:

    A. "Yes, many women become infertile after taking birth control pills."

    B. "No, this is unlikely."

    C. "There is no indication at this point that you are sterile."

    D. "There is a 30% chance that oral contraceptives decreased your ability to conceive."

104. Mr. Jackson, in confidence, expresses concern over the couple's inability to conceive. The nurse needs to be aware that he is *most* likely primarily concerned about:

    A. The possibility of not being able to have children.

    B. His inability to father children.

    C. The couple's overall sex life.

    D. His wife's inability to become pregnant.

Medical Diagnosis: Infertility/spontaneous abortion.

- *Nursing Problems/Diagnosis:*

    Risk for alteration in endocrine/metabolic processes.

    Altered health maintenance.

    Altered parenting.

    Sexual dysfunction.

- *Chief Complaint:*

    Joan and Mike Hamlin have been unable to conceive after attempting for 4 years.

- *Present Health History:*

    Joan is negative for chronic or concurrent disorders. Joan (27 years old; 5 feet, 6½ inches; 130 pounds) and Mike (27 years old; 5 feet, 11 inches; 165 pounds) have been married for 4 years. They had intended to have children as soon as possible after they married. As time went on without conception, they became concerned.

- *Past Health History:*

Joan had all the usual childhood infectious diseases. She has had no hospitalizations. She gets a cold about once every 3-4 years. Seven years ago she had an IUD inserted but then had it removed within 6 months. At that time, she started oral hormonal contraception, which she discontinued 1 month prior to marriage. Her normal menstrual cycle recurred within 8 months.

- *Family History:*

There is no history of infertility in maternal or paternal families or among Joan's siblings. Mike's family history is negative also. Joan's family history is negative for hypertension and diabetes mellitus. Her maternal grandmother died of breast cancer at age 76; her maternal grandfather is alive and well at 80 years. Her paternal grandmother is alive and well at the age of 79; her paternal grand-father died from a tractor accident on his farm at the age of 62.

- *Review of Systems:*

Nutrition assessment: Excellent.

Menarche at age 11. Periods regular at about 28 days; flow: x 4 days, heaviest for first 2 days. Denies dysmenorrhea. Couple has inter-course "regularly."

Findings negative for all organs and systems, except for the following: After IUD insertion, experienced intermittent heavy vaginal bleeding and uterine cramping. Within 2 months, experienced lower abdominal pain, which was treated by removal of the IUD and oral antibiotic therapy. Has had no recurrence of this symptomatology.

Has had two episodes of "yeast" infection, both successfully treated with nystatin (Mycostatin) vaginal cream. Does not douche.

- *Physical Exam:*

Within normal limits: vital signs, height, weight. Development of female anatomy. Indices for good nutritional status: hair, skin, eyes, teeth, hemoglobin, hematocrit.

Negative findings: All organs and systems.

- *Psychological Assessment:*

Alert, appropriate affect. Well-groomed, good posture, articulate. Couple sit close to each other, touch each other, and look at each other frequently. Both are "certain" that they want children.

---

105. The nurse is adding to the database for this couple. Which question provides the *least* relevant data?

   A. "How often do you have sexual intercourse?"

   B. "Do you experience orgasm each time you have inter-course?"

   C. "What is your husband's occupation?"

   D. "Was your pelvic inflammatory disease due to gonor-rhea?"

106. When taking Joan's history, the nurse in the fertility clinic knows that data relevant to infertility include:

    A. A 28-30-day menstrual cycle.

    B. Pubic hair and breast development at age 11.

    C. Epidemic parotitis at age 14.

    D. Gonorrhea treated 2 years ago.

107. Which finding during Joan's physical examination requires additional assessment when seeking the etiology of this couple's infertility?

    A. Uterus is anteverted.

    B. Abdominal scars noted in the right lower quadrant.

    C. Clitoral size is 0.5 cm.

    D. Pubic hair is thick and covers the mons and vulva.

108. Which statement is the *most* therapeutic nursing action to assist Joan and Mike to cope with infertility?

    A. "Your sexual relationship is considered normal."

    B. "Tell your friends and family that you have chosen not to have children."

    C. "Your angry feelings are understandable and an expected response."

    D. "When you are over your initial response, you may want to consider an alternative such as adoption."

109. Prior to instructing Joan and Mike in the procedure for assessing Joan's cervical mucus, the nurse's *first* action is to:

    A. Show her pictures of cervical mucus common to each phase of the menstrual cycle.

    B. Explain the effects of the ovarian hormones, estrogen and progesterone, on cervical mucus.

    C. Demonstrate, using a pelvic model, how a specimen is obtained.

    D. Assess her readiness to touch her external genitalia and her cervix.

110. Mike wants to know how to go about collecting semen for analysis. Using pelvic models, the nurse demonstrates and instructs him to:

    A. Apply a regular condom on the penis to collect ejaculate.

    B. Ejaculate directly into a clean specimen jar.

    C. Soak up ejaculate from Joan's vagina using sterile cotton balls.

    D. Remove ejaculated sperm from his wife's vagina with a vaginal spoon and place it directly into a clean test tube, which is then packed in ice.

111. The nurse knows that the couple understood which fertility test when Mike and Joan arrive at the clinic at the expected time of ovulation and within 6-8 hours after coitus?

    A. Complete semen analysis.

    B. Sims-Huhner test.

    C. Buccal smear.

    D. Rubin's test.

112. Joan's last normal menstrual period was March 18, but she spotted around April 15. Her estimated date of birth is:

    A. December 25.

    B. December 11.

    C. January 22.

    D. January 18.

113. Joan has been amenorrheic for two successive cycles, and has been experiencing some nausea, breast tenderness, and fatigue. Now she is admitted to the hospital for some spotting and cramping sensations. Vaginal examination reveals no cervical dilation. The nurse prepares Joan for diagnostic and therapeutic measures related to:

    A. Threatened abortion.

    B. Inevitable abortion.

    C. Tubal pregnancy.

    D. Incompetent cervical os.

Medical Diagnosis: Hemorrhage/placenta previa.

- *Nursing Problems/Diagnosis:*

    Risk for alteration in circulation.

    Altered feeling state: grief.

    Altered fluid volume: deficit.

    Impaired gas exchange.

    Knowledge deficit.

    Impaired physical mobility.

    Self-care deficit: medication administration.

- *Chief Complaint:*

    Parwinder Singh-Kaur, an expectant mother, is admitted to the labor unit via gurney. She is a 31-year-old Asian Indian primigravida at 36 weeks' gestation. Her husband, Donald, is with her. She reports vaginal bleeding that started 1½ hours ago.

- *Present Health History:*

"Immediately after getting out of bed this morning, blood started to run down my legs and into my slippers."

- *Past Health History:*

Negative for chronic or concurrent medical disorders.

- *Obstetric History:*

Course of pregnancy: Unremarkable.

Blood type: B, Rh (D) negative.

Coombs: Negative.

Husband: B, Rh positive.

BP: 132/84.

Weight gain: 26 pounds over baseline weight of 130.

Height: 5 feet, 5 inches.

Pelvic measurements: Gynecoid, adequate.

VDRL: Negative. Gonorrhea: Negative.

Plans to have a nonmedicated vaginal birth with husband acting as coach.

- *Review of Systems:*

Increasing fatigue.

Return of urinary frequency, mild constipation, itching and uncomfortable hemorrhoids.

Inability to sleep because of large abdominal size and fetal movements.

Difficulty sitting and walking because of sensation of pelvic looseness.

Good appetite. Last ate dinner 12½ hours ago; nothing by mouth since then.

No respiratory problems now, but had a cold 3 weeks ago.

- *Physical Exam:*

Vaginal discharge: Perineal pad contains one small blood spot.

Abdominal examination: Uterus relaxed. One fleeting mild contraction, 30–40 seconds in 10 minutes. Fetus active. Possible breech presentation. FHR in RUQ at 144 bpm.

Vaginal examination: Deferred.

Hct: 35%. Hgb: 11.5 g.

Sonogram: Placenta located in lower uterine segment over internal os, fetus in breech presentation.

Diagnosis: Complete (total) placenta previa with fetal breech presenting.

Plan: Cesarean birth after fetal lung maturity is ensured.

- *Psychological Status:*

Anxious and concerned for the fetus.

---

114. While transferring Parwinder Singh-Kaur from the gurney to the bed, the most appropriate question the nurse can ask regarding the vaginal bleeding is:

    A. "Was the vaginal bleeding accompanied by pain?"

    B. "Had you had intercourse just before the bleeding started?"

    C. "Has this happened before during your pregnancy?"

    D. "Do you usually bleed easily, like a bloody nose?"

115. The nurse settles Ms. Singh-Kaur in bed. Which appropriate nursing action is taken *first*?

    A. Auscultate and record fetal heart rate and rhythm.

    B. Palpate tone of uterine muscle.

    C. Assess amount of bleeding presently on the perineal pad.

    D. Complete the intake history and physical examination.

116. The intern arrives on the unit and asks for Ms. Singh-Kaur's room number. He asks the nurse to accompany him while he assesses Ms. Singh-Kaur for cervical dilation and effacement and fetal presentation. The nurse's best response is:

    A. "Ms. Singh-Kaur has just been given a sedative. Can you come back later?"

    B. "Ms. Singh-Kaur has had vaginal bleeding. Vaginal examinations are contraindicated."

    C. "You will need to check with the resident first."

    D. "I will be glad to go with you. She is very anxious."

117. To prepare Parwinder for a vaginal examination under double setup, the nurse prepares a sterile field:

    A. In the labor room.

    B. In the birthing room.

    C. In the operating room.

    D. Nowhere. Double setup refers to an intravenous infusion line suitable for regular fluids and for blood transfusion.

118. Vaginal bleeding has stopped. The tracing of the FHR indicates a baseline heart rate between 136 and 144; good long-term variability, accelerations present, no decelerations noted. In the presence of these findings, the nurse:

    A. Continues to monitor maternal and fetal status with no change in care plan.

    B. Starts oxygen by face mask at 10–12 L/min.

    C. Notifies the physician stat and prepares for cesarean birth.

D. Reassures the family that the crisis is over.

119. When providing nursing care to a woman with a fetal monitor in place, the nurse keeps in mind the following case:

> The physician ordered a fetal monitor for a woman in labor and then proceeded to meet his surgery schedule. The nurse applied the monitor. The physician returned to find a late deceleration pattern that had persisted for 2 hours and went unrecognized by the nurse. Within 30 minutes, a stillborn fetus was born.

In the situation described, which statement is true?

A. The physician is solely responsible/accountable.

B. The nurse accepted total responsibility/accountability for recognizing ominous FHR patterns.

C. The nurse was not expected to take independent action to prevent harm to the fetus.

D. The late deceleration pattern was unrelated to the intra-uterine fetal demise.

120. Ms. Singh-Kaur is not bleeding now. She and her husband appear to be—and state that they are—less anxious and more hopeful about continuing the pregnancy at this time. Mr. Kaur reveals he does not understand "about the Rh thing." He continues, "I heard the Rh can hurt the baby. How would we know if the baby is hurt?" Which is the *most* appropriately stated nursing problem to enter into Ms. Singh-Kaur 's record?

A. Mr. Kaur would like an explanation of Rh incompatibility.

B. The Kaurs want to know how the Rh factor affects the baby.

C. The Kaurs need to learn more about the Rh factor.

D. Mr. Kaur's concern is increased because he does not understand isoimmunization—its cause or diagnosis.

121. Ms. Singh-Kaur is to remain on bedrest for at least a week. Which nursing action is inappropriate?

A. Ask her to cough and deep breathe at least 4 times per day.

B. Encourage her to wiggle her toes and flex and extend her feet against the footboard whenever she thinks of it.

C. Prepare her for L/S ratio determination.

D. Assist her in choosing a diet high in roughage and fluids.

Two weeks later, Ms. Singh-Kaur begins to bleed slightly. A cesarean birth is performed. Mr. Kaur stayed with her during the birth. Both saw and held their newborn son before he was admitted to the nursery for observation. Baby Boy Kaur is assessed to be large for gestational age (LGA). Gestational age is estimated at 37 weeks.

Parwinder's glucose tolerance test is positive for (gestational) diabetes. Her hemoglobin A_{1c} at 10% or more, implies abnormal glucose metabolism over the past several weeks.

122. Based on these new findings, what is least relevant in the neonate's care?

    A. Observation for signs of respiratory distress syndrome (RDS).

    B. Evaluation for blood glucose below 40 mg/dL.

    C. Laboratory assessment for serum bilirubin above 15 mg/dL.

    D. Examination of diapers for pinkish staining.

123. At birth, Baby Boy Kaur's heart rate is 92; he has made no respiratory effort; his muscle tone shows some flexion; he grimaces in response to a slap on the soles of his feet; and his color is pale. Based on his assessment, the nurse:

    A. Does nothing.

    B. Takes him to the nursery for further observation.

    C. Administers oxygen by mask until he is pink.

    D. Begins resuscitative actions immediately.

124. At cesarean delivery, the diagnosis of complete placenta previa is confirmed. In the first 24 hours after birth, the nurse must know that the woman who had placenta previa is at greater risk for hemorrhage than other new mothers due to:

    A. Uterine atony.

    B. Retained placental fragments.

    C. Pelvic hematoma.

    D. Location of decidua basalis.

125. To prevent or treat postpartal hemorrhage, defined as the loss of 500 mL or more of blood within the first 24 hours after birth, which prescribed drug would the nurse administer?

    A. Metronidazole.

    B. Methylergonovine maleate.

    C. Estradiol valerate.

    D. Naloxone (Narcan).

126. Ms. Singh-Kaur and her husband feel that breast milk is better for their baby. She wants to supply milk for their son during his hospitalization and to have sufficient milk for him when he comes home. What is the most appropriate plan of action to help her establish and maintain lactation when the baby cannot nurse?

    A. Increase fluid and caloric intake.

    B. Empty the breasts every 3—4 hours.

    C. Receive an injection of oxytocin to stimulate the letdown reflex.

    D. Take oral estradiol valerate as prescribed.

127. The specimen of cord blood obtained from Baby Boy Kaur at delivery reveals he is Rh positive, Coomb's negative. Ms. Singh-Kaur is a candidate to receive Rho (D) immune globulin (i.e., RhoGAM). Rho (D) immune globulin protects a future Rh-positive fetus of Ms. Singh-Kaur by:

    A. Beginning to build maternal immunity to the Rh factor.

    B. Destroying fetal Rh-positive RBCs in the maternal blood system.

    C. Inactivating maternal anti-Rh factor antibodies.

    D. Supporting the maternal immunologic rejection of fetal Rh-positive RBCs.

128. Prematurity places the neonate at high risk. The nurse knows that prematurity is associated with:

    A. Moderate obesity, maternal age between 28 and 32 years, exercise such as swimming, or too much intercourse.

    B. High hemoglobin and hematocrit, increased water conservation by the kidneys, and constipation.

    C. Lack of surfactant and immaturity of retinal and other blood vessels.

    D. Parental preference for this child over the other normal-term siblings because of the emotional and financial investment.

Baby Boy Kaur dies.

---

129. When a neonate dies, the *initial* response of the parent(s) is often:

    A. Denial and shock.

    B. Anger.

    C. Depression and acute grief.

    D. Resolution.

130. The nurse can *best* comfort/reassure Ms. Singh-Kaur by saying:

    A. "It is God's will. He works in ways we sometimes do not understand."

    B. "It is better he died now before he suffered through any surgeries and before you got too attached to him."

    C. "You can be thankful that you are still young and can have another baby."

    D. "This must be a very difficult and sad time for you."

Medical Situation: Complications in pregnancy and labor: abruptio placentae.

- *Nursing Problem/Diagnosis:*

  Fluid volume deficit.

- *Chief Complaint:*

  Mavis Scott, a 31-year-old African-American woman, arrives in the emergency department complaining of severe abdominal cramping. She is 30 weeks pregnant and is experiencing intense pain during contractions.

- *History of Present Illness:*

  Ms. Scott's husband states that shortly after dinner his wife began complaining of cramps: "She began to hurt so bad that she couldn't walk." Mr. Scott called the physician, who told him to bring his wife to the hospital immediately. On arrival at the hospital, the nurse identified that the contractions were irregular, the uterus was not relaxing between contractions, and vaginal bleeding was apparent.

- *Past History and Family History:*

  This is Mr. and Ms. Scott's third pregnancy. They have a son, age 3, and a daughter, age 2. This pregnancy was unplanned, but the family wants this baby. Ms. Scott did not have problems with her other two pregnancies. Throughout this present pregnancy, she has "felt pretty good." Ms. Scott is healthy. Except for her two earlier births, the only time she was hospitalized was for a broken arm when she was 10 years old. Mr. Scott is very supportive of his wife and is concerned about both his wife and child. Mr. Scott is employed as a cab driver and Ms. Scott is a homemaker. Prior to having the children, Ms. Scott worked as a nursing assistant in a nursing home.

- *Physical Exam:*

  Vital signs: Temperature: 99°F, P: 88, R: 28, BP: 100/70.

  Lab values: Hct: 40%. Decrease in clotting time. Urine: Negative for protein, and blood.

  Lungs: Clear to auscultation.

  Heart: Pulse strong and regular; no murmurs or splitting noted. Abdomen: Spleen and liver nonpalpable; fundal height halfway between umbilicus and xiphoid process. Contractions hard and irregular, lasting 30–60 seconds; membranes intact.

  Extremities: No edema, pain, or tenderness; ROM intact. Head: All neurologic signs within normal limits.

  Eyes: PERL.

  Reflexes: Slightly hyperactive.

  Fetus: FHR: 140 bpm (steady rhythm noted); active.

■ *Psychological Status:*

Ms. Scott is very anxious; she is crying and shaking intermittently. Mr. Scott remains with his wife and refuses to leave her bedside. He appears as if he is "being strong for her."

131. A vaginal examination is contraindicated for Ms. Scott because she is bleeding during the last trimester of pregnancy. The nurse knows that an examination could:

   A. Cause hemorrhage from a low-lying placenta.

   B. Be painful and stimulate labor.

   C. Introduce infection.

   D. Rupture the membranes.

132. Ms. Scott is diagnosed as possibly having abruptio placentae. A major diagnostic sign to look for as part of the nursing assessment is:

   A. Painless bleeding.

   B. Hypotension.

   C. Painful bleeding.

   D. Nausea and vomiting.

133. A diagnosis of abruptio placentae is made. Abdominal palpation will reveal:

   A. A soft, boggy uterus with a distended bladder.

   B. A hard, tender, boardlike uterus.

   C. A distended bladder with hypertension.

   D. Mild contractions every 2 minutes, lasting 30 seconds.

134. What assessment does the nurse need to make because it is associated with abruptio placentae as a serious complication?

   A. Tachycardia.

   B. Decreased urinary output.

   C. Hypertension.

   D. Coagulopathy.

135. In providing care for Ms. Scott, in which position is it essential to maintain her?

   A. Semi-Fowler's.

   B. Prone.

   C. Side-lying.

   D. Supine.

Medical Situation: Normal labor and birth.

- *Nursing Problem/Diagnosis:*

Altered health maintenance.

- *Chief Complaint:*

Allene Nelson is a 25-year-old Caucasian woman who arrives at the hospital complaining of contractions occurring every 5-18 minutes and lasting for about 30 seconds.

- *Present Status:*

Allene is 40 weeks pregnant with her first child. Her pregnancy has been essentially unremarkable. She has gained 30 pounds and has "felt good" throughout her pregnancy. She experienced a slight amount of nausea during the first 2 months of pregnancy; however, she never vomited and has had a good appetite throughout the pregnancy. Her last prenatal visit was 2 days ago. The cervix was dilated 1 cm at that time, and she was experiencing a backache. Her husband, Tim, has accompanied her to every prenatal visit and has been very supportive.

- *Past Health History:*

Allene began menstruating at age 13. Her periods usually occur every 29 days and she experiences moderate abdominal cramps, which are relieved by taking ibuprofen every 4 hours for the first 24 hours. Allene has had all of her immunizations. She had chickenpox when she was 5 and does not remember being sick otherwise.

- *Family History:*

This pregnancy was planned. Both Allene and Tim are looking forward to the birth of their first baby. Allene and Tim have been married 4 years. Tim is a lab technician and Allene is a secretary at the same medical laboratory. Allene worked until last week and intends to return to work when the baby is 6 months old. The couple attended childbirth classes, and Tim is planning to be present throughout the birth.

- *Physical Exam:*

Vital signs: Temperature: 99.2°F, P:84, R:24, BP: 110/80.

FHR: 160 bpm.

Dilation: 4 cm; effacement: 100%; station: – 1 cm.

Contractions: Approximately every 8 minutes, lasting about 30 seconds; mild.

Membranes: Intact.

Bloody show: Present.

Overall physiologic status good.

- *Psychological Status:*

Allene is very excited and anxious for the baby to arrive. She is very talkative and appears to be enjoying her husband's attention. Tim appears somewhat anxious. He is providing support for Allene by massaging her back, getting the nurse when needed, and sponging her forehead with cool water.

---

136. On admission to the labor unit, Allene presents with the following signs: 100% effaced, 4 cm dilated, vertex at - 1 station, membranes intact. The nurse's *next* appropriate action is to:

    A. Start an intravenous infusion.

    B. Check the FHR.

    C. Set up for imminent birth.

    D. Prepare her for amniotomy.

137. While listening to the FHR, the nurse is least likely to hear:

    A. Funic souffle.

    B. Fetal respiratory movements.

    C. Uterine souffle.

    D. Maternal intestinal noises.

138. The nurse continues the admission assessment with palpation of Allene's abdomen. Palpation to assess for fetal presentation, position, lie, and engagement is known as the maneuver of:

    A. Leopold.

    B. Scanzoni.

    C. Ritgen.

    D. Shirodkar.

139. After entering the findings from the admission assessment, the nurse reviews Allene's prenatal record. The nurse notes that Allene's pelvis is described as gynecoid. When the patient asks the nurse what "gynecoid" means, since she heard the doctor use it to describe her pelvis, the nurse draws the following picture:

    A. Oval, widest from front to back.

    B. A transverse oval.

    C. Somewhat heart shaped, widest from side to side.

    D. Somewhat heart shaped, widest from front to back.

140. The nurse knows that the part(s) of the bony pelvis that serve(s) as a landmark for determining the station of the presenting part is (are) the:

    A. Ischial spines.

    B. Ischial tuberosities.

    C. Sacral promontory.

    D. Lower border of symphysis pubis.

141. The Nelsons inform the nurse that they are planning to use the Lamaze method for labor. To assist this couple, the nurse needs to know that the Lamaze method suggests the following breathing pattern during early labor:

    A. Deep chest.

    B. Shallow chest.

    C. Shallow abdominal.

    D. Deep chest at beginning and end of contraction; rapid and shallow chest during peak of contraction.

142. In planning care for Allene, the nurse need not be concerned with:

    A. Monitoring the FHR.

    B. Examining the vagina.

    C. Providing support for her husband.

    D. Rupturing the membranes.

143. Allene is becoming fatigued and more uncomfortable. Tim asks the nurse what he can do to help. The *most* appropriate response includes:

    A. "Relax and remain calm."

    B. "Call the physician whenever your wife needs her."

    C. "Reassure your wife."

    D. "Keep your eye on the fetal monitor."

144. Tim asks the nurse when he will know that Allene has entered the transitional stage of labor. The *most* appropriate response includes the information that his wife will become:

    A. More irritable and complain of nausea.

    B. Less talkative and more serene.

    C. More talkative and excited.

    D. More serious and less energetic.

145. Allene notices a leaking of clear fluid from her vagina. During the vaginal examination, the nurse cannot tell if the membranes have broken. To test whether the "bag of waters" has broken, which test may the nurse use?

    A. Phenaphthazine (Nitrazine).

    B. Guthrie assay.

    C. Gravindex.

    D. Pap smear.

146. The nurse applies the fetal monitor ordered by the physician, and the FHR and contractions are recorded continuously on a strip. Fetal monitor readings indicate a uniform shape of FHR deceleration pattern, which *coincides with* the uterine contraction; FHR returns to baseline as the contraction ends. The nurse:

A. Reports this pattern immediately to the physician.

B. Turns the woman onto her side, administers oxygen, and stops the oxytocin induction if induction is in progress.

C. Alerts surgery and anesthesiology departments that an emergency cesarean birth is pending.

D. Does nothing; there is no clinical significance to this pattern.

147. Allene has had no regional anesthesia. Which symptom indicates that she is approaching the second stage?

A. Elevation of temperature and pulse.

B. Nausea, shaking legs, increased irritability.

C. Malar flush, increasing seriousness.

D. Tingling or numbness of the fingers and/or toes.

148. Allene begins to complain of nausea, belches, and begins to perspire over her upper lip, and her legs begin to shake. The nurse's *first* action is to:

A. Notify the physician because she is starting to convulse.

B. Check to see if the cervix is dilated 10 cm.

C. Check for hypotension.

D. Cover her with extra blankets and keep her quiet.

Medical Situation: Complications during labor and birth: placenta previa; cesarean surgery.

- *Nursing Problem/Diagnosis:*

Altered family processes.

Anxiety.

Fluid volume deficit.

Impaired gas exchange.

Risk for injury.

Altered tissue perfusion.

- *Chief Complaint:*

Dorothy Toth, a 31-year-old African-American woman, is 38 weeks pregnant with her third baby. She woke up this morning and discovered that she had vaginal bleeding.

- *Present Status:*

Ms. Toth called her obstetrician, who suggested that she come into the hospital to be examined. Ms. Toth was not experiencing any cramping or pain; however, the bleeding was continuous and Ms. Toth was very apprehensive.

- *Past Health History:*

Ms. Toth had no complications during her other two pregnancies. During this pregnancy, she felt unusually tired. However, she felt this was related to having two small boys, ages 6 and 4, to care for while being pregnant.

- *Family History:*

Mr. and Ms. Toth have been married for 8 years. They did not plan the three pregnancies; however, "they only used the diaphragm whenever they felt like it." They enjoy children but do not feel they can afford more than three. Mr. and Ms. Toth attended childbirth classes with all three pregnancies, and Mr. Toth has attended both previous births and intends to be present for this birth. Mr. and Ms. Toth have decided that Ms. Toth will have her tubes ligated following the birth of this baby.

- *Physical Exam:*

Vital signs: Temperature: 99.4°F, P: 98, R: 30, BP: 110/70.

Hct: 33%.

FHR: 130 bpm.

Bleeding: Moderate.

Heart: Regular rate and rhythm, no murmur or splitting.

Lungs: No congestion, wheezes, rales, or rhonchi noted.

Elimination: Urine: Negative for protein and blood; bowel sounds present.

Abdomen: Liver and spleen nonpalpable. Fundus: No contractions; membranes intact.

Neurologic signs: Eyes: PERL. Reflex: Normoreflexive.

- *Psychological Status:*

Ms. Toth is very anxious. She appears afraid and has verbalized fear of possibly losing this baby. Mr. Toth paces constantly and questions everybody about the care his wife is receiving. He appears very concerned about his wife and baby.

---

149. In assessing Mr. Toth's constant questioning of the care his wife is receiving, the nurse needs to realize that Mr. Toth is:

    A. Anxious about the hospital procedures being utilized.

    B. Concerned about the medical staff's level of competence.

    C. Anxious about his wife and baby's condition.

    D. Concerned about not being able to remain with his wife.

150. In assessing Ms. Toth's condition, the nurse needs to realize that the signs and symptoms of placenta previa are:

    A. Contractions occurring every 5–6 minutes.

    B. Low abdominal pain.

    C. Painless vaginal bleeding.

    D. Increased uterine muscle tonus.

151. In implementing care for Ms. Toth, the nurse should avoid:

    A. Positioning Ms. Toth in a high Fowler's position.

    B. Monitoring maternal and fetal vital signs.

    C. Permitting vaginal examinations.

    D. Providing a quiet environment.

152. Ms. Toth begins crying uncontrollably. The *most* appropriate nursing intervention includes:

    A. Telling Mr. Toth to ask his wife what is wrong.

    B. Sitting quietly with the couple.

    C. Assessing Ms. Toth's reasons for crying.

    D. Asking the physician to order her a sedative.

153. Electronic fetal monitoring is initiated. Fetal monitor readings indicate a uniform shape of FHR deceleration pattern, which *begins after* the contraction is established and returns to baseline after the contraction ends. The nurse:

    A. Does nothing; there is no clinical significance to this pattern.

    B. Turns Ms. Toth onto her side, administers oxygen, and stops oxytocin induction if induction is in progress.

    C. Alerts the surgery and anesthesiology departments that an emergency cesarean birth is pending.

    D. Prepares Ms. Toth for immediate birth, either vaginal or abdominal.

154. Ms. Toth is scheduled for cesarean birth. In preparing her for the cesarean birth, which order would the nurse question?

    A. Observe for contractions and ruptured membranes.

    B. Continue fetal monitoring prior to surgery.

    C. Insert an indwelling catheter.

    D. Give meperidine hydrochloride, 100 mg IM 1 hour prior to surgery.

155. The nurse checks Ms. Toth's vital signs; 8 hours ago she gave birth by cesarean surgery. She is restless, but has no specific complaints. Her pulse is 94 and her BP is 108/70. The nurse should be suspicious of:

    A. Anxiety over the birth.

    B. Beginning shock.

    C. Preeclampsia.

    D. "Postpartum blues."

Medical Situation: Postpartum.

- *Nursing Problems/Diagnosis:*

  Risk for altered feeling processes (anxiety).

  Risk for fluid volume excess.

  Health-seeking behavior (contraception).

  Altered role performance.

- *Present Status:*

  Ann Bayless is 24-years-old, gravida 2, para 2. She has just given birth to a 7½ pound boy and is being moved into the recovery room.

- *Past History:*

  Normal prenatal course. Husband and wife attended childbirth classes and looked forward to their roles during labor and birth. They did not attend prenatal classes for their first child.

- *Family History:*

  Both parents are only children and are college graduates. Joe Bayless teaches English in a local high school and Ann is a registered nurse, although she has never worked as a nurse. They have no religious preference.

- *Physical Exam:*

  Breasts: Erect nipples, free of cracks or fissures.

  Fundus: Firm at umbilicus.

  Lochia: Moderate rubra.

  Perineum: Episiotomy (midline); moderate pain.

  Legs: Negative Homans' sign.

  Reflexes: Normoreflexive.

  Vital signs: Within normal limits.

  Urinalysis: Negative for sugar, protein, and blood.

  Hematocrit: 37%.

156. In assessing Ann, the nurse should determine that the behavior which demonstrates postpartum response to a *normal* birth is:

   A. Anxiousness to discuss her labor and birth.

   B. Difficulty in relating to her labor experience.

   C. Seriousness and weariness.

   D. Concern about the postpartum environment.

157. The nurse finds Ann's fundus to be "atonic and boggy." The *first* nursing intervention is to:

    A. Check Ann's blood pressure and pulse.

    B. Catheterize the bladder for urinary retention.

    C. Administer an oxytocic drug.

    D. Massage the uterine fundus.

158. Fifteen minutes later the nurse checks Ann and finds her fundus firm, 2 fingerbreadths above the umbilicus, and shifted to the right. The nursing intervention is to:

    A. Check for a distended bladder and catheterize Ann if it is distended and she cannot void adequately.

    B. Take her vital signs.

    C. Get an order for methylergonovine maleate (Methergine).

    D. Chart that her fundus has failed to involute.

159. Due to religious convictions, the nurse is not in favor of artificial means of family planning. Ann asks the nurse, "What contraceptive would you recommend?" The nurse's most appropriate response is:

    A. "I don't believe in contraceptives, so you will have to ask somebody else."

    B. "Contraceptives have bad side effects; I don't recommend them."

    C. "There are several contraceptives. I will give you the pros and cons so that you can make the decision. Also, consult your doctor about what is best for you."

    D. "The pill is the most effective and I recommend you start taking it right away so that you will be protected when you begin having intercourse."

160. Ann confides to the nurse that she does not know how she will be able to give enough attention to her husband, her 2-year-old, and her newborn. The nurse's most appropriate response is:

    A. "This is the time your newborn needs you most; your husband and child will understand."

    B. "Plan times when you can be with each one alone for a certain period."

    C. "Ask your husband to assume the care of your 2-year-old."

    D. "Suggest to your husband that this is a time when he can be free to go out with the boys and not worry about you."

Medical Situation: Postpartum.

- **Nursing Problems/Diagnosis:**

  Ineffective breastfeeding.

  Altered comfort (pain related to engorged breasts).

  Health-seeking behaviors (exercises, breastfeeding).

  Psychomotor retardation.

  Management of therapeutic regime: effective individual.

- **Present Status:**

  Audrey Johnson is 31-years-old, gravida 2, para 2. She had a normal birth 8 hours ago. She is anxious to start caring for herself and her infant, and is excited about breastfeeding.

- **Past and Family History:**

  Ms. Johnson had a normal prenatal course. She has a 5-year-old son. Her husband works as a plumber and she works as a bookkeeper part-time. There are no health problems on either side of the family.

- **Physical Exam:**

  Breasts: Soft, erect nipples; no fissures or bleeding.

  Fundus: Firm at umbilicus.

  Lochia: Moderate rubra.

  Extremities: Negative Homans' sign; no edema.

  Reflexes: Normoreflexive.

  Perineum: Episiotomy (mediolateral) approximated, minimal pain, ice to area.

  Vital signs: Within normal limits.

  Hematocrit: 36.5%.

  Urine: Negative for protein, sugar and ketones.

---

161. Ms. Johnson is anxious to learn postpartum exercises. Which exercise is inappropriate for the nurse to instruct?

    A. Kegels.

    B. Pelvic tilt.

    C. Sit-ups.

    D. Head raising.

162. Ms. Johnson wants to breastfeed and assume care of her newborn. The nurse determines that she is in the "taking-hold" phase due to her:

    A. Self-centeredness.

    B. Readiness to concern herself with her infant.

    C. Concern about personal weight gain and diet.

    D. Reluctance to assume mothering role.

163. The nurse instructs Ms. Johnson that during the postpartum period a brassiere should:

    A. Not be worn.

    B. Be worn to support and lift the breasts.

    C. Be worn to press the breasts flat against the chest wall.

    D. Be worn to apply constant, firm pressure toward the midline.

164. Ms. Johnson develops engorged breasts. The nurse teaches her to:

    A. Apply heat to the breasts prior to nursing and express some milk.

    B. Apply heat to the breasts after nursing.

    C. Apply cold packs to the breasts prior to nursing.

    D. Take pain medication 1 hour prior to nursing.

165. Ms. Johnson experiences "postpartum blues" due to feelings of inadequacy about breastfeeding. The nurse's most appropriate response is to:

    A. Make inquiries about a psychiatric consult.

    B. Explain that these feelings are normal and why they occur.

    C. Separate mother and infants until the depression ceases.

    D. Utilize suicidal precautions.

166. In preparation for Ms. Johnson's discharge, which instruction by the nurse is inappropriate?

    A. Resuming her prepregnancy life-style within 1 week.

    B. Strategies for dealing with new responsibilities.

    C. Plans for her own rest and relaxation.

    D. Resources to call in an emergency.

167. One week later Ms. Johnson phones the clinic and says, "I decided not to continue breastfeeding because the baby liked the bottle better." The nurse's most appropriate response would be:

    A. "You should feed the baby the way that works best for both of you."

    B. "You should not have given up breastfeeding so soon."

    C. "Breastfeeding is better for the baby, but you may as well stay with bottlefeeding now."

    D. "Your baby won't gain weight and may develop milk allergies."

Medical Situation: Postpartum complications/neonatal complications.

- **Nursing Problems/Diagnosis:**

  Altered family processes.

  Altered feeling state: grief.

  Altered parenting.

- **Chief Complaint:**

  Henrietta Young is a 36-year-old woman who has just given birth via cesarean surgery to a stillborn infant at 28 weeks' gestation.

- **Present Health History:**

  Ms. Young began experiencing contractions early this morning around 4 A.M. She started bleeding profusely and her husband took her to the hospital immediately. Upon admission, her vital signs were: temperature: 97.6°F, P: 88, and R: 28; BP was 100/60; her pulse was very weak and thready. She was taken to the birthing room immediately because the FHR was not audible. She gave birth to a baby boy who was stillborn at 5:15 A.M.

- **Past Health History:**

  Ms. Young has one child, Bryant, age 6. She has experienced two miscarriages; one occurred about 8 years ago and another occurred approximately 2 years ago. Both of these miscarriages occurred at about 14 weeks' gestation. Her physician told her that the miscarriages were due to a hormone imbalance. However, her pregnancy with Bryant was essentially unremarkable, with the exception of 2 days of slight spotting at 8 weeks' gestation. Ms. Young had planned to have a tubal ligation immediately following this birth because she felt that she did not want to subject herself and family to other pregnancies.

- **Family History:**

  Mr. and Ms. Young have been married 10 years. Both of their parents are living and have no major health problems. Bryant attends a private school and is doing very well; that is, he is in the first grade doing second-grade reading and math. Mr. Young is employed as a graphic designer and Ms. Young is employed as a home economics teacher at a junior college.

- **Physical Exam:** First hour postpartum

  Vital signs: Temperature: 97.8°F, P: 84, R: 26, BP = 100/70. Pulse is stronger and steadier than it was on admission.

  Lochia: Scant.

  Incision site: Inflamed, edematous, and draining small amounts of sanguineous liquid; area is tender to touch.

  Bladder: Catheter draining well. SG: 1.015.

  Analgesia-anesthesia: Spinal.

IV therapy: IV fluids infusing well; IV site not tender, no edema or inflammation.

Level of consciousness: Ms. Young was given an analgesic immediately following surgery. She is responsive when stimulated. However, she is generally nonverbal. Her husband is visiting. He is visibly upset and has been quietly crying intermittently.

168. The nurse observes Mr. Young quietly crying. The *most* appropriate nursing action is to:

   A. Give him privacy.

   B. Talk with him about his wife's condition.

   C. Assess his plans for the baby.

   D. Ask him to leave the room.

169. Mr. Young asks the nurse what she thinks his wife's reaction will be to the loss of their baby. The *most* therapeutic response is to:

   A. Ask Mr. Young how he thinks she will react.

   B. Tell him you are not sure.

   C. Inform him that there is no uniform pattern of reaction.

   D. Validate with him how his wife usually copes with losses.

170. Mr. Young asks the nurse what he should tell his son, Bryant. The *most* appropriate response the nurse could suggest is to:

   A. Tell Bryant what has occurred at a level he can comprehend.

   B. Ask Bryant what he thinks death involves.

   C. Wait until Bryant's mother comes home so that both parents can tell him about his brother's death.

   D. Inform Bryant that his brother is now in heaven.

Medical Situation: Normal–term neonate.

- *Nursing Problems/Diagnosis:*

   Altered comfort (discomfort related to inverted nipples).

   Health-seeking behavior: infant nutrition.

- *Present Status:*

   Michael, a newborn, is 2 hours old, and weighs 7½ pounds (3405 g). Normal newborn; 39 weeks' gestation; uncomplicated labor and birth. Apgar scores of 9-9; second child of 34-year-old mother.

■ *Past History:*

Mother stopped working at the 28th week of this gestation; she does not plan to return to work. Father has a position in a law firm. Mother is anxious to care for her newborn.

■ *Physical Exam:*

Fontanelles: Within normal limits.

Reflexes: Appropriate and intact.

Muscles: Good tone; attitude of general flexion.

Color: Good oxygenation; hands and feet slightly blue when at rest.

Activity: Cries vigorously.

Stool: One meconium passed at 1 hour of age.

Urine: None observed.

Chest: Clear.

Temperature: 36.8°C (axillary).

Respirations: 45 irregular; without grunting, flaring, or retractions.

Bowel sounds: Present.

Extremities: No hip clicks.

Genitalia: Descended testicles; scrotum well creased.

Buttocks: Nickel-size mongolian spot.

---

171. The nurse instructs Michael's mother that in comparison with commercial formulas, breast milk:

    A. Has a higher protein content.

    B. Has a lower protein content.

    C. Has a lower carbohydrate content.

    D. Can cause milk allergy.

172. The nurse continues her health teaching and states that infants who are breastfed normally do not:

    A. Have less chance of GI infection than infants who are formula-fed..

    B. Gain more weight than infants who are formula-fed.

    C. Have an increased chance of loose stools.

    D. Have less chance of milk allergy.

173. Because of severely inverted nipples, Michael's mother wishes to decrease the milk in her breasts and bottlefeed. The nurse would teach her to:

    A. Decrease stimulation to the breasts.

    B. Stimulate the nipples every 4 hours.

    C. Place heat on the breasts.

    D. Put the infant to the breast once a day.

174. The nurse bases her instruction to Michael's mother on knowledge that a 7½-pound (3.4-kg) infant from birth to 5 months of age needs approximately the following calories per kilogram per day (FDA guidelines):

    A. 100-110.

    B. 115-120.

    C. 150-160.

    D. 180-185.

175. It is determined that Michael needs 120 cal/kg/day. Commercial formulas are prepared to supply 20 cal/oz. How many ounces should Michael receive per feeding if he is fed every 4 hours?

    A. 2-3.

    B. 3-4.

    C. 4-5.

    D. 5-6.

Medical Situation: Normal-term neonates.

- *Nursing Problem/Diagnosis:*

    Ineffective airway clearance.

    Risk for disorganized infant behavior.

    Risk for altered endocrine/metabolic processes.

    Health-seeking behaviors related to effective breastfeeding, nutritional needs of infants.

    Impaired home maintenance management.

    Risk for infection.

    Risk for injury.

    Knowledge deficit (infant feeding and care).

    Risk for altered neurologic/sensory processes.

    Altered nutrition.

    Risk for impaired skin integrity.

- *Chief Concern:*

    Baby Boy Zale is one baby in a neonate nursery. Baby Boys Allen, Bohack, and Chelain are also in the neonate nursery at this time. The chief concern is establishing health supervision for these normal neonates. The history below applies to Baby Boy Zale.

- *Present Health History:*

    Baby Boy Zale was born 2 hours ago with an Apgar score of 9 at 1 minute and 9 at 5 minutes. The vertex birth was spontaneous. He nursed at the breast soon after the cord was cut. No gross abnormalities were noted at birth. Prophylactic eye care was completed and vitamin K was administered at 1 hour of age.

- *Past Health History:*

Baby Boy Zale is the product of the second pregnancy of a 23-year-old married woman. The mother was not anemic, took no drugs, does not smoke, had no concurrent medical problems, and availed herself of early and continuous prenatal care. Labor was spontaneous and unmedicated.

- *Family History:*

The family history is essentially negative. The maternal grandmother died of endometrial carcinoma at age 75. The father of the baby is 25 years old, blood type A, Rh positive, and works as a certified public accountant. The older brother is 3 years old, has had all immunizations, is followed routinely at the well baby clinic, and is apparently healthy.

- *Physical Exam:*

Gestational age: 40 weeks.

Apical pulse: 132-144 in left midclavicular line, fifth intercostal space.

Posture: General flexion.

Respirations: 56/min (taken when active).

Weight: 3515 g (7 pounds, 12 ounces); length: 50 cm (20 inches).

Head circumference: 34 cm (13½ inches).

Chest circumference: 32 cm (12½ inches).

Axillary temperature: 36.5°C (97.6°F).

Findings of physical assessment: Reflexes within normal limits. Genitals: male, testes descended. Passed meconium and voided during physical exam.

---

176. Which statement related to administration of prophylactic eye care to the newborn is not accurate?

    A. Eye prophylaxis is a legal requirement.

    B. Ophthalmia neonatorum may be caused by gonococcal or pneumococcal infection.

    C. Eye prophylaxis may be delayed up to 1 hour after birth to facilitate parent-child attachment.

    D. The medication is placed into the conjunctival sac of the lower lid.

177. When providing eye prophylaxis, the nurse keeps in mind the following case:

    The nurse handed the physician an incorrect strength of eye medication drops for instillation into the neonate's eyes. The physician instilled the medication, and the infant's vision was impaired.

The possible outcome of this situation may be that a charge of negligence can legally be brought against:

A. The nurse.

B. The physician.

C. Both the nurse and the physician.

D. The pharmacist for supplying an incorrect strength.

178. Vitamin K_1 (Aquamephyton) is injected intramuscularly to Baby Boy Zale because his GI tract is incapable of producing it for several days. Vitamin K_1 acts to catalyze the synthesis of prothrombin in the liver. The nurse giving vitamin K_1 to the neonate needs to know that which of the following may be unsafe?

A. Using the greater trochanter and posterior superior iliac spine as landmarks.

B. Using the vastus lateralis muscle as the injection site.

C. Injecting the needle at a 45-degree angle.

D. Injecting the needle in the direction of the knee.

179. Baby Boy Zale has been sleeping quietly since he fell asleep at 1 hour after birth. Now, 4½ hours after birth, he awakens, regurgitates mucus, and has a gagging episode. His mother calls out for the nurse. The nurse:

A. Holds the infant upright and pats him on his back.

B. Immediately takes him to the nursery for suctioning.

C. Helps the mother hold him face down with the head lower than the buttocks.

D. Reassures the mother that this is normal and not to worry.

180. To measure Baby Boy Zale's head circumference, the nurse places the measuring tape:

A. From the bregma, around the lower portion of the occiput, and back to the bregma.

B. On the forehead just above the eyebrows, over the junction of the ear on the head, and back to the forehead.

C. Over the eyebrows, over the top of the earlobes, and back over the eyebrows.

D. From the mentum to the vertex and back to the mentum.

181. Baby Boy Zale's head circumference is 34 cm; his chest circumference, 32 cm. Based on the findings, the nurse:

A. Refers him to be appraised for psychomotor retardation.

B. Knows that the physician will want to transilluminate his cranial vault.

C. Measures his occipitofrontal circumference daily.

D. Records the findings and does nothing further.

182. The nurse assesses each neonate to identify existing or potential problems. If an examination of Baby Boy Zale revealed the following findings, which requires further assessment and/or therapy?

    A. Flat hemangiomas, head circumference between 31 and 36 cm, hemoglobin between 14 and 19 g.

    B. Acute hearing, erythema toxicum, wrinkles covering the soles of the feet.

    C. Single palmar crease, snuffles, apical pulse between 120 and 140/min at rest.

    D. Molding, smegma, acrocyanosis, respiratory rate of 40/min at rest.

183. As the charge nurse, your responsibilities include checking all orders for feeding the neonates in your nursery. Which information is the most important in evaluating the nutrient needs of a normal-term neonate such as Baby Boy Zale?

    A. Kilograms of body weight.

    B. Percentage of body fat.

    C. Route of feedings, for example, oral versus gavage.

    D. Crown-to-heel length in centimeters.

184. In the plan of care for a normal newborn like Baby Boy Zale, the nurse incorporates knowledge that:

    A. The neonate may vomit if his bottle is propped.

    B. He may lose up to 4 ounces within the first days of life.

    C. His stomach holds about 120 mL at any one time.

    D. He needs about 90 cal/kg/24 hours or 45 cal/pound/24 hours.

185. When an object touches the newborn's cheek and/or lips, he turns toward the stimulus and opens his mouth. This reflex is known as:

    A. Babinski.

    B. Suck and swallow.

    C. Rooting.

    D. Moro.

186. Baby Boy Allen, a full-term neonate, was born 16 hours ago. Birth weight: 7 pounds, 6 ounces. Length: 20 cm. He is very active when awake and is on oral feedings. The fluid requirement for Baby Boy Allen is:

    A. 32 oz. (960 mL) per day.

    B. 24 oz. (720 mL) per day.

    C. 16 oz. (480 mL) per day.

    D. 12 oz. (360 mL) per day.

187. Ms. Bohack, 2 days postpartum, seems preoccupied. Her baby has just eaten and is now back in the nursery. She tells you the baby weighed 8 pounds, 2 ounces (3685 g) at birth; today he weighs 7 pounds, 10 ounces (3459 g). Ms. Bohack is worried because the baby "lost so much." The nurse's reply is based on the knowledge that Baby Boy Bohack can lose up to how many ounces and still be within normal range?

    A. 7 ounces.

    B. 9 ounces.

    C. 11 ounces.

    D. 13 ounces.

188. Baby Boy Chelain, birth weight 9 pounds, 10 ounces, was born 3 hours ago. Apgar scores are 8 at 1 minute and 9 at 5 minutes. At this time, the nurse notes athetoid posturing and movements, with slight tremors of the arms. The nurse's first response is:

    A. Feed him glucose water because these behaviors could be signs of hypoglycemia.

    B. Swaddle him because these are signs of drug (heroin or alcohol) dependence.

    C. Notify the physician because these behaviors are signs of increased intracranial pressure.

    D. Obtain and assess a blood sample by heelstick because these behaviors could be signs of hypoglycemia.

189. Ms. Allen is concerned because she thinks her son has lost too much weight. She adds, "Maybe I should just give him a bottle and not try to breastfeed. That way I know what he gets." Baby Boy Allen's weight was 7 pounds, 6 ounces (3345 g). Today, 2 days later, he weighs 6 pounds, 14 ounces (3118 g). Which is the best way for the nurse to deal with this situation?

    A. Explain to Ms. Allen that he can lose 3 more ounces and still be within normal limits for weight loss.

    B. Bring a bottle of glucose water for Ms. Allen to give after breastfeeding, until her milk comes in.

    C. Tell her he is OK and that you will ask her pediatrician to come by to see her.

    D. Support Ms. Allen's statement about the fact that an accurate record is possible when feeding is by bottle.

190. Ms. Zale is sitting up in bed, looking comfortable. She is holding her son and feeding him a formula. Ms. Zale says he seems to get full fast and he has regurgitated some of the formula already. She adds, "Maybe I just don't know how to feed him." As the baby sucks on the nipple, large bubbles are seen in the bottle. The nurse tells the mother:

    A. "Tighten the bottle cap a little."

B. "Hold the baby in a more upright position."

C. "Bubble (burp) him after each ½ oz. of formula."

D. "Let me show you how. Then you can try it again."

191. Which *best* demonstrates that Ms. Allen has incorporated knowledge about breastfeeding?

    A. She weighs her baby and records his weight before and after feeding.

    B. She touches her nipple to the baby's cheek at the start of the feeding.

    C. She bubbles (burps) her baby after his feeding.

    D. She protects her clothing by placing small squares of cellophane wrap in her nursing bra.

192. A heelstick is performed before discharge of Baby Boy Zale to obtain a blood specimen to rule out:

    A. Kernicterus.

    B. Hypoglycemia.

    C. Thrush.

    D. Phenylketonuria (PKU).

193. The nurse determines that Ms. Allen needs further health instruction in appropriate care for her son when the nurse observes her:

    A. Cleanse each eye with a different cotton swab or corner of a washcloth from the inner canthus outward.

    B. Retract his prepuce completely to cleanse the glans penis of smegma and other debris.

    C. Rinse shampooed hair thoroughly, then use a fine-toothed comb or brush.

    D. Cleanse his nares and ears with twists of moistened cotton.

194. Nurses often work with people from a wide variety of cultures, both within the United States and in other countries. Nurses are asked questions about the preparation of formulas to meet the nutritional needs of infants. Which information about the infant's digestive capabilities and about formula preparation is inaccurate?

    A. Fat is not easily digested by the gastric fluids.

    B. Milk sugar (lactose) is not digested in the stomach.

    C. Corn and coconut oil mixtures are not absorbed to the same extent as the fat in human milk.

    D. The infant is developmentally ready for solid foods at about 4–6 months. There are no nutritional advantages to giving him solids before that time.

195. The postpartum nurse is asked to evaluate a pamphlet to be used to provide anticipatory guidance regarding breast-feeding. Which is the only accurate statement?

    A. Breastfeeding provides immune bodies to the neonate and contraception for the mother for 8 months.

    B. Breast milk jaundice is a possible complication that necessitates weaning.

    C. Breast milk contains more protein and less carbohydrate than cow's milk.

    D. Women who have breastfed are less prone to develop breast cancer later in life.

196. Which commonly occurring neonatal problem is due to overdressing or excessive warmth?

    A. Diaper rash.

    B. Miliaria.

    C. Seborrheic dermatitis.

    D. Diarrhea.

197. When working in the newborn nursery, the nurse keeps the following case in mind:

    > The newborn nursery is desperately short of staff. The nurse agrees to work an extra shift. During the 14th hour on duty, the nurse makes a medication error.

    Since the nurse was filling a "desperate" staffing need and therefore was fatigued, the outcome may be that:

    A. The hospital accepts the responsibility for the negligent act.

    B. The nurse is held to the same standard of care as always.

    C. No problem exists if the client does not bring legal action.

    D. Legal responsibilities are met if an incident report is filed.

Answers and Rationale

1. **A. Tuning in to own feelings and values about the topic.**

    A is correct; before beginning a class for adolescents, the nurse needs to assess own feelings. If these feelings are negative, this attitude will be conveyed to the adolescents. *B* is incorrect because adolescents assume their own style of dress and language to assert their difference and independence from adults. In addition, adolescents still want to have adults there to provide some limits, to give direction, and so forth. Adolescents prefer to have adults behave like adults. *C* is incorrect because the adult focusing on own experience as an adolescent does not help the adolescent focus on own reality now. *D* is incorrect because the younger adolescent is still operating on the concrete level of cognition (Piaget); that is, the adolescent has to have an experience first before she can understand it or its implications for the future.

2. **C. When the ovum is present.**

   C is correct; a woman is fertile only during the time that an egg is present. The egg lives for 24 hours but is thought to be most fertilizable for 12 of those hours. The precise moment of ovulation is difficult to determine. In general, ovulation occurs 14 days before the next menstrual flow begins. *A* is incorrect because ovulation occurs on day 14 of a *28-day cycle only*. *B* is incorrect because ovulation occurs 14 days before the next cycle begins. Just before menstruation, the endometrium is beginning to die. *D* is incorrect because day 1 of the cycle is the first day of menstrual flow, that is, when the endometrium is being sloughed off.

3. **D. Is about to ovulate.**

   D is correct. Just before ovulation, the cervical mucus is clear, copious, stretchable (good spinnbarkeit), and slippery. This is the characteristic assessment in the presence of high levels of estrogen. *A* is incorrect. During pregnancy, high levels of estrogen and progesterone are present; therefore, the cervical mucus does not have the consistency of egg white and is not stretchable. *B* is incorrect; leukorrhea is a white or yellowish discharge that does not have all the characteristics listed. *C* is incorrect; just before menstruation, when the levels of progesterone and estrogen fall, the mucus is sticky and less copious.

4. **A. 8 through 24.**

   A is correct. To calculate the fertile period, subtract 18 from the shortest cycle in the previous 12 months, and 11 from the longest. 26 – 18 = 8; 35 – 11 = 24. This formula works in the following manner: In the 26-day cycle, ovulation occurs on day 12; sperm live for 3 days, so there should be no sperm in the vaginal vault for 3 days before ovulation. For added protection, subtract 1 more day. Therefore, the fertile period begins on day 8. In the 35-day cycle, ovulation occurs on day 21; the ovum lives for 1 day (or so); add another 2 days for added protection. The fertile period then ends on day 24. *B*, *C*, and *D* are incorrect because of the explanation for *A*.

5. **A. Chloasma.**

   A is correct. Chloasma, or mask of pregnancy, consists of brownish blotches, irregular in shape and size, caused by the high levels of estrogen. Estrogen stimulates production of melanin-stimulating hormone (MSH), which increases the level of anterior pituitary melanotropin. *B* and *C* are incorrect. Although both palmar erythema and spider nevi (telangiectasia) result from high levels of estrogen, they *do* fade after birth and when the oral contraceptive estrogen dosage is changed or discontinued. *D* is incorrect; pruritus is due to excretion of bile salts through the skin in some women during pregnancy. Treatment for mild cases is bathing. For more severe cases, phenobarbital is prescribed. Phenobarbital works in the liver to stimulate the production of an enzyme that relieves this condition.

6. **D. Thromboembolic disease.**

    D is correct; thromboembolic disease is the most serious of the side effects and carries an increased risk of morbidity and mortality. Pulmonary embolism and cerebral thrombosis may occur, especially in women over 35 years old. However, there is a much higher risk—6–10% higher—of thromboembolic disease during pregnancy than when one is taking the pill. *A*, *B*, and *C* are incorrect because ectopic pregnancy, cholelithiasis, and gastroenteritis are not associated with the ingestion of oral contraceptive hormones. *A*, ectopic pregnancy, is sometimes related to the presence of an IUD. Ovulation continues to occur with this contraceptive method and there is an increased incidence of pelvic inflammatory disease in IUD wearers. When inflammation heals, scar tissue forms. This scar tissue may partially occlude the fallopian tubes, preventing a fertilized egg from moving into the uterine cavity.

7. **A. Appearance of a chancre.**

    A is correct; appearance of a chancre brings most people in for treatment. This primary lesion usually forms at the initial site of infection. The chancre is a dull red, firm, and painless papule that will heal spontaneously. *B* is incorrect; within a few hours, organisms multiply and spread to all tissues, but the chancre does not appear until 3-4 weeks after infection. *C* is incorrect because the tests for serology are not positive until at least 1 week after the chancre appears. The test is for antibodies to *Treponema pallidum*. *D* is incorrect because pain in the joints and loss of position sense are two characteristics of tertiary syphilis, known as tabes dorsalis.

8. **D. The spirochete crosses the placenta after the 16th week of gestation.**

    D is correct. The spirochete can cross the placenta after the 16th-18th week; however, treatment with high doses of penicillin now should cure the disease for the parents and the fetus. If treated now, there will be no residual fetal damage. *A* is incorrect; secondary lesions, called condylomata lata, appear about 4-6 weeks after the chancre heals and are extremely infectious. Skin lesions can occur anywhere over the body, but are characteristic over the palms of the hands and soles of the feet. *B* is incorrect; obliterative endarteritis, destruction of the arteries and arterioles, causes cell damage to the eyes, cardiovascular system, brain, and spinal cord, and is characteristic of tertiary syphilis. *C* is incorrect;

gummas, hard nodules of dead tissue throughout the body, are characteristic of tertiary syphilis.

9. **A. It can result in pharyngitis, tonsillitis, perianal pruritus, and burning.**

    A is correct. In addition to pharyngitis, tonsillitis, and perianal pruritus, gonorrhea may result in pelvic inflammatory disease and sterility; thick, purulent vaginal discharge; infection of Skene's and Bartholin's glands; and infection of the urinary tract. Arthritis, meningitis, and endocarditis may be systemic infections. *B* is incorrect; systemic congenital gonorrhea results in purulent discharge from the newborn's eyes, nose, and vagina or anus. The infant may have a cough, be lethargic, and be a poor feeder. He or she may also be born prematurely from premature rupture of the membranes. *C* is incorrect; symptoms of vaginal infection are profuse, purulent drainage and bartholinitis. The man may experience dysuria, a discharge from the urinary meatus, penile pain, and frequency. Blisterlike lesions are characteristic of herpes. *D* is incorrect; if infected drainage soils bed linens and clothing, one can become infected through contact with these soiled articles. Also, the newborn may receive a systemic infection via the placenta or by direct contact with the infected birth canal.

10. **C. Is a candidate for rubella vaccination shortly after birth.**

    C is correct; Wendy has not had rubella or is serologically negative because her rubella titer is less than 1:8. She is scheduled for rubella vaccine shortly after birth. Because the live, attenuated rubella virus is not communicable, she may receive the vaccine even if she is lactating. However, the virus can be teratogenic, so contraception is mandatory for 2 months following vaccination. *A*, *B*, and *D* are incorrect because of the rationale given for *C*.

11. **A. Coach her to keep eyes, mouth, and hands open.**

    A is correct because while keeping one's eyes, mouth, and hands open, it is almost impossible to contract the perineal musculature. *B* is incorrect because squeezing anything facilitates tensing all other parts of the body. *C* and *D* are both therapeutic nursing actions, but *A* *best* assists Wendy to relax her perineal muscles.

12. **D. An assignment on another unit.**

    D is correct because Wendy needs to avoid inhalant anesthetics that leak out into the surgical suites. An increased incidence of spontaneous abortion and congenital disorders has been noted among women who are in contact with air polluted with anesthetic gases. *A*, *B*, and *C* are incorrect because the seriousness of exposure to anesthetic gases is the most important consideration in this instance.

13. **D. Nurse 0: "Changes in female hormone levels occur in both pregnancy and menopause."**

   D is correct because the changes in female hormone levels that occur in both pregnancy and menopause cause vasomotor instability. *A* is incorrect; although identification between mother and daughter may occur, shared feelings of increased body warmth have not been noted. *B* is incorrect because the data as stated do not support an infectious process as the etiologic factor. *C* is incorrect; although feelings of increased perspiration and warmth do accompany anxiety, the data given here do not support that conclusion.

14. **A. Avoids bending at the waist and does "flying" exercises.**

   A is correct. Heartburn occurs when food is regurgitated from the stomach into the esophagus through the relaxed cardiac sphincter. The "flying" exercise promotes good posture, thus permitting food to reenter the stomach; avoidance of bending at the waist prevents food from spilling out of the stomach into the esophagus. *B* is incorrect because eating some type of dry (not fatty) carbohydrate before getting out of bed is a method for relieving *nausea*, not heartburn. *C* is incorrect because it has nothing to do with heartburn; the unusual (usually culturally influenced) practice of eating starch or red clay is termed pica. *D* is incorrect because health habits that include getting plenty of fluids, exercise, and food with roughage help to prevent or minimize *constipation*, not heartburn.

15. **C. "Avoid taking any drug unless it is prescribed by your physician."**

   C is correct; drugs ingested by the mother cross the placenta and may adversely affect fetal development or function. *A* is incorrect. Lying on one's side does take the weight of the uterus off the ascending vena cava, but the positive physiologic effect of the left lateral position is not due to placental function. *B* is incorrect because not all vitamins and minerals can be stored. The baby's nutritional needs require the mother's daily intake of certain nutrients—for example, vitamin C. *D* is incorrect because infectious agents of small molecular size do cross the placenta. In addition, maternal fever has an adverse effect on the fetus. Because of this, all maternal infections must be diagnosed and treated appropriately.

16. **C. Help Wendy to place her full weight on the affected leg and lean forward on it.**

   C is correct. Stretching the affected muscles—by standing on the affected leg and leaning forward, by extending the knee and flexing the toes toward the tibia, or by standing on a cold floor—forces the muscle to relax. *A* is incorrect because the pain may be from thrombophlebitis or a thrombus, and massage could dislodge the clot into the bloodstream. *B* would be correct *only* if pain were felt when the muscle was stretched; in that case the physician should be notified immediately. *D* is incorrect because pointing one's toes may cause cramping of the gastrocnemius (Charley horse). One should remember to point the heel, not the toes.

17. **A. Feelings and attitudes toward pregnancy.**

A is correct; feelings and attitudes toward the pregnancy are important during the first trimester. Other concerns and questions at this time include the discomforts being experienced (such as nausea, frequency of urination, fatigue, and increase in vaginal mucus) and content pertaining to general hygiene (such as rest, sleep, douching, and marital relations). Financial problems are also a major concern for many now. The Bradley method of preparation for childbirth features an "early bird" class to answer these questions. *B* is incorrect because preparation for labor and childcare is begun in the eighth month by childbirth educators. *C* is incorrect because it is more appropriate to the middle trimester. At that time the mother is very interested in fetal growth and development and in learning what discomforts are normal, how long they will last, and what can be done to relieve them. The nurse instructs the mother regarding danger signals at that time. *D* is incorrect because most discussions regarding questions and concerns about the new baby and the new role as parents are most appropriate during the last trimester. Most preparation for labor is done during the last trimester, as well.

18. **C. Ptyalism and gums that bleed when teeth are brushed.**

C is the answer; ptyalism and gums that bleed easily result from hyperemia due to the increased vascularization during pregnancy. It is not necessary to notify the physician about them; gentle brushing and good oral hygiene are the only treatments recommended. Excessive salivation may increase the discomforts of nausea. If bleeding of the gums becomes severe, however, the physician should be notified immediately. *A* is incorrect because severe, persistent headache is one of the symptoms of preeclampsia -- probably due to generalized arteriospasm and edema of the CNS. *B* is incorrect because tight finger rings and puffy eyes are symptomatic of preeclampsia. Edema with weight gain in excess of 1 pound per week is one of the three cardinal symptoms/signs. The other two are hypertension and proteinuria. *D* is incorrect because a change in the woman's facial expression or affect, often accompanied by a puffy, edematous appearance, is seen with severe preeclampsia.

19. **B. Grapefruit juice, beef liver with scrambled egg, toast, coffee.**

B is correct because the breakfast described is high in both vitamin C and protein. The *A* breakfast is high in vitamin *C*, but the Cream of Wheat is lower in protein than the liver in the *B* breakfast. *C* is incorrect because the fried tomato has less vitamin *C* than orange or grapefruit juice. D is incorrect because this breakfast has less vitamin *C* and less protein than the other three choices.

20. **A. *Cottage cheese and tomatoes, peanut butter sandwich, milk.***

    A is correct because this combination contains the most protein (peanut butter), vitamin C (tomato), and calcium (milk). *B*, *C*, and *D* all have less protein than choice *A*.

21. **A. *Pork chops, sweet potatoes, cooked dried beans, raisin pudding.***

    A is correct because it has the most iron. *B*, *C*, and *D* are incorrect because all have less iron than choice *A*.

22. **B. *300.***

    B is correct; a calorie increase of 300 is recommended for (1) growth of fetus, placenta, and maternal tissues; (2) sparing of protein for tissue synthesis; and (3) weight gain needed as a buffer against food deprivation (also prevents catabolism of maternal tissues). *A* is incorrect because 200 calories is too small an increase. *C* and *D* are incorrect because each is much too large an increase.

23. **A. *Maintenance of a trim figure to promote good body image.***

    A is the answer; the nurse should not counsel any pregnant woman on maintaining a trim figure during pregnancy; this is an impossibility. The factors in *B* (cultural, economic, and educational background) will affect each teenager differently and must be considered to provide a healthy prenatal course. *C*, growth needs of the mother and the infant, will vary with each mother and should be considered. *D*, dietary habits, will vary and must be considered for each individual.

24. **D. *Egg yolk and deep-yellow or green vegetables.***

    D is correct. In the American diet fat-soluble vitamin A is easily acquired through sources other than whole milk— egg yolk, deep-yellow or green fruits and vegetables, milk products, and liver. *A* and *C* are incorrect because they are not as complete as *D*. *B* is incorrect because wheat germ oil is a source of vitamin B, not vitamin A.

25. **D. *3 cups of vanilla ice cream.***

    D is the answer; substitution of ice cream would add many extra calories and too many carbohydrates, and could leave little appetite for other essential food groups, perhaps leading to poor nourishment. *A*, *B*, and *C* are not the answers because each is acceptable as a milk substitute to meet nutritional requirements.

26. **C. *Is gaining the desired amount of weight.***

    C is correct; Wendy is meeting her nutritional needs if her weight gain is appropriate. *A* is incorrect; if she is at her prepregnant weight, she is not maintaining a nutritional state that is meeting her pregnancy needs or the growth needs of her infant. *B* is incorrect; increasing the amount of meat in her diet may not meet her RDA requirements. *D* is incorrect; she may need nutritional between-meal snacks to meet both her and the baby's needs.

27. **C. Dried apricots, prune juice, chili con carne.**

C is correct because all these foods are high in iron. Egg yolk, liver, and Fe-enriched bread and bread products are also good food sources. Use of iron frying pans and pots adds some iron to one's intake. Steaming vegetables, rather than boiling them, and using all the fluid from cooking conserve the iron content. Spinach, *A*, is not as good a source of iron because its high bulk content decreases absorption. *B* and *D* are incorrect because *C* supplies more iron.

Note: Some people with nutritional iron deficiency anemia have normocytic, normochromic RBCs.

28. **C. Take divided doses after meals, with a glass of fruit juice.**

C is correct because vitamin C seems to enhance iron absorption, and because ingestion after meals seems to lessen GI irritation. Also, since bulk in food decreases absorption, iron medications are taken after the meal. *A* is incorrect because milk and phytic acid (found in some whole-grain cereals like oatmeal) prevent absorption. *B* and *D* are incorrect because of the rationale given for *C*. A normal diet contains about 6 mg of iron per 1000 cal, so 3000 cal (well above the intake of most women) is needed to meet the RDA of 18 mg of iron. Pregnancy increases the demand for iron; therefore, supplementation is still being recommended even though there is some concern about possible effects on embryonic/fetal development.

29. **C. Prepare for childbirth.**

C is correct; preparation for childbirth is the primary purpose of the classes, although this preparation may be instrumental in helping the woman (couple) achieve some success with *A* and *B*. *D* is incorrect because some forms of dystocia are unavoidable. There are no guarantees regarding childbirth or its outcome. Childbirth preparation classes counter ignorance and misconceptions, and offer alternatives. This is ego building for the woman (couple) and increases her (their) ability to solve problems and to cope.

30. **A. Nonpain signals from other parts of the nervous system can greatly alter the degree of transmission of pain signals.**

A is the correct definition of the "gating" mechanism. *B*, *C*, and *D* are incorrect; the specific details of the "gating" mechanism are as yet unknown.

31. **C. Trying to resolve previously repressed conflicts.**

C is correct; previously unresolved (repressed) issues can be revived during pregnancy. During this time, the woman is vulnerable, but she is also open to assistance in resolving unfinished developmental tasks or emotional problems, so that the experience can be one of maturation and growth. The woman may be concerned that her thoughts are bizarre. She can, however, distinguish fantasy from reality, which clearly distinguishes her from the psychotic. Therefore, *A*, *B*, and *D* are incorrect.

32. **A. Puts on a sterile glove and inserts litmus paper into the vagina, placing it near the cervix.**

   A is correct; phenaphthazine (Nitrazine) paper is litmus paper used to determine pH values. Therefore, the paper turns blue-green if the membranes have ruptured. The litmus paper must be placed near the cervix so that the color will change in response to the presence of amniotic fluid and to avoid false readings from urine or mucus. *B*, *C*, and *D* are all incorrect because they do not pertain to testing for amniotic fluid.

33. **A. Fever.**

   A is correct because fever is an indication of a possible complication of PROM—namely, chorioamnionitis. Intrauterine infection can cause intrauterine fetal death or neonatal pneumonia. *B* is incorrect. Vaginal examinations are avoided, if possible, for two reasons: (1) There is an increased risk of infection and (2) touching the cervix may elicit Ferguson's reflex, for example, uterine contractions. *C* is incorrect because coagulopathy (i.e., DIC) is not associated with PROM. *D* is incorrect. Only when the physician is considering effecting birth, perhaps after treatment with betamethasone, is the risk of amniocentesis considered, to estimate fetal lung maturity (L/S ratio).

34. **B. "Would you like to talk about what you mean when you say you are afraid?"**

   B is correct because it encourages the mother-to-be to communicate her feelings and concerns. *A*, *C*, and *D* ignore Wendy's concerns, deny her right to have concerns, and try to offer reassurance for as-yet-unidentified fears—fears that may have nothing to do with the "doctor's examinations."

35. **A. Determine fetal presentation, position, lie, and engagement.**

   A is correct. Abdominal palpation, the four maneuvers of Leopold, provides data regarding fetal presentation, position, lie, and engagement. After determining fetal position, the nurse then also knows approximately where the FHR may be heard the loudest. *B*, *C*, and *D* are incorrect descriptions of Leopold's maneuvers.

36. **A. Abandonment.**

   A is correct; the woman who chooses to return home soon after birth needs to have signed an informed consent and to have been prepared for her physical recovery and care of the neonate through some educational program during her pregnancy. Many hospitals arrange for RNs to make home visits during the early days after birth. A woman in labor must be attended at all times. *B*, *C*, and *D* are incorrect statements of the woman's legal rights.

37. *A. "I'll walk you to the bathroom and stay with you."*

A is correct. Even if the woman has had an unmedicated labor, she is subject to orthostatic hypotension, which can develop during the first 48 hours after birth. The rapid change in intraabdominal pressure at birth results in splanchnic engorgement. The woman must be forewarned about the possibility of light-headedness and should be instructed to sit down immediately anywhere if she feels faint. *B* is incorrect because of the danger of orthostatic hypotension after birth. *C* and *D* are incorrect because orthostatic hypotension poses a safety hazard for the new mother. However, the instructions to wash hands, to wipe from front to back, and to lean forward when voiding are all appropriate after the woman's safety is ensured.

38. *B. Increased circulation of blood and lymph in the mammary glands.*

B is correct because primary breast engorgement represents an increase in the normal venous and lymph system of the breasts. It is not due to an overaccumulation of milk, to increased fluid intake, or to production of more milk with successive pregnancies. Therefore, *A*, *C*, and *D* are incorrect.

39. *D. Preoccupied with her own needs.*

D is correct; the mother generally has a great need to talk about her perceptions of labor and birth. *A* is incorrect because the mother tends to be passive and somewhat dependent after a normal birth. *B* is incorrect because a new mother's hearing is very acute; she thinks everything she hears refers to her. *C* is incorrect because the new mother follows suggestions and is hesitant about making decisions.

40. *B. Firm, below the umbilicus in the midline.*

B is correct because vasoconstriction is causing firmness and descent of the uterus into the pelvis. *A* indicates a possible full bladder, which could eventually affect involution by preventing descent of the uterus into the pelvis. *C*, a slightly boggy fundus two finger-widths above the umbilicus, indicates vasodilation, with the possibility of hemorrhage; it would also mean a full bladder with urinary stasis. *D*, a boggy fundus below the umbilicus in the midline, indicates vasodilation, with the possibility of hemorrhage.

41. *B. Herself and her needs.*

B is correct because the mother needs mothering before she can nurture. *A* is incorrect because in the taking-in phase the mother is concerned about herself first, and her infant only *after* her own needs are met. *C* and *D* occur, not in the taking-in period, but in the taking-hold period.

42. **C. Massaging the perineum promotes absorption of the hematoma.**

    C is the least relevant and therefore the answer of choice. *A*, *B*, and *D* are not the answers because they *are* all good nursing actions to increase the comfort of episiotomy repair.

43. **A. Of the possibility of discomfort and infection in the mother.**

    A is correct. Until small tears are healed, there is the possibility of infection and discomfort. Discomfort may also occur because the vagina is hormone poor at this time. Healing is usually complete by 3 weeks, which corresponds with the cessation of lochial flow. *B* is incorrect; whether this is an unsafe time to become pregnant would depend on the person and the circumstances. *C* is incorrect because if the episiotomy is correctly repaired, tearing will not occur. Some episiotomies or tears are purposely not repaired; intercourse is dependent on the comfort of the couple. *D* is incorrect because intercourse actually aids in involution due to the uterine contractions that occur during intercourse.

44. **C. Abdominal enlargement.**

    C is correct because abdominal enlargement does not generally occur *until the end* of the first trimester; it could also be due to rapid weight gain or "gas." *A*, *B*, and *D* are incorrect because they are all presumptive symptoms of pregnancy; *A* and *D* are *subjective* symptoms, and *B* is an *early* objective sign.

45. **B. Urine test for pregnancy, protein, sugar, estriol levels.**

    B is correct because a urine test for *estriol* levels was often used in the past to assess for fetal placental-maternal well-being, but it is not used currently, and would *not* be indicated at the *first* prenatal visit. *A* and *C* are not the answers because they *are* appropriate tests to perform. *D* is less correct than *B*. If the pregnancy is under 10 weeks, fetal heart rate and fundal height may not be appropriate; however, some women wait much longer than the second missed menstrual cycle before "suspecting" pregnancy.

46. **C. X-ray pelvimetry prior to the onset of labor.**

    C is correct because x-ray pelvimetry is not ordered prior to the onset of labor. *A*, *B*, and *D* are all *appropriate* procedures performed during routine prenatal care.

47. **C. Gravida 2, para 0.**

    C is correct because "Gravida" refers to a pregnancy regardless of its duration. "Para" refers to past pregnancies carried to 20 weeks. Since this is the second pregnancy, the woman is gravida 2. The first pregnancy was approximately 14 weeks' gestation, and therefore was not carried to 20 weeks.. Ms. Primings is classified as gravida 2, para 0. *A*, *B*, and *D* are all incorrect based on the explanation for *C*.

48. ***C. Acts as the fetus's organ of respiration, nutrition, and elimination.***

C is correct because movement of nutrients, gases, and wastes is by diffusion and osmosis. This exchange occurs through the chorionic portion. The hormones secreted include human chorionic gonadotropin (HCG), human chorionic somatomammotropin (HCS), estrogen, and progesterone, which is called pregnanediol during pregnancy. The placenta is a barrier against larger molecules of infectious agents and many drugs, preventing their passage through to the fetus. Generally, maternal and fetal blood do not mix. At term, the placenta weighs about 1 pound (or one-sixth of the newborn's weight) and is 7–8 inches in diameter. The word *placenta* is a Greek word meaning "flat cake." *A* is incorrect because the amniotic fluid acts as the shock absorber. *B* is incorrect because nutrients are not secreted. They are passively received from the mother and actively transported to the fetus. *D* is incorrect because all blood elements are produced within the fetal system.

49. ***A. Coaches her on breathing normally and keeping her hands relaxed.***

A is correct because it is almost impossible to tense the abdominal and perineal muscles if the mouth and hands are relaxed and when one is concentrating on breathing. *B*, *C*, and *D* are incorrect because they contribute to increased tension without reassurance or therapeutic value.

50. ***A. Leg cramps.***

A is correct; increased absorption of phosphorus upsets the calcium-phosphorus ratio. Treatment consists of discouraging ingestion of more than 1 quart of milk and prescribing calcium pills. *B*, *C*, and *D* are unrelated to the calcium-phosphorus ratio.

51. ***B. Umbilical vein.***

B is correct; the umbilical vein conveys oxygenated blood from the placenta to the fetus. The two umbilical arteries, *A*, return depleted blood from the fetus to the placenta for replenishment. Both the left ventricle, *C*, and the arch of the aorta, *D*, contain blood from the umbilical vein, which has been diluted with deoxygenated fetal blood.

52. ***B. Palpitation.***

B is correct; palpitation, a subjective symptom, may occur occasionally during a normal pregnancy; the pulse rate may increase by as much as 10 bpm. *A*, *C*, and *D* are incorrect because physiologic anemia, increased blood pressure, and increase in the anterior-posterior chest diameter (all objective signs) are not changes that the woman will necessarily notice. She may become aware that she needs a larger bra, but probably attributes this to the increased size of the breasts.

53. B. Heartburn.

B is correct because heartburn is caused by the compression and displacement of the stomach upward with the increasing size of the uterus and from progesterone-provoked reverse peristalsis, which results in reflux of stomach contents into the esophagus. It has nothing to do with the heart. *A* is incorrect; morning sickness occurs in about 50% of women and is thought to be caused by both hormonal and psychological influences. Eating small amounts of dry carbohydrate before getting out of bed or during the day may suffice to relieve this distressing symptom. *C* is incorrect; pica is a craving for unusual nonfood substances such as red clay, plaster, or cornstarch. It is sometimes associated with anemia. Pica is a culturally controlled phenomenon. *D* is incorrect; backache is relieved by rest, good posture, sturdy shoes, and pelvic rock exercises.

54. D. Lightening.

D is correct; lightening is the descent or settling of the presenting part into the pelvis, which then results in the pressure symptoms given. Lightening is expected to occur about 2 weeks before labor in the nullipara and to occur at the time of labor in the multipara. *A* is incorrect; transition is the period between 8 and 10 cm. This period is usually described as the most difficult time during labor. The powerful, overwhelming contractions are closer together and longer; the mother may have the urge to push and is instructed not to do so until the cervix is completely (10 cm) dilated. *B* is incorrect; quickening is the feeling of life, a stirring that is felt by the nullipara about the 18th–20th week, but may be felt by the multipara earlier. Some women describe these early movements as similar to the fluttering of butterfly wings. *C* is incorrect; effacement is the process by which the cervix becomes incorporated into the lower uterine segment. Effacement is caused by contractions of the muscle layer, the middle layer of the uterus, and pressure from the amniotic sac and presenting fetal part.

55. C. Introspection.

C is correct because introspection is characteristic of the seventh month of pregnancy for the woman (and for most prospective fathers, also). Introspection allows the prospective parent to reflect on and experiment with different philosophies regarding child rearing, religion, sexuality and sexual expression, and relations with others, including one's parents, spouse, etc. *A* is incorrect because irritability is more characteristic of early pregnancy. *B* is incorrect because anxiety regarding labor is generally not seen at this time; labor is still far in the future. *D* is incorrect because ambivalence is usually more characteristic of early pregnancy.

56. D. The mother's blood volume is increased during pregnancy, so there might normally be a decrease in hematocrit.

D is correct; the nurse must determine if anemia is actually due to low hematocrit or to increased volume of fluid in pregnancy. *A* is incorrect; mothers are *not* supposed to be anemic during pregnancy but may appear anemic as determined by hematocrit, due to hypervolemia. *B* is incorrect; the mother's blood volume is not decreased, but increased, so this is not necessarily a true anemia. *C* is incorrect because the mother's blood volume is not decreased, but increased, during pregnancy.

57. **A. Stools will be loose.**

A is the best answer; the nurse would *not* inform Bertha that her stools will be loose. If Bertha is taking iron, her stools will be hard and constipating. *B*, *C*, and *D* are not the answers because these three statements *are true.* Iron can be irritating to the GI tract, and food will provide a buffer against irritation. Iron will also cause the stools to be black. Fluids and exercise will aid in preventing constipation, which often occurs with iron ingestion.

58. **B. Increase roughage in the diet.**

B is correct because increasing roughage in the diet will help prevent constipation. *A* is incorrect because only a physician can prescribe drugs. *C* is incorrect because milk can cause further constipation. *D* is incorrect because activity will increase circulation throughout the body and will have an effect on the overall muscle tone of the body.

59. **A. Decrease her milk intake to 1 quart a day.**

A is correct because too much milk can produce a calcium-phosphorus imbalance, causing leg cramps. *B* is incorrect because increased milk intake will aggravate the problem. *C*, decreasing ambulation, will increase the pain and decrease circulation. *D*, use of skim milk, will not alleviate the calcium-phosphorus imbalance.

60. **A. Asparagus and kidney beans.**

A is correct because the best sources of folic acid are organ meats (liver, kidney), yeast, and mushrooms; asparagus, broccoli, lima beans, and spinach; and lemons, bananas, strawberries, and cantaloupes. *B*, *C*, and *D* are poorer sources of folacin, with milk lowest in folacin content.

Note: Absorption of folacin is decreased in pregnancy, in women taking the pill, and with alcholism.

61. **C. 25-30 pounds.**

C is the correct gain for a woman of normal weight. *A* and *B* are incorrect because low weight gain tends to be associated with infants who are small for their gestational age. *D* is incorrect; dieting during pregnancy is contraindicated because of the danger of insufficient nutrients to meet the demands of pregnancy and because of the danger of ketoacidosis. Women who are underweight need to gain more than 25-30 pounds.

62. *D. Is experiencing nausea and vomiting.*

    D is correct because nausea and vomiting may prevent adequate intake and therefore predispose the person who is diabetic to ketosis and acidosis. *A* is incorrect because it is a value judgment that may be irrelevant unless the woman perceives this as a problem. *B* is incorrect; as the mother with diabetes becomes older, there is an increased risk of complications. *C*, although significant, is incorrect because fatigue and restlessness during the first trimester are normal.

63. *C. Assess Ms. Osborne's feelings about this pregnancy.*

    C is correct because asking Ms. Osborne about her feelings and needs provides an opportunity for her to be involved in decisions about her life. The nurse functions as a facilitator of decision-making by offering support and guidance. *A*, *B*, and *D* are incorrect because the nurse is making assumptions about Ms. Osborne's needs and feelings. Ms. Osborne needs to be encouraged to participate in decision-making so that she will arrive at a decision that is "right" for her and to increase her own coping ability.

64. *C. Attempt to carry the baby to term to ensure adequate fetal lung maturity.*

    C is correct because mothers with diabetes give birth by *induction or cesarean surgery* when fetal lung maturity has been determined, to prevent fetal death if the diabetic condition is poorly controlled. *A*, *B*, and *D are all appropriate* to tell the mother to expect. The goal of all intervention is to control her diabetes for her own sake and for the well-being of her fetus.

65. *A. Assess the frequency and amount she vomits each day.*

    A is correct because it is essential to determine if any medical or nursing intervention is needed, such as for starvation and dehydration (hyperemesis gravidarum). Usually, no intervention is warranted. Health teaching includes instructing her to avoid an empty stomach; eat small, frequent meals; and eat dry carbohydrate prior to rising. *B* is incorrect. Teaching her active relaxation may be appropriate after validating the frequency, type, and amount of vomitus and assessing her pattern of weight gain. *C* is incorrect because instead of assessing, the nurse merely encourages the woman to share her complaints with the physician. *D* is inappropriate because it does not assist in alleviating her symptoms and anxiety now. This statement may be false reassurance if Ms. Osborne continues to experience nausea and vomiting.

66. *D. Hospitalization may be required to adjust insulin requirements.*

    D is correct because any stress can lead to acidosis, which is hazardous to fetal well-being. Tolbutamide does not protect against acidosis-ketosis. Oral hypoglycemics are generally not used during pregnancy because they may be teratogenic. *A* is incorrect because insulin requirements remain the *same* or *decrease* during the first trimester, increase rapidly during the second and third trimesters, and are variable during the early puerperium. *B* is incorrect because fetal macrosomia is due to excessive growth of all tissues except the brain. Maternal hyperglycemia results in fetal hyperinsulinism and excessive fetal growth. *C* is incorrect because if the intrauterine fetus is not at risk and lung maturity has not been achieved, birth is *not* indicated.

67. *C. Frequent glucose monitoring.*

C is correct because frequent blood sugar monitoring is indicated if glucosuria is found. *A* and *B* are incorrect because alterations in the management of diabetes during pregnancy are accurate only if based on serum values of glucose. *D* is incorrect because creatinine clearance and 24-hour total urine protein level are obtained to assess *renal* status.

68. *C. That the mother may go into ketoacidosis.*

C is correct; ketoacidosis is detrimental to the mother and the infant. *A*, deprivation of nourishment to the infant, might eventually be a concern, but it is not a serious problem at this point unless the mother goes into acidosis due to an inadequate carbohydrate intake. *B* is incorrect because it is merely conjecture at this point, although some research indicates this to be true. *D* is incorrect because it is not the *most* serious concern, although it is an important nursing action.

69. *B. Have irregular menstrual cycles.*

B is correct because menstrual cycle irregularity makes it difficult to estimate the date of birth. *A* is incorrect because it has nothing to do with the date of birth. *C* is not true; mothers who have diabetes are sometimes overweight in pregnancy. (Also, this has nothing to do with date of birth.) *D* is not necessarily true, unless severe atherosclerosis is present; mothers who have diabetes usually give birth to infants weighing more than 9 pounds. Also, this has nothing to do with date of birth.

70. *A. Atherosclerosis of the placenta.*

A is the correct cause of small infants in mothers who are diabetic. *B* is incorrect; increased blood sugar will cause the infant to be large. *C* is incorrect because the size of the mother has no bearing on the size of the infant. *D* is incorrect; hypoglycemia in utero does not necessarily follow; the infant will tend to be large.

71. *C. Inadequate.*

C is correct; her inadequate weight gain puts this pregnancy at risk. An inadequate prenatal weight gain is 0.9 kg (2 pounds) or less per month during the second and third trimesters. *A*, *B*, and *D* are all incorrect because of the rationale given for *C*.

72. **D. Age at 29 years.**

     D is the answer. Her age places her in the low-risk category under usual conditions. *A*, *B*, and *C* are not the answers because all of these statements are *true*. Inadequate weight gain, poor reproductive history with several pregnancies in rapid succession, and a dropping hematocrit indicate inadequate nutrition and depleted maternal stores, both of which are associated with lowered birth weight, intrauterine growth retardation (IUGR), and fetal loss.

73. **A. Discuss with her how nutrition affected her pregnancies in the past, because she wants a good pregnancy now.**

     A is correct. A discussion about how her poor nutrition most likely led to her poor reproductive history indicates to Ms. Garvey that she has been "bad," and leaves her with a sense of lowered self-esteem and perhaps guilt. The negative feelings can alienate her from medical-nursing supervision and counseling. *B*, *C*, and *D* are not the answers because all of these statements *are* helpful. In addition, the nurse needs to identify her learning needs and, ultimately, to evaluate whether Ms. Garvey has actually gained the knowledge she needs.

74. **D. Hematocrit.**

     D is correct because hematocrit levels provide data for nutritional assessment and evaluation of therapy simply and for the least expense. *A*, *B*, and *C* are incorrect because although these values add important data, they are expensive to obtain and require laboratory examination.

75. **A. Vitamin D.**

     A is the best choice because vitamin *D* promotes a positive *calcium* balance during pregnancy. *B*, *C*, and *D* are not the answers because iron, folacin, and vitamin B_6 *are* all *blood-forming* nutrients.

76. **D. Animal proteins such as meat and organs.**

     D is correct; animal proteins such as meat and organs provide protein of high biologic value, as well as iron, folacin and vitamin B_6. *A* is incorrect; although leafy green vegetables are an exchange group containing folacin, meat provides a better supply and balance of all the nutrients needed to form blood. These vegetables do supply iron and magnesium and several vitamins, for example, A, E, B_6, and riboflavin. *B* is incorrect because of the rationale for *D*. Grain products do provide vitamins (niacin, riboflavin, and thiamine) and minerals (iron, phosphorus, and zinc), however. *C* is incorrect; yellow fruits do not have the necessary protein, iron, and B vitamins, but they do provide significant amounts of vitamin A.

77. **C. Hypertension.**

     C is the answer because hypertension *is not a consequence of anemia*. *A*, *B*, and *D* are not good because maternal anemia *can* result in SGA neonates, hemorrhage, and perinatal infection.

78. **B. "It is important to gain weight with good food to feed the baby and fix your anemia first."**

   B is correct because the immediate need is to feed this fetus and to resolve maternal anemia for both the mother and the fetus. A poor reproductive experience now, added to previous ones, further decreases her self-esteem as a woman and her feelings of self-worth. *A* is incorrect; Ms. Garvey needs to take in sufficient calories to prevent ketonemia—a condition incompatible with fetal enzyme function. *C* is incorrect because the first priority is to meet maternal and fetal nutritional needs. The nurse may plan to spend some time later allowing Ms. Garvey to ventilate and to identify her real concerns and probable ways of solving them. Poor nutritional status can result in depression. *D* is incorrect because the nurse is not meeting her role expectations by referring this type of problem to another professional person.

79. **D. The consent form must be written in English, but an interpreter should be used when needed for the person's comprehension.**

   D is correct because the consent form can be written in any language. The important issue is the assurance that the involved person understands it thoroughly. *A*, *B*, and *C* are incorrect because all of these conditions must be met for an informed consent.

80. **B. Battery.**

   B is correct; the person (physician) is liable for battery, unless the consent form provides for reasonable and necessary extensions. *A*, *C*, and *D* are incorrect because they are not the legal actions that can be initiated in this situation.

81. **D. FHR: 154.**

   D is correct because an FHR of 154 is common at this gestational age. The parasympathetic system takes longer to mature—that is, the faster-maturing sympathetic system is not controlled by the heart rate, lowering effects of the parasympathetic system until later in gestational life. *A* is incorrect; by itself, a weight of 169 pounds does not place the pregnancy at risk. However, loss of weight since the onset of pregnancy indicates that she has not taken in the number of calories needed for optimum protein utilization (3000 cal/kg/24 hours). The result is catabolism of fat stores, which in turn produces ketonemia. Fetal enzyme systems cease in an acidotic environment. *B* is incorrect because by mid-pregnancy, the systolic and diastolic values are expected to drop by 10–15 mm Hg. If the diastolic value is over 75 mm Hg during the second trimester, there is a statistically significant rise in fetal mortality. *C* is incorrect. Fundal height at 20 weeks is expected to be between 18 cm and 20 cm.

82. **B. Swollen fingers, increased diastolic blood pressure, 1 + proteinuria.**

   B is correct because swollen fingers, increased diastolic blood pressure, and 1+ proteinuria are all signs of preeclampsia.

A is incorrect because not all the items listed are signs of preeclampsia; the blood pressure should be elevated, rather than decreased. *C* is incorrect because sugar in the urine is not indicative of preeclampsia. *D* is incorrect because not all signs listed are indicative of preeclampsia.

83.   A. *Place in a room with mothers to keep her company.*

A is the best answer because the nurse should *not* take this action. The mother needs quiet, decreased stimulation, and privacy. *B*, *C*, and *D* are not the answers to the question because they *are* good nursing measures.

84.   A. *Suction apparatus.*

A is correct because suction may be needed to maintain a clear airway if the woman convulses. Other essential equipment includes oxygen, tubing, and mask; intravenous fluids and infusion sets readied for use; emergency delivery pack; plastic airway; drugs such as magnesium sulfate, phenobarbital, calcium gluconate, morphine, and antihypertensives; a reflex hammer; indwelling catheter and collection bag; ophthalmoscope and an electronic FHR monitor. *B* and *C* are incorrect because sudden noise may precipitate a convulsion. *D* is incorrect because this test is unrelated. However, the amount of urine she produces is crucial. An increased urinary output is indicative of decreasing severity of the disease. Urine must be checked for protein.

85.   B. *Decreasing urinary output.*

B is correct because magnesium sulfate is eliminated through the kidneys; if it is not eliminated, it may increase CNS problems and cause respiratory depression. *A*, *C*, and *D* are incorrect because these signs would indicate that the drug should be continued; the drug is intended to decrease these signs.

86.   A. *Calcium gluconate.*

A is the correct antidote for magnesium sulfate. *B* is an antidote for meperidine (Demerol) or morphine. *C* is an electrolyte, not an antidote for magnesium sulfate. *D* is a drug that can be used to stop labor contractions.

87.   B. *24-26.*

B is correct. *A* is too slow a rate and would not correct the problem. *C* and *D* are too fast; these rates will give too much and could cause too severe depressive effects.

88.   D. *Her systolic pressure has increased by 30 mm Hg; the diastolic, by 15 mm Hg.*

D is correct because the significance of the blood pressure can be determined only by assessing any reading in relation to previous readings and to other findings. *A* is incorrect; a rapid weight gain can be caused by overeating. *B* is incorrect because although hydatidiform mole does present with signs of preeclampsia, these and other signs generally appear by weeks 12-14. Preeclamptic changes in blood pressure are still assessed on the basis of *D*. The signs of true preeclampsia of pregnancy appear after week 24. *C* is incorrect because ankle swelling, without pretibial pitting, may occur during hot weather or in the woman who is on her feet for many hours each day.

89. **C. Phlebitis.**

   C is correct because pain in the calf can reflect phlebitis. *A*, *B*, and *D* are incorrect because pain in the calf does not necessarily reflect infection, edema, or hemorrhage.

90. **B. Preeclampsia.**

   B is correct; methylergonovine maleate (which increases the blood pressure) is not given to a woman with a history of preeclampsia because one indication of preeclampsia is high blood pressure. Administration of the drug could obscure the symptoms of preeclampsia. *A*, *C*, and *D* are incorrect because none of these conditions involves high blood pressure.

91. **A. Mother-infant bonding.**

   A is correct; it is important to foster a strong mother-child relationship to prevent or at least minimize problems as the child gets older. *B*, breastfeeding to prevent engorgement, is important, but secondary to *A*; also, not all mothers breastfeed. *C* is important; however, not all mothers breastfeed and oxytocin can be given orally. *D* is incorrect because the mother cannot be active in the early phase of recovery due to her physical condition.

92. **D. Medication should be given at such a time that it will not be in the breast milk when nursing.**

   D is the correct choice. *A* is incorrect because it is not an accurate statement. *B* is incorrect because medication can be given to mothers who are nursing, but not at times that would coincide with the medication being in the breast milk at the time of feeding. *C* is incorrect because giving medication an hour before breastfeeding could cause CNS depression in the newborn.

93. **B. The mother to try various breastfeeding positions to find the one that is most comfortable for her.**

   B is correct; a mother who has a cesarean birth can breastfeed with comfort if given assistance. The "football hold" is used by many mothers. *A* is incorrect because it would lead to the mother's milk supply drying up. *C* is not the best answer, because the infant is deprived of bonding. *D* is incorrect because the healing process is enhanced by breastfeeding due to oxytocin stimulation to the uterus.

94. **C. "You are upset because you did not have a vaginal birth. It must have been hard for you to accept."**

   C is the correct answer because it gives the mother an opportunity to respond. *A* is incorrect; it is the nurse's responsibility to provide an opportunity for the mother to ventilate her feelings and not put the mother's statement off for the doctor to answer. *B* is incorrect because the nurse is inferring that the mother feels guilty. In *D*, also incorrect, the nurse is again not giving the mother an opportunity to vent her feelings, but rather is hoping another mother will give assistance.

95. **A. "I'm so tired; the baby breastfeeds every hour."**

A is correct; this comment indicates that the mother is not getting enough rest, and that the baby is feeding too often and may not be getting enough milk at each feeding. *B, C*, and *D* are not correct; these comments indicate that the nurse's discharge planning *was* effective. *B* is a good way for the mother to recover from surgery. *C* indicates that the mother is rested and happy in her postpartum period. *D* indicates normal status for lochia at this time.

96. **A. He understands that no change in testosterone levels will result.**

A is correct; Mr. Garvey should have no change in levels of testosterone, follicle-stimulating hormone, or luteinizing hormone after vasectomy. *B* is incorrect; reinstating *tubal patency* through a reanastomosis is successful in many men who have a vasectomy, but if he develops autoimmunity to his own sperm, he would still remain sterile. *C* is incorrect because both conditions are unrelated to vasectomy. Balanitis is an inflammation or infection of the glans penis. Phimosis is a narrowed foreskin or prepuce, a condition that prevents its easy movement over the glans. Vasectomy is performed through a small incision in each scrotal sac. *D* is incorrect. Following vasectomy, the man is cautioned that because of the sperm already in the upper part of the sperm duct, he is not considered sterile until after 10 ejaculations or after 3-6 months.

97. **C. Formation of the corpus luteum.**

C is the answer because progesterone is produced by the corpus luteum. Stimulus for the formation of the corpus luteum comes from the anterior pituitary and is known as the luteinizing hormone. *A, B*, and *D* are physiologic effects of progesterone.

98. **C. Inhibition of uterine contractility during pregnancy.**

C is correct because uterine contractility is inhibited by *progesterone* during pregnancy. *A* is incorrect because estrogen begins the process of developing the spiral arteries in the innermost lining of the uterus, the endometrium; progesterone assists estrogen in this function during the second half of the cycle. *B* and *D* are incorrect because they are physiologic effects of estrogen.

99. **A. Estrogen and luteinizing hormone (LH).**

A is correct; after ovulation, luteinizing hormone is responsible for the development of the corpus luteum from the now-empty graafian follicle. The corpus luteum continues to produce progesterone until about the end of the third month, when the placenta takes over this function. *B* is incorrect because the follicle-stimulating hormone (FSH) is produced by the anterior pituitary in response to a low circulating level of estrogen and progesterone toward the end of a cycle if conception has not occurred. Its target organ is the ovary, where it stimulates the maturation of the graafian follicle in which an egg is beginning to be prepared for ovulation. *C* is incorrect because progesterone is the main hormone during the last half of the cycle, known as the secretory phase, when the endometrium is readied for implantation if an egg is fertilized. *D* is incorrect because human chorionic gonadotropin (HCG) is produced as soon as nidation (also called implantation) occurs; chorionic villi continue to produce this throughout the pregnancy. This hormone stimulates the production of pituitary growth hormone. The presence of HCG in the mother's urine from the third week after conception is the basis for pregnancy tests.

100. C. Further physiologic assessment.

C is correct; a complete physical assessment of both the man and the woman needs to be performed to rule out any physiologic abnormalities that may prevent conception. *A* and *B* are incorrect because they are not the *primary* tests required. Both may need to be performed after completing the physical exams to ensure physical capability. *D* is less correct than *C*. Many clinics will perform preliminary health teaching in the area of conception during the initial screening process; psychotherapy may be appropriate if the couple perceives this as a need and the health team identifies this as an appropriate health action.

101. B. Ms. Jackson's history of taking oral contraceptives.

B is of primary importance because many couples experience some degree of difficulty conceiving for several months when the wife has taken oral contraceptives. With a little more time for hormonal readjustment, this couple may find that they will have little difficulty conceiving. *A* is insignificant because the couple are at the optimum fertility age. The fact that Ms. Jackson started taking oral contraceptives about 7 years ago is more significant. *C* probably has little to do with the possibility of Ms. Jackson's being sterile or infertile. *D*, the fact that Ms. Jackson's mother died during childbirth, is significant, but not the *most* significant factor at this time. A family history of problems with pregnancy may be of more significance if Ms. Jackson is unable to conceive within another year, provided that her husband's sperm analysis is within normal limits. In assessing the reason for death, it appears that Ms. Jackson's mother died due to preeclampsia. The cause of death would be highly relevant if Ms. Jackson becomes pregnant.

102. A. *Sperm analysis.*

A is correct because it is generally a less complicated procedure and less expensive than testing the woman. *B* and *C* are incorrect because these tests are more expensive and time-consuming. Also, these tests may not be necessary if the sperm count is found to be too low for conception or the percentage of abnormal sperm is not within normal limits and the woman is experiencing no other problems. *D* is incorrect because although not expensive, this test is usually performed by the client over several months. Basal body temperature monitoring can be a very frustrating procedure and can be highly inaccurate.

103. C. *"There is no indication at this point that you are sterile."*

C is the correct response; more data need to be collected and analyzed before Ms. Jackson is told (by the physician) that she may be infertile or sterile. *A* is untrue; there are no definitive studies to support this assumption. There is, however, a small chance that permanent suppression of the anterior pituitary may occur. *B* is incorrect because there are no data to support this statement. *D* is incorrect because there are no concise statistical data to support what percentage of women taking oral contraceptives may have miscarriages, have problems becoming pregnant, or become infertile.

104. B. *His inability to father children.*

B is correct; many men fear being a failure as a man if they are unable to produce offspring. This is probably why Mr. Jackson wanted to see the nurse confidentially. *A* is probably a concern, but is secondary to his self-image and perception of his role as a man. C may be a problem if the couple is experiencing frustration. However, some of the frustration may be enhanced by Mr. Jackson's feelings regarding his own self-esteem and "manly" image. *D* is important but secondary to the man's feelings of uncertainty about himself. In fact, the man will probably blame the woman for the couple's inability to conceive if he is unable to face the possibility of his own deficits.

105. B. *"Do you experience orgasm each time you have intercourse?"*

B is correct because this question is *irrelevant*. Orgasm in women is unnecessary for fertilization; male ejaculation is essential. *A* is incorrect because both frequency and timing of intercourse affect fertility. Intercourse with ejaculation must occur during the 12-24 hours after ovulation. *C* is incorrect; the husband's occupation is relevant. The man's sperm count decreases if he wears tight-fitting or thermal clothing or if he sits for long hours, such as while driving a truck long distances. Excessive heat to the testicles is the etiologic factor. *D* is incorrect. Pelvic inflammatory disease (PID) due to gonorrhea (or any other cause) heals by scar tissue formation. Scar tissue may obliterate or distort the fallopian tubes, thus preventing the passage of sex cells (ova and sperm) and fertilization.

106. D. Gonorrhea treated 2 years ago.

D is correct because if the upper reproductive tract (i.e., the uterus, tubes, and ovaries) is infected, scar tissue forms as the inflammation subsides. Scar tissue in the fallopian tubes prevents normal passage of sperm, ova, or a fertilized egg. *A* is incorrect; a 28–30-day menstrual cycle is normal and unless the cycles are anovulatory, the time of her ovulation or her period of fertility is easily determined. *B* is incorrect; the appearance of pubic hair and breast development are pubescent changes that appeared at the expected time, that is, between the ages of 11 and 14 years. *C* is incorrect; epidemic parotitis, or mumps, in *men*, especially during adolescence, leads to sterility if both testes are affected. There is no analogous occurrence in women.

107. B. Abdominal scars noted in the right lower quadrant.

B is correct because the presence of abdominal scars indicates a possibility of scar formation or adhesions, which may interfere with reproductive capacity. *A* is incorrect because an anteverted uterus is a normal finding. *C* is incorrect because clitoral size of 0.5 cm is within normal limits. *D* is incorrect because the hair pattern described is within normal limits for the woman of childbearing age.

108. C. "Your angry feelings are understandable and an expected response."

C is correct because it is the only response that acknowledges this couple's feelings and their right to have these feelings. *A*, *B*, and *D* are not therapeutic.

109. D. Assess her readiness to touch her external genitalia and her cervix.

D is correct because until Joan is able to come to terms with her feelings about touching herself, she will be unable to hear how to obtain and assess a specimen of cervical mucus. *A*, *B*, and *C* would all be appropriate nursing actions *after* the nurse has determined whether Joan is able to obtain a specimen.

110. B. Ejaculate directly into a clean specimen jar.

B is the correct way to collect semen for analysis. The man ejaculates directly into a specimen jar, seals it, and takes it to the laboratory without either chilling it or warming it. *A* is incorrect because the residual rubber solvents and sulfur in condoms adversely affect sperm; however, there is a condom made especially for collecting semen for analysis. C is incorrect because the total volume of semen and number of sperm could not be retrieved from the cotton balls. *D* is incorrect; although retrieval of sperm from the vaginal vault with a special spoon (Doyle) is acceptable, the semen is to be neither chilled nor warmed.

111. B. Sims-Huhner test.

B is correct. The Sims-Huhner test is a postcoital test to determine sperm movement and survival in the vaginal environment. *A* is incorrect; to prepare for a semen analysis, a specimen must be obtained from the man either by masturbation or by coitus (with special precautions) and examined for volume, pH, sperm density and motility, and percentage of sperm with normal morphology. *C* is incorrect; a scraping of the buccal mucosal cells is examined for chromosomal aberrations that cause infertility (e.g., Klinefelter's syndrome). *D* is incorrect; a Rubin's test is performed to ascertain tubal patency. With the woman in the lithotomy position, carbon dioxide gas is administered under pressure through the cervix. The woman prepares for this test by voiding.

112. A. December 25.

A is the correct calculation. Naegele's rule states, "From the last menstrual period, count back 3 months, then add 7 days." *B* is incorrect; if you calculated December 11, you have subtracted 7 days instead of adding them. *C* and *D* are incorrect; if you calculated January 22 or 18, you assumed that the spotting Joan experienced was a menstrual period. It is not uncommon for the expectant mother to have some small amount of *spotting* during the time she would have experienced menstruation if she had not conceived.

113. A. Threatened abortion.

A is correct; with threatened abortion, some vaginal bleeding and cramping are noted but no cervical dilation is seen. Treatment would probably be bedrest and the avoidance of orgasm, sexual intercourse, and vaginal examinations. *B* is incorrect because with inevitable abortion, considerable bleeding and cramping are noted. The cervix is dilating and the membranes may have ruptured. *C* is incorrect because the symptoms of a tubal pregnancy usually occur after the first missed period. Rupture of the tube usually results in a sudden, sharp pain in the lower abdominal quadrant, with symptoms of acute shock out of proportion to the amount of vaginal bleeding observed. *D* is incorrect; incompetent cervical os is the most common cause of second-trimester abortion. Treatment consists of the application of a purse-string suture, using the technique of Shirodkar or McDonald, applied prior to cervical dilation. This is intended to prevent premature delivery, which would probably occur in the sixth month, when the fetus weighs between 1¼ and 1½ pounds. An incompetent cervix tends to occur more frequently when the cervix has been forcibly dilated in the past, such as for elective abortion.

114. A. "Was the vaginal bleeding accompanied by pain?"

A is correct. The bleeding of placenta previa is usually painless; premature separation of the placenta is usually accompanied by pain. The answer to this question adds to the database. *B* is incorrect; although coitus may result in a few drops of dark blood because of increased cervical friability, frank bleeding is uncommon. Also, this question sounds intimidating and accusatory. *C* is incorrect because it is not as appropriate a question as *A*. Episodes of spotting (a few drops of dark bleeding) may have occurred during the pregnancy, but it is unlikely that a frank hemorrhage had occurred previously. It is most important to determine the presence or absence of pain. *D* is incorrect because the question does not address the most commonly seen causes of hemorrhage during late pregnancy—placenta previa and premature separation of the placenta.

115. *C. Assess amount of bleeding presently on the perineal pad.*

C is the nurse's first action. With severe hemorrhage, oxygen is delivered by face mask at 10–12 L/min, and the woman is prepared quickly for examination under double setup. Blood work is needed stat. An intravenous infusion is begun, to facilitate stabilization of fluid and hematologic status. The woman is prepared for a possible emergency cesarean birth. *A* is incorrect because time should not be wasted in trying to find the FHR if hemorrhage is brisk. Both mother and fetus are best served by the rationale for *C*. As soon as possible, institute electronic fetal monitoring. *B* is incorrect because tone of uterine muscle is irrelevant if bleeding is brisk. (See rationale for *C*.) If hemorrhage has stopped or is minimal, the FHR is obtained first, then uterine tone is assessed. Increased uterine tone or rigidity is indicative of premature separation of the placenta (abruptio placentae); a uterus that relaxes well is found with placenta previa. *D* is incorrect because the history and physical examination are the last on this priority list.

116. *B. "Ms. Singh-Kaur has had vaginal bleeding. Vaginal examinations are contraindicated."*

B is correct; that vaginal examination, except under double setup, is contraindicated is expected knowledge of the "reasonably prudent" nurse. To allow the intern to proceed could result in a massive hemorrhage for Ms. Singh-Kaur and a lawsuit against the nurse. *A* and *C* are incorrect because they do not communicate clearly the rationale for *B*. Answer *D* is incorrect because it implies the nurse lacks knowledge of Ms. Singh-Kaur 's condition.

117. *C. In the operating room.*

C is correct. Double setup refers to a sterile vaginal examination in an operating room. Staff and equipment are ready for either a vaginal or an abdominal birth if profound hemorrhage occurs. *A*, *B*, and *D* are incorrect because double setup refers to readiness for immediate birth should profound hemorrhage occur.

118. *A. Continues to monitor maternal and fetal status with no change in care plan.*

A is correct; FHR tracings indicate adequate fetal oxygenation, so no change in the care plan is indicated. *B* is incorrect because the maternal-placental-fetal unit is adequately oxygenated at the moment. *C* is incorrect because no crisis exists at the moment. *D* is incorrect because no one can predict accurately the outcome of a "normal" labor, let alone the outcome of a possibly compromised pregnancy.

119. **B. The nurse accepted total responsibility/accountability for recognizing ominous FHR patterns.**

     B is correct. Nurses who perform in highly specialized areas of care are expected to perform as a nurse who is comparably trained and reasonably prudent would perform in that area, and the nurse must take appropriate action to prevent harm to the infant. *A* and *C* are incorrect because the nurse is responsible for recognizing an ominous FHR pattern and taking appropriate action. *D* is incorrect because a late deceleration pattern is associated with fetal jeopardy, which requires medical-nursing intervention.

120. **D. Mr. Kaur's concern is increased because he does not understand isoimmunization—its cause or diagnosis.**

     D is correct. An appropriately stated nursing problem has three components: the person involved, the condition or problem that is increased or decreased, and an intervention that can be initiated by a nurse without a physician's order. *A*, *B*, and *C* are incorrect because they lack the three components of a nursing problem.

121. **C. Prepare her for L/S ratio determination.**

     C is correct. Amniocentesis for an L/S ratio for this 36-37-week pregnancy is not warranted. Even if the ratio is below 2:1, the fetus would be delivered if hemorrhage were to occur. *A*, *B*, and *D* are incorrect because anyone on bedrest is prone to respiratory, cardiovascular, and GI problems associated with immobility. Coughing and deep breathing, *A*, are interventions to prevent hypostatic pneumonia; *B*, wiggling toes, prevents thrombus formation; and *D*, diet with roughage and fluids, prevents constipation and stimulates appetite.

122. **D. Examination of diapers for pinkish staining.**

     D is the answer because pinkish staining is due to the presence of urates, a common variation in normal newborn characteristics. *A* is not the answer because an increased incidence of RDS *is* associated with maternal diabetic condition regardless of gestational age. *B* is not the answer because hypoglycemia *is* an expected response. During fetal life, persistent maternal hyperglycemia results in fetal hyperinsulinism. At birth, the maternal supply of glucose stops abruptly and hypoglycemia occurs. *C* is not the answer because hyperbilirubinemia *is* associated with maternal diabetes. The cause is not fully understood.

123. **D. Begins resuscitative actions immediately.**

     D is correct. This neonate is severely depressed and requires immediate resuscitation. In addition, he is suffering from asphyxia neonatorum, which is defined as the absence of respiratory effort for 30-60 seconds after birth. Asphyxia neonatorum may be due to anoxia from prolapsed cord or placenta previa or abruptio placentae; from cerebral injury, such as intracranial hemorrhage; or from narcosis from the analgesics or anesthetics given to the mother. If respiratory depression is due to narcotics, nalorphine (Nalline), levallorphan tartrate (Lorfan), or naloxone (Narcan) may be administered. As resuscitation procedures are being done, the neonate must be kept warm or the rapidly developing acidosis will be increased because of the effects of chilling. If the infant is born with thick meconium and no respiratory effort, an endotracheal tube may need to be inserted to suction out the tenacious meconium and other debris from the upper respiratory tract prior to the administration of oxygen. *A* and *B* are incorrect because the infant is severely depressed and requires immediate intervention. *C* is incorrect because the infant is severely depressed and requires active resuscitation, starting with tracheal suctioning.

124. *D. Location of decidua basalis.*

D is correct. Because the placenta has been implanted in the lower uterine segment, there is a greater possibility of hemorrhage. The "living ligature" uterine muscles are located mostly in the body (corpus) of the uterus. The muscle fibers in the lower uterine segment do not contract as strongly. Hemorrhage may occur even when the fundus feels firmly contracted. *A* is incorrect; Ms. Singh-Kaur has just as great a chance of uterine atony followed by hemorrhage as any other new mother, especially those mothers who had spinal anesthesia for delivery. *B* is incorrect; the possibility of retained placental fragments is almost nonexistent when birth is by cesarean surgery. *C* is incorrect; pelvic hematoma may occur in any new mother, especially when birth is surgical or if a vaginal birth was very difficult.

125. *B. Methylergonovine maleate.*

B is correct. Methylergonovine maleate (Methergine) produces progressive contractions of uterine muscle. This derivative of ergonovine stimulates stronger and lengthier contractions and has less tendency to raise the blood pressure. However, do not give to the woman if she is hypertensive. Notify the physician if she needs an alternative oxytocic. *A* is incorrect; metronidazole (Flagyl), is specific for the treatment of *Trichomonas vaginalis*. *C* is incorrect; estradiol valerate is an estrogen-androgen combination that exerts an antilactogenic effect. There is only a negligible incidence of engorgement if this drug is injected just before or just as the placenta separates, before the release of lactogenic hormone from the posterior pituitary. It is contraindicated in women with thrombophlebitis, epilepsy, migraines, cardiac or renal disease, and asthma. Because exogenous estrogen has been implicated in endometrial carcinoma, the woman signs an informed consent prior to receiving it. *D* is incorrect.

Naloxone (Narcan) is a narcotic antagonist that can be given to the mother along with the narcotic during labor without affecting pain relief; or it may be given to an infant whose respiratory depression is due to narcotics. Nalorphine and levallorphan titrate (Lorfan) are not the narcotic antagonists of choice because if the neonate's depression is not due to narcosis, the neonate will become more depressed. Naloxone is a narcotic antagonist that if given to a neonate whose depression is not due to narcosis, does not deepen the depression.

126. B. Empty the breasts every 3–4 hours.

B is correct. The empty breast is the appropriate stimulus to establish and maintain lactation. *A* is incorrect; additional added fluids and calories and good general nutrition do facilitate lactation, but emptying the breast is the specific stimulus needed. **C** is incorrect. On rare occasions, a woman does not lactate spontaneously; for the woman who is affected, one injection of oxytocin may be needed to initiate lactation and to stim-ulate the let-down reflex. *D* is incorrect; estradiol valerate (Delestrogen) is a depoestrogen, which is an antilactogenic drug.

127. B. Destroys fetal Rh-positive RBCs in the maternal blood system.

B is correct. Rho (D) immune globulin promotes lysis of fetal Rh-positive RBCs circulating in the maternal bloodstream before the mother can produce antibodies. RhoGAM is administered, within 72 hours of birth, to the woman who is Rh-negative who gives birth to a fetus who is Rh-positive if she is Coombs negative, that is, does not have antibodies against the Rh factor. *A*, **C**, and *D* are incorrect. Rho (D) immune globulin provides passive immunity by acting like antibodies. Following any future pregnancy, whether it terminates in abortion or the birth at term of an infant who is Rh-positive, Ms. Singh-Kaur will receive another injection of Rho (D) immune globulin.

128. C. Lack of surfactant and immaturity of retinal and other blood vessels.

C is correct. Lack of surfactant predisposes the infant born at 37 weeks or less to respiratory distress syndrome (hyaline membrane disease). Immature retinal blood vessels in the presence of high arterial oxygen tension may result in visual impairment due to retrolental fibroplasia. Immature vessels elsewhere may rupture and cause thrombosis and hemor-rhage. *A* is incorrect because none of these factors is related to the incidence of prematurity. Related factors include: maternal age 17 years or less, multiple gestation, high parity, poor nutrition, severe physical or emotional stress, premature rupture of membranes due to infections such as beta strep or gonorrhea, incompetent cervical os, fetal congenital anomalies, preeclampsia, and diabetes. *B* is incorrect because infants who are premature tend to be anemic due primarily to fragile capillary walls and hemorrhage and to poorly developed ability to form new erythrocytes. The premature kidneys do not conserve water well. Water retention and edema may occur. The infant who is premature does not absorb nutrients from the intestine efficiently. *D* is incorrect because children who are ill or premature at birth and require early and prolonged separation from the parents are more often victims of child abuse and neglect. Early and consistent contact to facilitate bonding, involvement in the care of the infant, and assistance with finances are necessary to prevent this unhealthy result.

129. A. Denial and shock.

A is correct; denial and shock are often the *first* responses to loss. *B*, *C*, and *D* are often the next steps in the grieving process, in that order. The nurse's role is to evaluate the grieving process so that the involved people can move toward resolving the loss. The acute phase lasts about 6 weeks; the total process, about 1 year. Parents need to be reassured that what they are or will be experiencing is symptomatic of this process.

130. D. "This must be a very difficult and sad time for you."

D is correct. The nurse is serving as a role-model in facing grief, open communication, and feeling safe and comfortable in dealing with unpleasant situations. *This* baby is important now—the woman does not want or need to focus on other children. Occasionally a mother must withdraw, as if to take the experience a small piece at a time. *A*, *B*, and *C* are incorrect because of the rationale given for *D*.

131. A. Cause hemorrhage from a low-lying placenta.

A is the correct reason why vaginal examinations are contraindicated when bleeding is present in the last trimester. *B* is untrue; vaginal examinations are not more painful, and an exam does not stimulate labor. *C* is incorrect; an examination using sterile techniques does not cause infection and is not contraindicated. *D* is not true; correctly administered vaginal examinations do not rupture membranes.

132. C. Painful bleeding.

C is correct; painful bleeding—and particularly, the element of abdominal pain—is a major sign of abruptio placentae. *A*, *B*, and *D* are incorrect because they are not specific to this condition. *A* is a symptom of previa. *B* could be a sign of *any* hemorrhage, vena cava syndrome, or bacteremic shock. *D* could be a sign of various conditions.

133. B. A hard, tender, boardlike uterus.

B is the correct answer because the uterus reacts to placental abruption with a sustained tetanic contraction. *A* is incorrect because it is not related to abruption. *C* could be present in other conditions; one would not necessarily find this with abruptio placentae. Also, abruptio tends to lower blood pressure. *D*, mild contractions, is highly unlikely; the woman would have severe pain.

134. D. Coagulopathy.

D is the correct answer because clotting factors, especially platelets, are used up and disseminated intravascular coagulation (DIC) can occur. *A* is not a complication, but a sign, of abruptio placentae; thus, it is incorrect. *B* is incorrect because decreased urinary output might be a compensatory mechanism in early shock. *C* is incorrect because hypertension is one *etiologic* factor for abruption, *not a result* of abruption.

135. C. Side-lying.

C is correct because this position prevents pressure on the vena cava, which contributes to a diminished blood supply to the heart, thereby decreasing cardiac output and causing hypotension and decreased perfusion of the uterus and fetus. *A* is incorrect because it could increase discomfort and pain. *B* is incorrect because lying on one's stomach is highly uncomfortable during the 30th week of pregnancy and could depress the vena cava, thereby contributing to shock. *D* is incorrect because it is uncomfortable, may cause difficulties in breathing, and could result in the vena caval syndrome described in the rationale for *C*.

136. B. Check the FHR.

B is the correct choice at this time. *A*, *C*, and *D* are incorrect because Allene is still early enough in labor that these actions are not indicated.

137. B. Fetal respiratory movements.

B is best because although the fetus does inhale and exhale amniotic fluid within the upper respiratory tree and even makes crying motions, no sound is heard since there is no air available to force through the larynx. *A*, *C*, and *D* are not the answers because these sounds can be heard. Both the funic and the uterine souffle may be heard. The funic souffle is identical to the FHR and represents the sound of blood rushing through the umbilical vessels. The uterine souffle is identical to the mother's heart rate and represents her pumping blood to the placenta. To differentiate between the two, listen to the fetal heart tones and palpate the maternal pulse simultaneously. This is especially important if the FHR has decelerated to about the level of the maternal pulse, or vice versa. Maternal intestinal noises can also be heard.

138. A. Leopold.

A is correct; Leopold's maneuver refers to the palpation of the uterine contents through the abdominal wall to assess fetal presentation, position, lie, and ballottement. *B* is incorrect; the Scanzoni maneuver involves the rotation of the fetal head to the occiput anterior position with forceps such as Luikart's. *C* is incorrect; during normal spontaneous vertex birth, the Ritgen maneuver is used to control the birth of the infant's head between contractions. Pressure is applied to the infant's chin through the mother's perineum with one hand while applying pressure to the occiput or crown with the other. *D* is incorrect; Shirodkar refers to the application of a purse-string suture around the internal cervical os to support an incompetent cervix until the time of birth.

139. C. Somewhat heart shaped, widest from side to side.

C is correct; the fetal head enters the true pelvis in the transverse position. The configuration of the mid-pelvis and pelvic outlet direct the internal rotation of the presenting part during descent. *A* describes the anthropoid pelvis. *B*, a transverse oval, describes the platypelloid pelvis. *D* describes the mixed pelvis (i.e., gynecoid-android).

140. A. Ischial spines.

A is correct; the ischial spines serve as a landmark. *B*, *C*, and *D* are incorrect. The tuberosities and symphysis pubis form part of the outlet of the pelvis and the sacral promontory cannot be felt during vaginal examination in the normal gynecoid pelvis.

141. B. Shallow chest.

B is correct; the Lamaze method suggests this breathing pattern during early labor. *A*, *C*, and *D* do not facilitate optimal relaxation and comfort, the goal for early labor.

142. D. Rupturing the membranes.

D is best because this is the *physician's* responsibility. *A*, *B*, and *C* are all appropriate *nursing* actions based on the nurse's responsibility and obligations.

143. C. "Reassure your wife."

C is correct because this is the most important function of the husband throughout labor and birth. *A* is an evasive and ineffective response and does not allow the husband to feel needed. *B* is incorrect because this is the nurse's responsibility, and the nurse should be readily available to the woman in labor. *D* is incorrect because it is a nursing function that should not be delegated to the husband. However, if the husband is interested, he can be informed about how the monitor works. In childbirth classes, both parents are taught the monitor's purpose during childbirth. The nurse in the labor room needs to assess and reinforce this information.

144. A. More irritable and complain of nausea.

A is correct; during the transitional phase (8–10-cm dilation), most women begin feeling as if they cannot make it; become more irritable; experience nausea, vomiting, and belching; and begin to perspire more over their upper lip and between their breasts. *B* and *D* are incorrect because they are seen during the active phase (4–8 cm). *C* is incorrect because it is seen during the latent and early phases (0–4 cm).

145. A. Phenaphthazine (Nitrazine).

A is correct; phenaphthazine (Nitrazine) paper is litmus paper used to determine pH values. Vaginal secretions are acidic and amniotic fluid is basic; therefore the paper turns a blue-green to deep blue. To do the test, the nurse puts on a sterile glove and inserts the paper into the vagina near the cervix. *B* is incorrect because the Guthrie method tests for the phenylalanine concentration in blood drawn from a heelstick. It is usually done on the third or fourth day (after the child has ingested some milk), and should be repeated in 4 weeks' time. *C* is incorrect because Gravindex is a simple slide test for pregnancy whereby a drop of urine is placed on a slide and mixed with antiserum for 30 seconds. More antiserum is added and the slide is rocked gently for 2 minutes. If no agglutination occurs, the test is positive for pregnancy; it is accurate 90% of the time. *D* is incorrect because the Pap smear is the examination of cells from the squamocolumnar junction of the cervix to identify cytologic changes that may be indicative of malignancy.

146. D. Does nothing; there is no clinical significance to this pattern.

D is correct because this pattern represents early deceleration caused by head compression. In general, perfusion of the placenta and fetus and normotension are enhanced by the side-lying (or semi-Fowler's) position during labor. *A*, *B*, and *C* are not relevant for this FHR pattern.

147. B. Nausea, shaking legs, increased irritability.

B is correct; these are a few of the symptoms of second stage, when the cervix is drawn up to become part of the lower uterine segment. Other symptoms may include feelings that she cannot go on, perspiration, belching, and the urge to defecate. *A* is incorrect because elevation of temperature and pulse are indicative of increasing exhaustion due to prolonged labor and to a lack of fluid intake, as well as of infection. *C* is incorrect because malar flush, increasing introspection, and seriousness are characteristics of about 5-cm dilation. *D* is incorrect because tingling or numbness of the fingers and/or toes and carpopedal spasms are indicative of a decreased Pco_2 due to hyperventilation. Treatment is to change the breathing pattern through coaching and role modeling, and to ask her to breathe into a paper bag.

148. B. Check to see if the cervix is dilated 10 cm.

B is correct because the symptoms described are signs of complete dilation and Allene will need to be coached for pushing. *A*, *C*, and *D* are incorrect since the signs herald the beginning of the second stage of labor and are not pathologic.

149. C. Anxious about his wife and baby's condition.

C is correct; Mr. Toth is concerned about his wife and infant's condition. *A* is incorrect; although this may be an underlying factor, he is *primarily* concerned about his wife and the baby's condition. *B* may be a contributing factor, but he has not questioned the staff's level of competency. He is concerned about the baby and his wife's condition and treatment of those conditions. *D* is incorrect because there is nothing to indicate that he cannot be with his wife. In fact, he may be able to provide support for her and help lower her anxiety level.

150. *C. Painless vaginal bleeding.*

C is correct because it is one of the primary symptoms of placenta previa. *A* and *B* are incorrect because there are usually no contractions and the bleeding is usually painless. *D* is incorrect because it is a symptom of abruptio placentae.

151. *C. Permitting vaginal examinations.*

C is correct because vaginal examinations may initiate hemorrhage and/or labor. *A* is incorrect because it is an *appropriate* action if the placenta is marginal. *B* is incorrect because this action is absolutely essential to provide optimum nursing management. *D* is incorrect because a quiet environment is important to maintain a low level of anxiety and prevent an increase in bleeding.

152. *C. Assessing Ms. Toth's reasons for crying.*

C is correct because it is important to ascertain her reasons for crying so that the nurse can provide the appropriate intervention. *A* is incorrect; the burden of assessing Ms. Toth's condition should not be transferred to her husband. He may assist in comforting his wife and identifying her feelings, but the nurse is the primary caretaker. *B* may be appropriate, but only after the nurse has assessed Ms. Toth's condition. *D* is inappropriate because further assessment is required before any intervention is initiated.

153. *B. Turns Ms. Toth onto her side, administers oxygen, and stops oxytocin induction if induction is in progress.*

B is correct because the FHR pattern describes late deceleration, an indication of uteroplacental insufficiency. To increase perfusion of the uteroplacental unit, keep the uterus off the vena cava, oxygenate maternal blood, and hydrate. *A* is incorrect; the nurse who "does nothing" or does not recognize the implications of this tracing is negligent. *C* is not as correct as *B*; although there may be occasions when the nurse initiates contact with surgery, this is normally within the physician's role. *D* is incorrect because the immediate need is to deliver oxygen to the fetus. Preparation for birth may follow immediately in some cases.

154. *D. Give meperidine hydrochloride, 100 mg intramuscularly 1 hour prior to surgery.*

D is correct; a nurse should *question* this order because the drug has an adverse effect on the newborn, causing respiratory depression. *A*, *B*, and *C* are incorrect choices because *A* is a *correct* assessment for the safety of the fetus; *B* is an *appropriate* nursing action for the safety of the fetus; and *C* is an *appropriate* nursing action following a doctor's order.

155. B. Beginning shock.

B is correct; the restlessness and tachycardia alert the nurse to shock. *A* is incorrect because the blood pressure is not appropriate to a person who is anxious; she may be anxious, but the data presented do not relate to anxiety. *C* is incorrect because these are not the correct vital signs for preeclampsia (the blood pressure is too low). *D* is incorrect because postpartum blues do not necessarily change vital signs and usually do not occur so soon after birth.

156. A. Anxiousness to discuss her labor and birth.

A is correct; it is important for mothers to go over the details of the labor and birth, to realize and integrate their accomplishment. *B* is incorrect; mothers usually do not have difficulty remembering their labor and are anxious to talk about it, even if they feel they did not do what they wanted or it did not go as planned—it is an important time for catharsis. *C* is incorrect; after a *normal* birth mothers usually gain new energy and are less weary and tired than during labor; a mother might be weary and serious after a *problem* birth. *D* is incorrect; as long as she is satisfied with her performance, the mother is not too concerned about her environment.

157. D. Massage the uterine fundus.

D is correct because massage might solve the problem without the need for drugs or other measures. However, the nurse should avoid overmassage, which may fatigue the muscle. *A* is not the *first* nursing intervention; while the nurse is making these checks, the woman could be hemorrhaging; this would be a later intervention. *B* is incorrect; catheterization is not indicated unless there is evidence of a distended bladder. *C* is incorrect; this would not be the *first* intervention, but might be ordered by the doctor.

158. A. Check for a distended bladder and catheterize Ann if it is distended and she cannot void adequately.

A is correct; a full bladder elevates the uterus, but because the uterus is firm, the nurse should not worry about hemorrhage. *B* is incorrect; these data do not give information about the fundus. *C* is incorrect; Ann does not need methylergonovine maleate (Methergine) because there is no evidence of uterine relaxation. *D* is incorrect; the uterus is not failing to involute; it is high simply because of a full bladder.

159. C. "There are several contraceptives. I will give you the pros and cons so that you can make the decision. Also, consult your doctor about what is best for you."

C is correct because the nurse gives the facts and lets the woman, in consultation with her physician, make the decision. *A* is incorrect; the woman's question is ignored due to the nurse's bias. *B* is incorrect; the statement is not completely true and should be explained. *D* is incorrect; the nurse cannot decide what is best for the woman.

160. B. *"Plan times when you can be with each one alone for a certain period."*

B is correct because this approach includes each member of the family and all will feel that they are accepted and cared about. *A* is incorrect; the entire family must be included in caring for and accepting the newborn to avoid the husband's and child's feeling left out. *C* is incorrect; the husband and child will feel replaced by the newborn, and they may have problems accepting the newborn. *D* is incorrect; the husband will feel rejected and may go outside of the home for support and not return; he may feel that the relationship has changed and cannot be healed in the future.

161. C. *Sit-ups*

C is best because sit-ups are too strenuous immediately postpartum. The exercises in choices *A*, *B*, and *D* are all *appropriate* at this time and will not harm the mother. Kegels strengthen perineal muscles and enhance sensation and muscle tone. Pelvic tilt will help her regain muscle tone and good posture. Head raising will strengthen abdominal muscles.

162. B. *Readiness to concern herself with her infant.*

B is correct because having met her own needs during the "taking-in" phase, the mother is ready to concern herself with her infant. *A*, *C*, and *D* are incorrect; these behaviors are characteristic of the "taking-in" phase.

163. B. *Be worn to support and lift the breasts.*

B is the correct answer; a brassiere gives support and comfort. *A* is incorrect; not wearing a brassiere can lead to sagging breasts and discomfort in the shoulders and back from heavy breasts. *C* and *D* are incorrect because they will not support the breasts in the breastfeeding state and could cause pain and possible injury to the breasts.

164. A. *Apply heat to the breasts prior to nursing and express some milk.*

A is correct; this will soften the breasts, and manual removal of some milk will allow the baby to take hold of the nipple more easily and remove more milk. *B* is incorrect; this will fill the breasts with more milk, which will not be removed until the next feeding, causing more discomfort and possibly increasing the problem. *C* is incorrect because it will cause vasoconstriction, inhibiting the release of milk and adding to the problem. *D* is incorrect because the mother may not be in pain, and taking medication at this time could mean that the medication will be in the breast milk at the time of feeding.

165. B. *Explain that these feelings are normal and why they occur.*

B is correct; the nurse should offer an explanation for the mother's feelings and present her with options to correct the problem. *A* is incorrect; this condition is normal and can be helped by consideration, support, and health teaching. *C* is incorrect because bonding is essential at this time and can help to solve the problem, although the mother may need additional rest. *D* is inappropriate; it is an extreme solution to a normal situation.

166. **A. *Resuming her prepregnancy life-style within 1 week.***

    A is the incorrect instruction because the nurse has no way of knowing whether the mother's prepregnancy life-style is appropriate; even if this information were known to the nurse, resumption of the prepregnancy life-style after 1 week most likely is inappropriate. *B*, *C*, and *D* are appropriate instructions. The mother should be given health teaching regarding herself, the baby, and family responsibilities. Planning for rest and relaxation helps the mother avoid exhaustion and frustration. And knowing that she has planned ahead for emergencies is reassuring and could be life-saving.

167. **A. *"You should feed the baby the way that works best for both of you."***

    A is correct; since the mother has changed the method of feeding, she should be supported in her choice, since it probably is best for her situation. *B* is judgmental and could cause the mother to feel guilty. *C* is untrue; whether breastfeeding or bottlefeeding is better for a baby depends on the circumstances. *D* is an inappropriate response; it could make the mother feel guilty and it is not necessarily true; the baby may or may not gain more weight and may or may not be allergic.

168. **A. *Give him privacy.***

    A is the most appropriate response of the four choices given. However, the nurse still needs to be readily available so that the woman does not feel isolated. *B* is inappropriate because Mr. Young also needs time to grieve for his loss. *C* is incorrect; it is too premature, will serve to stimulate his anxiety, and may lead to feelings of hostility or depression. *D* is inappropriate because these parents may feel the need to be close to each other at this time.

169. **D. *Validate with him how his wife usually copes with losses.***

    D is correct because each individual reacts differently to various stressors. It is important to identify past reactions in order to begin to identify how an individual *may* react or attempt to cope with a new crisis. *A* is incorrect because it places pressure on Mr. Young to answer his own question, without providing adequate emotional support. *B* may be true, but is not an appropriate nursing response. The nurse needs to attempt to identify how the woman may react to this stressor in order to facilitate planning for nursing intervention. *C* is also a true statement, but this is not an individualized response and tends to be perceived as nonempathetic.

170. A. Tell Bryant what has occurred at a level he can comprehend.

A is correct; it is important to provide Bryant with an accurate explanation that he can understand, to alleviate any fears and assist him in coping with his feelings. *B* is incorrect because it is too abstract and evasive an approach for a 6-year-old child. *C* is incorrect because while Bryant is waiting for his mother to return home, all types of anxieties and fears will build up; he needs to be informed now in order to prevent this. Also, it may be too stressful for Bryant's mother to have to come home and tell him of this loss. *D* is incorrect because it is too abstract and assumes that this family has this belief.

171. B. Has a lower protein content.

B is correct; breast milk has a lower protein content, but its protein is more easily digested and more fully utilized than that in formula. *A* is incorrect because breast milk has a lower, not a higher, protein content. *C* is incorrect; breast milk has a higher carbohydrate content; formulas must have carbohydrates added. *D* is incorrect; ingestion of commercial formulas may lead to milk allergy.

172. B. Gain more weight than formula-fed infants.

B is the incorrect instruction; infants who are breastfed gain weight less rapidly than do infants who are formula-fed. *A*, *C*, and *D* are true of infants who are breast-fed. *A* is due to the immunoglobins of breast milk. *C* is due to the consistency of breast milk and more frequent feeding. *D* is true because breast milk is more compatible with the infant's metabolism and digestive system.

173. A. Decrease stimulation to the breasts.

A is correct; lack of stimulation will aid in decreasing milk let-down and negative lactogenic hormone feedback. *B*, *C*, and *D* are all incorrect because these activities support lactation. *B* increases milk production. *C* increases vasodilation and stimulates the let-down reflex. *D*, emptying the breasts, stimulates milk production.

174. B. 115-120.

B is the correct answer because the correct amount is 117 cal/kg/day. *A* is an inadequate number of calories for growth. *C* and *D* are too many calories; the infant will gain too much weight, which can lead to adult obesity.

175. B. 3–4.

B is the correct answer. Michael is fed 6 times a day. He requires 20 oz./day to provide 120 cal/kg/day (400 cal total). 20 oz. divided by 6 = $3^1/_3$ oz. per feeding. *A* is incorrect because 2–3 oz. x 6 = 12–18 oz.—less than Michael's needs. *C* and *D* are incorrect because both would exceed Michael's needs and lead to diarrhea or to obesity from overfeeding.

176. C. Eye prophylaxis may be delayed up to 1 hour after birth to facilitate parent-child attachment.

C is the correct answer because it is *not* true. Eye prophylaxis may be delayed up to 2 *hours* after birth to facilitate parent-child attachment through eye-to-eye contact. *A*, *B*, and *D* are not the answers because each of these statements is *true* about prophylactic eye care of the newborn.

177. C. Both the nurse and the physician.

C is correct because both the nurse and the physician are responsible and accountable for checking the label prior to using a medication. *A*, *B*, and *D* are therefore incorrect.

178. A. Using the greater trochanter and posterior superior iliac spine as landmarks.

A is the best choice; the landmarks for IM injections are *not* the greater trochanter and the posterior superior iliac spine. That would place the needle in the posterior gluteal muscle, which, in neonates, is small, poorly developed, and close to the sciatic nerve. The landmarks for IM injection in neonates are the greater trochanter and the knee. *B*, *C*, and *D* are not the answers because all of these are true about giving a neonate an IM injection.

179. C. Helps the mother hold him face down with the head lower than the buttocks.

C is correct. Between the fourth and eighth hour after birth, the infant experiences the second period of reactivity. This period is characterized by alertness, gagging with regurgitation of mucus, and passage of meconium. Although the infant's response is normal, to prevent aspiration, the infant is held face down with the head lower than the buttocks to assist gravity drainage. At this time, the nurse increases the mother's confidence by assisting the mother to take the appropriate action. *A* is incorrect; holding the infant upright and patting his back encourages inhalation and aspiration. *B* is incorrect; the infant's mucus must be drained stat and the nurse's racing the infant to the nursery would be very frightening for the mother. The mother may then feel she is not capable of appropriate action. *D* is incorrect because the infant's mucus must be drained stat. Also, the mother is rightly concerned; telling her not to worry is false reassurance.

180. B. On the forehead just above the eyebrows, over the junction of the ear on the head, and back to the forehead.

B is correct; head circumference is measured by placing the tape on the forehead just over the eyebrows and then around the head over the junction of the ear with the head. The head circumference may need to be remeasured after molding and caput succedaneum have resolved, usually after 2-3 days. *A*, *C*, and *D* are incorrect because of the rationale given for *B*.

181. D. Records the findings and does nothing further.

D is correct. The head (occipitofrontal) circumference is about 2 cm (³/₄ inch) more than the chest circumference at the nipple line. If the head measures under 32 cm, microcephaly must be ruled out. If the head is 4 cm or more larger than the chest, hydrocephaly is suspected. *A*, *B*, and *C* are all inappropriate actions because the head and chest circumferences are within normal limits.

182. C. Single palmar crease, snuffles, apical pulse between 120 and 140/min at rest.

C is correct because single palmar creases are associated with genetic defect, Down syndrome, or trisomy 21. Assess for incurvature of the fifth fingers, thick tongue, extra epicanthal folds, excessive joint motility, and poor feeding. Snuffles refers to the irritating rhinitis of syphilis, which cause excoriation and formation of scar tissue called rhagades. Assess for other symptoms of syphilis, and wear gloves when working with this infant. The pulse is within the normal limits. *A* is incorrect. Flat hemangiomas are also known as stork bites, and are the small, irregular red blotches over the bridge of the nose, upper eyelids, and the nape of the neck caused by rupture of capillaries from the stress of vaginal birth. Head circumference and hemoglobin levels are within normal levels. *B* is incorrect because all findings are within normal limits. Erythema toxicum is not fully understood and seems to have no clinical significance. *D* is incorrect. Molding is the overlapping of cranial bones to accommodate the head to the birth canal. Smegma is the white mucus formed between the labia majora and under the prepuce. Acrocyanosis is blueness of the hands and feet, primarily within the first week of life, especially when the neonate is chilled and at rest. Acrocyanosis is due to immaturity of the peripheral vascular system. Respirations are within normal limits for a neonate at rest.

183. A. Kilograms of body weight.

A is correct; nutrient needs for the neonate are calculated as kilocalories per kilogram of body weight. *B*, *C*, and *D* are incorrect because nutrient needs are calculated per kilogram of body weight.

184. A. The neonate may vomit if his bottle is propped.

A is correct. In addition to the increased hazard of aspiration, if the bottle is propped, formula may enter the neonate's eustachian tube and predispose the baby to ear infections. *B* is incorrect. The neonate may lose 5–10% of his birth weight normally. To determine the percentage of weight loss, multiply the number of pounds by 16 ounces and divide by 10. Example: Birth weight is 8 pounds. 8 x 16 = 128 ounces. 10% of 128 ounces = 12.8 ounces. *C* is incorrect; the neonate's stomach capacity is between 50 and 60 mL, or about 2 oz. *D* is incorrect; the neonate's caloric needs are high—about 115 kcal/kg/day for the first 6 months, or about 52 cal/pound/day. The gastrocolic reflex is stimulated during feeding, and he may have a bowel movement immediately following each feeding.

185. C. Rooting

C is correct; the rooting reflex is activated whenever the cheek and lips are touched, and the infant is awake and hungry. The mother is advised to use the reflex for introducing the nipple into the infant's mouth. *A* is incorrect; the Babinski reflex is normally present in early neonatal life. When the plantar surface of the neonate's foot is stroked firmly, the toes fan out. *B* is incorrect; suck and swallow reflexes are present and complete in the full-term infant. However, even in the full-term infant, suck and swallow may not be synchronized at birth, and may result in gagging and coughing. *D* is incorrect; the Moro reflex is a response to a falling sensation, a disorientation in space, or a noise. The arms and legs are extended, then returned to the midline in an embracing motion, and the fingers form the letter "C." The newborn usually cries. Adequate reflex responses indicate an intact musculoskeletal and neurologic system from the brain stem downward. Reflexes disappear as myelinization is completed.

186. D. 12 oz. (360) mL per day.

D is correct. 7 pounds, 6 ounces = 3.345 kg x 105 mL per day = 12 oz. (360 mL) per day. *A*, *B*, and *C* are incorrect because the full-term neonate's fluid requirement per day is 105 mL per kilogram of body weight.

187. D. 13 ounces.

D is correct. The baby can lose up to 10% of his birth weight, or 13 ounces. 8 pounds, 2 ounces = 130 oz. 10% of 130 = 13 ounces. *A*, *B*, and *C* are incorrect calculations.

188. D. Obtain and assess a blood sample by heelstick because these behaviors could be signs of hypoglycemia.

D is correct; slight, persistent tremors could be signs of hypoglycemia. This baby is larger but still within normal limits and the movements described *are within normal limit*s for newborns. If any doubt exists, the nurse gathers more data (assesses for blood glucose level according to protocol, e.g., heelsticks at 1, 2, 4, and 6 hours) prior to initiating an intervention. *A* is incorrect because the nurse acts *prior to completing an assessment*. *B* is incorrect because the data do not correlate with drug dependence. Signs of drug dependence, such as hypertonicity, high-pitched cry, frantic fist sucking, and poor feeding, likely will have been evident prior to this episode of tremors. *C* is incorrect because signs of increased intracranial pressure are a full, bulging fontanelle, abnormal respirations with cyanosis, and reduced responsiveness.

189. A. Explain to Ms. Allen that he can lose 3 more ounces and still be within normal limits for weight loss.

A is correct; the full-term neonate of average weight for gestational age can lose up to 10% of body weight after birth. A matter-of-fact answer such as this can be very reassuring to the mother. *B* is incorrect; the neonate is born with enough fluids and energy (usually) to sustain him until his mother's milk comes in. By bringing a bottle of glucose to the mother, the nurse implies that Ms. Allen is inadequate as a breastfeeding mother. In addition, the baby may be too satisfied to empty his mother's breast completely, thus preventing adequate lactation; and some are questioning whether giving glucose at this early age sets a pattern for the ingestion of refined sugar. *C* is incorrect; the nurse is giving false reassurance and is passing the responsibility for explaining the situation to the physician. *D* is incorrect; an accurate record is not the answer to the mother's concern about the well-being of her newborn.

190. A. *"Tighten the bottle cap a little."*

A is correct; a loose bottle cap pulls in extra air. The baby swallows the air, filling his stomach rapidly and causing regurgitation of formula and gagging. If the cap is too tight, the bubbles are tiny and the baby has to work hard to get any milk. *B* is incorrect; an upright position does facilitate burping, but the amount of air the baby is taking in must be decreased first. *C* is incorrect; the baby is burped often during feeding, but usually once after each ounce is sufficient. *D* is incorrect; by this behavior, the nurse is implying that the mother cannot feed her child correctly. The nurse is going to show the mother how well she can do it.

191. B. *She touches her nipple to the baby's cheek at the start of the feeding.*

B is correct; Ms. Allen elicits the rooting reflex by allowing her nipple to touch the baby's cheek or mouth. The baby turns his head toward the nipple and opens his mouth to receive it. *A* is incorrect; ritualistic weighing of the baby to note "how much the baby took" detracts from the naturalness of breastfeeding, and can increase the mother's anxiety. Anxiety has an antilactogenic effect. *C* is incorrect. Even babies who are breastfed take in air during feeding, even though it is less than the amount of air taken in during bottlefeeding. Babies who are breastfed are burped *at least* when changing them from one breast to the other and also at the end of the feeding. *D* is incorrect; placing any nonabsorbent material over the nipple does not let the nipples dry well. This causes maceration and possibly mastitis.

192. D. *Phenylketonuria (PKU).*

D is correct; PKU is an inherited recessive error of metabolism. The enzyme that is missing is phenylalanine hydroxylase, which is needed to convert phenylalanine, one of the 26 essential amino acids, into tyrosine. Tyrosine is needed for the production of melanin; therefore, those with this affliction tend to have light skin and hair. Lofenelac is a phenylalanine-poor formula for the neonate. *A* is incorrect; kernicterus results when the breakdown products of bilirubin are deposited in the nuclear masses and basal ganglia of the medulla. This area is responsible for muscle coordination. Kernicterus is usually associated with Rh incompatibility, but may result from jaundice from any cause. However, the jaundice associated with breastfeeding has never been known to result in kernicterus. *B* is incorrect; hypoglycemia is a condition characterized by an excessive lowering of blood sugar due to high levels of circulating insulin in the infant of the mother who is diabetic. It may also be due to the rapid utilization of glucose, to sepsis, or to exertion from respiratory distress and the like. *C* is incorrect; thrush is a fungal disease caused by the organism *Candida albicans*. It is usually found only in the neonate's mouth but may spread throughout the GI tract or become generalized with septicemia. Septicemia usually occurs only in a neonate who is very sick and debilitated.

193. B. Retract his prepuce completely to cleanse the glans penis of smegma and other debris.

B is the answer. Retraction of the foreskin (prepuce) of the baby boy who is uncircumcised must be done gently and not forced. It is common to find the foreskin adherent to the glans penis for at least 3 months to several years. The foreskin is replaced after the glans penis is washed with mild soap and warm water. *A*, *C*, and *D* are not the answers because they are all *appropriate* care activities. Each eye is washed with a clean material from the inner canthus outward to prevent spread of any infection from one eye to the other. The hair must be rinsed of soap thoroughly and then combed with either a fine-toothed comb or a brush to prevent the development of cradle cap (seborrheic dermatitis). The nares and ears are washed with a soft, pliable material to avoid trauma to delicate tissues.

194. C. Corn and coconut oil mixtures are not absorbed to the same extent as the fat in human milk.

C is the answer because corn and coconut oil mixtures *are* absorbed to the same extent as the fat in human milk; both oils are therefore used in the preparation of formulas. *A*, *B*, and *D* are not the answers because each of these statements is *true* about the neonate's digestive capabilities and formula preparation.

195. D. Women who have breastfed are less prone to develop breast cancer later in life.

D is correct. Studies have shown that women who have breastfed are less prone to develop breast cancer later in life than are women who have not lactated. *A* is incorrect; immune bodies *do* cross the placenta to the fetus during the last trimester to protect the neonate against diseases that the mother herself has had. These immune bodies last only about 6-8 months. Breastfeeding is a most unreliable contraceptive. Ovulation may occur while lactating as early as the 39th day or as late as 12 months. The average time of the first ovulation is about 8 months. The woman who assesses her cervical mucus can identify impending ovulation. *B* is incorrect. Breastfeeding jaundice results from the presence of pregnanediol or progesterone in the mother's milk. Pregnanediol inhibits the enzyme glucuronyl transferase and is needed to convert bilirubin to its soluble excretable form. Even severe breast milk jaundice is not known to cause kernicterus. However, most physicians suggest that the mother wean the infant. *C* is incorrect; breast milk contains less (not more) protein and more carbohydrate than cow's milk. The protein and carbohydrate in breast milk, which is bluish-white in color, are utilized much more efficiently and are better tolerated by the neonate than those from cow's milk. Prepared formulas, such as Similac, Enfamil, and Good Start, approximate breast milk more closely than does cow's milk.

196. B. Miliaria.

B is correct. Miliaria, more commonly known as prickly heat, is due either to overdressing the neonate or to a hot, humid environment. Treatment includes removing excess clothing and giving tepid baths, being especially careful to rinse and dry thoroughly all skinfolds. *A* is incorrect; diaper rash is a chemical dermatitis due to ammonia and nitrogen products in the urine or stool and/or due to cloth diapers from which the soap was not completely removed. Changing diapers often, rinsing them well, drying diapers in a hot dryer or in direct sunlight, and exposing the infant's buttocks to air for periods of time cure the rash. *C* is incorrect; seborrheic dermatitis is more commonly known as cradle cap. Although it starts on the scalp above the forehead, it spreads downward over the cheek, neck, and then chest. It often occurs because mothers shy away from washing over the anterior fontanelle. Treatment is daily washing with mild soap and water. *D* is incorrect; diarrhea may be due to overfeeding, high sugar content in formula, or GI or other infections. This stool is usually forcefully expelled, may be greenish, and leaves a watery ring on the diaper around the loose stool. This is a potentially fatal condition, since the neonates tolerate this water loss poorly. The parent is advised to notify the physician.

197. B. The nurse is held to the same standard of care as always.

B is correct; regardless of when or for how long nursing care is given, the nurse is held to the same standards that apply during normal shifts. Fatigue does not excuse poor performance. *A*, *C*, and *D* are incorrect assessments of the nurse's responsibility.

9. Adult Health Problems

Case Management Scenarios and Critical–Thinking Exercises

Medical Diagnosis: Diabetic ketoacidosis.

- *Nursing Problems/Diagnosis:*

  Electrolyte imbalance: hypokalemia.

  Fluid volume deficit.

  Altered nutrition.

- *Chief Complaint:*

  Dennis Rose, who is 18-years old and a high school basketball star, was admitted to the hospital for treatment of polyuria, polydipsia, and dry cough.

- *History of Present Illness:*

  The patient was well until 10 days prior to admission, when he developed gastroenteritis followed by bronchitis. He had diarrhea, abdominal pain, intermittent vomiting, and dry cough.

- *Past History:*

  Measles at age 7. No allergies.

- *Family History:*

  Hyperthyroidism in maternal grandmother. Adult-onset diabetes mellitus in maternal uncle.

- *Review of Symptoms:*

  10 pound weight loss over the past 6 days.

- *Physical Exam:*

  Head and neck: Eyes sunken. Tongue dry. Fruity breath odor.

  Lungs: Clear on auscultation.

  Abdomen: Benign.

  Extremities: Skin dry with decreased turgor.

  Vital signs: BP: 110/70. Temperature: 100.6°F. P: 110. R: 40.

- *Laboratory Data:*

  Na^+: 138. →

  K^+: 3.2. ↓

  CO_2: 6. ↓

  Cl^-: 102.

  Glucose: 860. ↑

  WBC: 17,000/mL. ↑

  Hgb: 18.1g. ↑

  Hct: 54%.

  Urinalysis: 4 + glucose; ketones—large. ✗

---

1. The nurse knows that the condition that does not *precipitate* diabetic ketoacidosis in the client is:

   A. Diarrhea.

   B. Intermittent vomiting.

   C. Bronchitis.

   D. Dehydration.

2. The nurse knows that Dennis will require insulin injections. Which statement best explains the rationale for insulin therapy?

   A. The person with diabetes, type 1 requires insulin to supplement circulating insulin.

   B. The person with diabetes, type 1 is insulin-dependent.

   C. The injections are temporary until the pancreas increases insulin production.

   D. All people who have diabetes must receive insulin.

3. Which admitting symptom indicates the incomplete lipid metabolism that occurs in diabetes?

   A. Polyuria.

   B. Polydipsia.

   C. Fruity breath.

   D. Weight loss.

4. The nurse knows that the presence of hypokalemia (after treatment with insulin) increases the risk of the client developing:

   A. Cardiac irritability.

   B. Renal failure.

   C. Cardiac depression.

   D. Respiratory failure.

5. Dennis has lost approximately 10 pounds in 6 days. He has been started on a 2800-calorie ADA diet. Which food is included in his diet?

   A. Whole-grain cereal with milk.

   B. Seafood casserole.

   C. Banana cream pie.

   D. Fried chicken.

6. Dennis has been asked to save his urine for testing. Which instruction should the nurse give him to ensure an accurate test?

   A. Supply only a single specimen of urine.

   B. Ingest at least 2 glasses of water before voiding specimen.

   C. Empty bladder ½ hour before testing and also supply a second voided specimen for testing.

   D. Test urine that has collected in bladder for 2–3 hours.

7. Blood glucose fingersticks are usually done for daily diabetic testing. Which test is done to assess a client's compliance for the previous 3 months?

   A. Glycosylated hemoglobin measurement.

   B. Glucose tolerance test.

   C. Postprandial blood sugar measurement.

   D. Connecting peptide test.

8. Dennis is concerned about returning to basketball. The nurse needs to tell him that he will be able to continue the sport, but the exercise will require him to make the following adjustments:

   A. Increase his caloric intake, but continue the same insulin dosage.

   B. Reduce both his caloric intake and the insulin dosage.

   C. Continue the same diet, but increase the insulin dosage.

   D. Reduce his caloric intake and continue the same insulin dosage.

9. The nurse anticipates that the major problem for a person who is diabetic of this age following discharge will be:

   A. Learning self-injection of insulin.

   B. Remembering to test his urine.

   C. Compliance with the dietary restrictions.

   D. Limiting his activities.

10. Following instructions on self-administration of insulin, the client should be able to demonstrate his knowledge that

tissue hypertrophy or atrophy (lipodystrophies) is prevented by:

A. Using the same injection site.

B. Administering room-temperature insulin.

C. Injecting the insulin into the adipose tissue.

D. Chilling the insulin before injection.

11. Dennis is being maintained on 12 units of NPH before breakfast, and 6 units before dinner. Which sign of an insulin reaction should the nurse watch for?

A. Diaphoresis during the night.

B. Kussmaul breathing in the late afternoon.

C. Flushed, dry skin 6 hours after administration.

D. Excessive hunger at meals and between meals.

Medical Diagnosis: Fracture of C–7 vertebra and multiple trauma.

- *Surgical Treatment:*

  Immobilization of fractured vertebra.

- *Nursing Problems/Diagnosis:*

  Impaired physical mobility.

  Knowledge deficit: about treatment.

- *Chief Complaint:*

  Jack Jenkins, a 19-year-old student, is seen in the emergency department after a motorcycle accident. He has suffered multiple traumatic in-juries.

- *History of Present Illness:*

  Loss of consciousness at time of accident. Skin lacerations on face and forearm. No obvious long bone injuries. When alert, complains of loss of feeling in lower legs.

- *Past History:*

  Usual childhood illnesses.

- *Family History:*

  No history of diabetes, cancer, or mental illnesses.

- *Review of Systems:*

  Unable to answer questions at time of exam.

- *Physical Exam:*

  Vital signs: BP: 90/60. P: 88. R: 24.

Head laceration 5 cm.

Pupils equal and reactive to light.

No sensation in legs and feet.

No respiratory distress.

Vomited undigested food; no abdominal distention or tenderness. Urine clear.

- *Laboratory and X-ray Data: X-ray:*

Fracture of C-7 vertebra.

Hgb: 13 g.

Hct: 40%.

Urinalysis: No RBCs.

---

12. In setting initial priorities of care for Jack, the nurse should spend the least amount of time:

    A. Maintaining proper body alignment.

    B. Immobilizing fractures of the long bones.

    C. Establishing and maintaining an airway.

    D. Scrubbing superficial lacerations.

13. It is determined that Jack has a head and back injury. A Stryker frame has been ordered for him. The nurse explains to Jack that the advantage of the frame is that:

    A. He can be turned while his spine is kept immobilized.

    B. It has automatic support in a position of good anatomic alignment.

    C. It provides even weight distribution.

    D. He will be able to turn himself.

14. Jack's area of permanent complete spinal cord damage is at the lowest end of the cervical spine. The nurse knows that it is unrealistic for Jack to expect to achieve the rehabilitative goal of:

    A. Walking.

    B. Writing.

    C. Feeding himself.

    D. Driving a car.

15. When testing the motor strength of a client with a head injury, it is best for the nurse to:

    A. Observe the client feeding himself or herself.

    B. Ask the client to cross the legs.

    C. Ask the client to squeeze the nurse's hands.

    D. Ask the client to identify a pinprick on the foot.

Medical Diagnosis: Fracture of the right radius and ulna.

- *Nursing Problems/Diagnosis:*

  Altered health maintenance.

  Risk of injury.

  Knowledge deficit: cast management.

- *Chief Complaint:*

  Sally Peters, a 20-year-old student, received an injury to her right arm when she fell off a chair while hanging curtains.

- *History of Present Illness:*

  Pain, swelling, tenderness, and loss of motor function in the right arm. No other reported injuries.

- *Past History:*

  No diabetes or cancer. No other siblings in family.

- *Review of Systems:*

  Healthy until this injury. Attending school. No unusual childhood illnesses.

- *Physical Exam:*

  Vital signs: BP: 120/66. P: 72. R: 16.

  Obvious deformity of right forearm; able to feel sensations when touched.

  No cyanosis noted.

  Right radial pulse: 72.

- *Laboratory Data:*

  Fracture, right radius and ulna.

---

16. X-ray reports document that a bone is broken into several fragments. The nurse knows that this type of fracture is known as:

    A. Impacted.

    B. Greenstick.

    C. Transverse.

    D. Comminuted.

17. While Sally is being examined, another client is brought in to the emergency department by a friend. His left arm has an obvious deformity. There is some bleeding at the site, and when the nurse moves the client's sleeve, the bone ends are penetrating the skin surface. The nurse should first:

    A. Reduce the fracture if possible.

    B. Leave the wound open to allow drainage and prevent hematoma.

C. Immobilize the left arm.

D. Thoroughly cleanse the wound.

18. The client in the bed next to Sally's is in traction. The nurse caring for the client in traction:

A. Allows the weights of her traction to hang freely on the pulleys. —

B. Decreases the amount of weight on her traction each day.

C. Removes the weight to inspect the site daily.

D. Lifts the weights to help her move in bed.

19. The nurse is planning Sally's discharge teaching. Which statement should the nurse omit from Sally's health care instructions?

A. Careful attention must be paid to monitoring circulation. ✓

B. There should be no exercise of the affected extremity.

C. The cast should be kept dry at all times. ✓

D. Pain will be lessened if the arm remains elevated. ✓

20. Sally's roommates bring her back to the emergency department because of a possible cast complication. Their action was most likely based on Sally's complaint that:

A. The cast was too heavy.

B. She felt irritable and depressed.

C. The cast was still damp 6 hours after application.

D. Her fingers were blue and felt cold. ✓

21. The nurse and Sally discuss the importance of a good diet to help bone healing. The nurse knows that the food substance determined to be least helpful in promoting healing is:

A. Iron.

B. Sodium.—

C. Calcium.

D. Vitamin D.

Medical Diagnosis: Partial-thickness and full-thickness burns.

- *Nursing Problems/Diagnosis:*

Risk of altered fluid volume.

Risk of infection.

Altered nutrition: less than body requirements.

Self-care deficit: medication administration.

- *Chief Complaint:*

    Jim Harte, a 24-year-old construction worker, enters the emergency department with burns resulting from a fire in the auto engine he was repairing.

- *History of Present Illness:*

    Burns 30 minutes ago. Partial-thickness burns of face and chest; full-thickness burns of left leg.

- *Past Health History:*

    Usual childhood illnesses. Weight 180 pounds. No history of drug or alcohol abuse.

- *Family History:*

    No significant findings.

- *Review of Systems:*

    No respiratory or cardiac problems. No major illnesses or infections.

- *Physical Exam:*

    Head, neck, and chest: Partial-thickness (second-degree) burns.

    Left leg: Full-thickness (third-degree) burns over entire leg.

    No other burns noted. No fractures. Breathing patterns normal; no crackles or wheezes.

---

22. The nurse is notified that Jim Harte, who has received burns, is on his way to the emergency department. The nurse remembers that characteristic signs of a partial-thickness (or second-degree) burn include:

    A. Blisters covering the entire burn site.

    B. Mild erythema.

    C. Absence of pain when touched.

    D. Color of the skin is white or black.

23. Jim's brother was with him at the time of the burn. He demonstrated incorrect burn first aid by:

    A. Sending immediately for the ambulance.

    B. Applying cold water to the area.

    C. Applying first aid cream to the burn.

    D. Preventing Jim from being chilled by getting him a blanket.

24. Besides the burns on his torso, Jim also has a full-thickness (or third-degree) circumferential burn on his left leg. The nurse should anticipate that he may need an escharotomy, which can be described as:

    A. Debridement of the burn area.

    B. A skin graft to the burn site.

C. Tube insertion for irrigation of the wound.

D. A lengthwise incision through the burn area.

25. The nurse explains to Jim that the disadvantage of silver sulfadiazine (Silvadene) ointment in burn therapy is due to the fact that:

A. Application is fast.

B. The ointment does not affect electrolyte imbalance.

C. The ointment depresses granulocyte formation.

D. Application is painless.

26. During the first 48 hours after a major burn, the nurse should see evidence of:

A. Plasma to interstitial fluid shift.

B. Interstitial tissue to plasma shift.

C. Potassium deficit.

D. Metabolic alkalosis.

27. During the recovery stage, the nurse plans the ideal diet with Jim. The nurse will be able to determine that Jim's caloric intake is adequate if he tells her that he takes in:

A. 3500–5000 calories.

B. 2000–2500 calories.

C. 1800–2500 calories.

D. 2000–3000 calories.

28. The nurse plans a high-protein diet with Jim to counteract his negative nitrogen balance. The nurse knows that this condition is not caused by:

A. Tissue destruction and protein loss.

B. Stress response.

C. Decreased protein intake during initial burn phase.

D. Tissue anabolism resulting from immobility.

Medical Diagnosis: Acute viral hepatitis.

- *Nursing Problems/Diagnosis:*

Risk of injury related to biochemical regulatory impairment.

Impairment of digestion.

Risk of infection.

Altered nutrition: less than body requirements.

Self-esteem disturbance.

Sensory/perceptual alterations related to chemical alterations.

- *Chief Complaint:*

  Ms. Bee is a 25-year-old real estate agent. She complains of fatigue, weakness, dark-yellow urine, and clay-colored stools.

- *History of Present Illness:*

  Two weeks prior to Ms. Bee's hospitalization, she felt very fatigued and weak. She complained of uncomfortable joint pains, frequent headaches, poor appetite, and nausea. On the fourth day of Ms. Bee's hospitalization, she developed jaundice, and strongly insisted that her visitors be restricted to her immediate family.

- *Past History:*

  Healthy young adult. No previous hospitalizations.

- *Family History:*

  Father, age 48; mother, age 45; both relatively well.

- *Physical Exam:*

  Neck: Supple; no pain or stiffness on movement; trachea midline.

  Chest: Symmetric chest expansion; adequate chest excursion.

  Lungs: Clear on auscultation.

  Heart: S_1 and distinct; regular rhythm; no S_3 or S_4.

  Abdomen: Flat, soft; active bowel sounds; tympanic sound in four quadrants; smooth liver edge with tenderness, palpated 3 cm below right costal margin.

  Extremities: No rashes or irritation; jaundice of skin noted on fourth hospitalization day; range of motion of all extremities adequate, without pain or discomfort on movement; strong hand grasps bilaterally.

- *Laboratory and X-ray Data:*

  Chest x-ray: Normal.

  Blood gases: Normal limits.

  ECG: Normal sinus rhythm.

---

29. Which client problem is the nurse least likely to encounter?

    A. Bleeding.

    B. Pruritus.

    C. Weight loss.

    D. Hyperglycemia. —

30. Based on the data given, the *most* common nursing problem is:

    A. Depression related to feelings of guilt.

    B. Anxiety related to a fear of impending doom.

    C. Body image change related to altered skin appearance. —

    D. Anger and hostility related to restriction of physical activity.

31. Which laboratory result may the nurse expect to find during the <u>initial phases</u> of hepatitis?

    A. Increased LDH and CK

    B. Normal prothrombin time.

    C. Elevated serum transaminases. —

    D. Decreased alkaline phosphatase.

32. The nurse observes that Ms. Bee has clay-colored stools. The reason is that:

    A. Hepatic uptake of bilirubin is impaired.

    B. Excretion of fecal urobilinogen is increased.

    C. Conjugated bilirubin reenters the bloodstream.

    D. Excretion of conjugated bilirubin into the intestines is decreased. —

33. The greatest risk of the spread of hepatitis B is from contaminated:

    A. Urine and feces.

    B. Nasogastric secretions.

    C. Used needles and syringes. —

    D. Feces and oral secretions.

34. Pruritus, caused by the accumulation of bile salts in the skin, can be relieved by administering prescribed:

    A. Valium to help the client relax.

    B. Benadryl to promote sleep during the night.

    C. Questran to stimulate the reabsorption of bile salts.

    D. Cholestyramine to bind bile salts in the intestines.

35. Which neurologic assessment parameter(s) would <u>least</u> likely indicate to the nurse the occurrence of impending hepatic coma?

    A. Flapping tremors.

    B. Decorticate rigidity. —

    C. Hyperactive reflexes.

    D. Irritability and drowsiness.

36. An ineffective nursing measure to prevent the progress of hepatic coma is:

    A. Giving diuretics.

    B. Making certain that a low-protein diet is served.

    C. Assessing if there is adequate renal perfusion.

    D. Assessing for a patent airway and oxygenation.

37. The nurse needs to know that lactulose and neomycin are given to clients with hepatic encephalopathy to:

    A. Decrease fecal pH and ammonia absorption.

    B. Induce peristalsis and promote bowel movement.

    C. Reduce antibacterial activity in the intestines.

    D. Remove potassium and magnesium in the intestines.

38. If the client with severe liver damage is retaining nitrogen waste products, the nurse will note in the lab reports an increase in serum:

    A. Ammonia.

    B. Leukocytes.

    C. Creatinine.

    D. Urea nitrogen.

Medical Diagnosis: Probable Graves' disease (hyperthyroidism).

- *Nursing Problem/Diagnosis:*

    Altered nutrition: less than body requirements.

- *Chief Complaint:*

    Ms. Wise is a 26-year-old woman who is a homemaker and mother of two. She complains of insomnia, and a weight loss of 20 pounds in 4 months.

- *Past History:*

    Has remained healthy; no surgeries.

- *Family History:*

    Father: Hypertensive cardiovascular disease.

    Mother: Unremarkable.

    Sibling: Unremarkable.

- *Review of Symptoms:*

    Ravenous appetite; heat intolerance.

- *Physical Exam:*

    Neck: Carotid pulse bounding.

    Skin: Moist with perspiration.

    Lungs: Clear A-P. Sinus tachycardia.

    Abdomen: Hyperactive bowel sounds.

    Extremities: Mild tremors.

    Mental status: Alert and agitated. Complete sentences for interviewer.

Vital signs: BP: 120/80. P: 120. R: 30. Temperature: 100°F orally.

ECG: Sinus tachycardia.

■ *Laboratory Data:*

Urinalysis: Normal.

---

39. During Ms. Wise's admission to the unit, the nurse begins the initial assessment. She notices an anxious facial expression, pulse of 120, respirations of 30, and skin moist with perspiration. The nurse knows that the most probable rationale for these symptoms is that:

    A. Ms. Wise is experiencing normal anxiety associated with her admission.

    B. Increased levels of thyroxine and triiodothyronine stimulate metabolic rate.

    C. Reduced iodine intake produces hypertrophy and overactivity of the thyroid gland.

    D. Ms. Wise was rushing to avoid being late for hospital admission.

40. A protein-bound iodide test has been scheduled. Before the test, it is important that the nurse:

    A. Have the client void.

    B. Inquire whether the client has had an x-ray for which opaque dye was administered.

    C. Instruct the client to get 8 hours of sleep the night before the test.

    D. See that the client receives a meal high in iodine.

41. A radioactive iodine uptake test is performed. The nurse should:

    A. Inform the client that there is no danger of radiating herself or others.

    B. See that the urine is collected in a lead container.

    C. Wear a radiation detection badge when the nurse is near the client.

    D. Avoid prolonged contact with the client for 6 hours after the test.

42. A diagnosis of hyperthyroidism is confirmed. The nurse instructs the client in a diet that has:

    A. 4000–5000 calories; 100–125 g of protein.

    B. 2000–3000 calories; 70–90 g of protein.

    C. Low calcium; high vitamin D.

    D. 1000–2000 g of carbohydrate; 60–80 g of protein.

43. Based on the pathophysiology of hyperthyroidism, it is important that the nurse:

    A. Have several blankets available for Ms. Wise's use.

    B. Place Ms. Wise in a room with an electric fan and windows.

    C. Provide a 300-piece puzzle for diversion.

    D. Insist that Ms. Wise rest 2 hours in the morning and in the afternoon.

44. Propylthiouracil is ordered. Which observation indicates to the nurse that the medication was having a therapeutic effect?

    A. A weight loss of ¼ pound per week.

    B. Apical pulse of 90 and reduction in urine output.

    C. Ability to sleep 8 hours at night without awakening.

    D. Inability to complete a paint-by-number picture.

45. Ms. Wise will be readmitted for surgery in about 2 weeks. She is now discharged on saturated solution of potassium iodide (SSKI). The nurse instructs Ms. Wise that the purpose of this medication is to:

    A. Produce a sedative effect so that she can sleep at night.

    B. Reduce exophthalmos.

    C. Minimize postoperative bleeding.

    D. Replace depleted iodine stores.

46. While planning preoperative teaching, the nurse realizes that Ms. Wise should be taught to maintain head elevation at a 15-degree Fowler's position. The nurse tells her that the purpose of this position is to:

    A. Prevent hemorrhage.

    B. Reduce pooling of respiratory secretions.

    C. Prevent strain on the suture line.

    D. Prevent hoarseness.

47. Ms. Wise has a subtotal thyroidectomy. The nurse can detect early hemorrhage by noting:

    A. A BP of 90/50, apical pulse of 150, and clammy skin.

    B. Muscle twitching and tremors.

    C. Hoarseness and weakness of the voice.

    D. Complaints of difficulty swallowing and sensation that the dressing is tight.

48. Ms. Wise exhibits hoarseness, crowing respirations, and retraction of the tissues of the neck. The nurse should have which of the following for initial emergency use?

    A. Calcium gluconate, 1 ampule.

    B. Synthroid sodium, 1 vial.

    C. Tracheostomy set.

    D. Thoracentesis tray.

49. Which observation might indicate to the nurse the therapeutic effect of calcium gluconate?

    A. Reduction in size of the thyroid gland from 4-2 cm.

    B. Curtailment of blood loss.

    C. Absent Trousseau's sign.

    D. Reduction in hoarseness.

50. Which client should the nurse anticipate to be prone to develop tetany?

    A. Ms. J with hyperparathyroidism.

    B. Mr. W with hypothyroidism.

    C. Mr. S in metabolic acidosis.

    D. Mr. X with metabolic alkalosis.

51. Hoarseness may occur during the immediate postoperative period. The client should be instructed that:

    A. It is important to refrain from speaking.

    B. This is a permanent, untoward response to surgery.

    C. Humidification and antitussives hasten the return of the voice.

    D. Even after the voice returns, it will never have the pitch and strength of the preoperative voice.

Medical Diagnosis: Burns.

- *Nursing Problems/Diagnosis:*

  Altered body temperature.

  Altered nutrition.

  Self-care deficit: medication administration.

  Impaired skin integrity.

- *Chief Complaint:*

  Mr. Green is a 35-year-old oil field supervisor who was burned on the job.

- *History of Present Illness:*

  Explosion on job started flash fire, producing partial-thickness and full-thickness burns of face, arms, and chest. Client presents 45 minutes after the thermal injury occurred.

- *Past History:*

  No allergies. Considered in good general health before accident.

- *Family History:*

Parents: Unremarkable.

One sibling: Diabetes mellitus, maturity onset.

- *Physical Exam:*

HEENT: Singed nares. Skin around nose and mouth red. Palate red.

Neck: Carotid pulse present; reddened.

Heart: Sinus tachycardia.

Lungs: Clear A-P.

Chest: Burned areas appear white, with redder areas on periphery. Burn extends from clavicle to umbilicus.

Extremities: Right arm: Circumferential burn on forearm, red and weeping. Upper left arm: Burn area found medially; appears white, with redder areas on periphery.

Vital signs: Temperature: 97°F. BP: 90/70. P: 100. R: 30.

- *Laboratory Data:*

Hct: 56%.

Urine: Specific gravity = 1.030. pH: 6. Positive for hemoglobin.

---

52. Before Mr. Green's arrival at the emergency department, which action should the industrial nurse perform *first*?

    A. Cover Mr. Green with a blanket.

    B. Apply a topical antibiotic ointment to the burned areas.

    C. Apply tepid to cold water to the burn surface.

    D. Excise eschar with scalpel and scissors.

53. What could the nurse do as emergency treatment if there is a chemical burn to the eye?

    A. Apply a sterile 4 x 4 bandage over the injured eye to prevent infection.

    B. Administer an antidote to slow down the chemical reaction.

    C. Apply ice packs to retard absorption of the chemical.

    D. Flush with water continuously.

54. Mr. Green arrives at the hospital emergency department. The nurse needs to prepare all medications for intravenous administration at this time because:

    A. Rapid excretion is needed to prevent overdose.

    B. There is a lack of sufficient available sites.

    C. Peripheral perfusion is poor.

    D. Reduction in pain and additional stresses is needed.

55. During the initial stage of burn therapy, the nurse expects Mr. Green's body temperature to be:

    A. 97°F

    B. 98.6°F.

    C. 100°F.

    D. 102°F.

Mr. Green is transferred to the burn unit.

---

56. A student in the burn unit asks the nurse why the surgeon wants to wait 24 hours before giving colloids. Which rationale does the nurse offer for that action at that time?

    A. To enhance interstitial edema.

    B. To improve cardiac output.

    C. To maintain renal perfusion.

    D. Capillary permeability is reduced.

57. Which nursing observation indicates a good prognosis 36 hours after the burn?

    A. Bounding pulse.

    B. CVP of 10.

    C. Urine output of 20 mL/hour.

    D. Reduction in size of blisters.

58. The nurse should avoid giving clients with burns anything by mouth in the first 48 hours after the burn because the client may develop:

    A. Productive cough with yellow mucus.

    B. A fall in blood pressure, with widening pulse pressure.

    C. Hematuria accompanied by decreasing output.

    D. Abdominal distention with absent bowel sounds.

59. Because of the location of Mr. Green's burns, which nursing observation requires immediate action?

    A. Urine output 30 mL/hour for the first 4 hours. Urine red to chocolate in color.

    B. Absent bowel sounds.

    C. Respiratory stridor.

    D. Blisters and white, leathery appearance of burned areas.

60. Mafenide (Sulfamylon) is ordered to be applied over the burned areas. Select the nursing measure to be used when this medication is administered:

    A. Give analgesic 30 minutes before application.

    B. Observe laboratory reports for leukopenia.

C. Observe creatinine and BUN levels.

D. Have Mr. Green's hearing checked by an otologist.

61. If gentamicin is used to treat a *Pseudomonas* infection, the nurse should:

A. Give analgesic 30 minutes before application.

B. Check laboratory reports for leukopenia.

C. Observe any changes in renal function.

D. Check deep-tendon reflexes for hyporeflexia.

62. The nurse knows that an important disadvantage of 5% silver nitrate as a treatment for burns is that it:

A. Prevents eschar formation.

B. Causes the loss of potassium and sodium.

C. Stains the floor, walls, and skin.

D. Cannot be used on children who are burned.

63. Curling's ulcer is a complication of severe burns. Early acute symptoms the nurse should look for include:

A. Pain in the right upper quadrant and flatus.

B. Hypotension and hematemesis.

C. Dyspepsia and hyperperistalsis.

D. Abdominal distention and decrease in hematocrit.

64. Which nursing observation indicates that zinc stores are adequately met?

A. A decrease in wound circumference from 4 to 2 cm.

B. Reduction in muscle twitching.

C. A urinary output free of acetone and glucose.

D. Adequate peripheral vision and color perception.

65. The closed method of treatment for burns involves occlusive dressings. Nursing measures relative to the care of a client with occlusive dressings include:

A. Avoid evenly distributed pressure on the wrapped part.

B. Submerge the dressed part in a pHisoHex solution before changing the dressing.

C. Keep the wrapped part in a dependent position.

D. Prevent two body surfaces from touching.

66. The nurse knows that which of the following is necessary for protein synthesis to proceed at an optimum rate?

A. Protein reserve.

B. Glucagon.

C. Adequacy of lipoproteins.

D. Adequate caloric intake.

67. In selecting a diet for the client with burns who is to receive a high-protein mid-evening snack, the nurse encourages the client to eat:

    A. $^{1}/_{3}$ cup yogurt.

    B. Broth.

    C. Jell-O with 8 crushed nuts.

    D. 1 cup of whole milk.

68. To minimize psychological stress, the nurse can:

    A. Insist that Mr. Green participate in his wound care.

    B. Schedule nursing care procedures to allow periods of uninterrupted sleep.

    C. Compare his progress with that of the other client in the unit.

    D. Ignore his periods of enuresis.

69. Which would the nurse assess to be an inappropriate response to thermal injury?

    A. Episodic depression or anger.

    B. Periodic anorexia.

    C. Reluctance to disrobe before the nursing staff.

    D. Continuous open masturbation.

70. Mr. Green is fitted for an elasticized garment during the rehabilitative phase. The nurse explains that the purpose of this mode of therapy is to:

    A. Reduce protein loss through the wound.

    B. Minimize evaporation and convection of heat.

    C. Reduce scar hypertrophy.

    D. Reduce collection of edema fluid under the graft.

Medical Diagnosis: Hyperthyroidism.

- *Surgical Treatment:*

  Thyroidectomy.

- *Nursing Problems/Diagnosis:*

  Risk of inadequate breathing patterns.

  Risk of fluid volume excess.

  Risk of injury: postoperative complications.

- *Chief Complaint:*

  Ms. Mary Easley, a 36-year-old woman who is Caucasian, seeks health care for palpitations and breathlessness.

- *History of Present Illness:*

  Weight loss over the past 6 months despite increases in appetite and food intake. Medication for diagnosed hyperthyroidism was propylthiouracil. Symptoms continued despite medical intervention.

- *Family History:*

  No history of thyroid disease. One sister has diabetes. No history of cancer.

- *Review of Systems:*

  Weakness, fatigue, weight loss, increased appetite; heat intolerance, diarrhea, and insomnia.

- *Physical Exam:*

  Fine tremors of hands.

  Skin fine textured and smooth and moist to touch.

  Exophthalmos.

  Jittery and tense.

- *Laboratory and X-ray Data:*

  Radioactive iodine uptake: 25% in 6 hours.

  Thyroid scan: Enlargement of thyroid gland.

---

71. Ms. Easley seeks health care for hyperthyroidism. Which is an uncharacteristic sign or symptom of this condition?

    A. Enlargement of the front of her neck.

    B. Increasing protrusion of her eyes.

    C. Weight gain.

    D. Feelings of nervousness and irritability.

72. Medical intervention has not been successful and Mary Easley has a subtotal thyroidectomy. Because the nurse knows that a complication of this surgery may be calcium deficit, the nurse cautions Ms. Easley to report:

    A. Sharp decrease in urinary output.

    B. Pain in her kidney region.

    C. Continuous toniclike muscle spasms.

    D. Loss of sensation in extremities.

73. Ms. Easley received 3000 mL of IV fluid, containing saline, during the past 24 hours. The nurse identified Ms. Easley's problem as potential fluid overload. The nurse based that decision on which assessment data?

    A. Scanty urine and burning on urination.

    B. Dry skin and mucous membranes.

    C. Increased RBC count and hemoglobin.

    D. Puffy eyelids and shortness of breath.

74. Anticipating Ms. Easley's return to her room postoperatively, the nurse gathers specific equipment for her care. Which is the least necessary item to have at the bedside?

    A. Airway.

    B. Tracheotomy set.

    C. IV equipment.

    D. Gastric suction apparatus.

Medical Diagnosis: Cancer of the right breast.

- *Surgical Treatment:*

  Modified radical mastectomy.

- *Nursing Problems/Diagnosis:*

  Fear.

  Altered feeling state: anger.

  Health-seeking behaviors: interpretation of lab data, skin care after radiation treatment.

  Knowledge deficit: about treatment.

  Self-care deficit: medication administration: outcome, toxic effects, disadvantages.

  Self-esteem disturbance.

- *Chief Complaint:*

  Marion Mulvrey, a 40-year-old homemaker who is married, entered the hospital for treatment of a breast lesion discovered 1 month ago during routine breast self-examination.

- *History of Present Illness:*

  Examines breasts monthly. Noticed a small lump at upper outer region of right breast.

- *Past History:*

  Two children, ages 12 and 15, living and well. Phlebitis after delivery of second child; treated medically with no complications. Auto accident at age 33; concussion with resulting headaches for approximately 6 months after the accident. Usual childhood illnesses.

- *Family History:*

  No known history of breast cancer. No diabetes, tuberculosis, or mental disorders. Mother living; history of arthritis. Father recently retired after myocardial infarction. Brother, age 46; history of duodenal ulcers. Two older sisters living and well.

- *Review of Systems:*

  Has lost 10 pounds in past year. Has noticed increased tiredness during the past 3 months. No respiratory problems noted. No high blood pressure. Usual health checkup every year; periodic dental exam every 6 months.

- *Physical Exam:*

    BP: 146/92. P: 88. R: 26.

    Apprehensive about finding lesion right upper quadrant, right breast, approximately 2 cm in size, painless. Boundaries on palpation seem to be irregular.

- *Laboratory and X-ray Data:*

    Mammography: Irregularly shaped lesion of 2 cm. Breast biopsy necessary to confirm diagnosis.

    Hgb: 13 g.

    Hct: 42%.

    Chest x-ray: Lungs clear.

---

75. `The nurse helps Ms. Mulvrey to be aware that of all the following women, the group that is least likely to be at risk for breast cancer is:

    A. Women over 50 years old.

    B. Women whose mothers or sisters have breast cancer.

    C. Women who had a child before the age of 30.

    D. Women who are overweight.

76. The nurse explains to the client that the most important reason for women to perform breast self-examination is:

    A. The woman is able to determine what is serious and what is not serious.

    B. Women have great fears about having a physician perform breast exams, so it is best if they do it themselves.

    C. It eliminates the need for costly periodic health checkups.

    D. Most breast abnormalities can be detected early by the woman or her partner and reported to the physician.

77. The nurse helps Ms. Mulvrey to decide that the best time to do breast self-examination is:

    A. When her menstrual period begins.

    B. One week after her period begins.

    C. On the first day of the month.

    D. On the 14th day of her menstrual cycle.

78. When Ms. Mulvrey finds a lump in her right breast, the nurse advises her to:

    A. Make an appointment with her physician as soon as possible.

    B. Wait another month and evaluate.

    C. Call relatives to determine if there is a family history of breast cancer.

    D. Ignore it because she is not in the high-risk group.

79. Ms. Mulvrey is scheduled for a breast biopsy. The nurse explains that:

    A. This is the treatment for cancer of the breast.

    B. Most biopsies lead to mastectomies.

    C. There will be no scar from this procedure.

    D. This is part of the diagnostic workup.

80. The biopsy specimen is positive for breast cancer. Ms. Mulvrey is scheduled for a modified radical mastectomy. The nurse explains that the tissue that will be removed will be:

    A. Breast and axillary nodes.

    B. Breast, pectoral muscles, and axillary nodes.

    C. Breast alone.

    D. The portion of the breast involved.

81. The nurse realizes that Ms. Mulvrey has demonstrated the first step toward acceptance of her altered body image by:

    A. Looking at the incision when the nurse is changing the dressing.

    B. Touching the operative site when the dressing is removed.

    C. Changing the subject each time the nurse attempts to discuss it.

    D. Asking her husband to bring in her sheer nightgown.

82. Ms. Mulvrey is scheduled for radiation therapy. When she asks if there are any special precautions she should plan to take, the nurse replies:

    A. "Use talcum powder for comfort."

    B. "Apply a soothing ointment to the skin."

    C. "Wash the skin with water and pat dry."

    D. "Sunbathe as usual."

83. The nurse has identified that the local tissue response to radiation is normal because Ms. Mulvrey's site shows:

    A. Redness of the surface tissue.

    B. Atrophy of the skin.

    C. Scattered pustule formation.

    D. Sloughing of two layers of the skin.

84. Six months after surgery, Ms. Mulvrey was found to have a positive liver scan. It was decided to begin a course of antimetabolite chemotherapy. The nurse recognizes that the expected action of this drug is to:

    A. Decrease blood supply to malignant cells.

    B. Produce a toxic substance absorbed by malignant cells.

    C. Interfere with nucleic acid synthesis.

    D. Destroy the capsule surrounding malignant cells.

85. The nurse knows that drugs commonly used to treat malignant tumors are often toxic. Her observations will show the most toxic effects on:

    A. Hair follicles.

    B. Lung alveoli.

    C. Muscle cells.

    D. Kidney tissue.

86. The nurse knows that the major disadvantage of antineoplastic drugs is that they:

    A. Tend to enhance the immune response.

    B. Do not discriminate between cancer cells and normal cells.

    C. Substitute for normal substances in the body and are absorbed by cancer cells.

    D. Always require the client to be hospitalized.

87. One of the potential side effects of cancer chemotherapy is thrombocytopenia. Which data confirm to the nurse the presence of this problem?

    A. Low lymphocyte count.

    B. Low platelet count.

    C. High RBC count.

    D. High eosinophil count.

88. Ms. Mulvrey is readmitted to the hospital 1 year later in a terminal stage of illness. At this time, the nurse planning care with Ms. Mulvrey should recognize that she is most likely to fear:

    A. Diagnosis.

    B. Further therapy.

    C. Being socially inadequate.

    D. Being isolated.

89. When Ms. Mulvrey's husband expresses his anger, it is best for the nurse to:

    A. Offer to call a friend to be with him.

    B. Leave him alone so he can have privacy.

    C. Stay with him and listen to his concerns.

    D. Explain that all that can be done has been done.

Medical Diagnosis: Fibroid uterus.

- *Surgical Treatment:*

  Abdominal hysterectomy.

- *Nursing Problems/Diagnosis:*

  Inadequate breathing patterns.

  Altered comfort pattern (discomfort-related to postop breathing).

  Fear.

  Risk for infection.

  Risk for injury: complications.

  Knowledge deficit: about diagnostic test.

  Self-care deficit: medication administration.

  Impaired skin integrity.

- *Chief Complaint:*

  Ms. Salisbury, a schoolteacher who is 42-years-old, enters the hospital for a planned abdominal hysterectomy.

- *History of Present Illness:*

  Ms. Salisbury has had a history of abnormal menstrual symptoms for the past 6 months. She has had menorrhagia for the past 6 months and metrorrhagia for the past 3 months. She has had low back discomfort and pain, constipation, and increasing dysmenorrhea.

- *Past History:*

  Ms. Salisbury has one daughter, age 19. She had three other pregnancies, which ended in spontaneous abortions in the first trimester. There was no history of inflammatory disease. She has been using a diaphragm and contraceptive jelly for birth control.

- *Family History:*

  One sister, age 46, had a hysterectomy at age 44 for similar problems. There was no history of ovarian or uterine cancer in the family.

- *Review of Systems:*

  Weight loss of 5 pounds during the past year. No rashes or skin lesions.

  Head and neck: No complaints of vertigo. Two colds during the past 3 months.

  Breasts: Periodic self-examination. No abnormalities.

  Respiratory: No distress at present. No cough.

  Cardiac: No known heart disease. One episode of palpitation after first bleeding episode.

  GI: Appetite fair; concern over weight loss.

  Urinary tract: Cystitis with first pregnancy. No other problems.

Genitoreproductive: Menarche at 13. Periods regular every 28 days for 5 days. Heavy bleeding at periods for past 6 months. Bleeding between periods past 3 months. D & C 2 months ago; bleeding pattern continued after D & C.

- **Physical Exam:**

Respiratory: No crackles or wheezes noted on auscultation.

Abdomen: Soft to palpation. Bowel sounds present.

Genitalia/vulva: Normal. Uterus: Anterior, enlarged, abnormal contour. Pap smear negative at time of D & C.

- **Laboratory Data:**

Pap smear: Negative.

D & C scrapings: Tissue consistent with leiomyoma formations.

Hct: 34%.

Hgb: 10 g.

---

90. Ms. Salisbury is discussing the report of the Papanicolaou smear she received from her physician. She asks the reason why such a test is done yearly. The nurse answers that this test helps to determine:

    A. Precancerous and cancerous conditions of the cervix.

    B. Fibrous and other benign tumors of the uterus.

    C. Inflammatory processes present in the pelvis.

    D. Infections of Bartholin's gland.

91. Ms. Salisbury expresses fear about her upcoming abdominal hysterectomy. The nurse should:

    A. Tell her that her physician is competent.

    B. Allow her an opportunity to express her fears.

    C. Change the subject when fear is obvious.

    D. Teach her that fear stands in the way of recovery.

92. Preoperative medications ordered for Ms. Salisbury were meperidine, 75 mg, and atropine, 0.3 mg. Dosages available were: meperidine, 50 mg/mL, and atropine, 0.4 mg/mL. The nurse prepares:

    A. Meperidine, 0.75 mL; atropine, 1.2 mL.

    B. Meperidine, 1.5 mL; atropine, 0.5 mL.

    C. Meperidine, 2 mL; atropine, 1 mL.

    D. Meperidine, 1.5 mL; atropine, 0.75 mL.

93. The nurse gives atropine sulfate preoperatively to achieve:

    A. General muscular relaxation.

    B. Decrease in pulse and respiratory rate.

C. Decrease in oral and respiratory secretions.

D. Blood pressure within normal range.

94. Considering the potential discomfort level during postoperative deep breathing and coughing, the nurse should prepare Ms. Salisbury to:

A. Support her abdomen with a pillow or with her hands.

B. Support her rib cage with a binder or with her hands.

C. Lie on her abdomen with her arms at her side.

D. Lie flat in bed with her hands behind her head.

95. Ms. Salisbury returns from the recovery room. The nurse observes that the site of the intravenous infusion is pale and edematous. The nurse should examine for further evidence of:

A. Phlebitis.

B. Air embolism.

C. Infiltration.

D. Allergic reaction.

96. When changing the dressing, the nurse noted a small separation at the base of the wound. Suddenly Ms. Salisbury coughs and the wound completely separates. The nurse's most appropriate initial action is to:

A. Cover the incision with a sterile, moist towel.

B. Pack the intestines back into the abdominal cavity.

C. Irrigate the exposed area with sterile water.

D. Document the sequence of events in the nurse's notes.

97. If Ms. Salisbury had her ovaries removed at the same time as she had her hysterectomy, the nurse would explain that she could expect to experience:

A. Decreased perspiration.

B. Increased desire to sleep.

C. Pallor of head, neck, and throat.

D. Increased sensitivity to heat loss.

98. Later in Ms. Salisbury's postoperative course, the nurse identifies that she has a possible infection of the wound. Which assessment parameter could the nurse eliminate in making this observation?

A. Small amount of drainage on the dressing.

B. Pain at the upper edge of the incision.

C. Fever of 101.8°F.

D. Moist crackles at the base of her lungs.

99. Ms. Salisbury receives a prescription for cephalexin (Keflex) to take after discharge from the hospital. The nurse should instruct her to:

   A. Take all of the medication prescribed by her physician.

   B. Take all of the medication prescribed for 3 days and reevaluate how she is feeling.

   C. Take all of the medication as long as she has a fever.

   D. Take the medication until the pain subsides.

Medical Diagnosis: Leukemia.

- ***Nursing Problems/Diagnosis:***

  Anxiety.

  Body image disturbance.

  Risk for infection.

  High risk for injury: bleeding tendency.

  Altered nutrition requirements.

  Social isolation.

- ***Chief Complaint:***

  Ms. Ella Perry, a 45-year-old homemaker, suffered a severe bleeding episode after having a tooth extracted.

- ***History of Present Illness:***

  For approximately 6 months, Ms. Perry complained of weakness, easy fatigability, and pain in her arms. She attributed these complaints to the strenuous exercises in which she usually engages in. She plays tennis regularly. Later, she noticed increased bruising on her thighs and arms.

- ***Past History:***

  Hospitalized twice; normal pregnancies.

- ***Family History:***

  Father died at age 65; cancer of lungs. Mother, age 70, relatively healthy. Sister, age 50, anemia. Children ages 10 and 13, healthy.

- ***Physical Exam:***

  Neck: No enlargement or asymmetry; no mass or lymph nodes palpated; no limitation of movement.

  Chest: Normal anteroposterior diameter; bilateral and equal chest expansion and excursion.

  Lungs: Clear on auscultation.

  Heart: Point of maximal impulse (PMI) at fifth intercostal space (ICS), barely palpable; S_1 and S_2 within normal limits; no clicks or splitting; no extra heart sounds.

Abdomen: Soft, nondistended; fairly active bowel sounds; enlarged spleen.

Extremities: Joint pains, particularly in arms; strong hand grasps; adequate muscle strength in lower extremities.

Chest x-ray: Normal.

ECG: Normal sinus rhythm.

Blood gases: Within normal limits.

■ *Laboratory Data:*

WBC: 205,000/μL.

Philadelphia chromosome positive.

Decreased leukocyte alkaline phosphatase.

---

100. To confirm the diagnosis of chronic myelocytic leukemia, which laboratory test is not routine?

    A. Blood culture.

    B. Differential count.

    C. Bone marrow aspiration.

    D. WBC count.

101. What physical assessment information gathered from the client's records by the nurse confirms the presence of an enlarged spleen?

    A. Dullness is elicited when the splenic area is percussed.

    B. The spleen tip is difficult to palpate below the left costal margin.

    C. A notch is palpated along the medial border of the left lower quadrant.

    D. Tympanic sound is elicited when the anterior axillary line is percussed.

102. The nurse knows that the weakness, fatigue, and pallor common in clients with leukemia are due to:

    A. Deficiency of platelets.

    B. Presence of infective process.

    C. Decreased erythrocyte production.

    D. Infiltration of peripheral nerves by cancer.

103. The client with leukemia is given a low-bacteria diet, particularly during the acute episode of the disease process. Which does the nurse expect to be included in such a diet?

    A. Cooked spinach and celery.

    B. Lettuce and alfalfa sprouts.

    C. Fresh strawberries and carrots.

    D. Raw cauliflower or broccoli.

104. To prevent sensory deprivation in a client who is on protective isolation, the nurse should:

     A. Encourage friends and relatives to visit at the same time.

     B. Visit the client frequently and engage her in conversation.

     C. Repeatedly explain why protective isolation is necessary.

     D. Encourage the family to stay with the client for as long as they want.

105. A complication that the nurse must watch for in clients receiving chemotherapy is crystallization of uric acid. Which is normal and therefore not a manifestation of this complication?

     A. Specific gravity of 1.030.

     B. Urine output of 30–50 mL/hour.

     C. Serum creatinine of 3 mg/dL.

     D. Elevated BUN levels.

106. Which response is the *most* appropriate for the client who has alopecia as a result of chemotherapy?

     A. "All we have to do is to put a cap on your head."

     B. "I'm sorry but your hair will always be thin now."

     C. "Your hair will grow again after the chemotherapy is over."

     D. "Well, chemotherapy does that to most people, and we don't know why."

107. When a client is on cancer chemotherapy, the nurse should continuously assess for the presence of bone marrow depression, manifestations of which are:

     A. Night sweats and easy fatigability.

     B. Loss of skin turgor and weight loss.

     C. Low urine output and elevated BUN levels.

     D. Ecchymosis and weakness.

108. The nurse expects that a client with leukemia is in "remission" when:

     A. The client's immune system is stimulated to fight the organism.

     B. There is an increased amount of myeloblasts in the bone marrow.

     C. No cancer cells are microscopically evident in the bone marrow.

     D. Clinical manifestations of cancer are absent for more than 3 years.

109. The least helpful nursing approach in the care of a client who is terminally ill is to:

    A. Maintain the client's self-esteem and well-being.

    B. Keep the client from making decisions regarding his or her care.

    C. Provide open communication between the client and the staff.

    D. Allow family members to participate in the care of the client.

Medical Diagnosis: Bleeding duodenal ulcer.

- *Surgical Treatment:*

Gastrectomy.

- *Nursing Problems/Diagnosis:*

Altered bowel elimination.

Altered cardiac output.

Altered comfort (pain).

Effective individual management of therapeutic regimen.

Altered nutrition: less than body requirements.

Self-care deficit: medication administration.

- *Chief Complaint:*

Mr. Earl Williams, the 46-year-old owner of a small business, is admitted to the hospital complaining of vomiting a large amount of bright red blood.

- *History of Present Illness:*

History of gastric disorders for the past 2 years. Current episode consisted of several days of consumption of some alcohol; death of brother (cancer of the lungs); inability to sleep, then epigastric pain, nausea, vomiting gastric contents; and then vomiting bright red blood.

- *Past History:*

Stomach disorders for several years. Weight loss of 6 pounds. Complaining of gnawing, aching, and burning pain, usually relieved by proper diet and antacids.

- *Family History:*

One brother died age 48, heart attack; one brother died, cancer of the lungs; one sister, living and well. Wife has multiple sclerosis, early stages. Son is unemployed and had dropped out of high school. Two daughters: one married (18-years-old) and living at home with husband and 2-month-old daughter; the other daughter is in high school and doing well.

- *Review of Systems:*

Weight loss. GI history (see **History of Present Illness** and **Past History**). No difficulty in breathing or palpitations.

- *Physical Exam:*

Vital signs: BP: 112/60. P: 92. R: 18.

Skin pale.

Acute pain.

Breath sounds clear.

Abdomen: complains of burning pain in mid-epigastric area.

- *Laboratory and X-ray Data:*

GI series shows abnormality of tissue in the duodenal region.

Endoscopy: positive for duodenal ulcer.

Stool: positive for occult blood.

Hgb: 12g.

Hct: 30%.

---

110. `Mr. Williams goes to the drugstore to buy an antacid. The nurse should teach him of the laxative effect of:

    A. Calcium carbonate (Titralac).

    B. Aluminum hydroxide gel (Amphojel).

    C. Magaldrate (Riopan).

    D. Magnesium hydroxide (magnesium magma).

111. Clients with duodenal ulcers are sometimes given drugs such as propantheline bromide (Pro-Banthine). The nurse knows that the desired effect of these drugs is to:

    A. Decrease gastric motility.

    B. Tranquilize the client.

    C. Increase gastric secretions.

    D. Directly stimulate mucosal cell growth.

112. Mr. Williams enters the hospital reporting that he has vomited a very large amount of blood. The nurse should expect which sign to be present?

    A. Decreased blood pressure.

    B. Decreased pulse.

    C. Decreased respirations.

    D. Increased urinary output.

113. The nurse needs to teach Mr. Williams that if he is having bleeding from his stomach ulcer, his stools will be:

    A. Claylike in color.

    B. Tarry.

C. Bright red.

D. Light brown.

114. Mr. Williams begins to hemorrhage from his ulcer and will have surgery. The nurse considers that the urgency of this surgery is:

A. Planned.

B. Imperative.

C. Emergency.

D. Optional.

115. The nurse is observing for the possible complication of postoperative peritonitis. Which sign or symptom is *least* indicative of peritonitis?

A. Hyperactive bowel sounds.

B. Pain, local or general.

C. Abdominal rigidity.

D. Shallow respirations.

116. Mr. Williams complains of postoperative pain. The nurse administers the analgesic as ordered. What nursing actions will help reduce the pain while the analgesic is taking its effect?

A. Move the client quickly; administer stimulating backrub.

B. Encourage the client to discuss his feelings.

C. Position comfortably; subdue the lighting.

D. Give the client a bath; change bed linens.

117. Mr. Williams demonstrates that he is aware of dietary influences in the prevention of the dumping syndrome when he adjusts his intake by:

A. Decreasing fats.

B. Decreasing proteins.

C. Increasing fluids at mealtimes.

D. Decreasing carbohydrates.

Medical Diagnosis: Cholelithiasis.

- *Surgical Treatment:*

  Open cholecystectomy.

- *Nursing Problems/Diagnosis:*

  Altered comfort (pain).

  Fluid volume deficit.

  Health-seeking behaviors: preparation for diagnostic procedures.

Effective individual management of therapeutic regimen.

Risk for injury: postoperative complications.

Altered nutrition: less than body requirements.

Self-care deficit: medication administration.

- **Chief Complaint:**

Adele Norfolk, 47-years-old, was admitted to the hospital, complaining of severe pain in her right upper quadrant.

- **History of Present Illness:**

Ms. Norfolk has noticed an intolerance to fatty foods over the past few months. She has also noted general indigestion. Prior to this admission, no serious episodes of pain were noted. Her present pain began 6 hours ago; its onset was sudden and the pain increased in severity. She complained of nausea and vomited twice prior to admission.

- **Past Health History:**

Twenty-five pounds overweight. Three normal deliveries; all children living and well. Appendectomy at age 14. Smokes 1 pack of cigarettes a day.

- **Family History:**

No history of gallbladder disease in mother, father, two brothers, or one sister. Diet has been high in fat content throughout lifetime.

- **Review of Systems:**

Weight gain gradual over past 5 years. Unsuccessful in own attempts to control weight. Distress when eating fatty foods; complains of "bloating feeling." Denies cough.

- **Physical Exam:**

Vital signs: BP: 140/92. Temperature: 101°F. P: 92. R: 26.

Head and neck: Tongue dry; face flushed; no jaundice noted.

Chest: Some wheezing noted at base of lungs. Difficulty in coughing due to acute distress.

Abdomen: Severe pain and tenderness in right upper quadrant. Positive Murphy's sign.

Extremities: Some evidence of varicosities in posterior aspect of lower legs.

- **Laboratory and X-ray Data:**

X-ray: Absence of opaque materials in the gallbladder—cholecystography.

Chest x-ray: Within normal limits.

GI series: Negative.

WBC: 12,500/μL.

Cholesterol level: 290 mg/dL.

Urine specific gravity: 1.040.

118. Which drug may increase biliary colic pain if given to a client with cholecystitis?

    A. Meperidine (Demerol).

    B. Nitroglycerin.

    C. Morphine.

    D. Ibuprofen.

119. Ms. Norfolk is having an oral cholecystogram. She asks the nurse if there are any special preparations for this type of x-ray. The nurse tells her that she will:

    A. Have a regular diet the evening before the test.

    B. Eat a full meal the morning of the test.

    C. Take iodine dye capsules by mouth the evening before the test.

    D. Have this test done after her scheduled GI series.

120. Ms. Norfolk is discharged from the hospital. She must follow a low-fat diet until her readmission for surgery. The nurse knows that the client is demonstrating her dietary knowledge when she eliminates:

    A. Fruit juices.

    B. Broiled chicken.

    C. Chocolate pudding.

    D. Carrots and spinach.

121. In preparing Ms. Norfolk for the surgical experience, the nurse is least likely to initiate teaching about:

    A. The reason for being NPO after midnight prior to surgery.

    B. Deep breathing, coughing, and turning techniques.

    C. The expected results of the surgical procedure.

    D. The availability of pain medication prn.

122. Ms. Norfolk returns from surgery. Which nursing action has the highest priority during the recovery room period?

    A. Checking vital signs every 15 minutes.

    B. Recording intake and output.

    C. Explaining procedures to her family.

    D. Maintaining a patent airway.

123. Ms. Norfolk is to receive 3000 mL of solution intravenously in each 24-hour period. If there is a drop factor of 15 drops/mL, at approximately how many drops per minute should the nurse regulate the IV?

    A. 22 drops.

    B. 31 drops.

    C. 42 drops.

    D. 51 drops.

124. The first IV infusion began at 8 A.M. At 11 A.M., given a correct flow rate and no interference, the nurse expects the first 1000-mL container to contain:

    A. 625 mL.

    B. 736 mL.

    C. 840 mL.

    D. 437 mL.

125. Because of Ms. Norfolk's weight and the location of her incision, the nurse can anticipate that the most likely complication will be:

    A. Fluid and electrolyte imbalance.

    B. Atelectasis.

    C. Infection.

    D. Nausea and vomiting.

126. Ms. Norfolk has a T-tube inserted in the surgical wound. The most important nursing function in caring for this tube is:

    A. Recording quantity and color of drainage.

    B. Changing the dressing every shift.

    C. Preventing the tube from kinking.

    D. Teaching the client about the reason for the tube.

127. Ms. Norfolk develops a paralytic ileus postoperatively. The nurse should question which medical order before carrying it out?

    A. Begin intermittent nasogastric suction.

    B. Encourage the client to take carbonated beverages.

    C. Neostigmine (Prostigmin), 500 µg IM.

    D. Continuous IV therapy, 3000 mL in 24 hours; alternate 5% dextrose in water with Ringer's lactate.

128. As she is preparing for discharge, Ms. Norfolk reports to the nurse that she has pain in the calf of her left leg. The nurse assesses the situation and finds a positive Homans' sign. The nurse's decision is to:

    A. Put Ms. Norfolk on bedrest.

    B. Measure her left calf and reassess in 4 hours.

    C. Assist Ms. Norfolk in ambulation.

    D. Massage the cramp in her calf.

Medical Diagnosis: Essential hypertension.

- **Nursing Problems/Diagnosis:**

  Altered cardiac output.

  Risk for alteration in circulation.

  Altered nutrition: less than body requirements.

  Self-care deficit: medication administration.

- **Chief Complaint:**

  Harry Amos, 52-years-old, works in a steel mill. He complains of dizziness and headache.

- **Past History:**

  Pneumonia, resolved 2 years ago. No surgeries or allergies.

- **Family History:**

  Father: Deceased, myocardial infarction. Mother: Deceased, senility.

  Siblings: Sister with glaucoma.

- **Review of Symptoms:**

  Currently 20 pounds overweight.

  Nocturia.

  Vital signs: R: 30. P: 90. Temperature: 98°F. BP: 180/100.

- **Physical Exam:**

  Neck: Mild jugular venous distention to 8 cm.

  Lung: Slight bilateral crackles in both lower lung fields; moderate dyspnea on exertion.

  Heart: Angina pain. S_4 heard. PMI palpated at 6th intercostal space, left of the left midclavicular line.

  Abdomen: Liver palpable 4 cm below right costal margin.

  Extremities: No pitting of 1+ pedal edema.

  Fundoscopic: Retinal vessel dilated; exudate, hemorrhages, papilledema absent.

- **Laboratory and X-ray Data:**

  Chest x-ray: Left ventricular hypertrophy bilateral infiltration in lung field.

  Creatinine: 0.5 mg/L.

  BUN: 15 mg/dL.

  Urinary protein: Absent.

---

129. The nurse considers Mr. Amos a good historian. Based on the review of symptoms and the initial physical exam, which nursing order is appropriate to write?

     A. Keep side rails up at all times.

    B. Assist with meals.

    C. Allow a rest period between activities.

    D. Ensure meticulous skin care.

130. Mr. Amos is placed on hydrochlorothiazide. Postural hypotension is a frequent complication of hydrochlorothiazide administration. The nurse should tell him that the probability of developing this complication increases:

    A. During the cold winter months.

    B. After alcohol ingestion.

    C. With sodium retention.

    D. After ingestion of seafood.

131. The most important nursing action for a client on diuretic therapy is:

    A. Recording daily weight.

    B. Reducing sodium in diet.

    C. Increasing oral fluid intake.

    D. Measuring intake and output.

132. Methyldopa (Aldomet), an antihypertensive drug, is ordered for Mr. Amos. In teaching him about the drug, the nurse should emphasize that:

    A. He should rise slowly from a lying to a sitting position and from a sitting to a standing position.

    B. He should skip a dosage of medication if he begins feeling dizzy, weak, and sleepy.

    C. He can alter his diet if necessary, as long as he takes the anti-hypertensive drug.

    D. Alcohol consumption does not affect the action of anti-hypertensive drugs.

133. While assisting Mr. Amos in getting out of bed, what objective indicator (other than a manometer) can the nurse use to evaluate the effect of ambulation and to detect early postural hypotension?

    A. Pupil response.

    B. Pulse rate.

    C. State of orientation.

    D. Increased muscle rigidity.

134. Mr. Amos explains that he is a quiet man and that he keeps all his feelings inside. Which activity is the most beneficial for the nurse to suggest to help Mr. Amos express himself?

    A. Watching a football game.

    B. Asking him what is bothering him.

    C. Nailing a table together.

    D. Playing chess.

135. Mr. Amos is to be discharged soon. What instruction does the nurse give him that is commonly given to all clients receiving diuretic therapy?

    A. Keep the bath water at 140°-150°F.

    B. Teach the client to take his weight and mark it down.

    C. Restrict fluids in the winter to avoid overhydration.

    D. Be alert for episodes of disorientation.

136. The nurse will need to tell Mr. Amos to make which adjustment in food preparation?

    A. Use more herbs and spices for flavoring.

    B. Purchase all low-sodium dietetic foods.

    C. Cook all of his food separately from the rest of the family's.

    D. Prepare foods such as biscuits and cakes from mixes.

The following two questions are on the subject of hypertension, but are not related to Mr. Amos's situation.

---

137. Ms. Root receives furosemide (Lasix), 80 mg PO every day. Her usual blood pressure is 120/76. This morning while taking her blood pressure prior to the furosemide, the nurse finds a reading of 90/60. What is the most appropriate nursing action?

    A. Withhold the dose and call the doctor.

    B. Give the drug but check her periodically.

    C. Give the drug and let the doctor know the blood pressure reading.

    D. Withhold the drug until the blood pressure rises.

138. Ms. Francisco is receiving pargyline (Eutonyl), an MAO inhibitor. The nurse instructs her to refrain from eating foods high in tyramine because these foods:

    A. Produce marked vasodilatation.

    B. Stimulate the myocardium, increasing its workload and output.

    C. Decrease the concentration of norepinephrine.

    D. Produce severe vasoconstriction.

Medical Diagnosis: Myocardial infarction.

- **Nursing Problems/Diagnosis:**

Altered cardiac output: decreased.

Risk of alteration in circulation.

Altered comfort (pain).

Altered fluid volume: excess.

Risk for injury.

Self-care deficit: medication administration.

- **Chief Complaint:**

Anthony Zingale, 52-years-old, has been experiencing tightness in the chest, dyspnea, diaphoresis, and weakness.

- **History of Present Illness:**

Approximately 2 weeks prior to admission, noted substernal tightness and pain radiating down both arms during exertion and excitement. Chest pain now unrelieved by rest.

- **Past History:**

Treated for hypertension for the past 3-4 years. No known history of diabetes or renal disease.

- **Family History:**

Mother died of a heart attack. Father died of liver cancer. Has an aunt with diabetes.

- **Review of Symptoms:**

Smokes 1 pack of cigarettes a day. Fifty pounds overweight.

- **Physical Exam:**

Head and neck: No neck vein distention.

Skin: Pale, cool, clammy. Lips slightly bluish.

Lungs: Clear, with faint breath sounds.

Heart: Heart sounds distant.

Abdomen: Rotund, soft.

Extremities: No cyanosis or edema. Weak pedal pulses.

- **Laboratory and X-ray Data:**

Na^+: 141.

K^+: 5.45.

BUN: 28.

Glucose: 280.

ECG: Sinus rhythm with occasional PVCs.

CK: 550.

MB: Greater than 35%.

Troponin T > 10 ng/mL.

Troponin I > 30 ng/mL.

---

139. Mr. Zingale has been experiencing the pain associated with angina pectoris prior to admission. For what characteristic picture of anginal pain should the nurse look?

   A. Requires a narcotic for relief.

B. Is relieved by rest.

C. Tends to radiate to the jaw.

D. Lasts at least 30 minutes.

140. Nitroglycerin was placed at the client's bedside in the event of an anginal attack. The nurse knows that the goal of care includes giving this drug to relieve chest pain by:

A. Increasing myocardial contractility.

B. Increasing the heart rate.

C. Decreasing myocardial contractility.

D. Decreasing venous return to the heart.

141. On review of the client's history and physical, which factor does not make Mr. Zingale a high-risk candidate for coronary artery disease?

A. Family history of cardiac disease.

B. Hypertension.

C. Smoking.

D. Family history of cancer.

142. When a colleague asks about it, which is the best explanation the nurse could give for the elevated serum potassium following myocardial damage?

A. Potassium is retained due to decreased renal function.

B. Sodium ions are excreted to relieve edema, and potassium is retained.

C. Potassium is released from the cells following destruction.

D. Potassium increases with metabolic alkalosis.

143. Nursing care for the client who is post–myocardial infarction is directed toward reducing the work of the heart and oxygen consumption. Which nursing action best accomplishes this goal?

A. Position flat in bed with pillow under head.

B. If possible, allow use of bedside commode.

C. Assist client in eating a regular diet.

D. Restrict all activity for 72 hours.

144. Mr. Zingale has been in the hospital for 24 hours. His temperature has increased from 98.6° to 100.2°F. The nurse's response to the increase is to:

A. Assume an infection is developing.

B. Increase fluid intake.

C. Consider it a normal occurrence.

D. Apply cooling measures.

145. Mr. Zingale tells the nurse that he is concerned about being able to eat his favorite Italian foods now that he is on a low fat, low sodium diet. Which foods does the nurse recommend as lowest in fat content?

    A. Cannelloni with part-skim ricotta cheese (1 cup).

    B. Canned spaghetti in tomato sauce (1 cup).

    C. Olive oil (1 tablespoon) and Italian herb bread.

    D. Dry salami sandwich (4 slices).

146. Mr. Zingale shows signs of congestive heart failure. He is started on a regime of digoxin and furosemide (Lasix). The signs of effectiveness that the nurse looks for include:

    A. Slowed heart rate and elevated urine specific gravity.

    B. Increased heart rate and lowered urine specific gravity.

    C. Clear breath sounds and slowed pulse.

    D. Regular heart rhythm and increased urine specific gravity.

147. Discharge teaching for the client who is post–myocardial infarction is an important nursing function. Of the following areas for discussion, which one includes *inaccurate* counseling?

    A. Stress reduction is useful in reducing the risk of subsequent attacks.

    B. Sexual activity can resume, but it will need to be limited compared with the pre–myocardial infarction activity.

    C. Weight reduction decreases the workload of the heart.

    D. All antiarrhythmic drugs can cause arrhythmias; therefore, the client and/or family should know how to check the pulse.

Medical Diagnosis: Laënnec's cirrhosis; hepatic encephalopathy.

- *Nursing Problems/Diagnosis:*

    Inadequate breathing patterns.

    Impairment of digestion.

    Fluid volume deficit.

    Altered nutrition: less than body requirements.

    Altered thought processes.

- *Chief Complaint:*

    Joseph Mesta, is 55-years-old and married. He complains of vomiting, confusion, restlessness, and increased abdominal size.

- *History of Present Illness:*

    Six episodes of coffee-ground emesis in past 24 hours. According to wife, he has intermittent disorientation to place and time. Also reports an 18-pound weight gain in past 6 months and a gradual increase in abdominal girth.

- *Past History:*

Discharged from hospital 6 months ago with diagnosis of Laënnec's cirrhosis. Responded well to treatment with diuretics and salt and protein restrictions.

- *Family History:*

Mother and father died of "old age" in their 80s.

- *Review of Symptoms:*

Admits to difficulty following doctor's prescribed diet. Avoids hard liquor but consumes 4–6 beers each night.

- *Physical Exam:*

Lungs: Bilateral, basilar crackles.

Abdomen: Marked distention; liver barely palpable; distended veins visible in right and left upper quadrants.

Rectal: Black, tarry stool; hematest positive.

Extremities: 2 + pitting edema both legs; 1+ arms.

Skin: Jaundice; multiple abrasions on forearms which bleed easily.

Neurologic: Lethargic; disoriented to time and place; tremor, both upper arms.

- *Laboratory and X-ray Data:*

Hgb: 10.1 g.

Hct: 31.3%.

WBC: 10,200/μL.

BUN: 62 mg/dL.

Creatinine: 3.3 mg/dL.

Total bilirubin: 7.3 mg/dL.

Albumin: 2.3 g/dL.

CK: 460 mU/mL.

AST: 180 U/mL.

LDH: 451 U/mL.

ALT: 488 U/mL.

Uric acid: 10.5 mg/dL.

UGI: Varices of esophagus and stomach.

Paracentesis: 400 mL clear, straw-colored fluid.

---

148. Which area should the nurse examine to look for jaundice in a person with a dark complexion?

    A. Nailbeds.

    B. Palms of hands.

    C. Hard palate. —

    D. Soles of feet.

149. Which goal of care is inappropriate when a lowered blood ammonia level is the desired outcome?

    A. Prevention of GI bleeding.

    B. Reduction of dietary protein intake.

    C. Avoidance of enemas and cathartics.

    D. Decrease in bacterial flora in the intestine.

150. Which drug might the nurse be asked to give to decrease ammonia levels in a client with liver disease?

    A. Diazepam (Valium).

    B. Diphenoxylate hydrochloride and atropine sulfate (Lomotil).

    C. Furosemide (Lasix).

    D. Lactulose.

151. Which is irrelevant in the nursing evaluation of the effectiveness of the treatment for hepatic encephalopathy?

    A. Lessening of flapping tremors of the hands.

    B. Decreases in pedal edema.

    C. Improved levels of consciousness.

    D. Increased cooperativeness.

152. Which nursing observation is an inappropriate indicator of GI bleeding?

    A. Elevated BUN.

    B. Coffee-ground emesis.

    C. Black, tarry stools.

    D. Lowered hemoglobin.

153. A Sengstaken-Blakemore (S-B) tube was inserted in Mr. Mesta to control bleeding of esophageal varices. On entering the room, the nurse notices that he is gasping for breath. His color has become cyanotic and his respirations are rapid and shallow. What should the nurse *first* suspect?

    A. A pulmonary embolus has probably developed.

    B. The S-B tube has dislodged and one of its balloons is obstructing the airway.

    C. The client is air hungry due to anemia.

    D. The client is anxious and this can cause changes in respiratory status.

154. Mr. Mesta is restless and uncooperative in the early days of his treatment. His wife asks the nurse if he could be medicated to "calm him down." Which statement should guide the nurse's response?

A. Sedatives are never given to clients with liver disease because damaged liver cells cannot metabolize the drug.

B. Sedatives are usually metabolized by the kidneys, so this request is feasible.

C. Sedatives have an excitant, rather than a calming, effect on clients with liver disease.

D. A few sedatives that are not metabolized in the liver exist, but they should be used cautiously. ✓

155. As Mr. Mesta's condition improves, he mentions his dislike for the low-sodium, low-protein diet ordered by his doctor. He states, "That food is not fit for a man to eat!" The best response that the nurse could make at this time is:

A. "It must be difficult for you to accept these changes in your diet, Mr. Mesta."

B. "Well, you've got to make the best of it, Mr. Mesta. You've really no choice but to follow the doctor's orders."

C. "It could be worse, Mr. Mesta. That poor person in the next bed isn't allowed to eat anything at all!"

D. "Maybe we could talk to your doctor, Mr. Mesta. We could ask him to put you on a regular diet since you will be going home soon."

Medical Diagnosis: Brain attack.

- **Nursing Problems/Diagnosis:**

  Impaired breathing patterns.

  Family coping: potential for growth.

  Risk for injury.

  Altered nutrition: more than body requirements.

  Impaired physical mobility.

  Self-care deficit.

  Altered thought processes.

  Altered verbal communication.

  Altered urinary elimination.

- **Chief Complaint:**

  George Lewis is 58-years-old and a businessperson. He is brought to the medical center due to sudden loss of consciousness.

- **History of Present Illness:**

  While playing golf with his business associate, Mr. Lewis complained of severe headache, which lasted for 5 minutes. He then suddenly fell to the ground and became comatose. At the medical center, he was tentatively diagnosed as having a left-sided stroke caused by intracerebral hemorrhage.

- *Past History:*

  Hypertension, age 42 to present.

- *Family History:*

  Father, age 80, relatively well. Mother died age 54, stroke. Brother, age 54, hypertension.

- *Physical Exam:*

  Face: Drooping, right side.

  Eyes: Paresis, right lateral gaze; negative doll's eye.

  Neck: Nuchal rigidity; bruit on right carotid artery.

  Chest: Periods of hyperpnea alternate with periods of apnea.

  Heart: Apical impulse extends to fifth and sixth intercostal spaces; forceful and thrusting.

  Abdomen: Soft, nondistended; hypoactive bowel sounds.

  Extremities: Left upper and lower extremities flaccid; positive Babinski sign.

- *Laboratory and X-ray Data:*

  Chest x-ray: Cardiac enlargement with left ventricular prominence.

  ECG: Increased QRS complexes, increased R wave in limb leads; deep S wave in lead V_1.

  Blood gases: Slight respiratory alkalosis.

  CAT scan: Hemorrhage in foramen, with involvement of adjacent internal capsule.

---

156. Which neurologic check may the nurse elicit from Mr. Lewis, who is in deep coma?

    A. Response to deep pain.

    B. Deep, gasping respirations.

    C. Eyes turned toward his left side.

    D. Purposeful movement of his right leg.

157. The nurse assesses that Mr. Lewis has decorticate posturing if he manifests:

    A. Flaccid arms and legs; fully extended legs; and flexed feet.

    B. A rhythmic contraction and relaxation of the muscles of one arm.

    C. Flexed fingers, wrists, and arms; fully extended legs; and flexed feet.

    D. Fully extended arms with clenched fists and arms rotated away from the body.

158. For which neurologic test should the nurse prepare the client to best determine the location of cerebral hemorrhage?

    A. Myelography.

    B. Electromyogram.

    C. Lumbar puncture.

    D. Computerized tomography.

159. Based on the information given about Mr. Lewis, the nursing problem that deserves immediate attention is:

    A. Brain attack (stroke) caused by intracerebral hemorrhage.

    B. Inability to communicate related to altered level of consciousness.

    C. Potential for respiratory insufficiency related to severely depressed level of consciousness.

    D. Ineffective communication related to inability to find words to express himself adequately.

160. The short-term nursing goal that has the *least* priority when responsiveness is decreased is to maintain adequate:

    A. Nutrition and fluids.

    B. Rest and relaxation.

    C. Expansion of both lungs.

    D. Protection from injury.

161. The nurse knows that when the client with a stroke is unable to appropriately express his needs verbally and to understand spoken or written words, he has:

    A. Aphasia.

    B. Agnosia.

    C. Apraxia.

    D. Ataxia.

162. The nursing care plan for urinary incontinence and retention in clients rehabilitating from the acute phase of stroke includes:

    A. A restricted fluid intake.

    B. Intermittent catheterization.

    C. Prolonged use of Foley catheter.

    D. Use of an external condom drainage system.

163. To provide caloric intake, supplemental feedings through the nasogastric tube were ordered. Which outcome criterion clearly indicates to the nurse the presence of the nasogastric tube in the stomach?

    A. White, thin mucus is aspirated.

B. Air is heard at the end of the nasogastric tube.

C. Light-brown or light-yellow liquid drainage is aspirated, with pH of 4 or less.

D. Bubbles are seen when the end tip of the nasogastric tube is immersed in water.

164. Before he is allowed to drink or eat, the ability of the client with a stroke to swallow is elicited by testing which cranial nerve?

A. Facial.

B. Trigeminal.

C. Hypoglossal.

D. Glossopharyngeal.

165. Which statement by a family member or significant other *best* indicates to the nurse the individual's acceptance of participation in the rehabilitation of the client with stroke?

A. "I wish with all my heart that this had not happened."

B. "I can take much better care of him than you did here."

C. "I am willing to be shown how to dress and feed him."

D. "I have not been well myself. Why doesn't he just stay in the hospital?"

Medical Diagnosis: Acute myocardial infarction.

- *Nursing Problems/Diagnosis:*

Altered cardiac output.

Altered comfort (pain).

Altered nutrition: less than body requirements.

Self-care deficit: medication administration.

- *Chief Complaint:*

Larry Simpson, 63-years-old, is a top real estate salesman for a large firm in the city. He complains of crushing substernal pain.

- *Past History:*

Hypertensive for the past 3 years. Treated with hydralazine hydrochloride (Apresoline), 20 mg qid.

- *Family History:*

Brother: Hypertensive cardiovascular disease.

Father: Deceased, myocardial infarction.

- *Review of Symptoms:*

Smokes 1½ packs of cigarettes a day.

Weight gain of 30 pounds over the past year.

- *Physical Exam:*

  Neck: Carotid pulse weak and thready.

  Skin: Cool, moist, pallor.

  Lungs: Bibasilar crackles.

  Heart: Ventricular gallop; loud S_3 sound.

  Chest: Use of accessory muscles of thorax to breathe.

  Abdomen: Diminished bowel sounds.

  Mental status: Alert, restless, apprehensive.

  Extremities: Dusty nailbeds.

  Vital signs: BP: 90/60. Apical pulse: 100 (irregular).

- *Laboratory Data:*

  ECG: ST segment elevation; inverted T wave.

  Blood gases: PO_2: 70. Pco_2: 48. HCO_3: 20. pH: 7.30.

  Mr. Simpson hails a cab to the local hospital and collapses in the emergency department.

---

166. The arterial blood gases for Mr. Simpson reflect which acid-base status?

     A. Compensated respiratory acidosis.

     B. Metabolic acidosis.

     C. Respiratory acidosis.

     D. Both metabolic and respiratory acidosis.

Mr. Simpson is admitted to the CCU and is diagnosed with acute myocardial infarction. The following orders are written:

Morphine sulfate, 3 mg IV prn.

Nitroglycerin, 1/150 prn sublingual.

Lidocaine drip for 5 or more PVCs/min. May give 50-mg bolus x 2.

Bedrest: May use commode.

Nasal 0_2 at 5 L/min.

Digoxin, 1 mg PO x 2d.

167. A pulmonary artery catheter is inserted. Which observation indicates to the nurse that there is a complication related to the device that requires immediate action?

     A. Temperature 100.2°F.

     B. Ecchymosis on back and thorax.

     C. Urinary output 25 mL at 10 A.M.

     D. Nausea and indigestion.

168. The current CVP readings have been 11–13 cm H_2O. Select the nursing action that is most appropriate at this time:

    A. Reduce IV infusion rate.

    B. Increase nasal O_2 to 8 L/min.

    C. Increase IV infusion rate.

    D. Raise head of bed.

169. The nurse caring for Mr. Simpson recognizes that the relief of pain is a primary objective because:

    A. The accumulation of unoxidized metabolites irritates nerve endings.

    B. Severe pain can produce shock and increase cardiac workload.

    C. The client should be comfortable at all times.

    D. Pain stimulates the vagus, which dangerously slows the conduction system of the heart.

170. Intramuscular injections are usually not ordered following a myocardial infarction because:

    A. A larger dosage would be required.

    B. The pain of the needle stick only increases stress.

    C. The tissues are poorly perfused and venous return is diminished.

    D. The client may also be receiving anticoagulants.

171. Atropine is ordered for a pulse rate of 40 and below. At this time, the nurse gives this drug to:

    A. Dry oral and tracheobronchial secretions.

    B. Accelerate the heart rate by interfering with vagal impulses.

    C. Stimulate the SA node and sympathetic fibers to increase the rate.

    D. Reduce peristalsis and urinary bladder tone.

172. An intra-aortic balloon pump is inserted. Mr. Simpson's primary nurse writes his nursing orders. Which should the nurse include?

    A. Monitor pedal pulses.

    B. ROM to all extremities.

    C. Keep affected leg flexed.

    D. Elevate the head of the bed 45 degrees.

173. Mr. Simpson is taking digoxin, 1 mg PO qid. On day 3, he complains of nausea and states that the objects in his room have a yellowish tinge. Select the most appropriate nursing action at this time:

    A. Administer the medication, but observe him for further nausea.

    B. Count the apical pulse; if it is regular and above 60, administer the drug as ordered.

    C. Hold the drug and call the doctor.

    D. Administer the drug, but leave a note on the front of the chart regarding his complaints.

174. The nurse could anticipate that the client who is most likely to develop digitalis intoxication is:

    A. Mr. W, who is constipated.

    B. Ms. S, with a serum K^+ of 4 mEq/L.

    C. Mr. A, who is receiving hydrochlorothiazide.

    D. Mr. B, who is taking an oral hypoglycemic agent.

175. The cardiac glycosides are essential in the therapy of the client with a myocardial infarction. Which would indicate to the nurse that a therapeutic response to this medication had been attained?

    A. A 15% increase in apical pulse rate.

    B. A rise in CVP from 12 to 15 cm H_2O.

    C. Urine output 30 mL/hour (previously 40–50 mL/hour).

    D. Diminished crackles.

176. Mr. Simpson has been in the CCU for 2 weeks. Which statement by the client demands the most immediate action by the nurse?

    A. "Nurse, I haven't had a BM in 2 days."

    B. "This has been a rough 2 weeks for me."

    C. "When am I going to get some real food?"

    D. "I have to walk this pain out of my leg."

177. When heparin is being administered, which drug must the nurse have on hand?

    A. Protamine sulfate.

    B. Sodium citrate.

    C. Vitamin K (Aquamephyton).

    D. Warfarin sodium.

Mr. Simpson is suddenly dyspneic: pulse 110; respirations 30 and moist.

He is coughing and expectorates frothy, blood-streaked mucus. Diagnosis: Acute heart failure with pulmonary edema.

---

178. Furosemide (Lasix), 40 mg IVP, is given. Which observation indicates to the nurse that the therapeutic objectives of this medication have been met?

    A. Respiration 20 and pulse 80.

    B. Mr. Simpson voids 200 mL.

    C. Bilateral moist crackles.

    D. BP 90/60 and skin moist and cool.

179. Nitroglycerin, 1/150 gr. sublingual tablets, is given to Mr. Simpson at discharge. Instructions the nurse should give regarding home use of this drug are:

    A. Store this medication in a well-lighted, well-ventilated area.

    B. If flushing of the skin develops after administration, discontinue the drug.

    C. If chest pain persists after 3 or more tablets have been taken, the physician should be notified.

    D. Alcohol ingestion produces no deleterious effects in combination with this drug.

180. Mr. Simpson is discharged on a 2-g sodium-restricted diet. Following the nurse's instructions, he should select which appropriate lunch menu?

    A. 2 hot dogs with mustard, tossed salad, iced tea.

    B. 1 bowl of consommé, 4 unsalted crackers, 1 oz. of cheddar cheese.

    C. Corned beef sandwich, kosher dill pickle, ginger ale.

    D. Sliced broiled chicken, macaroni, 1 glass of orange juice.

Medical Diagnosis: Chronic renal failure; secondary hyperkalemia; metabolic acidosis; anemia.

- *Nursing Problems/Diagnosis:*

Risk for alteration in endocrine/metabolic processes.

Altered nutrition: less than body requirements.

Altered urinary elimination.

- *Chief Complaint:*

C. S. Toy is 64-years-old and Chinese. He is brought to the emergency department by his wife and oldest son. He has been feeling ill and tired, has been unable to eat, and has been losing weight.

- *History of Present Illness:*

Mr. Toy has been ill for about a week with vomiting, diarrhea, and

progressively increasing fatigue.

- *Past History:*

Episode of epistaxis 4 years ago, which brought him to the outpatient clinic. Diagnosed at that time with hypertension. Treated with unknown medications, which he has taken sporadically.

- *Family History:*

  None significant.

- *Review of Symptoms:*

  Weight loss of 8 pounds with illness. Dry, itchy skin. "Passing a lot of water." Complains of thirst.

- *Physical Exam:*

  Head: Bilateral cataracts; dry, furrowed tongue; teeth in poor repair.

  Lungs: Deep, rapid respirations; lungs clear.

  Heart: Grade 2 systolic murmur.

  Abdomen: Decreased bowel sounds; rotund.

  Extremities: 1+ pedal edema.

  Skin: White, flaky residue on skin; poor skin turgor.

  Neuro: Lethargic; oriented to person and place but not to time.

  Vital signs: BP: 120/60. P: 108. R: 30. Temperature: 97.8°F.

- *Laboratory Data:*

  Hct: 21%.

  WBC: 11,200/μL.

  Na^+: 138 mEq/L.

  K^+: 8.1 mEq/L.

  Cl^-: 108 mEq/L.

  CO_2: 9 mEq/L.

  BUN: 214 mg/dL.

  Creatinine: 12.2 mg/dL.

  Arterial blood gases: pH: 7.10.

  PCO_2: 19.

  HCO_3: 16.

  PO_2: 90.

- *Abdominal X-ray:*

  Small left kidney (probable etiology: chronic glomerulonephritis).

---

181. What laboratory finding *best* supports the diagnosis of renal failure?

     A. Elevated blood pH.

     B. Elevated serum calcium.

     C. Elevated BUN.

     D. Elevated serum creatinine.

182. Mr. Toy is treated with sodium polystyrene sulfonate (Kayexalate) enemas. What should the nurse tell a student nurse who asks about the desired action of this drug?

   A. Eliminates excess sodium and water.

   B. Causes potassium to be excreted in increased amounts in the feces.

   C. Causes potassium to reenter the cells, thereby lowering serum levels.

   D. Corrects for the lowered pH of metabolic acidosis.

183. Mr. Toy's serum potassium is elevated to 8.1 mEq/L. Which pair of observations should the nurse look for to support this fact?

   ✱ ↑K = ↓VS
   ↓K = ↑VS

   A. Muscle atony and cardiac irregularities.

   B. Blurred vision and headaches.

   C. Pruritus and jaundice.

   D. Anuria and hyperuricemia.

184. A meeting is held with Mr. and Mrs. Toy to explain the need to reduce dietary intake of potassium. The nurse suggests restricting which food from the list below that is highest in potassium?

   A. Rice.

   B. Butter cookies. *(pastry) very low*

   C. Chicken.

   D. Dried peaches.

185. Additional dietary restrictions are often placed on clients with chronic renal failure. Which diet is the nurse most likely to suggest to Mr. Toy?

   A. Six small, bland feedings.

   B. High protein, high fat, low sodium.

   C. High carbohydrate, high fat, low protein.

   D. Low residue.

186. Mr. Toy's hematocrit suggests he is anemic. What other clinical data should the nurse look for to support this?

   A. Complains of feeling flushed and warm.

   B. Increased tolerance for exercise.

   C. Pale conjunctival sacs.

   D. Dusky skin color.

187. Which observation indicates to the nurse that metabolic acidosis is resolving?

   A. Decrease in blood pH and respiratory rate.

   B. Increase in blood pH and respiratory rate.

     C. Increase in blood pH and decrease in respiratory rate.

     D. Decrease in blood pH and increase in respiratory rate.

188. An inappropriate nursing action in administering peritoneal dialysis to a client in renal failure involves:

     A. Warming the dialysate before administration.

     B. Checking to see if the volume of dialysate returns exceeds the volume infused.

     C. Monitoring vital signs for changes.

     D. Ensuring that the area around the peritoneal catheter insertion site is open to the air and observed regularly.

189. Which finding suggests to the nurse that the client has peritonitis as a complication of peritoneal dialysis?

     A. Abdominal pain.

     B. Clear dialysate returns.

     C. Soft abdomen on palpation.

     D. Active bowel sounds.

Answers and Rationale

1. **D. Dehydration.**

   As the glucose level increases in diabetic ketoacidosis, the client develops polyuria, which leads to dehydration—a consequence, *not* a precipitating factor. *A*, *B*, and *C* all stress the body and stimulate the release of glucocorticoids. The increase in circulating glucose exceeds the amount of insulin in the body.

2. **B. The person with diabetes, type 1, is insulin dependent.**

   The person has little or no insulin production by the pancreas, and cannot be controlled without added insulin. *A* is incorrect because not all people with diabetes, type 1, have circulating insulin. The pancreatic deficiency is permanent; therefore *C* is not correct. *D* is not correct because the person with diabetes, type 2, has some circulating insulin and can be controlled with diet alone.

3. **C. Fruity breath.**

   As ketone bodies, the product of fat metabolism, exceed the body's capacity for oxidation, they are excreted into the urine, and acetone is blown off in the breath. If metabolism is complete, ketones are oxidized, buffered, and excreted as CO_2 and water. *A*, *B*, and *D*—polyuria (dehydration), polydipsia (thirst), and weight loss (protein and fat breakdown)—are due to the excessive glucose, which causes osmotic diuresis.

4. *A. Cardiac irritability.*

Potassium is an essential electrolyte for normal cellular depolarization and repolarization. Low potassium leads to cardiac irritability and arrhythmias. *B*, renal failure, is a cause of hyperkalemia. *C*, cardiac depression, occurs with hyperkalemia. *D*, respiratory failure, can be caused by hypokalemia during general anesthesia, but otherwise hypokalemia is not commonly associated with respiratory problems.

5. *A. Whole-grain cereal with milk.*

Although the diet must meet the high caloric need for weight gain, the client with diabetes must avoid high-carbohydrate foods, such as casseroles, sweet desserts, and fried foods, *B*, *C*, and *D*. The calories should be derived primarily from protein sources and complex carbohydrates.

6. *C. Empty bladder ½ hour before testing and also supply a second voided specimen for testing.*

Urine that has collected in the bladder for more than 30 minutes may reflect an inaccurate picture of the glucose level in the urine. The double-voided specimen is the most accurate method for testing. Both specimens should be tested, in case the client is unable to void a second time. A single specimen, *A*, may reflect an accumulation of glucose. Ingestion of more than 8 oz. of water, *B*, will dilute the concentration of glucose excessively. *D* is also incorrect because of the accumulation of glucose over the period of time.

7. *A. Glycosylated hemoglobin measurement.*

Glucose attaches to the hemoglobin molecule. Once attached, it cannot dissociate. The higher the blood glucose levels have been, the higher the glycosylated hemoglobin. Glycosylated hemoglobin level is the average of blood glucose control over the previous 3 months. *B*, considered to be one of the best methods of *diagnosing* diabetes mellitus, is a 3-hour blood test following glucose ingestion. *C* is done 2 hours after eating to determine *how well carbohydrates are digested*. *D*, connecting peptide test, measures the *level of endogenous insulin production*. A normal C-peptide level may mean inadequate or no insulin production.

8. *A. Increase his caloric intake, but continue the same insulin dosage.*

Exercise *decreases* the need for insulin; therefore, additional calories must be ingested to prevent insulin shock. *B* does not solve the problem of the diminished need for insulin. *C* is the opposite of the adjustment that is indicated. *D* will only intensify the insulin reaction.

9. **C. Compliance with the dietary restrictions.**

    The peer pressure for this age group to eat junk foods is intense. *A* and *B* may occur, but are not related as closely to the role of peers at this age. *D* is incorrect because there is no indication of the need to limit normal activities.

10. **B. Administering room-temperature insulin.**

    B is the only correct answer for preventing tissue hypertrophy or atrophy. *A*, *C*, and *D* are all causes of lipodystrophies.

11. **A. Diaphoresis during the night.**

    NPH is an intermediate-acting insulin that peaks in 6-12 hours after administration. Signs of an insulin reaction (hypoglycemia) include diaphoresis, weakness, and nervousness. *B*, *C*, and *D* all include signs and symptoms of hyperglycemia (diabetic ketoacidosis).

12. **D. Scrubbing superficial lacerations.**

    D is the correct answer; lacerations are not a life-threatening problem so they can wait while other priority nursing actions take place. *A*, *B*, and *C* take priority. *A* prevents further trauma to a possible spinal injury. *B* prevents simple fractures from becoming compound. *C*, establishing a patent airway, is always a priority.

13. **A. He can be turned while his spine is kept immobilized.**

    A Stryker frame permits horizontal turning in prone and supine positions while keeping the spine immobilized. *B* is incorrect because body alignment is not automatic; special attention must be given to ensure this. *C* is incorrect because the weight distribution provided by the frame is no different from that of a bed; however, because the client can be turned frequently, the chance of skin breakdown is lessened. *D* is incorrect; the staff must turn the client.

14. **A. Walking.**

    A is correct because muscle function has been lost below the chest. Since some arm and finger movement can be expected, Jack could possibly write, feed himself, and drive a car with special apparatus, *B*, *C*, and *D*.

15. **C. Ask the client to squeeze the nurse's hands.**

    C is correct because the nurse should determine strength by feeling or by measuring with evaluation equipment. *A* demonstrates function, not strength. *B* tests motor function. *D* tests sensation, not strength.

16. **D. Comminuted.**

    D is correct; a comminuted fracture is one involving several fragments from a traumatic injury. A pathologic fracture also has several fragments; it is caused by a weakness in the bone due to disease. In an impacted fracture, *A*, one portion of the bone is pushed into the other. A greenstick, *B*, is a fracture on one side of the bone. A transverse fracture, *C*, is a break straight across the bone.

17. **C. Immobilize the left arm.**

Immobilization prevents further tissue and vascular injury. *A* is incorrect because it is not a nursing function. *B* could result in potential hemorrhage and hypovolemia from loss of fluids. *D* is part of the medical treatment of a compound fracture, but it is not the *first* action.

18. **A. Allows the weights of her traction to hang freely on the pulleys.**

Traction weight is prescribed and will assist the bone in healing properly. *B*, *C*, and *D* are incorrect because the weights must be maintained constantly, to prevent fracture from overriding or disturbing alignment.

19. **B. There should be no exercise of the affected extremity.**

B is the incorrect statement, and *therefore* the best answer. The client *should* demonstrate movement and *should* exercise the fingers. Nonmovement is a sign that the cast may be too tight and potential problems exist. *A*, *C*, and *D* are not the best answers because they do represent correct nursing instructions. Monitoring circulation, *A*, is a good indicator of potential problems. A plaster cast will not maintain proper position and contour if allowed to get wet, *C*. The bone is placed in the proper position at the time it is set and should be maintained in that position while healing, *D*. Swelling increases pain; elevation decreases swelling.

20. **D. Her fingers were blue and felt cold.**

These are signs that the cast is too tight. The nurse should check for sensation, motion, and circulation. *A*, *B*, and *C* are normally associated with casts and should not cause concern. The cast will be heavy until it is completely dry, *A*. It is not unusual to feel irritable and depressed, *B*, when something unexpected, especially traumas, occurs. It takes a long time for a plaster cast to dry completely, *C*.

21. **B. Sodium.**

Sodium could increase edema and is therefore the least helpful in promoting healing. *A*, *C*, and *D* are all helpful in promoting healing.

22. **A. Blisters covering the entire burn site.**

A is a sign of partial-thickness (second-degree) burns and therefore is the correct answer. *B* is a sign of superficial (first-degree) burns. *C* and *D* are signs of full-thickness (third-degree) burns.

23. **C. Applying first aid cream to the burn.**

     C is the incorrect first aid action and therefore the best answer. Ointments or creams should *never* be applied as part of first aid; they will have to be removed for accurate assessment when the client reaches the health care facility. *A*, transportation to health care, is important. The burn victim is in danger of shock from loss of fluids at the burn site and will need attention. *B* stops the burn by reducing the heat. The burn site will continue to be damaged until it is cooled. *D* prevents further shock.

24. **D. A lengthwise incision through the burn area.**

     D is the correct description of an escharotomy. *A* describes a procedure that removes old tissue to aid healing. *B* describes application of client's own or donor tissue or synthetic grafts to cover the burn area. *C* is incorrect; no tubes are inserted in this procedure.

25. **C. The ointment depresses granulocyte formation.**

     C is correct because it is a disadvantage, rather than an advantage, of silver sulfadiazine (Silvadene) ointment. *A*, *B*, and *D* are advantages of this treatment.

26. **A. Plasma to interstitial fluid shift.**

     A is correct because the fluid called to the burn site leaves the vascular system. *B* is incorrect because this shift happens more than 48 hours after a major burn. *C* is incorrect because the problem in major burns is potassium excess, not deficiency. *D* is incorrect because metabolic acidosis, not alkalosis, is associated with major burns.

27. **A. 3500–5000 calories.**

     A is the correct number of calories needed to aid in the tissue rebuilding and healing process. The amounts in *B*, *C*, and *D* are inadequate for the adult with major burns.

28. **D. Tissue anabolism resulting from immobility.**

     D is the best answer because it is *not* a cause of his negative nitrogen balance. The problem is catabolism, not anabolism. Immobility leads to breakdown of tissue. *A*, *B*, and *C* are all examples of conditions that lead to negative nitrogen balance.

29. **D. Hyperglycemia.**

     D is the best answer because hypoglycemia, not hyperglycemia, occurs in acute hepatitis. This is due to an inadequate hepatic glycogen reserve. In addition, inadequate carbohydrate intake, prolonged nausea, and vomiting are also contributory factors. *A*, *B*, and *C* do occur. These are problems that are encountered because of *A*, prolonged prothrombin time; *B*, jaundice; and *C*, anorexia.

30. **C. Body image change related to altered skin appearance.**

     C is correct because the appearance of Ms. Bee's jaundice and her insistence on visitor restrictions occurred concurrently. Because of the jaundice, she became more self-conscious of her appearance, suggesting a change in her perception of her body image. *A*, *B*, and *D* are incorrect. The data do not reflect the presence of depression, *A*; anxiety, *B*; or anger and hostility, *D*. It is possible, however, that the nurse may encounter these nursing problems during the hospitalization of a client with hepatitis.

31. **C. Elevated serum transaminases.**

C is correct because the serum transaminases, ALT and AST, increase during the initial stage of the disease process, reflecting the liver cell injury present. *A* is incorrect because although moderate elevation of LDH levels is common in acute viral hepatitis, the CK level remains unchanged. CK is elevated in myocardial infarction, *not* in liver disease. *B* is also incorrect. Prothrombin is synthesized in the liver and variations in the prothrombin time can be expected because the liver cells are injured. *D* is incorrect because there is an *increased* release of, not a decrease in, alkaline phosphatase. Because of an impaired hepatic excretory function, enzyme synthesis is increased—subsequently, an increased release of alkaline phosphatase.

32. **D. Excretion of conjugated bilirubin into the intestines is decreased.**

D is correct because decreased excretion of conjugated bilirubin into the intestines is a common occurrence in viral hepatitis. It causes lack of bile pigments in the stools—thus, the clay-colored stools seen. *A* and *C* are incorrect. Although both can also occur in hepatitis, they do not have any effect on the color of the stools. The life span of the RBCs in clients with liver diseases is shortened, causing an impaired hepatic uptake of bilirubin, *A*. The reentry of conjugated bilirubin into the bloodstream, *C*, results in jaundice. *B* is also incorrect. Increased excretion of fecal urobilinogen occurs in hemolytic anemia, not in hepatitis.

33. **C. Used needles and syringes.**

Ms. Bee has acute viral hepatitis, type B. Her disease is spread mainly through contaminated needles and blood products, choice *C*. Some theorize, however, that it is possible that the disease also spreads through body excretions such as saliva, tears, intestinal fluids, and gastric juice. Hepatitis A is transmitted by the oral-fecal route. Based on this explanation, *A*, *B*, and *D* are incorrect.

34. **D. Cholestyramine to bind bile salts in the intestines**

Cholestyramine, a bile acid–sequestering resin, increases fecal bile excretion, resulting in the reduction of excess bile salt deposits in the skin. Questran, *C*, is another bile acid sequestrant, but it stimulates the excretion, not the reabsorption, of bile salts, so *C* is incorrect. *A* and *B* are incorrect. As stated, they do not relieve the pruritus of the client with hepatitis.

35. **B. Decorticate rigidity.**

B is correct because decorticate rigidity is a neurologic manifestation indicative of lesions in the cerebral white matter, internal capsules, and thalamus—*not* impending hepatic coma. Flexion of the fingers, wrists, and arms is seen in the client with this neurologic dysfunction. *A*, *C*, and *D* are incorrect answers because in the presence of advanced hepatocellular disease, these parameters *do* indicate impending hepatic coma.

36. **A. Giving diuretics.**

A is the incorrect nursing measure and *therefore* the correct answer. Diuretics stimulate the excretion of urine. They are not used in clients who are in hepatic coma because they precipitate the occurrence of hypovolemia. Hypovolemia decreases the perfusion of the liver, causing further injury to the already damaged liver cells and potentiating hepatic coma. *B*, *C*, and *D* are appropriate nursing measures, but they are incorrect responses to the question asked. Any source of increase in blood ammonia, such as a high-protein diet and a markedly decreased urine output, should be prevented. Poor tissue oxygenation to the liver cells should also be prevented.

37. **A. Decrease fecal pH and ammonia absorption.**

Lactulose, a synthetic disaccharide that contains galactose and fructose, reduces the ammonia level by expelling the ammonia into the bowel through its laxative action. Neomycin reduces the ammonia-forming bacteria in the intestinal tract. Thus, lactulose and neomycin are effective drugs used in clients with hepatic encephalopathy because they reduce the ammonia level in the body. The pharmacologic actions of lactulose and neomycin are not included in *B*, *C*, and *D*; they are incorrect responses.

38. **A. Ammonia.**

Ammonia is formed by the decomposition of nitrogen-containing substances, such as proteins and amino acid. It is markedly elevated in clients with a severely damaged liver—specifically, hepatocellular necrosis. The damaged liver is unable to convert ammonia to urea; thus, an increased ammonia level is seen. *B* is a general indication of infection, and is not specific to liver damage. *C* and *D* are incorrect. They indicate dysfunction of the kidneys.

39. **B. Increased levels of thyroxine and triiodothyronine stimulate metabolic rate.**

B is correct because too much thyroxine and triiodothyronine, which is the problem in Graves' disease due to overactivity of the thyroid gland, causes a dangerous speeding of metabolism and a high rate of oxygen consumption. *A* is incorrect. Admission to the hospital can be an anxiety-producing situation and can alter vital signs. However, in light of all the data presented, including the probable diagnosis, the most feasible rationale for her symptoms is *B*. *C* is incorrect. Iodine is necessary for the thyroid gland to manufacture and secrete its hormone. Insufficient amounts of iodine produce hypertrophy as a compensatory mechanism—not overactivity of the thyroid gland itself. *D* is incorrect because it is an unverified assumption.

40. **B. Inquire whether the client has had an x-ray for which opaque dye was administered.**

    B is correct because opaque dye contains iodine, which will produce an abnormal finding on x-rays. Since the protein-bound iodide test measures the amount of iodine attached to protein molecules within the body, any intake of iodine will skew laboratory findings. *A* is incorrect since samples of venous blood are taken for analysis in this test. *C* is incorrect because the amount of rest and sleep does not influence the findings of this test. *D* is incorrect because any ingestion of iodine will produce a false high reading.

41. **A. Inform the client that there is no danger of radiating herself or others.**

    The dosage of radioiodine is so small that it is not harmful; therefore, *A* is correct. *B* is incorrect because no special precautions need to be taken with the collected specimen. *C* and *D* are incorrect because the dosage of radioactive iodine is too small to be dangerous and there is no danger of radioactive emission after this test.

42. **A. 4000–5000 calories; 100–125 g of protein.**

    A is correct because an increase in metabolic rate increases carbohydrate, fat, and protein metabolism, as well as vitamin requirements. *B* is incorrect; insufficient calories are provided in this diet. *C* is incorrect because it does not meet the client's high mineral requirements. *D* is incorrect because it does not provide sufficient grams of carbohydrates and protein.

43. **B. Place Ms. Wise in a room with an electric fan and windows.**

    An increase in metabolic rate increases body heat production; consequently Ms. Wise will feel hot and *B* is the correct answer. *A* is incorrect because using several blankets will only make Ms. Wise hotter; this choice indicates lack of understanding of the underlying pathophysiology of her disorder. *C* is incorrect since a puzzle will only frustrate Ms. Wise and produce further agitation. The speeded metabolic rate of Graves' disease is also accompanied by impatience and mood swings. *D* is incorrect; the nurse's insistence will be interpreted as an additional stress, increasing Ms. Wise's agitation.

44. *C. Ability to sleep 8 hours at night without awakening.*

Propylthiouracil is an antithyroid drug that corrects hyperthyroidism by blocking thyroid hormone synthesis. Symptoms of Graves' disease are relieved within 4–8 weeks, and the client is placed in a euthyroid state. *C* is the only option that reflects the euthyroid state. *A* is incorrect; the observation illustrates a manifestation of the overactive thyroid gland and speeded metabolic processes. *B* is incorrect because the drug does not curtail urine output. *D* is incorrect because impatience and inability to concentrate are manifestations of Graves' disease.

45. *C. Minimize postoperative bleeding.*

C is correct because iodine therapy is used preoperatively to reduce the vascularity of the thyroid gland. *A* is incorrect; SSKI is not a sedative. *B* is incorrect; exophthalmos is due to a number of causes, probably from oversecretion of a hormone by the anterior pituitary called exophthalmos-producing substance. *D* is incorrect; reduced iodine stores are not the underlying disturbance in Graves' disease.

46. *C. Prevent strain on the suture line.*

C is correct since Fowler's position minimizes strain on the suture line when the client moves from a reclining to a sitting position. Ms. Wise should not extend or hyperextend the neck. *A* is incorrect because Fowler's position alone will not prevent hemorrhage. *B* is incorrect; to reduce pooling of respiratory secretions, the nurse can perform gentle suctioning and see that a humidifier is used, if ordered. *D* is incorrect because the cause of postoperative hoarseness is injury to the pharyngeal nerve.

47. *D. Complaints of difficulty swallowing and sensation that the dressing is tight.*

D is correct because slight bleeding within the soft tissues of the neck can produce complaints of difficulty swallowing. *A* is incorrect because these observations indicate shock; they are *not early* signs of hemorrhage. *B* is incorrect; muscle twitching and tremors are often produced by the accidental removal of one or more of the parathyroid glands, producing a fall in serum calcium. *C* is incorrect; hoarseness may result from damage to the pharyngeal nerve, but is not an early sign of hemorrhage.

48. *C. Tracheostomy set.*

C is correct because Ms. Wise is showing signs of acute respiratory obstruction. In this acute emergency, the maintenance of the client's airway is of paramount importance. The cause of this obstruction may be hemorrhage or tetany; insufficient information is given to determine which is the cause. *A* is incorrect because patency of the airway must be the *first* priority. Calcium gluconate *may* be given later if the need for it is determined. *B* is incorrect; thyroid replacement hormone is not a priority at this time. *D* is incorrect because Ms. Wise is showing signs of *upper* airway obstruction.

49. **C. Absent Trousseau's sign.**

Trousseau's sign, which is carpal spasm of the fingers and hand following application of a pressure cuff to the arm, illustrates hyperirritability due to hypocalcemia. Restoration of calcium to normal levels relieves such symptoms of tetany as muscle twitching and hyperirritability of the nervous system. *A* is incorrect because calcium replacement does not reduce the size of the thyroid gland. Medications such as SSKI or levothyroxine sodium (Synthroid) accomplish this. *B* is incorrect because calcium gluconate does not curtail blood loss. *D* is incorrect; the cause of hoarseness is damage to the pharyngeal nerve and it is best treated by voice rest and humidification.

50. **D. Mr. X with metabolic alkalosis.**

Symptoms of hypoparathyroidism and tetany are more severe in clients who have elevated serum pH (alkalosis). Symptoms are exaggerated because only ionized calcium can be used by the body. When alkalosis is present, the amount of ionized calcium ions drops, even though the serum calcium level may be normal. Therefore, tetany remains severe until alkalosis is corrected and *D* is the correct answer. *A* is incorrect; clients with hyperparathyroidism tend to have high serum calcium levels, which is not the problem in tetany. *B* is incorrect; clients with hypothyroidism (myxedema) tend to have slowed metabolic rates, rather than reduced serum calcium levels as in tetany. *C* is incorrect; symptoms of tetany are more pronounced in alkalosis than in acidosis.

51. **A. The client should refrain from speaking.**

Hoarseness occurs if there is injury to the pharyngeal nerve during surgery. This condition is usually temporary and should subside in a few days. Overuse of the vocal cords prolongs hoarseness, so *A* is correct. *B* is an incorrect statement since hoarseness is a temporary complication. *C* is incorrect because antitussives have no effect in hastening the return of the voice. *D* is also incorrect; the voice returns within a few days and there are no further complications in speaking.

52. **C. Apply tepid to cold water to the burn surface.**

Application of cold to tepid water to the burn surface produces vasoconstriction, reduces fluid loss, and minimizes the depth or degree of damage. *A* is incorrect; covering Mr. Green with a clean sheet may be done second. *B* is incorrect because applying topical antimicrobial ointment fosters the growth of anaerobic microorganisms. *D* is incorrect because eschar development does not occur during the first few minutes after burn.

53. **D. Flush with water continuously.**

Chemical burns to the eye are treated best by continuous flushing with copious amounts of water. This dilutes the chemical's concentration. *A* is incorrect; a sterile dressing can be applied *after* the eye is flushed with water. Without dilution of the chemical first, thermal injury will continue. *B* is incorrect because administration of an antidote is quite dangerous. The amount and percent concentration to use are difficult to determine. Also, the antidote itself may be caustic. *C* is incorrect because application of ice packs will not halt tissue destruction.

54. **C. Peripheral perfusion is poor.**

Hypovolemia associated with increased capillary permeability, plasma to interstitial fluid shift, and stasis of blood in the peripheral tissue occur during the shock stage. Cutaneous vasoconstriction may exist concomitantly. Peripheral perfusion during the initial stage is therefore quite poor and medications will not be absorbed, so *C* is correct. *A* is incorrect because rapid excretion is not possible during the burn shock phase in light of stasis and capillary permeability. *B* is incorrect because it is not the best answer. It is true that the availability of appropriate sites may be limited, but the primary reason for this route of administration of medication is to ensure absorption. *D* is incorrect because it is not the primary reason. Minimization of pain is needed. However, if analgesics are given by another route, absorption will not take place and the client will not reap the benefits.

55. **A. 97°F.**

The function of the skin is to assist in the maintenance of body temperature by preventing heat and water loss. Without this protective covering (as in thermal injury), heat is lost via conduction, convection, and radiation. Mr. Green's temperature would therefore be subnormal and the correct answer is *A*. This is one major reason why skin grafting is done early during the treatment regimen. Further application of this principle is illustrated in the use of sunlamps and bed cradles. *B*, *C*, and *D* are incorrect because it is very difficult to maintain a normal or certainly an above-normal body temperature in the face of continual heat loss.

56. **D. Capillary permeability is reduced.**

Many surgeons give minimal to no colloids during the first 24 hours after burns because much of their therapeutic value is lost due to increased permeability—that is, the colloids leak into the interstitial space. During the fluid restitution phase, in which interstitial fluid (edema) remobilizes to the vascular space, colloids are better able to exert their osmotic "pull" and "draw" fluids back into the vascular compartment. As a result, cardiac output and renal perfusion improve, barring any other complications. *A* is incorrect because colloids reduce, not enhance, interstitial edema. *B*, an improvement in cardiac output, occurs as a *result* of the interstitial to plasma fluid shift and the administration of colloids; it is not the rationale for this action. *C*, improvement of renal perfusion, also occurs as a result of fluid remobilization and is not the rationale for this action.

57. **B. CVP of 10.**

During the fluid remobilization phase of interstitial fluid to plasma shift, venous return, and hence the CVP, improves. *A* is incorrect; it may indicate vascular overload. *C* is incorrect because it is a poor prognostic indicator, possibly pointing to renal damage. *D* is incorrect because blister size is not relevant.

58. **D. Abdominal distention with absent bowel sounds.**

Paralytic ileus, which is characterized by absent bowel sounds and abdominal distention, often occurs during this time. Clients are therefore NPO. This is a normal response of the flight or fight mechanism. *A* is incorrect; these are signs that a pneumonia may be present but this is not related to oral intake. *B* is incorrect; this is a sign of hypovolemic shock and is not the best response. *C* is incorrect; this is a sign of renal failure and is not related to oral intake.

59. **C. Respiratory stridor.**

Mr. Green's burns are on his neck and chest. Eschar formation over these areas may restrict respiratory movement due to its hard, leatherlike characteristics. *A*, *B*, and *D* are incorrect because they are all normal occurrences with third-degree burns. Chocolate to red-colored urine, *A*, is due to the presence of myoglobulin and, although normal with burns, should be closely observed.

60. **A. Give analgesic 30 minutes before application.**

Since mafenide burns on application, the thoughtful nurse should administer analgesic before dressing change. *B*, *C*, and *D* are *not* side effects of mafenide.

61. **C. Observe any changes in renal function.**

Gentamicin is nephrotoxic and ototoxic. The nurse should ensure that baseline renal function tests have been done, that is, creatinine clearance and BUN (not WBC count, *B*). If the client is conscious, the nurse should determine whether any hearing impairment exists initially. *A* applies to mafenide. *D* is incorrect because there is no effect on the spinal nerves (although damage occurs to *cranial* nerve VIII).

62. **B. Causes the loss of potassium and sodium.**

The hypotonicity of 5% silver nitrate encourages the loss of electrolytes, so *B* is correct. *A* is incorrect because prevention of eschar formation is not an effect of silver nitrate. *C* is incorrect because although silver nitrate does stain everything it touches, this is not its *major* disadvantage. *D* is an incorrect statement; silver nitrate *can be used* in the treatment of children with burns.

63. ***D. Abdominal distention and decrease in hematocrit.***

Curling's ulcer, or stress ulcer, is a constant concern for the nurse and can occur as early as 4 days after burn. *D* lists the symptoms. *A* is incorrect because pain may not always occur. *B* is incorrect; hematemesis is a late sign. *C* is incorrect because hyperperistalsis does not occur; rather, hypotonia is a sign of stress ulcer.

64. ***A. A decrease in wound circumference from 4 to 2 cm.***

Zinc is needed to promote wound healing: *A* is the only statement that illustrates this action of zinc.

65. ***D. Prevent two body surfaces from touching.***

Preventing two body surfaces from touching maintains the integrity of each healing surface. For example, two fingers will not share the same surface. *A* is incorrect; dressings should be applied with even distribution of pressure. Uneven areas where pressure is greater act much like a tourniquet. *B* is incorrect; saline is a better solution to use to remove adherent dressings. *C* is incorrect because keeping the affected part in a dependent position will foster the development of dependent edema.

66. ***D. Adequate caloric intake.***

Adequate calories ensure that protein will not be utilized for energy and heat production, thereby maintaining a positive nitrogen balance. The body uses carbohydrates first for energy, and then proteins. *A* is incorrect because the high metabolic needs of the client with burns will quickly utilize any reserve stores. *B* is incorrect; glucagon is a substance secreted by the alpha cells of the pancreas. It stimulates the breakdown of glucogen and the release of glucose by the liver. In this way, glucagon influences blood sugar levels. Its protein-sparing function is limited. *C* is incorrect; lipoproteins are simple proteins combined with a lipid component such as cholesterol.

67. ***D. 1 cup of whole milk.***

The best-quality protein is from animal sources and dairy products. Whole milk contains the cream (fat source) and has the highest amount of protein—9 g—of the choices. *A* is incorrect because although nuts are high in calories, they are low in protein value (3 g). *B* is incorrect because broth is a clear liquid supplying no grams of protein. *C* is incorrect because yogurt from partially skimmed milk is low in protein (3 g).

68. **B. Schedule nursing care procedures to allow periods of uninterrupted sleep.**

A source of psychological stress for all clients with burns is sensory deprivation—lack of touch sensation—due to deep burns, and over-stimulation and sleep deprivation due to the constant monitoring, pain, etc. Allowance for periods of rest and sleep is helpful to maintain orientation. Many studies support the importance of sleep. *A* is incorrect; insistence that Mr. Green participate in wound care before he is ready is unwise. This will only increase anxiety. *C* is incorrect; comparing his progress with that of other clients in the unit is unethical. *D* is incorrect; all behavior has meaning, and ignoring enuresis overlooks possible dependency or regression. Urine is also a source of wound contamination.

69. **D. Continuous open masturbation.**

Inappropriate behavior may result from many sources. The stress of thermal injury is an assault to one's body image and a threat to economic and social well-being. These clients are often in various stages of the mourning process. *A* and *B* are incorrect choices since they are illustrations of *normal* behavior associated with the mourning process. *C* is incorrect because concepts regarding nudity are influenced by personal, cultural, and family mores.

70. **C. Reduce scar hypertrophy.**

Wound contraction and scar tissue formation are normal parts of wound healing. Scar tissue can produce disabling contractures, deformity, and disfigurement. This type of tissue is metabolically active and continually rearranges itself. An elasticized garment prevents tissue hypertrophy. *A* is incorrect because wound closure has occurred during the rehabilitative period; loss of protein through the wound surface is impossible. *B* is incorrect because heat loss via evaporation cannot occur during this period because the wound surface is now grafted or healed closed. *D* is incorrect because the accumulation of edema fluid under a skin graft cannot be controlled by elastic garments.

71. **C. Weight gain.**

According to the case situation, the client has *lost* weight despite a ravenous appetite, so *C* is the answer. This weight loss is due to increases in metabolism. *A*, *B*, and *D*—goiter symptom, exophthalmos, and irritability—*are* all symptoms of excess secretion of thyroid hormone.

72. **C. Continuous toniclike muscle spasms.**

If one or both of the parathyroid glands are damaged or removed during thyroidectomy, there will be an alteration in the amount of calcium produced. This alteration may cause continuous toniclike muscle spasms (also known as tetany). *A*, urinary output, is not related to calcium metabolism. *B*, flank pain, is a sign of calcium excess. *D* is incorrect because sensations *increase* with calcium deficit.

73. **D. Puffy eyelids and shortness of breath.**

   D is correct because these signs are due to retention of fluid and edema. *A*, *B*, and *C* are incorrect because they are signs of fluid deficit.

74. **D. Gastric suction apparatus.**

   D is correct because clients who have a thyroidectomy do not usually have a Levin tube in place, and therefore do not require gastric suction. *A* and *B* *are* necessary because of possible respiratory problems due to edema. *C* is necessary because clients with major surgery usually return from the operating room with an IV line in place.

75. **C. Women who had a child before the age of 30.**

   The risk of breast cancer increases if a woman has never had a child or had a child *after* the age of 30; therefore *C* is correct. *A*, *B*, and *D* are incorrect because they list women who *are* more likely to be at risk. Risk increases with age, if female family members have or have had breast cancer, and if a woman is obese.

76. **D. Most breast abnormalities can be detected early by the woman or her partner and reported to the physician.**

   D is correct because monthly examination can determine changes in normal tissue, which can be reported quickly. *A* is incorrect since only a professional can determine what is serious. All lesions should be evaluated. *B* is incorrect because not all women fear a physician's exam. *C* is untrue; although breast self-examinations should be performed, women still need yearly checkups for other possible problems.

77. **B. One week after her period begins.**

   B is correct because breast tissue is in its most normal state at this time. *A* is incorrect because breast tissue is painful and swollen due to hormonal changes at the beginning of the period. *C* is incorrect for a *pre*menopausal woman such as this client; the first day of the month or another significant date is appropriate for a *post*menopausal woman. *D* is incorrect because midway through the cycle is not an optimum time; tissue is not in its most normal state.

78. **A. Make an appointment with her physician as soon as possible.**

   A is correct because the earliest diagnosis and treatment of breast cancer produces the best possible survival rate. Waiting, *B*, wastes valuable time. *C* is important, but the physician's exam is more important. *D* is incorrect; *all* lumps should be investigated.

79. *D. This is part of the diagnostic workup.*

   Biopsy is a diagnostic process, not a treatment, so *D* is correct. *A* is incorrect; the treatment is surgery, chemotherapy, radiation, or a combination of these treatments. *B* is not true; most biopsies reveal negative findings. *C* is incorrect; a small scar remains on the breast after this procedure.

80. *A. Breast and axillary nodes.*

   A is the correct definition of a modified radical mastectomy. *B* describes a Halsted's; *C*, a simple mastectomy; and *D*, a lumpectomy.

81. *A. Looking at the incision when the nurse is changing the dressing.*

   A is correct because the *first* step to acceptance of altered body image is viewing the site. *B*, touching, is the second step toward accepting altered body image. *C* and *D* are examples of denying that the problem exists.

82. *C. "Wash the skin with water and pat dry."*

   C is the correct response. The client should avoid increasing or decreasing the dosage of radiation by utilizing any lotions or creams. Unless specifically ordered, she should use water only and pat dry to prevent trauma. *A*, *B*, and *D* should be avoided because they alter the dosage of radiation.

83. *A. Redness of the surface tissue.*

   A is correct; redness is a local tissue reaction. *B*, *C*, and *D* show that radiation has caused excessive damage to local tissue.

84. *C. Interfere with nucleic acid synthesis.*

   C is correct because this form of chemotherapy exerts its effect by interfering with cell metabolism. *A* is incorrect because the drug does not directly interfere with blood supply. *B* is incorrect because both cancerous and normal cells absorb antimetabolite drugs. *D* is incorrect because the drug does not specifically affect the capsule.

85. *A. Hair follicles.*

   A is correct because the drugs affect rapidly dividing cells. Epithelial tissue is affected more often and earlier than other tissue. Cells in *B*, *C*, and *D* are affected, but not at the same rate as hair follicles.

86. *B. Do not discriminate between cancer cells and normal cells.*

   B is correct; as the drugs are influencing the cancer cells, they are also being detrimental to normal cells—a major disadvantage. *A* is incorrect; the drugs *interfere* with the immune response. *C* is incorrect because the drugs are absorbed by both cancer cells and normal cells. *D* is untrue; many clients have chemotherapy as outpatients.

87. ***B. Low platelet count.***

B is correct because a low platelet count and the tendency to bleed confirm thrombocytopenia. *A* is incorrect because although a low lymphocyte count is a side effect of chemotherapy, it does not confirm thrombocytopenia. *C* and *D* are incorrect because neither confirms thrombocytopenia. Side effects of chemotherapy are anemia (*not* high RBC count) and a decrease (*not* an increase) in eosinophils.

88. ***D. Being isolated.***

There is a sense of isolation, *D*, and clients are afraid of being left alone. *A*, *B*, and *C* are other possible fears, but the greatest fear is isolation.

89. ***C. Stay with him and listen to his concerns.***

C is the correct action. The nurse recognizes Mr. Mulvrey and his need to discuss his concerns. *A*, *B*, and *D* are incorrect because they do not allow him the opportunity to express his concerns, and leaving him alone when he is expressing his anger tells him that the nurse does not want to listen.

90. ***A. Precancerous and cancerous conditions of the cervix.***

The Papanicolaou smear is a cytologic test for diagnosing cervical cancer. *B*, *C*, and *D* are possible gynecologic problems that are diagnosed by methods other than the Papanicolaou smear.

91. ***B. Allow her an opportunity to express her fears.***

Allowing the client to discuss what is concerning her is the best way to reduce fear. *A* is an inappropriate response. Ms. Salisbury has made a decision about the surgery and the surgeon, and the nurse should say nothing that might raise a doubt about competency at this time. *C*, changing the subject, tells the client that the nurse is unavailable for discussion. *D* is not the best response. Fear does stand in the way of recovery, but when the client is in this state, she cannot learn. The nurse must first try to reduce her fears.

92. ***D. Meperidine, 1.5 mL; atropine, 0.75 mL.***

To arrive at the correct amount of medication:

$75/50 \times 1 = 1.5$ mL $0.3/0.4 \times 1 = 0.75$

93. ***C. Decrease in oral and respiratory secretions.***

Atropine sulfate is used for its ability to dry bronchial secretions, to prevent pooling of secretions during anesthesia. *A*, relaxation, is produced by tranquilizers. *B* and *D* are incorrect because atropine blocks vagal transmission, thereby preventing bradycardia and hypotension.

94. ***A. Support her abdomen with a pillow or with her hands.***

This provides support and assists in comfort during coughing and deep breathing. *B* is incorrect because the rib cage is not involved in this surgery. *C* is incorrect because Ms. Salisbury can lie on either side or on her back, but not on her abdomen. *D* is incorrect because it puts undue strain on the incision.

95. **C. Infiltration.**

   The dislodging of the needle will cause fluid to infiltrate into the tissues. The nurse should look for edema, discomfort, blanching of the skin, and fluid not dripping in the chamber. *A*, *B*, and *D* are incorrect. Signs of phlebitis are redness and heat. Symptoms of embolism are hypotension, cyanosis, and tachycardia. Respiratory problems, skin reactions, hives, and feelings of warmth are symptoms of allergic reaction.

96. **A. Cover the incision with a sterile, moist towel.**

   The use of a large sterile, moist covering prevents trauma of a dry object on the bowel, and also prevents small non-radiopaque objects from entering the cavity. *B* is not a nursing action. *C* increases the risk of infection and electrolyte imbalance. *D* is not a priority; life-saving actions should be performed first.

97. **D. Increased sensitivity to heat loss.**

   Hot flashes are common due to lowered estrogen levels. *A* is incorrect because perspiration increases, not decreases. *B* is incorrect since insomnia is common. *C* is incorrect because the skin increases in color due to flushing.

98. **D. Moist crackles at the base of her lungs.**

   D is the answer because it is a sign of respiratory complication, not wound infection. *A*, *B*, and *C* are all signs of wound infections.

99. **A. Take all of the medication prescribed by her physician.**

   Completing the entire prescription reduces chances of drug reactions in the future and also prevents the bacterium from reasserting itself. *B*, *C*, and *D* are incorrect because the client does not complete the entire course of medication.

100. **A. Blood culture.**

   The laboratory test that does not show leukemic cells is blood culture; thus, *A* is the answer. Blood culture is used to determine the type(s) of organism(s) that cause the infection. With a laboratory media, the causative organisms are induced to grow. Leukemia is not caused by an organism that can be identified through a blood culture. Rather, the characteristic abnormal proliferation of leukocytes is confirmed through diagnostic tests such as differential count, *B*; bone marrow aspiration, *C*; and WBC count, *D*. These tests determine which WBC component is proliferative, if immature WBCs have invaded the bone marrow, and if there is a marked increase of WBCs.

101. C. A notch is palpated along the medial border of the left lower quadrant.

C describes a markedly enlarged spleen that descends into the left lower quadrant. The findings in *A*, *B*, and *D* are normal physical findings; thus, these are incorrect responses.

102. C. Decreased erythrocyte production.

The weakness, fatigue, and pallor seen in clients with leukemia are due to a decreased production of erythrocytes. There is a reduction of RBC mass and a corresponding decrease in the oxygen-carrying capacity of the blood. *A*, *B*, and *D* are incorrect. Bleeding occurs if there is a deficiency of platelets, *A*. A febrile response is one indication of an infective process, *B*. Alteration in sensation occurs if cancer cells infiltrated the peripheral nerves, *D*.

103. A. Cooked spinach and celery.

A therapeutic goal in the care of clients with leukemia is the reduction of potentials for infection. Bacteria are normally present in the human colon. Because this can become a source of infection in the client with leukemia, a low-bacteria diet is served in conjunction with the use of gut sterilizers, such as polymyxin B, vancomycin, and colistin. Foods eaten in a low-bacteria diet are cooked. Some also advocate the use of canned soft drinks. Thus, *A* is the correct answer. *B*, *C*, and *D* are incorrect. Raw foods such as those mentioned in these items contain bacteria that normally can be handled by the average person who has adequate defense mechanisms to fight infection. The client with leukemia who is acutely ill has a markedly decreased resistance to infection; therefore, raw foods should not be served because they could become potential sources of infection.

104. B. Visit the client frequently and engage her in conversation.

When the client is ill, the potential for depression to occur is increased, particularly when the prognosis of the illness is poor and when room isolation is required. Frequent, short visits by the nurse allow opportunities for the client to communicate needs, worries, and anxieties. To prevent sensory deprivation, an open communication and frequent contact with the client must be maintained. Thus, *B* is the correct answer. *A*, *C*, and *D* are incorrect. Caution must be taken that the client does not acquire respiratory infection through contact with numerous family members or visitors, *A*, or through prolonged contact with them, *D*. The resistance to infection is low in clients with leukemia. Measures should be taken to minimize the potential for infection. Once the nurse has elicited a verbal response from the client demonstrating her understanding of the rationale for the need of protective isolation, repeated explanation of why this is done, *C*, is unnecessary.

105. B. Urine output of 30–50 mL/hour.

A urine output of 30–50 mL/hour reflects an adequate amount of urine excreted by the kidneys. Frequently, kidney dysfunction is a complication of chemotherapy. This is caused by the crystallization of uric acid in the kidney tubules, causing obstruction, decreased glomerular filtration, and eventually anuria. Signs of kidney dysfunction include an elevated or nonchanging urine specific gravity, *A*; elevated serum creatinine, *C*; and elevated BUN levels, *D*.

106. C. "Your hair will grow again after the chemotherapy is over."

This is a factual statement. The loss of hair during chemotherapy is only temporary. The hair grows back after chemotherapy is over. *A* is a misleading statement that does not reassure the client. Loss of body image is a problem that these clients are faced with. *B* and *D* are incorrect statements. Factual, honest information, rather than vague, incorrect information, should be communicated to them by the health personnel.

107. D. Ecchymosis and weakness.

When the bone marrow is depressed, there is also a decreased production of RBCs and platelets. Spontaneous bleeding into the skin occurs, as manifested by the formation of ecchymosis. The weakness and fatigue are attributed to the anemia present. There is a significant reduction in RBC mass and a corresponding decrease in the oxygen-carrying capacity of the blood. *A*, *B*, and *C* are incorrect. Night sweats and easy fatigability, *A*, are possible manifestations of pulmonary tuberculosis. *B* occurs when fluid imbalance is present, and *C* indicates kidney dysfunction.

108. C. No cancer cells are microscopically evident in the bone marrow.

A refers to immunotherapy; *B* refers to an acute episode of the disease process; and *D* refers to a "cure." Therefore, *C* is the correct answer.

109. B. Keep the client from making decisions regarding his or her care.

Keeping the client from making decisions regarding care leads to feelings of powerlessness, anxiety, fear, or hostility. The client must participate in the decision-making process, especially in matters that concern treatment and care. When the client is physically or psychologically unable, the immediate family is consulted. *A*, *C*, and *D* *are* appropriate nursing approaches, and therefore are not the answers to the question asked.

110. D. Magnesium hydroxide (magnesium magma).

Milk of magnesia (magnesium hydroxide) has a laxative effect. *A*, *B*, and *C* all have a constipating effect.

111. A. To decrease gastric motility.

These drugs decrease gastric secretions by decreasing gastric motility. *B*, *C*, and *D* are incorrect because the drugs have no tranquilizing effect; decrease, rather than increase, secretions; and do not influence cell growth.

112. A. Decreased blood pressure.

The decreased blood pressure is due to a fall in cardiac output because of loss of volume. *B* and *C* are incorrect because both pulse and respirations are increased. *D* is incorrect because urinary output is decreased.

113. B. Tarry.

The tarry color indicates digested blood. Stools that are the color of clay, *A*, indicate a diet with excess fat. Bright red stools, *C*, indicate bleeding low in the large intestine or rectum. Light brown stools, *D*, indicate a diet too high in milk and low in meat.

114. C. Emergency.

This is a life-threatening situation because of the blood loss. The client's surgery is an emergency and must take priority over other surgeries scheduled. Surgery can be described as planned, *A*, when conditions necessitate it but it can be scheduled at a convenient time. Imperative surgery, *B*, must be done within 24 hours. Optional surgery, *D*, is done at the client's request. The client can survive without having this surgery performed.

115. A. Hyperactive bowel sounds.

Absence of bowel sounds is indicative of peritonitis, as in *B*, *C*, and *D*.

116. C. Position comfortably; subdue the lighting.

These actions encourage relaxation and provide a quiet environment, which should help reduce pain until the analgesic takes effect. *A*, *B*, and *D* produce a stimulating effect and are unlikely to help alleviate the client's pain.

117. D. Decreasing carbohydrates.

The food mass is a concentrated hyperosmolar solution in relation to surrounding extracellular fluid. Water is drawn from the blood into the intestines, and symptoms of distress occur. *A* and *B* are incorrect; fats should be increased because they slow passage of food into the intestines, and protein should be increased. *C* is incorrect, as fluids with meals should be decreased or eliminated so that food will stay in the stomach longer.

118. C. Morphine.

Morphine is thought to stimulate the sphincter of Oddi, causing biliary pain; therefore, it is usually avoided. *A*, meperidine, is the drug of choice for pain. *B*, nitroglycerin, is given to relax smooth muscle and decrease colic pain. *D*, ibuprofen, an NSAID, most likely will have no significant effect on biliary colic.

119. C. Take iodine dye capsules by mouth the evening before the test.

Telepaque capsules, usually six, are administered the evening prior to the test. It takes about 13 hours for the dye to reach the liver and be excreted into the bile, where it is stored in the gallbladder. *A* is incorrect; the diet should be fat free, since fat is the prin-cipal cause of contraction of the diseased organ and should be avoided. *B* is incorrect; the client is given no food after the evening meal, to prevent contraction of the gallbladder and expulsion of the dye. *D* is incorrect; barium studies should be performed *after*, not before, the gall-bladder series because the barium may shadow normal structures if it is not excreted completely.

120. C. Chocolate pudding.

Chocolate and milk are eliminated from the diet because of their fat content. *A*, *B*, and *D* are allowed in a fat-free diet.

121. C. The expected results of the surgical procedure.

The surgeon usually initiates this information; the nurse reinforces the information as needed by the client. *A*, *B*, and *D are* all included by the *nurse* in routine preop teaching, and are therefore not the correct answers.

122. D. Maintaining a patent airway.

D is correct because life-threatening factors always have priority. *A*, *B*, and *C* are all important functions, but the airway has priority.

123. B. 31 drops.

To determine the number of drops per minute, the nurse uses the following calculation:

(total amount of solution x drop factor) ÷ (total time x minutes)
(3000 x 15) ÷ (24 x 60) = 31 drops.

124. A. 625 mL.

3000 mL in 24 hours = 125 mL per hour.

125 mL x 3 hours = 375 mL.

1000 – 375 = 625 mL.

125. B. Atelectasis.

Respiratory complications are the most probable due to the unwillingness of the client to cough and deep breathe because of the high incision. This inhibits ventilatory movement, and the incidence of postop pneumonia is very high. *A*, *C*, and *D* are all possible complications, but respiratory complications are the most common.

126. C. Preventing the tube from kinking.

For any tube to function properly, the opening must remain patent for drainage of fluid. *A* and *D* are important functions but do not have the highest priority. *B* is incorrect because dressings should be changed only when necessary due to wetness.

127. B. Encourage the client to take carbonated beverages.

B is the order that should be questioned because nothing should be given by mouth when nonfunctioning bowel is suspected. *A*, *C*, and *D* are all appropriate actions for such a client and are therefore not the answers.

128. A. Put Ms. Norfolk on bedrest.

Thrombophlebitis is a very serious complication and the client must be immobilized to prevent further life-threatening problems. *B* is incorrect because problems should be reported immediately. *C* and *D* are incorrect because they could assist a clot in traveling from the calf to a vital organ. The nurse should not ambulate and should never massage the client when thrombophlebitis is suspected.

129. C. Allow a rest period between activities.

Mr. Amos is in mild pulmonary edema. The lack of temperature indicates no active infections. Allowance for a rest period between activities helps to relieve dyspnea. *A* is incorrect because he is not confused and is considered a good historian. *B* is incorrect because his shortness of breath is not to the extent that it would interfere with eating and crackles are slight. *D* is incorrect because since no edema is present, he is not in acute danger of skin breakdown.

130. B. After alcohol ingestion.

Postural hypotension results from the vascular system's inability to adjust to sudden venous pooling when position is changed from a lying to a standing state. Peripheral vasodilation is promoted by alcohol. Alcohol has also been shown to potentiate the orthostatic hypotensive effects of the thiazides. *A* is incorrect because cold produces vasoconstriction, rather than dilation and pooling. *C* is incorrect because thiazides act by depressing tubular reabsorption of sodium and chloride, thereby reducing circulating blood volume. *D* is incorrect because the ingestion of seafood has no effect.

131. A. Recording daily weight.

Diuretics produce a net loss of fluids. Assessment of their effectiveness is reflected in weight change. Excess fluid loss indicates a reduction in fluid in the vascular and extravascular compartments. *B*, reducing sodium in the diet, is also important, but it is *not the first priority*. Sodium is usually limited to "no added salt," and the client is advised to avoid processed or ethnic foods. *C*, increasing oral fluid intake, is incorrect because fluids are *not* likely to be increased, and may actually be restricted, depending on the severity of the fluid retention. *D*, measuring intake and output, is important to the total management of a fluid imbalance; however, the question asks for the *most important* action.

132. A. He should rise slowly from a lying to a sitting position and from a sitting to a standing position.

Methyldopa lowers brain and heart norepinephrine and therefore reduces sympathetic activity. It lowers blood pressure by reducing peripheral resistance. Postural hypotension results from the vascular system's inability to adjust to sudden pooling when position is changed from lying to standing. Changing position slowly gives the vascular system the opportunity to adjust. *B* is incorrect because self-regulation of medication is always dangerous without medical consultation first. *C* is incorrect because alteration of the diet without medical consultation and specific guidelines may produce further complications. *D* is untrue; alcohol potentiates the action of antihypertensives and should therefore be avoided.

133. B. Pulse rate.

The cardiovascular system first tries to compensate for a sudden drop in circulatory blood volume by increasing the pulse rate by sympathetic stimulation. *A* is incorrect because pupillary change results from oxygen deficit after a severe drop in blood pressure. *C* is incorrect because it is not an *early* sign of postural hypo-tension. A drop in blood pressure alters the state of orientation (i.e., to fainting) due to diminished perfusion and oxygen lack, but this will not occur until later. *D* is incorrect because muscles become limp, rather than rigid, with postural hypotension.

134. C. Nailing a table together.

Nailing a table together encourages the client to use muscle strength and activity to dissipate anxiety. This is a very healthy means of expressing feelings. Hypertension is a psychosomatic disorder in which emotions play an important influence. Often these clients internalize anxiety. *A* and *D* are not the best responses because they do not attempt to assist Mr. Amos to express his feelings. In some clients, moreover, these activities may in themselves promote anxiety. *B* is incorrect. When anxiety is internalized, it is unconscious; asking a client directly what is bothering him would probably evoke a response denying the existence of such anxiety.

135. B. Teach the client to take his weight and mark it down.

B is correct because weight loss indicates a state of hydration Diuretics can produce dehydration through excessive water loss. *A* is incorrect because the water temperature is too hot and may produce burns or vasodilation and hypotension. *C* is not logical; restriction of fluids in clients receiving diuretics will produce dehydration. *D* is not common to *all* clients receiving diuretics; disorientation is seen only with extreme electrolyte disruption.

136. A. Use more herbs and spices for flavoring.

Flavoring foods with spices and herbs is one of the better alternatives to using sodium-based products. Low-sodium dietetic foods, *B*, are expensive and need not be used exclusively. Cooking Mr. Amos's foods separately, *C*, is an inconvenience for the cook and disrupts the family routine. Cake mixes and the like, *D*, are high in sodium.

137. A. Withhold the dose and call the doctor.

This is a question of nursing judgment. Furosemide is a rapid acting and potent diuretic. The client's blood pressure is below her usual level. After administration of furosemide, her blood pressure will drop markedly. *B* and *C* are incorrect because the drug should be withheld. Notification of the physician is important, to make him or her aware of the current status of the client in relation to the treatment regimen and of the possible need to change the dosage or drug. *D* does not include calling the physician.

138. D. Produce severe vasoconstriction.

MAO inhibitors increase the concentration of norepinephrine. Tyramine is a precursor of norepinephrine. When both are present, a flooding of the body with norepinephrine can result. Severe vasoconstriction with marked blood pressure elevation follows. *A* is incorrect because vasodilatation does not occur with norepinephrine stimulation. *B* is incorrect because norepinephrine tends to decrease cardiac output. *C* is incorrect because the concentration of norepinephrine is increased.

139. B. Is relieved by rest.

Angina, which is precipitated by the three "Es"—*eating, emotion, and exertion*—is relieved by rest. The pain of myocardial infarction does not resolve when the client stops what he or she was doing. *A* describes the treatment for myocardial infarction pain. Angina responds to nitroglycerin. *C* is a description fitting both angina and myocardial infarction pain. *D* is incorrect because angina characteristically lasts 5–20 minutes. Myo-cardial infarction pain lasts 30 minutes to hours.

140. D. *Decreasing venous return to the heart.*

Nitroglycerin is a vasodilator; the drug not only dilates the coronary arteries, but also causes a peripheral vasodilation, which decreases venous return. Therefore, the heart does not have to work as hard and there is less oxygen consumption. *A* describes the action of digitalis preparations. *B* is not an action of nitroglycerin, and drugs that do increase the heart rate need to be administered cautiously in clients with heart damage. *C* is incorrect because nitroglycerin does not affect the strength of cardiac contractions. An example of a drug that decreases myocardial contractility is propranolol (Inderal).

141. D. *Family history of cancer.*

A, *B*, and *C* are known risk factors in the development of coronary artery disease. *B* and *C* are two of the three major risk factors; hyperlipidemia is the third. There is no known correlation between cancer and coronary artery disease.

142. C. *Potassium is released from the cells following destruction.*

Potassium is an intracellular ion that is released in the extracellular space when cells are destroyed. *A* can occur if renal perfusion is severely impaired, but is not the initial cause of hyperkalemia. *B* is incorrect because treatment to relieve edema includes diuretic therapy, which results in sodium and potassium loss. *D* is incorrect because potassium increases in metabolic acidosis, not alkalosis.

143. B. *If possible, allow use of bedside commode.*

Use of a bedpan is a more strenuous activity than allowing the client up on a bedside commode. There is generally less straining and anxiety associated with the use of a commode. Positioning flat in bed, *A*, may be contraindicated, particularly if the client is short of breath or hypertensive. The diet of a client with a cardiac illness is progressive. A client who is not allowed to feed himself or herself, *C*, because of the exertion, most likely will be on a diet (such as liquids or soft foods) that does not consume excessive oxygen during digestion. Activity, like diet, is progressive, and will vary from client to client. Total activity restriction for 72 hours, *D*, may be more stressful for clients.

144. C. *Consider it a normal occurrence.*

The increase in temperature is a normal inflammatory response to tissue destruction and is expected 24–48 hours after infarction. Infection, *A*, needs to be ruled out if an elevated temperature occurred 72 hours or later after infarct. *B* and *D* are incorrect because they are actions for reduction of high fevers. Also, fluid intake must be increased cautiously in the client with cardiac weakness.

145. B. Canned spaghetti with tomato sauce.

A 1-cup serving of canned spaghetti with tomato sauce contains 2 g of fat. A home-cooked recipe has 9 g of fat. Cannelloni, *A*, has 19 g of fat from the ricotta cheese alone. The pasta adds only one more gram. Olive oil, *C*, contains 14 g of fat in 1 tablespoon. Dry salami, *D*, has 4 g of fat per slice, for a total of 16 g.

146. C. Clear breath sounds and slowed pulse.

In congestive heart failure the signs include tachycardia, crackles, and edema. The drug therapy improves myocardial contractility, slows the heart rate, and removes excess fluid. *A* and *D* are incorrect since diuresis will result in decreased urine specific gravity. *B* is incorrect because digoxin has a negative chronotropic effect and slows heart rate.

147. B. Sexual activity can resume, but it will need to be limited compared with the pre–myocardial infarction activity.

Resumption of sexual activity is a necessary topic for discharge teaching. The post–myocardial infarction activity will depend on the extent of the myocardial damage. In most cases the client can gradually return to the pre–myocardial infarction level (but not necessarily a level greater than the pre–myocardial infarction activity). *A*, *C*, and *D* are examples of accurate counseling. *A* is important because stress is linked closely to the risk of further disease or damage. *C* is an approach to decreasing the risk associated with obesity. *D* is appropriate counseling that allows the client greater control over his condition.

148. C. Hard palate.

Jaundice, in persons of various skin colors, can be readily viewed by examining the hard palate of the mouth with the aid of a flashlight. *A* is incorrect since some persons have naturally yellow, discolored nailbeds or very dark nailbeds, which prevents observation of color change. *B* and *D* are incorrect because they do not represent the best site for observing jaundice in dark-skinned persons. Some people have a yellow coloration to their skin because of ethnic background or sun exposure. Others may have such dark skin that jaundice is not clearly visible in these areas.

149. C. Avoidance of enemas and cathartics.

C is not indicated if a *lowering* of blood ammonia is desired, so it is the correct answer. Enemas and cathartics *may be given* to *hasten* the removal of protein materials from the intestine, thereby *lowering* blood ammonia. *A* and *B* lower ammonia levels by decreasing intestinal protein. *D* lowers ammonia levels by reducing the bacterial production of this substance.

150. D. Lactulose.

Lactulose is a drug that lowers the pH of the colon, which inhibits the diffusion of ammonia from the colon into the blood, reducing blood ammonia levels. *A*, *B*, and *C* do not have the desired effect on ammonia levels. Diazepam is a sedative and skeletal-muscle relaxant that should be used with much caution in a person with liver disease. Lomotil is an antidiarrheal drug that will slow the removal of protein materials from the intestine and thereby increase ammonia levels. Furosemide is a diuretic drug that inhibits reabsorption of sodium and water in renal tubules.

151. B. Decreases in pedal edema.

Pedal edema suggests circulatory disturbances rather than the cerebral disturbances that are characteristic of hepatic encephalopathy. *A*, *C*, and *D* are examples of improved cerebral functioning.

152. A. Elevated BUN.

BUN levels reflect the *kidney's* ability to excrete urea, an end product of protein metabolism. *B*, *C*, and *D* are classic signs of GI *bleeding*.

153. B. The S-B tube has dislodged and one of its balloons is obstructing the airway.

Each of the answers given could conceivably cause respiratory distress in a client like Mr. Mesta. *A* and *B* are the most likely to cause a sudden respiratory crisis. *B* should first be considered since Mr. Mesta has a S-B tube in place. Displacement of the tube constitutes a medical emergency. *A* is a less correct response since the case study makes no reference to chest pain or hemoptysis, classic signs of a pulmonary embolus. Also, the client's history does not suggest prolonged immobility or long bone fractures, conditions that often precipitate an embolus. *C* is incorrect because Mr. Mesta's anemia is unlikely to cause such a sudden respiratory change. *D* is incorrect because the case situation states that the client is lethargic and disoriented—not especially anxious.

154. D. A few sedatives that are not metabolized in the liver exist, but they should be used cautiously.

Clients with liver disease respond adversely to sedation. The inability of damaged liver cells to metabolize drugs is generally given as a reason for this. *A* is incorrect in that a few drugs—namely, phenobarbital and paraldehyde—are given to clients if absolutely necessary. *B* is incorrect since most opiates, short-acting barbiturates, and major tranquilizers are metabolized primarily in the liver. *C* is incorrect because "excitant" effects with sedatives are rarely, if ever, reported.

155. A. "It must be difficult for you to accept these changes in your diet, Mr. Mesta."

This response is the most supportive of the four choices given. It shows concern and understanding for Mr. Mesta's situation in a nonjudgmental way. *B* is a less desirable response since it focuses on telling the client what to do and suggests he is powerless in this situation. *C* is also an undesirable response if the nurse hopes to achieve long-term compliance with the prescribed diet. The fact that another client cannot eat may be true, but it is unlikely to motivate Mr. Mesta to change his dietary habits. *D* is incorrect and suggests that the nurse does not understand the need for long-term changes in dietary habits.

156. C. Eyes turned toward his left side.

The eyes of a client who is comatose with a cerebral lesion usually deviate toward the side of the lesion. Mr. Lewis has a left-sided stroke; therefore, his eyes deviate toward his left side. *A* and *D* are incorrect because clients who are in deep coma do not respond to deep pain or have any motor response, such as a purposeful movement of the nonparalyzed extremity. *B* is incorrect because deep, gasping respirations (Kussmaul respirations) are usually associated with diabetic coma.

157. C. Flexed fingers, wrists, and arms; fully extended legs; and flexed feet.

The client has decorticate posturing when his fingers, wrists, and arms are flexed, and when his legs are extended and his feet are flexed. This signifies severe dysfunction of the brain—specifically, lesions in the cerebral white matter, internal capsules, and thalamus. Thus, *C* is the correct answer. *A* and *D* are descriptions of decerebrate posturing. *B* is a description of a client with a motor focal seizure.

158. D. Computerized tomography.

Computerized tomography, such as CT or CAT scan, and EMI (electronic musical instrument) scan, is a noninvasive procedure that permits the visualization of the cranial contents in several horizontal planes. It confirms the presence of epidural, subdural, and internal hemorrhage of the ventricular system. *A* is incorrect because myelography detects the compression of the spinal cord and other cord pathologies, not cerebral hemorrhage. *B*, electromyogram, detects the presence of muscle disorders. Although lumbar puncture, *C*, may confirm cerebral hemorrhage and may provide clues to the location of the hemorrhage, it is not as reliable and efficient as computerized tomography. Lumbar puncture also increases intracranial pressure and can lead to herniation of the brain.

159. C. Potential for respiratory insufficiency related to severely depressed level of consciousness.

Because the respiratory status becomes depressed as the level of consciousness is decreased, support of the respiratory system must be given immediate attention. Adequate oxygenation is vital to life. When the brain is deprived of oxygen for longer than 5 minutes, irreversible brain damage occurs.

Mr. Lewis needs oxygen support because he already has compromised brain tissue oxygenation because of the cerebral hemorrhage. Thus, *C* is the correct answer. *B* and *D* are incorrect. These deal with communication problems—very important considerations, but they are not life-threatening. *A* is incorrect because it is a medical diagnosis. The question asks for a nursing problem.

160. *B. Rest and relaxation.*

The nursing goals that preserve the life of the client are the top priorities. For the client with decreased responsiveness, adequate lung expansion and nutrition and fluids are most important for sufficient gas exchange, nutrition, and perfusion of tissues. The client also needs to be protected from injury because he cannot defend himself from external threat. The *least* important of all the stated short-term goals is the provision of adequate rest and relaxation, *B*, because lack of this does not pose an immediate threat to the client's life. Thus, *A*, *C*, and *D* are not the answers.

161. *A. Aphasia.*

Because of a dysfunction in the speech center of the brain, the client with a stroke is unable to communicate verbally. There may also be a dysfunction in the area involved in auditory comprehension. This communication problem is called aphasia. The type of aphasia described in the stem of the question is global aphasia. Other common types include expressive, receptive, and jargon aphasia. *B* is incorrect; agnosia means the inability of a person to understand auditory, visual, or other types of sensation, although the sensory sphere is not damaged. *C* is incorrect; apraxia means the inability to perform movements that are purposeful, yet the sensory and motor functions are intact. *D* is incorrect; ataxia means muscular incoordination, particularly when voluntary movements are done.

162. *B. Intermittent catheterization.*

Repeated aseptic insertion and removal of the Foley catheter, *B*, is the preferred management of clients with chronic illnesses who have problems voiding or retaining urine. Because the catheter is not in the body for a prolonged period of time, the risk of urinary tract infection is lessened. *A* is incorrect. Decreased fluid intake eventually leads to dehydration, a problem that must be prevented in clients with stroke. An adequate fluid intake is necessary to produce urine, to enable the excretion of excess body fluids and waste products. Urine production should also be adequate to stimulate the micturition reflex. *C* is incorrect. Prolonged use of a Foley catheter increases the risk of urinary tract infection because of the presence of a foreign substance in the body cavity. *D* is incorrect. The use of an external drainage system solves the problem of urinary incontinence but not the urinary retention if also present.

163. C. Light-brown or light-yellow liquid drainage is aspirated, with a pH of 4 or less.

The two most currently accepted outcome criteria for correct placement of the nasogastric tube are: (1) aspiration of light-brown or light-yellow liquid drainage with a pH of 4 or less, by means of a 60cc catheter-tipped syringe; and (2) a chest x-ray. A rush of air heard on auscultation of the epigastric region, when 20–40 mL of air is rapidly introduced through the nasogastric tube, is *another* possible method of checking placement; however the nurse should follow agency policy when checking placement of a nasogastric tube. Thus, *C* is the correct response. *A*, *B*, and *D* are incorrect. These parameters indicate the presence of the nasogastric tube in the *lungs*.

164. D. Glossopharyngeal.

The cranial nerves responsible for swallowing movements are the glossopharyngeal and vagus nerves. Thus, *D* is the correct response. *A*, *B*, and *C* are incorrect. The facial nerve, *A*, makes changes in facial expressions possible. The trigeminal nerve, *B*, is responsible for chewing movements, and the hypoglossal nerve, *C*, for tongue movement.

165. C. "I am willing to be shown how to dress and feed him."

C is a matter-of-fact response indicating a desire by a family member or a significant other to be given direction in the care of the client. It is a realistic statement, and it indicates acceptance of participation in the rehabilitation of the client. *A*, *B*, and *D* are incorrect. These responses are evasive and nonaccepting of the responsibility of caring for the sick individual.

166. D. Both metabolic and respiratory acidosis.

The increase in CO_2, (above 45 mm Hg), the decrease in HCO_3 (below 22 mm Hg), and the low pH (below 7.35) are consistent with both metabolic and respiratory acidosis. If compensation were present, *A*, the metabolic level would be nearer to or above 26, and the pH would be within normal limits. *B* and *C* alone are not complete interpretations.

167. B. Ecchymosis on back and thorax.

When a pulmonary artery catheter is in place, thrombi development is a constant danger. Heparinization is usually done routinely to prevent this complication. Administering the heparin via infusion pump can reduce the risk of over-heparinization. Nevertheless, observation for signs of bleeding should still be done. *A* is incorrect because a low-grade fever can be expected after myocardial infarction. This is a manifestation of the inflammatory process associated with the destruction of myocardial tissue. *C* is incorrect because a one-time urinary output of 25 mL does not warrant immediate action. Oliguria may result due to shock and secondary poor renal perfusion. The urinary output should therefore be monitored closely. Consistent oliguria may indicate renal hypoxia. **D** is incorrect because nausea and indigestion are normal complaints after myocardial infarction. These complaints may be due to vasovagal reflexes conducted from the area of ischemia to the GI tract.

168. **A. Reduce IV infusion rate.**

The CVP reading is elevated, indicating cardiac decompensation and reflex of blood into the venous system. The most appropriate action at this time is one that reduces cardiac workload. **B** is incorrect; although additional O_2 would be helpful, it does not deal with the *cause* of the presenting symptom—that is, increasing venous pressure. **C** is incorrect; by increasing the IV infusion rate, the nurse will only increase cardiac workload to an already damaged myocardium. **D** is incorrect; raising the head of the bed will alter the CVP reading but does not deal with the true cause of the elevated reading—that is, increasing venous pressure.

169. **B. Severe pain can produce shock and increase cardiac workload.**

The pain associated with myocardial infarction is so terrifying, severe, and debilitating that the pain itself can produce shock. **A** is incorrect because it describes the basis for the pain, not the reason for relieving it. **C** is not the best explanation. **D** is incorrect because it is an erroneous statement. Pain stimulates the sympathetic, not the parasympathetic, system.

170. **C. The tissues are poorly perfused and venous return is diminished.**

Severe reduction in cardiac output and inadequate tissue perfusion produce pooling of any medication in the muscle mass. The client would not reap the benefit of the drug. Furthermore, when adequate perfusion is restored, the medication will be absorbed and overdosage may occur. **A** is incorrect; a larger dosage will have no effect due to poor venous return—the medication is not being absorbed. **B** is incorrect; the pain of the injection may increase stress, but at this time the *most* important consideration is venous pooling. Although **D** is basically a true statement, it is the incorrect answer; at this time it is more important to relieve the client's pain.

171. **B. Accelerate the heart rate by interfering with vagal impulses.**

Atropine exerts its effect on several body organs. In this instance, however, atropine is needed to accelerate the heart by interfering with the response of the heart muscle to vagal nerve impulses. **A** and **D** are incorrect; although both represent actions of atropine, they are not the rationale for its use in this instance. **C** is incorrect because atropine does not have a direct effect on the SA node.

172. A. Monitor pedal pulses.

The intra-aortic balloon pump is inserted in the femoral artery, and is positioned into the descending aorta. It inflates and deflates with the cardiac cycle, to increase perfusion of the coronary arteries. Because the femoral artery is obstructed, ischemia may result distal to the site of arteriotomy. *B* and *C* are incorrect because the affected leg should remain straight to prevent hip flexion and disruption of the balloon. *D* is incorrect; the head of the bed should not be raised more than 30 degrees. Greater elevations may force the balloon to the aortic notch.

173. C. Hold the drug and call the doctor.

This client is showing signs of digitalis toxicity. The most appropriate action is to hold the drug and call the doctor. Severe arrhythmias may develop. *A* is incorrect because further administration of this medication will only increase toxicity. *B* is incorrect; despite this evaluation of the client, continued administration of digitoxin can lead to complications such as heart block. *D* is incorrect because any administration of this medication will be perilous given the client's symptoms.

174. C. Mr. A, who is receiving hydrochlorothiazide.

Clients taking thiazide diuretics are prone to develop potassium loss. Since potassium inhibits the excitability of the heart, depletion of the body's myocardial potassium increases cardiac excitability. Low extracellular potassium is synergistic with digitalis and enhances ectopic pacemaker activity (arrhythmias). This question tests circumstances that produce digitalis intoxication. *A* is incorrect; constipation does not predispose the client to digitalis intoxication. *B* is incorrect because this is a normal serum potassium level. *D* is incorrect; the administration of oral hypoglycemic agents does not predispose the client to digitalis toxicity.

175. D. Diminished crackles.

Heart failure exists to some degree in all clients with myocardial infarction. Crackles exist due to left-sided failure and passive reflux of blood, producing pulmonary hypertension. Because digitoxin increases the force of systolic contraction, allows complete ventricular emptying, and improves cardiac output, pulmonary edema is reduced. *A* is incorrect; digitalis preparations slow the heart rate by depressing conduction through the bundle of His and facilitating the vagal effect on the SA node. *B* is incorrect because the CVP should fall, rather than rise. A rise in CVP indicates cardiac failure and worsening venous congestion. *C* is incorrect; urinary output should improve due to the diuretic action of this drug.

176. D. "I have to walk this pain out of my leg."

This is a question of judgment and priority setting. This client may have thrombophlebitis. Some clients think it is a cramp and try to exercise. Exercise could dislodge a clot and peril the client's life. The nurse should investigate this at once. *A* is incorrect as the priority action, although it is important to assess the client's elimination status. Straining at stool increases the workload on the heart. *B* is incorrect as the priority action. In this instance, the client is attempting to open the door of communication. *C* is incorrect because it does not warrant immediate action. Mr. Simpson may be feeling better physically or psychologically.

177. A. Protamine sulfate.

When protamine sulfate is given in the presence of heparin, they are attracted to each other instead of to the blood elements, and each neutralizes the anticoagulant activity of the other. *B* is incorrect; sodium citrate is an anticoagulant and systemic antacid. *C* is incorrect; vitamin K is most often given as an antidote for coumarin overdosage. *D* is incorrect; warfarin sodium is an anticoagulant.

178. A. Respiration 20 and pulse 80.

Furosemide exerts its diuretic action by inhibiting the reabsorption of sodium and chloride at the proximal and distal tubules, as well as at the loop of Henle. It is useful in the treatment of pulmonary edema and congestive heart failure by reducing circulatory blood volume and pulmonary congestion by the passive regurgitation of blood. Restoration of the vital signs to normal is indicative of reversal in the pathologic process and that therapeutic effect has taken place. *B* is incorrect; voiding 200 mL does not indicate that the therapeutic effects of this medication have been met. The purpose of furosemide is to reduce circulatory blood volume, *not* to stimulate voiding. *C* is incorrect because crackles indicate that passive lung congestion still persists. *D* is incorrect because these symptoms indicate that the client is getting "shocky"—an untoward reaction.

179. C. If chest pain persists after 3 or more tablets have been taken, the physician should be notified.

This precaution is necessary in case of myocardial ischemia. If 3 tablets of nitroglycerin in 15 minutes do not relieve the pain, the client may be experiencing an infarct. *A* is incorrect because nitroglycerin deteriorates with exposure to light. *B* is incorrect; flushing of the skin occurs due to the vasodilatory effect of the drug and is considered a normal reaction. *D* is incorrect; alcohol, like nitroglycerin, produces vasodilation of peripheral vessels.

180. D. Sliced broiled chicken, macaroni, 1 glass of orange juice.

A is incorrect because hot dogs with mustard are high in sodium. *B* is incorrect because consommé is high in sodium. *C* is incorrect because the corned beef sandwich with kosher dill pickle is high in sodium.

181. D. Elevated serum creatinine.

Serum creatinine is elevated in diseases of the kidney that result in significant nephron damage. Nonrenal causes of creatinine elevation are rare, so this is an excellent, specific test for renal failure. *A* is incorrect because renal failure precipitates a lowered blood pH, with metabolic acidosis. *B* is incorrect because serum calcium levels usually drop in response to increased levels of serum phosphorus. *C* is partially correct. BUN levels rise in renal failure, but they also rise with a high protein intake or protein catabolism in the body. Therefore, BUN is not the most accurate indicator of renal function.

182. B. Causes potassium to be excreted in increased amounts in the feces.

Sodium polystyrene sulfonate (Kayexalate) is a sodium compound that exchanges sodium and hydrogen ions for potassium in the GI tract. As a result, excess potassium is excreted in the feces. *A* is incorrect since diuretic drugs, rather than sodium polystyrene sulfonate, are likely to cause sodium and water excretion. *C* is incorrect since intravenous glucose and insulin cause potassium to reenter the cells. *D* is incorrect since sodium bicarbonate is usually given to correct for metabolic acidosis.

183. A. Muscle atony and cardiac irregularities.

Muscle weakness and paralysis and bradycardia proceeding to cardiac standstill are signs and symptoms associated with hyperkalemia. *B* and *C* are incorrect because these observations are not characteristic of hyperkalemia. *B* is likely to be associated with a neurologic problem. *C* is likely to occur in a person with liver disease. *D* is partially correct. Anuria may be a complication of hyperkalemia, but hyperuricemia is a result of the kidney's inability to excrete waste products of protein metabolism.

184. D. Dried peaches.

Fruits in general—and dried fruits in particular—are high in potassium content. *A* and *C* have lesser amounts of potassium. *B*, pastries, tend to be very low in potassium.

185. C. High carbohydrate, high fat, low protein.

Protein is often restricted since the kidneys have difficulty excreting the end products of protein metabolism. Extra quantities of carbohydrates and fats provide necessary calories. *A* and *D* are incorrect since they are diets more often prescribed for GI problems. *B* is partially correct. High fat and low sodium are components of prescribed diets in renal failure. High protein in the diet is contraindicated.

186. C. Pale conjunctival sacs.

Pallor in the conjunctiva of the eye is an excellent indicator of anemia in persons of various skin colors. *A* is incorrect because people who are anemic tend to be pale and complain of feeling cold. *B* is incorrect because fatigue and weakness often accompany anemia. *D* is incorrect because dusky coloring is a sign of hypoxia, rather than anemia.

187. C. Increase in blood pH and decrease in respiratory rate.

Resolving metabolic acidosis will result in an increase in the arterial pH. The compensatory respiratory response (Kussmaul breathing) will be unnecessary as pH returns to normal. As a result, respiratory rate and depth will decrease. *A* is partially correct, as it identifies a decrease in respiratory rate. *B* is partially correct, as it identifies an increase in blood pH. *D* is totally incorrect because it identifies decreasing pH and increasing respiratory rate as indicators of a resolving acidosis.

188. D. Ensuring that the area around the peritoneal catheter insertion site is open to the air and observed regularly.

D is the inappropriate nursing action. Special care and attention are directed toward preventing infection around the catheter site. A dry, sterile dressing is placed around the catheter and changed regularly. *A is* indicated to prevent chilling of the client and to dilate peritoneal blood vessels, thus facilitating the exchange of substances. *B is* important with peritoneal dialysis to prevent hypovolemia or retention of dialysate. *C is* important to monitor fluid balance and possible infections or peritonitis.

189. A. Abdominal pain.

Peritonitis is characterized by a rigid abdomen and pain with palpation or movement. *B* is incorrect because cloudy, rather than clear, dialysate returns signal peritonitis. *C* is incorrect because the abdomen is rigid, not soft. *D* is incorrect because bowel sounds tend to be absent.

10. Older Adults and Geriatrics

Case Management Scenarios and Critical–Thinking Exercises

Medical Diagnosis: Chronic obstructive pulmonary disease (COPD).

- **Nursing Problem/Diagnosis:**

  Impaired gas exchange.

- **Chief Complaint:**

  Ms. Beckus is 65-years-old, a widow and works in a cotton-processing plant. She was admitted with shortness of breath, productive cough, and weakness.

- **History of Present Illness:**

  Over the past week, Ms. Beckus experienced increasing difficulty breathing on exertion. Her cough was productive of large amounts of yellow, thick sputum.

- **Past History:**

  Heavy smoker—2 packs a day for 45 years. Diagnosed 5 years ago with chronic obstructive pulmonary disease (COPD). Pneumonia 1 year ago.

- **Family History:**

  No family history of pulmonary diseases.

- **Review of Symptoms:**

  No weight loss. Chest pain on inspiration.

- **Physical Exam:**

  Vital signs: BP: 145/95. Temperature: 102°F. P: 104. R: 32.

  Head/neck: Accessory breathing muscles enlarged.

  Chest: Increased anterior-posterior diameter.

  Lungs: Prolonged expiratory phase. Bilateral basilar crackles. Hyperresonant to percussion.

  Abdomen: Soft; no organomegaly.

  Extremities: Nailbeds dusky. Clubbing present.

- *Laboratory and X-ray Data:*

  Chest x-ray: Lungs are hyperinflated with scattered bullae. Infiltrated areas over left lower lobe.

  Na: 146.

  K: 4.3.

  Hgb: 12.8 g.

  Hct: 58%.

  WBC: 16,000/μL.

  Blood gases: Respiratory acidosis with moderate hypoxemia.

---

1. As the nurse enters the room, she notices that Ms. Beckus appears "air hungry." Which observation best indicates to the nurse that the client is having difficulty getting sufficient air?

   A. Rapid respiratory rate.

   B. Use of accessory neck muscles.

   C. Bluish appearance of nailbeds and lips.

   D. Audible expiratory wheezing.

2. Which laboratory and x-ray findings does the nurse expect to see, consistent with Ms. Beckus's condition?

   A. Decreased arterial PCO_2, decreased arterial PO_2, and decreased hematocrit.

   B. Increased arterial PCO_2, hypoinflated alveoli, and decreased arterial PO_2.

   C. Increased arterial PO_2 and hyperinflated alveoli.

   D. Increased arterial PCO_2, increased hematocrit, and hyperinflated alveoli.

3. Oxygen therapy has been ordered to assist the client with her breathing. Which principle should guide the nurse in managing the delivery of oxygen to Ms. Beckus?

   A. Clients with COPD require higher concentrations (6–8 L) of oxygen since hypoxemia is their stimulus to breathe.

   B. The concentration of oxygen should be high since the stimulus to breathe in clients with COPD is the elevated PCO_2.

   C. Clients with COPD should receive low concentrations (2–3 L) of oxygen since the stimulus to breathe is their low PO_2.

   D. The concentration of oxygen should be low since the stimulus to breathe in clients with COPD is the elevated PCO_2.

4. The client has been started on intravenous aminophylline, 500 mg every 6 hours. An indication to the nurse of the drug's effectiveness is:

   A. Clearing of the bibasilar crackles.

   B. Absent expiratory and inspiratory wheezing.

   C. Change in sputum color from yellow to white.

   D. A lowering of the hematocrit.

5. Ms. Beckus refuses to stop smoking despite her pulmonary disease. Which is the least plausible explanation?

   A. She feels better when she smokes.

   B. She may be denying the severity of her condition.

   C. Refusal to quit is an attempt to retain control of her condition.

   D. Neurotic reactions should be expected with COPD.

6. The nurse determines that Ms. Beckus is at greater risk of developing thromboembolism because of which compensatory response to COPD?

   A. Polycythemia.

   B. Hypercapnia.

   C. Hypoxemia.

   D. Leukocytosis.

7. The nurse is observing the client as she practices diaphragmatic and pursed lip breathing. The nurse explains that the purpose of the exercises is to:

   A. Strengthen the intercostals.

   B. Reduce the anterior-posterior diameter of the chest.

   C. Increase inspiratory volume.

   D. Facilitate complete exhalation.

8. The nurse knows that the prognosis for a client with COPD is related most directly to controlling and preventing:

   A. The incidence of respiratory infections.

   B. The development of carbon dioxide retention.

   C. Chronic hypoxemia.

   D. Irritation from cigarette smoking.

9. Adequate hydration is an important aspect of care for Ms. Beckus. Which assessment by the nurse is not an indication of a response to an increase in fluid intake?

   A. Thinning of the pulmonary secretions.

   B. A decrease in the WBC count.

   C. Reduction in body temperature.

   D. A lowering of the hematocrit level.

Medical Diagnosis: Cancer of the bowel.

- *Surgical Treatment:*

  Abdominal perineal resection with descending colostomy.

- *Nursing Problems/Diagnosis:*

  Altered bowel elimination.

  Altered comfort pattern.

  Risk for alteration in endocrine/metabolic processes.

  Knowledge deficit: about diagnostic test.

  Altered nutrition: more than body requirements.

  Self-care deficit: medication administration.

- *Chief Complaint:*

  Mr. Richmond is 67-years-old and a retired locomotive engineer. He enters the hospital complaining of passing blood in the stool and a change in bowel habits.

- *History of Present Illness:*

  During the past 3 months, Mr. Richmond has noticed that the contour of his stool has changed. He has had episodes of constipation and diarrhea, distention, and some lower abdominal cramping.

- *Past History:*

  Treated medically for duodenal ulcer at age 36. No bowel problems. Loss of 20 pounds over past year. Smoker. Periodic episodes of bronchitis. Treated at age 57 for rectal polyps.

- *Family History:*

  Grandfather died after being ill with a "bowel problem." No documented history of cancer.

- *Review of Systems:*

  Eyes: Uses glasses for reading.

  Ears: Some loss of hearing in past 10 years.

  Respiratory: Admits to cough in the morning; denies tuberculosis. Bronchitis documented three times.

  Cardiac: Denies high blood pressure, orthopnea, or chest pain.

  GI tract: Change in bowel habits; see History of Present Illness. Loss of appetite; lower abdominal pain. Weight loss of 20 pounds in past year. Rectal polyps treated at age 57.

  Urinary: No change in urinary habits. No nocturia.

  Musculoskeletal system: Generalized weakness past 2 months.

- *Physical Exam:*

  Respiratory: Crackles and wheezes in lower lobes. Thorax symmetric. Diaphragm descends 2 cm on inspiration.

  Abdomen: Soft; tenderness in lower abdomen. Lower spleen and kidneys not felt.

Rectal stool positive for occult blood. No mass felt on digital examination.

- *Laboratory and X-ray Data:*

Upper GI series: Within normal limits.

Barium enema: Mass noted in descending colon.

Colonoscopy: Abnormal tissue observed. Biopsy consistent with carcinoma of the bowel.

Hct: 38%.

Hgb: 12 g.

---

10. In preparing Mr. Richmond for his diagnostic tests, the nurse is teaching him what to expect at the time of his barium enema. The nurse tells him:

   A. Fecal matter must be cleansed from the bowel for good visualization.

   B. No restrictions will be made regarding food.

   C. He will be placed in one position during the entire procedure.

   D. He will be asked to drink some barium when in the x-ray department.

11. Which sign should the nurse look for as the most commonly associated with early detection of cancer of the colon?

   A. Abdominal distention.

   B. Vomiting of fecal material.

   C. Alteration in bowel habits.

   D. Presence of mucus in the stool.

12. Mr. Richmond has a tumor of the descending colon and needs surgery. The nurse administers neomycin sulfate prior to his surgery to reduce:

   A. Electrolyte imbalances.

   B. Bacterial content in the colon.

   C. Peristaltic action in the colon.

   D. Feces in the bowel.

13. In discussing the expected drainage that will come from the stoma site, the nurse tells Mr. Richmond that he can eventually anticipate:

   A. Constant green liquid drainage.

   B. Soft, brown, mushy feces.

   C. Solid, formed feces.

   D. Liquid, brown feces.

14. In preparation for surgery Mr. Richmond is placed on a low-residue diet. In discussing the kinds of foods he will be allowed to eat, the nurse lists:

    A. Ground lean beef, soft-boiled eggs, tea.

    B. Lettuce, spinach, corn.

    C. Prunes, grapes, apples.

    D. Bran cereal, whole-wheat toast, coffee.

15. One of the most common electrolyte imbalances associated with nasogastric tube suction that a nurse needs to be aware of is:

    A. Hypocalcemia.

    B. Hypermagnesemia.

    C. Hypokalemia.

    D. Hypoglycemia.

16. To prevent electrolyte imbalance, the nurse should:

    A. Irrigate the nasogastric tube with saline.

    B. Irrigate the nasogastric tube with water.

    C. Avoid irrigating the nasogastric tube.

    D. Change the suction from intermittent to continuous.

17. Threats to body image can affect the amount of pain or discomfort perceived by a client. This fact will be most important in planning care with the client who is undergoing a(n):

    A. Colonoscopy.

    B. Exploratory laparotomy.

    C. Colostomy.

    D. Barium enema.

18. The nurse knows that the type of ostomy following an abdominal perineal resection will most likely be a:

    A. Continent ileostomy.

    B. Permanent colostomy.

    C. Double-barreled colostomy.

    D. Transverse colostomy.

19. The appearance of a normal colostomy stoma should be:

    A. Red and raised.

    B. Pale and flat.

    C. Dusky and raised.

    D. Rosy and flat.

20. The nurse recognizes Mr. Richmond's willingness to be involved in his own care when he:

   A. Discusses the cost of his medical insurance.

   B. Asks what time the surgeon will be in.

   C. Asks questions about the equipment being used.

   D. Complains about the noise in the other room.

Medical Diagnosis: Brain Attack/Stroke.

- *Nursing Problems/Diagnosis:*

   Fluid volume deficit.

   Altered nutrition: less than body requirements.

   Impaired physical mobility.

   Sensory-perceptual alteration.

   Impaired skin integrity.

   Altered verbal communication (aphasia).

- *Chief Complaint:*

   Ms. Tweed is 78-years-old, obese, and has been transferred from an acute care hospital to a skilled nursing facility with the diagnosis of brain attack. She exhibits right hemiparesis, aphasia, and incontinence of stool and urine. Her two daughters, who are in their 50s, are unable to care for her at home.

- *History of Present Illness:*

   Hospitalized 2 weeks with no resolution of paralysis. Aphasia affects both expressive and receptive communication.

- *Past History:*

   Hypertension and mild congestive heart failure treated with hydrochlorothiazide and spironolactone.

- *Family History:*

   Mother died at an early age of tuberculosis. Father died in his 50s of pneumonia.

- *Review of Symptoms:*

   Weight loss of 15 pounds since hospitalization. Eats poorly and takes only sips of clear fluids with encouragement.

- *Physical Exam:*

   Head: Pale conjunctiva and mucous membranes in mouth; sunken cheeks; dry, furrowed tongue.

   Thorax: Marked kyphosis.

   Lungs: Scattered, fine crackles, which clear with coughing; shallow respirations.

Heart: Regular sinus rhythm with occasional premature ventricular beats.

Extremities: Flaccid paralysis of right arm and leg.

Skin: Gray color; dry, inelastic skin; small, red areas on both heels.

Neuro: Responds slowly but appropriately to commands; PERL; responds to name by opening eyes and attempting to speak.

Vital signs: BP: 170/100, P: 96, R: 20, Temperature: 98°F.

- **Laboratory Data:**

Hgb: 10.2 g.

Hct: 31.5%.

WBC: 10,800/µL.

Albumin: 2.5 g/dL.

---

21. Ms. Tweed is the focus of a nursing care conference soon after her admission. It is determined that she has a depletion of body fluids, which is to be corrected by increasing her daily oral intake. To evaluate the effectiveness of this plan, the nurses should monitor:

    A. Sugar, acetone, and specific gravity of urine.

    B. Color of mucous membranes and skin turgor.

    C. Body weight and urine specific gravity.

    D. Skin color and turgor.

22. Which nursing action is *inappropriate* when working with a client who is aphasic?

    A. Speak for the client as often as possible to minimize feelings of embarrassment.

    B. Repeat simple explanations until they are understood; use non-verbal clues when needed.

    C. Have client practice trying to repeat words and sounds after you say them.

    D. Caution family members against showing amusement or embarrassment after client attempts to communicate.

23. Ms. Tweed is repositioned every 2 hours, but the red pressure areas on the back of her heels worsen. She has also developed a pressure area over the sacrum. Which nursing action is *inappropriate*?

    A. Avoid positioning on back; turn side to side only.

    B. Put a sheepskin under her and heel pads on her feet.

    C. Place her on an alternating pressure mattress.

    D. Administer a sedative to promote rest and speed healing of tissues.

24. There is concern that Ms. Tweed is developing respiratory complications as a result of her immobility. Which source of data provides the nurse with the most reliable information on respiratory status?

    A. Breath sounds.

    B. Temperature.

    C. Pulse.

    D. Skin color.

25. Ms. Tweed complains of cold feet due to a draft blowing under the bed's foot cradle. What is the most appropriate action for the nurse to take?

    A. Remove the foot cradle so the covers can be snugly tucked around her feet.

    B. Prop hot water bottles by her feet.

    C. Vigorously massage the feet and lower legs to increase circulation and warmth.

    D. Help her into a pair of warm socks that she can wear while in bed.

26. In assessing Ms. Tweed's dietary intake, the nurse finds she is deficient in vitamin C and protein. Which breakfast menu should the nurse suggest to best meet the client's dietary needs?

    A. Cream of Wheat, whole milk, and toast.

    B. Strawberries with milk, cottage cheese, and toast.

    C. Orange juice and a sweet roll.

    D. Soft-cooked eggs, toast, and coffee.

27. Ms. Tweed continues to have fecal incontinence. She has 6–7 small, liquid, brown stools each day. She is on a soft diet and does not receive any stool softeners or laxatives. Her primary form of activity is sitting for 2 hours in a wheelchair twice a day. The nurse knows that a likely cause for this diarrhea is:

    A. Too much roughage in the diet.

    B. Overhydration with fluids.

    C. Excessive activity.

    D. Impaction.

28. Which nursing action is *inappropriate* in the prevention of thrombophlebitis in a client on bedrest?

    A. Elevate the knee gatch of the bed.

    B. Encourage exercises that dorsiflex and plantarflex the ankle.

    C. Apply antiembolism stockings.

    D. Prevent dehydration.

29. The purpose of proper positioning of the client's affected side following a stroke is to:

    A. Maintain extension of the limbs.

    B. Place the extremities in a flexed position.

    C. Preserve maximum functioning.

    D. Immobilize the joints.

Medical Diagnosis: Thrombophlebitis; deep-vein thrombosis.

- **Nursing Problems/Diagnosis:**

  Risk for alteration in circulation.

  Altered comfort (pain).

  Impaired physical mobility.

  Self-care deficit.

  Impaired skin integrity.

- **Chief Complaint:**

  Mr. Tell is 79-years-old, obese, and a retired bank manager. He complains of right leg pain and swelling.

- **History of Present Illness:**

  Mr. Tell sustained a right hip fracture, for which he had a closed reduction done, after a fall. He had been in the hospital for 4 days. Edema of his right calf was noted on his third day of hospitalization.

- **Past History:**

  Medical: Thrombophlebitis, age 70; pulmonary embolism, age 78.

- **Family History:**

  Father died at age 75, congestive heart failure. Mother died at age 60, stroke. One sister, age 68, apparently well except for chronic arterial insufficiency of lower extremities.

- **Physical Exam:**

  Neck: No lumps or pain; no limitation of movement; no bruit on carotid artery.

  Chest: Normal anterior-posterior diameter; symmetric chest expansion.

  Lungs: Diminished breath sounds in lung bases; bilateral upper lobes and right middle lobe resonant to percussion, bilateral lower lobes dull to percussion.

  Heart: No engorgement of neck veins on 30-degree head elevation; point of maximal impulse at fifth intercostal space and left mid-clavicular line; S_1 and S_2 within normal limits; no splitting, no extra heart sounds.

Abdomen: Flat, no unusual pigmentation or pulsation; active bowel sounds in four quadrants; soft, nontender, nondistended; no pain or guarding on light and deep palpation.

Extremities: Dry skin; right thigh and calf markedly edematous; marked tenderness on right femoral vein, particularly on right popliteal fossa on palpation; mottled erythema extends from back of right thigh down to popliteal fossa; right calf diameter 2.5 cm greater than left calf diameter.

- *Laboratory and X-ray Data:*

Chest x-ray: Mild density in lung bases.

ECG: Normal sinus rhythm with rare atrial premature beats.

Blood gases: Mild hypoxemia.

^{125}I fibrinogen test: Increased radioactivity in femoral and popliteal veins of right leg.

---

30. Why should the nurse maintain Mr. Tell, a client with deep-vein thrombo sis, on bedrest?

    A. To alleviate edema and pain.

    B. To prevent further venous stasis.

    C. To maintain adequate blood return flow.

    D. So that the thrombus firmly adheres to the vessel wall.

31. During the first critical days, venous return is increased in Mr. Tell's right leg through which nursing intervention?

    A. Elevation of the gatch of the bed.

    B. Encouragement of active exercises of the affected extremity.

    C. Raising the foot of the bed on blocks, up to 8 inches high.

    D. Assisting Mr. Tell to sit up in chair for 2 hours 3 times a day.

32. The nurse knows that administration of heparin in clients with deep-vein thrombosis is considered effective when it achieves all of the goals *except*:

    A. Dissolve a thrombus.

    B. Prevent the extension of existing clots.

    C. Prevent the activation of clotting factor IX.

    D. Inhibit the conversion of fibrinogen to fibrin.

33. Which laboratory test does the nurse expect the client to have to determine the effects of warfarin (Coumadin), another therapeutic drug used with deep-vein thrombosis?

    A. International Normalized Ratio (INR)

    B. Lee-White clotting time.

    C. Partial thromboplastin time (PTT).

    D. Activated partial thromboplastin time (APTT).

34. Which is least likely to be a contributing factor for Mr. Tell in developing deep-vein thrombosis?

    A. Obesity.

    B. Hemorrhage.

    C. Hip fracture.

    D. Immobilization.

35. The nurse should always be alert for the presence of pulmonary embolus, examples of which are sudden manifestations of:

    A. Restlessness and bradycardia.

    B. Dull chest pain and tachypnea.

    C. Subnormal temperature and hypotension.

    D. Localized, stabbing chest pain and dyspnea.

36. Should Mr. Tell develop an obstruction in the pulmonary artery due to a blood clot, the nurse should look for which arterial blood gas values?

    A. $pH = 7.52$; $PaCO_2 = 27$; $PaO_2 = 64$; $HCO_3 = 24$.

    B. $pH = 7.50$; $PaCO_2 = 38$; $PaO_2 = 90$; $HCO_3 = 30$.

    C. $pH = 7.40$; $PaCO_2 = 42$; $PaO_2 = 85$; $HCO_3 = 22$.

    D. $pH = 7.25$; $PaCO_2 = 40$; $PaO_2 = 68$; $HCO_3 = 15$.

37. A client with a long-standing arterial insufficiency will complain of:

    A. Paralysis or paresthesia.

    B. Intermittent claudication.

    C. Sudden onset of severe pain.

    D. Anesthesia or tingling sensation.

38. When assessing the pulses of a client with an occlusion of the left popliteal artery, the nurse may expect which pulse of the left extremity to be present?

    A. Femoral.

    B. Popliteal.

    C. Dorsalis pedis.

    D. Posterior tibial.

39. Neuromuscular parameters that the nurse must assess in all clients on bedrest are:

    A. Strength and movement of the extremities.

    B. Presence and quality of peripheral pulses.

    C. Color and sensation of affected extremity.

    D. Discoloration and temperature of the skin.

Medical Diagnosis: Fracture of the right hip.

- **Surgical Treatment:**

  Hip prosthesis.

- **Nursing Problems/Diagnosis:**

  Fluid volume excess.

  Impaired home maintenance management.

  Effective individual management of therapeutic regime: positioning.

  Risk for infection.

  Risk for injury: postoperative complications.

  Knowledge deficit: preoperative procedure.

  Impaired physical mobility.

- **Chief Complaint:**

  Ms. Berryville, 79-years-old, enters the hospital via ambulance complaining of pain in her right hip. She fell at home when she tripped over the open oven door.

- **History of Present Illness:**

  Pain in right hip area. Injured 3 hours ago. Alone in apartment at the time of the injury. Bruise on right shoulder.

- **Past History:**

  Digoxin, 0.125 mg daily, for history of congestive heart failure. Appendectomy at age 17; cholecystectomy at age 52. Two hospitalizations for congestive heart failure. Maintained on diuretics and digoxin for the past year. Symptom free for congestive heart problem at present.

- **Family History:**

  Mother died at age 76; history of diabetes. Father died of "old age." No history of cancer. One sister, age 72; arthritis.

- **Review of Systems:**

  Able to perform activities of daily living by herself. No complaints of headache, dizziness, or loss of consciousness at time of injury. No stiffness of neck. Pain in right hip; tenderness in right shoulder; no complaints of other discomforts. No orthopnea, dyspnea, or chest pain.

- **Physical Exam:**

  Vital signs: BP: 110/62, P: 66, R: 20.

  Right hip swollen, painful to touch, ecchymosis present, obvious deformity.

  Right shoulder swelling, with ecchymosis present, tender, able to perform limited range of motion.

  Abdomen tender, no apparent distress.

Head: no bruises or discolorations.

Alert, oriented to time, place, and person.

■ *X-ray Data:*

X-ray fracture of the neck of the right femur.

40. Ms. Berryville was seen in the emergency department because of injuries received in a fall in her home. She is suspected of having fractured her right hip. On examination the nurse expects to find that her right leg is:

   A. Shortened, with external rotation.

   B. Shortened, with internal rotation.

   C. Equal in length to the nonaffected limb.

   D. Abducted, with internal rotation.

41. The diagnosis of fractured hip is confirmed. Ms. Berryville has a skin prep for surgery. The nurse explains that the primary goal of this procedure is to:

   A. Render the operative area free of organisms.

   B. Enhance the skin's natural defense against infection.

   C. Decrease the number of organisms on the skin.

   D. Improve the field of vision for the procedure.

42. Due to the extent of Ms. Berryville's fracture, a hip prosthesis is inserted. The nurse should design strategies to prevent the most dreaded complication of implant surgery, which is:

   A. Infection.

   B. Phlebitis.

   C. Urinary retention.

   D. Narcotic addiction.

43. Ms. Berryville returns from the operating room. Her IV solution is running at 150 mL/hour. Her pulse is 100 and full. Her respirations are moist and wheezy. The nurse's initial action is to:

   A. Speed up the IV rate.

   B. Check the electrolyte level.

   C. Report the findings to the charge nurse.

   D. Slow down the IV rate.

44. The presence of tachycardia and moist breath sounds most likely indicates:

   A. Optimum fluid balance.

   B. Fluid overload.

   C. Electrolyte imbalance.

   D. Insufficient hydration.

45. Ms. Berryville's temperature rises on the second postoperative day. To confirm the nursing diagnosis of "risk of infection," the nurse should:

    A. Perform a lung assessment.

    B. Send a urine sample for culture.

    C. Remove the operative dressing.

    D. Rotate the affected hip.

46. The nurse instructs Ms. Berryville in proper transfer technique and body positioning. Ms. Berryville demonstrates correct understanding when she:

    A. Knows that her legs should be separated with a pillow.

    B. Puts first one leg and then the other on the floor when arising.

    C. Keeps her legs in a dependent position.

    D. Sits straight up in a low chair.

47. The nurse plans to give Ms. Berryville written instructions for home activities. Which direction is *incorrect* in this situation?

    A. Avoid sitting for more than 1 hour.

    B. Stand, walk, and stretch periodically.

    C. Avoid crossing legs.

    D. May tie own shoes in the usual manner.

Medical Diagnosis: Left cataract.

- **Surgical Treatment;**

    Cataract removal.

- **Nursing Problems/Diagnosis:**

    Fear.

    Risk of injuries.

    Knowledge deficit: regarding cataract glasses.

    Effective management of therapeutic regimen.

    Self-care deficit.

- **Chief Complaint:**

    Mr. Chesapeake, 84-years-old, enters the hospital for elective cataract surgery.

- **History of Present Illness:**

    Noticed blurring of vision at the time of his last eye exam (8 months ago). Cataract diagnosis at that time. No history of infections, trauma, or other eye diseases.

- *Past History:*

  Chronic obstructive lung disease, arthritis, controlled diabetes, 26 units of NPH insulin daily.

- *Family History:*

  Brother has diabetes. Family history of heart disease. One brother died of heart attack; one sister died of cancer.

- *Review of Systems:*

  Blurring vision; difficulty seeing at night; no pain in eyes; memory good. Joint pain in cold weather. On an 1800-calorie diabetic diet. Lives with daughter and her family. Morning cough.

- *Physical Exam:*

  Vital signs: BP: 182/90, P: 72, R: 20.

  Smokes 1 pack of cigarettes a day.

  Opacity of lens of left eye.

  Decreased vesicular breath sounds with prolonged expirations; no crackles or wheezes.

- *Laboratory Data:*

  FBS: 110 mg.

  RBC: Within normal limits.

  Urinalysis: Normal.

---

48. Mr. Chesapeake has a medical diagnosis of suspected cataracts. Which symptom should the nurse find consistent with this diagnosis?

    A. Objects are distorted and blurred.

    B. Vision is not affected by change in light.

    C. Objects have a halo around them.

    D. Single objects seem to be doubled.

49. Mr. Chesapeake tells the nurse that he does not like the idea of being awake during his eye surgery. Of the following responses, which is the most appropriate for the nurse?

    A. "I don't blame you. I would feel the same."

    B. "By receiving a local, you won't have nausea and vomiting after surgery."

    C. "There is nothing to fear. These operations are done every day."

    D. "Can you tell me more about not liking to be awake during surgery?"

50. The nurse knows that her teaching regarding prevention of intraocular pressure after cataract surgery has been achieved when she observes Mr. Chesapeake:

    A. Asking someone to pick up his robe from the floor.

B. Getting out of bed quickly in the morning.

C. Practicing his deep breathing and coughing exercise.

D. Tying his own shoes.

51. The nurse is planning to instruct Mr. Chesapeake about his new cataract glasses. Which statement by the nurse is not helpful to him in his adjustment?

A. "Objects will appear to be much darker than before."

B. "Initially, use the new glasses only while sitting down."

C. "Look through the center of the glasses."

D. "Turn your head to the side rather than looking toward the side."

52. Mr. Chesapeake's family should be instructed to recognize signs and symptoms of hemorrhage from the operative site. The nurse should tell them that most characteristic of this complication is:

A. Mild pain and discomfort.

B. Drainage of clear fluid.

C. Sharp pain in the eye.

D. Difficulty adjusting to new glasses.

Answers and Rationale

1. **B. Use of accessory neck muscles.**

   All of the choices are symptoms of COPD, but *B* is the response that indicates the effort required to breathe. Because the chest becomes rigid and fixed in a hyperexpanded position, the client is forced to use the accessory muscles of respiration to ventilate the lungs. *A* is incorrect because tachypnea, a response to hypoxemia, can be effortless. *C* indicates insufficient oxygenation of the available hemoglobin, and *D* is due to the degree of bronchitis and bronchospasm present.

2. **D. Increased arterial PCO_2, increased hematocrit, and hyperinflated alveoli.**

   Air trapping and alveolar destruction cause the typical ventilation-perfusion imbalances seen in COPD—increased arterial carbon dioxide and decreased oxygen. There is an increase in RBC production in response to the hypoxia. Hyperinflated alveoli occur with overdistention and air trapping. *A* is incorrect because PCO_2 increases and the hematocrit is increased, as discussed above. *B* is incorrect because alveoli are hyperinflated, and *C* is incorrect because the client is hypoxic—decreased PO_2.

3. *C. Clients with COPD should receive low concentrations (2–3 L) of oxygen since the stimulus to breathe is their low PO_2.*

In COPD the respiratory center loses its sensitivity to the elevated CO_2 concentration, which normally stimulates a healthy person to hyperventilate. Instead the stimulus to breathe becomes the chronic hypoxic drive. If high concentrations of oxygen are given, which increase the oxygen tension in the blood, the client will develop CO_2 narcosis and can ultimately die. A client with COPD should never receive more than 3 liters of oxygen. *A* and *B* are incorrect because the concentration of oxygen should be low. *D* is incorrect since the stimulus to breathe is a low PO_2.

4. *B. Absent expiratory and inspiratory wheezing.*

The primary use of aminophylline is to relieve broncho-spasms. It also has a secondary diuretic effect, which may assist in the clearing of fluid retention. *A* is due to the pulmonary congestion from infection and indicates effective antibiotic therapy and chest physiotherapy. *C* also is an indication of antibiotic effectiveness. *D* occurs as hydration status improves.

5. *D. Neurotic reactions should be expected with COPD.*

Although some sources explain the noncompliance behavior of COPD clients as psychopathologic, their refusal to quit smoking is considered to be a matter of free choice. *A* is a frequently used client excuse for not quitting. The initial response to the nicotine is bronchodilation. *B* is also a legitimate explanation, since clients with COPD experience stages similar to the grief process. *C* reinforces the idea that noncompliance is an attempt to retain control over one's condition.

6. *A. Polycythemia.*

Polycythemia, an increase in RBCs from hypoxia, increases the viscosity of the blood. Since dehydration is also a problem in COPD, the viscosity is increased even more, leading to sluggish circulation and stasis. *B*, *C*, and *D* do not alter the viscosity of the blood.

7. *D. Facilitate complete exhalation.*

The client with COPD has a problem with trapping of air. By strengthening the diaphragm and breathing against pursed lips, there is a more complete exhalation. Pursed lip breathing creates a backpressure in the airway, keeping the airway open longer. Tightening of the diaphragm helps to squeeze air out. *A* is incorrect because the intercostal muscles become overused and ineffective in COPD. *B* is an irreversible condition that necessitates the pursed lip and diaphragmatic breathing. *C* is incorrect because the problem in COPD is reduced expiratory volume.

8.   **A. The incidence of respiratory infections.**

Respiratory infections in the client with COPD cause further lung damage and can cause decompensation in a client who would otherwise tolerate the condition. Acute infections are often the precipitating cause of death. Changes in the carbon dioxide level, **B**, and oxygen level, **C**, are caused by factors that produce further lung destruction, as with **A**. Although **D** is associated with aggravation of the condition, the constant threat of infection is a *direct* threat to the client's prognosis.

9.   **B. A decrease in the WBC count.**

The WBC is not affected by fluid volume, as are other tests such as hematocrit, hemoglobin, and BUN. A decrease in the WBC occurs following antibiotic therapy or from the normal inflammatory response. Increased fluid will thin tenacious respiratory secretions, **A**, as well as lower body temperature through perspiration and cooling, **C**. As previously mentioned, hematocrit, **D**, responds to changes in fluid.

10.   **A. Fecal matter must be cleansed from the bowel for good visualization.**

A is correct because fecal material in the bowel can interfere with interpretation of the test. **B** is incorrect; Mr. Richmond will be given a low-residue diet the evening before the test and liquids the morning of the test. **C** is incorrect because the client will be moved into many positions, and will be asked to expel the enema. **D** is incorrect because barium is given by enema.

11.   **C. Alteration in bowel habits.**

C is one of the seven danger signals of cancer; other signs include bleeding, pain, weight loss, and anorexia. **A** and **B** are symptoms of obstruction. Mucus, **D**, appears in conditions of parasympathetic excitability.

12.   **B. Bacterial content in the colon.**

B is correct because neomycin sulfate helps to reduce the possibility of postoperative infections. Neomycin does *not* alter electrolyte balance, **A**; nor influence peristalsis, **C**; or cleanse the bowel, **D**.

13.   **C. Solid, formed feces.**

The type of stool described in **C** is usual in the descending portion of the colon. **A** is incorrect because it describes drainage from an ileostomy. **B** is incorrect because a soft, brown, mushy stool is found in the transverse colon. **D**, liquid stools, are found before the transverse colon.

14.   **A. Ground lean beef, soft-boiled eggs, tea.**

A is correct because all the foods listed are low-residue foods. Choices **B**, **C**, and **D** all contain foods *high* in residue.

15. *C. Hypokalemia.*

    C is correct because one source of potassium depletion is gastric and intestinal suction. The imbalances in *A*, *B*, and *D* are due to causes not related to gastric suctioning.

16. *A. Irrigate the nasogastric tube with saline.*

    A is correct because irrigating the tube with saline prevents potassium loss. *B* encourages potassium loss, as do multiple water enemas. *C* is incorrect since it may be necessary to irrigate to keep the tube patent. *D* is incorrect because changing the nasogastric tube from intermittent to continuous suction will not affect the client's electrolyte balance.

17. *C. Colostomy.*

    Of the choices, *C* is the greatest threat to body image presented because it is an alteration in normal function and a change in the normal pattern and because the client feels a lack of control. *A*, *B*, and *D* do not significantly alter body image, function, or control.

18. *B. Permanent colostomy.*

    The colon and usually a segment of the descending colon are removed, so the stoma is permanent. *A* is seen after total removal of the colon. *C* is usually seen with a reversible colostomy. *D* is more often the site for a double-barreled colostomy.

19. *A. Red and raised.*

    A normal stoma should be red (like the color of healthy oral mucosa). *B*, *C*, and *D* indicate some problem with the stoma.

20. *C. Asks questions about the equipment being used.*

    The beginning step to performing self-care is to question how and why procedures are being done. *A*, *B*, and *D* could be important to the client but do not demonstrate a willingness to be involved in self-care.

21. *C. Body weight and urine specific gravity.*

    Observing for increases in body weight and decreases in specific gravity of urine suggest rehydration of the client and are important sources of evaluative data. *A* is not totally true since sugar and acetone measurements are done to detect urinary clearance of glucose and ketone bodies, which are conditions characteristic of diabetes mellitus, *not* fluid depletion. *B* is not totally true, as color of mucous membranes is observed to detect cyanosis, pallor, and jaundice. Skin turgor is an appropriate indicator of fluid balance. *D* is not totally true, as skin color changes are not associated with fluid status.

22. **A. Speak for the client as often as possible to minimize feelings of embarrassment.**

   A is an inappropriate nursing action and therefore the best answer. Repeatedly speaking for the client who is aphasic discourages him or her from attempting to speak. *B* is a correct nursing action for a client with receptive aphasia, who has difficulty understanding the spoken word. *C* is a correct action for a client with expressive aphasia, who needs to practice speaking. *D* also is a correct action. It fosters supportive actions from the family that encourage attempts at speech and contribute to self-esteem.

23. **D. Administer a sedative to promote rest and speed healing of tissues.**

   D is the best answer since it is the one nursing action that is *not* indicated in this case. Sedating a client who is immobilized, such as Ms. Tweed, decreases spontaneous body movements and increases the risk of decubitus ulcers. *A* is an appropriate action. It keeps pressure off the heels and sacrum, yet allows for side-to-side changes in position. *B* is also a correct action. A sheepskin and heel pads prevent abrasive rubbing of the skin against the sheets and vary pressure points in the affected areas. *C* is a correct action because an alternating pressure mattress will prevent further tissue damage.

24. **A. Breath sounds.**

   Auscultating breath sounds provides information on the rate, depth, and character of respirations. Crackles and wheezes can indicate atelectasis and obstruction. Diminished breath sounds signify a need for deep breathing activities. *B*, *C*, and *D* generate information that may or may not relate to respiratory status. *B* is incorrect since an increased temperature can signify an infectious process anywhere in the body. Also, the reliability of temperature elevations as a sign of infection in older persons is questionable. *C* and *D* are incorrect since changes in pulse and skin color can suggest cardiac arrhythmias, anxiety, and a variety of other conditions unrelated to respiratory status.

25. **D. Help her into a pair of warm socks that she can wear while in bed.**

   Such a simple action can promote comfort without adversely affecting circulation to the legs. *A*, *B*, and *C* are inappropriate actions. Removing the foot cradle allows tight bedcovers to constrict circulation to the feet and may contribute to footdrop. Hot water bottles can result in burns to tender skin. Vigorous massage of feet and legs is always contraindicated in clients who are immobilized. Thrombi may become dislodged and result in pulmonary embolism.

26. **B. Strawberries with milk, cottage cheese, and toast.**

   B is correct. This was verified in the following reference:

Williams SR, Schlenker E. *Essentials of Nutrition and Diet Therapy* (8th ed). St. Louis: Mosby.

The food combinations in each option are assessed as to their protein and vitamin C contents as follows:

A. Cream of Wheat (¾ c.)   3.5 g protein
                                 0 mg vitamin C

   Whole milk (8 oz.)   8.5 g protein
                                 3 mg vitamin C

   Toast (1 slice wheat)   2.1 g protein
                                 0 mg vitamin C
                                 ─────────────
                                 14.1 g protein
                                 3 mg vitamin C

B. Strawberries (10 fresh)   0.8 g protein
                                 60 mg vitamin C

   Whole milk (4 oz.)   4.25 g protein
                                 1.5 mg vitamin C

   Cottage cheese (½ c.)   22 g protein
                                 0 mg vitamin C

   Toast (1 slice wheat)   2.1 g protein
                                 0 mg vitamin C
                                 ─────────────
                                 29.15 g protein
                                 61.5 mg vitamin C

C. Orange juice (3⅛ oz.)   0.8 g protein
                                 42 mg vitamin C

   Sweet roll   4.7 g protein
                                 0 mg vitamin C
                                 ─────────────
                                 5.5 g protein
                                 42 mg vitamin C

D. Soft-cooked eggs (2)   12.2 g protein
                                 0 mg vitamin C

   Toast (1 slice wheat)   2.1 g protein
                                 0 mg vitamin C

   Coffee   Trace amounts protein
                                 0 mg vitamin C
                                 ─────────────
                                 14.3 g protein
                                 0 mg vitamin C

27. **D. Impaction.**

Liquid stools in a person with limited activity, a diet low in roughage, and an absence of stool softeners or laxatives often suggest fecal leakage around impacted stool. **A** is incorrect since Ms. Tweed receives a soft diet, which is not high in roughage. **B** is incorrect since overhydration results in signs and symptoms different from those reported here. *C* is incorrect because brief periods of sitting in a wheelchair are not classified as extraordinary activity.

28. **A. Elevate the knee gatch of the bed.**

A is the inappropriate action and therefore the answer. Elevating the knee gatch slows circulation to the legs and is contraindicated for the client on bedrest. *B*, *C*, and *D* are appropriate nursing actions. Ankle exercises increase leg circulation. Antiembolism stockings decrease venous pooling and lessen the likelihood of thrombus formation. Adequate hydration also prevents thrombus formation.

29. **C. Preserve maximum functioning.**

C is correct because if use of the affected extremity is to be regained, it is necessary to prevent complicating deformities and contractures. Even if the client does not regain total use, functional positioning of the extremity can be adapted to numerous devices. *A*, *B*, and *D* are not conducive to normal functioning if a contracture formed in those positions.

30. **D. So that the thrombus firmly adheres to the vessel wall.**

Bedrest is maintained for clients with deep-vein thrombosis to allow the thrombus "tail" to become firmly adhered to the vessel wall, and to prevent venous pressure fluctuations. *A* and *C* are reasons why leg elevation must be maintained, but these are not the rationale for bedrest, which is what the question asks. *B* is incorrect because bedrest does *not* prevent venous stasis; rather, bedrest *potentiates* it.

31. **C. Raising the foot of the bed on blocks, up to 8 inches high.**

When the legs are elevated above the level of the heart, venous return is facilitated by the force of gravity. Raising the foot of the bed on blocks achieves this purpose. *A* is incorrect because the gatch of the bed elevates the knees above the foot, interfering with adequate blood flow. *B*, active exercises of the affected extremity, is not done because of the potential release of the thrombus. *D* is incorrect because this activity increases the hydrostatic pressure in the capillaries, which may result in edema.

32. **A. Dissolve a thrombus.**

Heparin is not a fibrinolytic drug; thus, it does *not* dissolve thrombi. *B*, *C*, and *D* are the pharmacologic actions of heparin.

33. **A. International Normalized Ratio (INR).**

The International Normalized Ratio (INR) is now used to monitor the effectiveness of therapy with coumarin derivative drugs. The INR adjusts for variability in types of tissue thromboplastin used for the prothrombin time

(PT). Warfarin (Coumadin) suppresses the synthesis of prothrombin in the liver. Since warfarin is a vitamin K–blocking drug, any change in the prothrombin level while the client is on warfarin therapy becomes significant and is reflected in the INR. Thus, *A* is the correct answer. *B*, *C*, and *D* are incorrect because these tests determine the effects of heparin, *not* warfarin.

34. **B. Hemorrhage.**

No data are given to support the presence of hemorrhage. Had hemorrhage been the problem, Mr. Tell would have manifested ecchymosis on his right leg. Thus, *B* is the best answer. *A*, *C*, and *D* are not the best answers, because they *are* causes. Mr. Tell *is* obese, *A*; he *has* hip fracture, *C*; and he *has* limited physical activity, causing immobilization, *D*. Obesity and immobilization contribute to the development of venous stasis; fracture results in endothelial injury. Deep-vein thrombosis occurs when venous stasis and endothelial injury are present. Furthermore, hypercoagulability can also be a contributory factor as to what happens in severe hemorrhage. Dehydration and, eventually, hypercoagulation result if no intervention is given.

35. **D. Localized, stabbing chest pain and dyspnea.**

Early signs of pulmonary embolism include: restlessness, anxiety, tachycardia, tachypnea, localized, stabbing chest pain, dyspnea, and cough. Pulmonary infarction has occurred if pleuritic chest pain, hemoptysis, cough, friction rub, and fever are present. *A*, *B*, and *C* are incorrect because bradycardia, dull chest pain, and subnormal temperature do not occur.

36. **A. pH = 7.52; $PaCO_2$ = 27; PO_2 = 64; HCO_3 = 24.**

Because of the embolic obstruction, the affected area of the lung becomes ventilated but not perfused ("dead space"). The cessation of the pulmonary capillary blood flow results in alveolar hypocapnia, resulting in the constriction of air spaces and the airways in the affected area. The ventilation-perfusion imbalance that results leads to hypoxemia. Thus, when there is pulmonary infarction, respiratory alkalosis and hypoxemia are seen. *B* is incorrect because the blood gas results show metabolic alkalosis. *C* shows arterial blood gas results that are within normal range. *D* shows metabolic acidosis and hypoxemia. These results are *not* associated with pulmonary infarction.

37. **B. Intermittent claudication.**

B is the correct answer; chronic or long-standing insufficiency of arterial blood supply is characterized by intermittent claudication. The client experiences a sensation of pain, fatigue, or cramps, particularly in the calf muscles when he walks or exercises. Pain is relieved when these activities are stopped. *A*, *C*, and *D* are incorrect answers because these are assessment parameters indicating the presence of acute arterial occlusion.

38. ***A. Femoral.***

A is the correct answer because pulses are lost distal to the site of the occlusion. The client has an occlusion in the left popliteal artery. The pulses distal to the occlusion are those in the dorsalis pedis, *C*, and posterior tibial, *D*, of the left extremity. Pulse is not felt on the popliteal artery, *B*, because it is occluded. The femoral pulse, which is *above* the area of occlusion, *is* present.

39. ***A. Strength and movement of the extremities.***

Assessing strength and movement of the extremities tests the ability of the muscles for movement and coordination. It also tests adequate nerve innervation to the muscles. *B*, *C*, and *D* are incorrect. These data are most appropriate for clients with peripheral vascular disease.

40. ***A. Shortened, with external rotation.***

A is correct because of the suspected right hip fracture. The signs are shortened, abducted, and in a position of external rotation. *B* and *D* are incorrect because they refer to internal, rather than external, rotation. *C* is incorrect because there will be a difference in the length of the legs.

41. ***C. Decrease the number of organisms on the skin.***

C is correct because although all organisms cannot be removed, their numbers can be decreased by removing the hair and scrubbing the site. *A* is incorrect because a skin prep is unable to render human skin free of organisms. *B* is incorrect because removing the hair actually decreases the natural defense of intact skin against infection but it helps to lower the amount of organisms in the area and reduces the possibility for infection in the operative area. *D* is not a goal of the skin prep.

42. ***A. Infection.***

A is correct; infection can lead to osteomyelitis, which is very difficult to clear up. *B*, *C*, and *D* may be possible complications after implant surgery, but are *not* as serious or as common as infection.

43. ***D. Slow down the IV rate.***

D is the *priority* action, for possible fluid overload. *A* is incorrect because it increases the problem. *B* might be important to look at in the total picture, but it is *not* the priority action. *C* is also an important action, but it is *not* as important as slowing the IV rate.

44. *B. Fluid overload.*

B is correct because moist breath sounds (crackles) and tachycardia are associated with fluid overload. On palpation, the pulse is bounding and full. Consequently *A* and *D* are incorrect. *C* most likely is associated with cardiac irregularity, not just tachycardia; and changes in the breath sounds are not expected.

45. *A. Perform a lung assessment.*

A is correct because respiratory problems are the first to exhibit postoperatively, usually within the first 24-48 hours. *B* is incorrect because urinary tract infections usually occur later, especially if the person has had a catheter. *C* is incorrect because the nurse usually reinforces the initial dressing, rather than removing it; there is no mention of hemorrhage; and it is too soon to expect any drainage from the incision that could be interpreted as infection. *D* is incorrect because correct positioning of the hip is very important; rotating the hip definitely is contraindicated.

46. *A. Knows that her legs should be separated with a pillow.*

A is correct; an abduction pillow is used between the legs to keep the hip in the proper position. *B*, *C*, and *D* are incorrect because they increase the risk of dislocation of the implant.

47. *D. May tie own shoes as usual.*

D is the incorrect instruction because tying her own shoes in the usual manner results in flexion and possible dislocation of the hip. *A*, *B*, and *C* *are* correct instructions to prevent dislocations.

48. *A. Objects are distorted and blurred.*

A is correct due to the opacity of the lens caused by chemical changes. *B* is incorrect; although difficulty seeing at night is common to all, clients with cataract development in the center portion of the lens can generally see better in dim light, when the pupil is dilated. *C* is a symptom of glaucoma. *D* is due to weakness of some extraocular muscles, *not* to a cataract.

49. *D. "Can you tell me more about not liking to be awake during surgery?"*

D is correct because it asks the client to discuss his concerns further. *A*, *B*, and *C* are incorrect because they do not help the client, nor do they allow him to discuss his fears. These responses close the discussion.

50. *A. Asking someone to pick up his robe from the floor.*

A is correct because it is important after cataract surgery to prevent increased intraocular pressure, which could put a strain on the suture line. *B*, *C*, and *D* are incorrect; all of these activities could increase pressure on the suture line.

51. **A. "Objects will appear to be much darker than before."**

    A is the incorrect statement and therefore the best answer. Opacity has been removed, so objects may seem *brighter*. *B* is true of cataract glasses; since the lenses magnify, the client should become accustomed to this before ambulation. *C* and *D* are also correct statements; cataract lenses distort peripheral vision. The wearer must learn to turn the head farther and more frequently to ensure safety.

52. **C. Sharp pain in the eye.**

    C is the correct answer; sharp pain is usually indicative that something is wrong. This symptom plus a half-moon of blood on the dependent position in the anterior chamber are indicative of hemorrhage. *A*, *B*, and *D* may be expected after cataract surgery and do not indicate hemorrhage.

11. Behavioral and Emotional Problems

Case Management Scenarios and Critical-Thinking Exercises

Medical Diagnosis: Leukemia, terminal stage.

- *Nursing Problem/Diagnosis:*

  Response to terminal illness.

- *Chief Complaint:*

  Betsy Banner, a 3-year-old, is on the pediatric unit dying of leukemia.

- *History of Present Illness:*

  Betsy had been in remission for 6 months, but recently her WBC was extremely elevated, she began having elevated body temperatures, and she was readmitted in a terminal stage.

- *Family History:*

  Betsy's parents are in their early 20s, and she is an only child. They are devastated by the fact that their "baby" is dying.

---

1. Betsy's mother tells the nurse that she just cannot stand to see her baby suffer and can only be in the room with her for a short time. Which approach is best for the relationship between Betsy and her mother?

    A. Support Mrs. Banner's feelings and encourage open communication.

    B. Tell Mrs. Banner she needs to spend more time with Betsy for the sake of the child's, as well as her own, well-being.

    C. Tell Mrs. Banner to have her husband visit more often if she is unable to do this.

    D. Let Mrs. Banner know that she is running away from her own guilt and projecting it onto her child.

2. In planning the nursing care for Betsy, it is not helpful for the nurse to:

   A. Hold and touch Betsy as much as possible.

   B. Leave Betsy alone as much as possible so that she can get adequate rest.

   C. Provide comfort and relief from pain, even if it means the child may become dependent on pain medication.

   D. Keep the environment as normal as possible, even though Betsy is dying.

3. One week after Betsy dies, Mrs. Banner comes to the unit to pick up her daughter's things. She keeps repeating to the nurse, "It can't be possible that Betsy is gone." The nurse's understanding of the normal grief process leads to the realization that Mrs. Banner is experiencing:

   A. Anger toward the nursing staff.

   B. Overwhelming guilt.

   C. Feelings of emptiness.

   D. Denial of reality.

Medical Diagnosis: Anorexia nervosa.

- *Nursing Problems/Diagnosis:*

  Body image disturbance.

  Altered eating: refusal to eat.

  Altered family processes.

- *Chief Complaint:*

  Angela McAdoo, 14-years-old, was admitted to the hospital 3 days ago. Angela has been diagnosed as having anorexia nervosa. She is in the hospital because of her persistent weight loss.

- *History of Present Illness:*

  Angela began to be concerned about gaining weight at the time of onset of her menstrual cycles. Her father teased Angela about her budding sexuality and implied that he preferred her to her mother. This terrified Angela and she refused to eat.

4. In the hospital the nurse should:

   A. Encourage verbalization about body functions and feelings concerning body functions.

   B. Insist that Angela eat at least one bite of everything on her tray.

   C. Ignore the fact that Angela is not eating.

   D. Tell Angela that she will be fed by tube if she does not eat.

5. Angela says to the nurse one day, "I promised my father that I would gain weight, but he did not notice the 2 pounds I gained. Why bother?" The nurse should:

   A. Discuss with Angela her wish to remain slim and the reasons growing up is painful.

   B. State she noticed that Angela had gained 2 pounds.

   C. Tell Angela to eat more for the next few days and that her father will then notice.

   D. Tell Angela that the important thing is not that her father notice her weight gain but that she has gained weight.

6. The most successful therapy used in treating eating disorders is:

   A. Individual therapy.

   B. Behavior modification therapy.

   C. Gestalt therapy.

   D. Reality therapy.

Medical Diagnosis: Anorexia nervosa.

- **Nursing Problem/Diagnosis:**

  Altered eating: refusal to eat.

- **Chief Complaint:**

  Carol Clifton, age 16, was admitted to the hospital with a diagnosis of anorexia nervosa. Her physical exam revealed an adolescent who is cachectic, weighing 80 pounds and whose menses had ceased.

- **Family History:**

  Carol's social history indicated that her parents were divorced a year ago and that she lives with her mother.

- **History of Present Illness:**

  Carol began to lose interest in her schoolwork shortly after the divorce, and 8 months prior to admission she began to curtail her food intake severely.

7. The nurse, in determining the client's care, realizes that a teenager like Carol should:

   A. Remain with her family.

   B. Be restricted to the hospital unit until at least 10 pounds is regained.

   C. Be allowed to eat when she desires.

   D. Be rewarded for eating.

8. Two weeks after admission, Carol opens up to her primary nurse. She asks, "Why would I just stop eating the way I did?" Which comment by the nurse will be most helpful to Carol?

    A. "Did your mother provoke you in any way?"

    B. "You will soon discover why in your therapy."

    C. "Were you depressed at the time?"

    D. "I don't know why, but I will try to help you find an answer."

9. What would be an inappropriate therapeutic approach for Carol?

    A. Setting limits.

    B. Providing support.

    C. Not allowing involvement in decision making.

    D. Avoiding staff conflicts.

Medical Diagnosis: Brief psychotic disorder.

- ***Nursing Problems/Diagnosis:***

    Risk of injury (self-inflicted).

    Altered thought processes.

- ***Situation:***

    Charles Adams is 19- years-old and was admitted to the hospital by his parents.

- ***History of Present Illness:***

    Charles's parents report that for the past 6 months he has not seen any of his friends, has eaten only bread crusts, and has hardly spoken to anyone. After extensive diagnostic studies, it was determined that Charles is exhibiting severe withdrawal as part of an acute schizophrenic reaction.

10. In planning the interventions for Charles's care, the nurse is aware that he will respond best to:

    A. Opportunities to make decisions.

    B. Being left alone.

    C. Clear, simple language.

    D. Small-group activities.

11. The nursing team determines that remotivation therapy will be most helpful for Charles's progress. The focus of remotivation therapy is to:

    A. Train for a job.

B. Share personal conflicts.

C. Prepare for discharge.

D. Increase interest in the everyday activities of life.

12. One morning Charles grabs sharp scissors from a nursing assistant and stabs his arm in several places. Which comment should the nurse immediately make?

A. "I see that you are still angry at yourself."

B. "How could you do this to yourself?"

C. "You are bleeding in several places. I will help you."

D. "Will you let me help you? I know I can stop your bleeding."

Medical Diagnosis: Schizophrenia.

- *Nursing Problem/Diagnosis:*

Altered thought processes.

- *Chief Complaint:*

John Arnold, a 20-year-old who seems several years younger than his stated age, has been a client on the mental health unit for the past 3 weeks. His diagnosis is schizophrenia, undifferentiated.

- *History of Present Illness:*

This is John's first hospitalization. He was brought to the hospital by his family after his behavior caused them concern. John had been withdrawn and mute for periods of a week and then would sing nonsense verses for hours at a time. At this time, John is verbalizing but is not joining in any ward activities. He is very obsessed with the idea of food and spends hours repeating sentences concerning food. An example of his verbalization is:

"You can't make a tomato. You can't make it yellow, squash is yellow. Mother doesn't like mustard. Brown doesn't go with ham. He doesn't handle ham."

13. The example of John's verbalization given in the case situation is called:

A. Neologism.

B. Delirium.

C. Clang association.

D. Flight of ideas.

14. When listening to John's constant flow of words, the nurse should:

A. Not interrupt him.

B. Attempt to stop the flow of words.

C. Interrupt occasionally to clarify what he is talking about.

D. Interrupt frequently and try to keep him on one topic.

15. The nurse should expect the relationship with John to:

A. Develop slowly, as it will take John time to trust.

B. Develop slowly because John is unable to communicate effectively.

C. Develop rapidly because John is verbal.

D. Develop rapidly because John seems attracted to the nurse.

Medical Diagnosis: Schizophreniform disorder.

- *Nursing Problems/Diagnosis:*

Sensory/perceptual alteration.

Altered thought processes.

- *Chief Complaint:*

Marlene Klein is 23-years-old, has lived with her parents, has no close friends, and could be considered a "loner." She was admitted to the psychiatric hospital when she refused to leave the house, neglected her personal appearance, and claimed she heard music all the time.

- *History of Present Illness:*

In the hospital she is quite regressed and refuses to attempt self-care. She is often found talking out loud to no one but herself. She was diagnosed as having an acute schizophrenic reaction. She was also put on chlorpromazine (Thorazine), 200 mg tid.

16. Understanding the side effects of chlorpromazine (Thorazine), the nurse realizes that which activity is contraindicated in planning Marlene's care?

A. Playing cards.

B. Shuffleboard.

C. Sunbathing.

D. Gardening.

17. Marlene was admitted to the hospital on a temporary, involuntary basis. In establishing goals, the nurse is aware that:

A. Marlene will be detained until her behavior is no longer a major problem.

B. A subsequent hearing must be scheduled if Marlene's problems necessitate additional hospitalization time.

C. Marlene will not have visitors until her behavior has stabilized.

D. Marlene must accept the prescribed treatment.

18. One afternoon, while the unit is particularly quiet, Marlene comes up to the nurse and says, "Listen to that music; it's so loud. Make it stop." Which is the best comment for the nurse to make?

    A. "I bet you feel like dancing to that music."

    B. "Music is nice, Marlene. Try relaxing as you hear it."

    C. "I don't hear any music on the unit now. Perhaps we can talk together about how you are feeling."

    D. "Let's play cards together. It will help you stop hearing the mu-sic."

Medical Diagnosis: Anxiety disorder; conversion disorder.

- *Nursing Problem/Diagnosis:*

  Anxiety.

- *Chief Complaint:*

  Sara Brownly, a 26-year-old fourth-year medical student, was admitted to the hospital for observation after complaining of tingling and frequent severe numbness in both hands.

- *History of Present Illness:*

  Sara was often unable to hold or even grasp an object. These symptoms became exacerbated after spending the Christmas holidays at home with her father.

- *Physical Exam:*

  A complete physical exam revealed no organic problems. Sara was generally in good spirits, but her conversation focused on her disability and the possibility of not returning to medical school.

- *Family History:*

  Sara's social history revealed that she was an only child and her father was a successful practicing surgeon. Their relationship was described as being very close. Her mother was killed in an automobile accident when Sara was 14. After the accident, Sara's father focused all his attentions on his daughter, pushing her academically so that she could enter medical school. Her father referred to how much he was looking forward to having his daughter in practice with him and called her the "future hands" in his practice.

  Sara was diagnosed as having a severe anxiety reaction with conversion symptomatology.

19. In assessing Sara's symptoms, the nurse should understand that the relationship between the paralysis of the hands and the underlying emotional conflict is:

    A. Not an important issue in planning her care.

    B. Symbolic in nature.

    C. Indirect and of questionable importance.

D. An expression of Sara's anger toward her father.

20. An important nursing intervention for Sara is to:

   A. Limit her social activity until she regains better use of her hands.

   B. Set limits on her behavior.

   C. Allow her to have all her dependency needs met.

   D. Decrease opportunities for secondary gain.

21. In planning for Sara's immediate needs, which is an inappropriate

   approach?

   A. Avoid displaying concern over Sara's symptoms.

   B. Involve Sara in planning a social activity.

   C. Give Sara opportunities to express her feelings.

   D. Encourage Sara to discuss her symptoms freely.

Medical Situation: Postmastectomy reaction.

- *Nursing Problems/Diagnosis:*

  Body image disturbance.

  Ineffective individual coping: denial.

- *Chief Complaint:*

  Linda Weber, a 29-year-old married homemaker with two children, discovered a lump in her left breast 2 weeks ago. On the advice of her physician she underwent a breast biopsy, and at that time the diagnosis of carcinoma was made. Linda chose to undergo a mastectomy. Her postoperative course has been uneventful.

- *Past History:*

  Linda has been in good health. This is her only hospitalization other than for the birth of her two children.

- *Family History:*

  Linda and her husband have been married for 8 years and have a good marital relationship. They have a boy, Jason, age 6, and a girl, Lisa, age 4. Linda worked as a court reporter before the birth of her children.

---

22. Linda could not look at her incision on the first postoperative day, although she carefully watched and listened to the doctor and the nurse as the dressing was changed. This reaction indicates that:

   A. Linda will have difficulty adapting to her change in body image.

   B. Linda is testing how others will react to her altered body image.

C. Linda feels mutilated and ugly.

D. Linda is denying that anything is different.

23. The nurse's response to Linda should be:

   A. "Maybe you'd like to look at your incision tomorrow when we change the dressing."

   B. "The incision looks beautiful. You really should see it."

   C. "It will be hard for you to look at the incision the first time."

   D. "Everyone has to look at his or her incision sooner or later."

24. Linda expresses angry feelings toward her surgeon: "Why did he remove my entire breast when the cancer was so small?" The nurse should respond:

   A. "Don't be angry with your doctor. He was doing what he had to do."

   B. "Your doctor is one of the best on the hospital staff."

   C. "You sound angry. Would you like to talk about it?"

   D. "Ask your doctor why he had to remove so much."

Medical Diagnosis: Possible breast malignancy.

- *Nursing Problem/Diagnosis:*

   Body image disturbance.

- *Chief Complaint:*

   Ellen Sands, age 32, was admitted to the hospital unit for a breast biopsy to rule out a malignancy. On the day of her biopsy, she tells the nurse that she was up all night and feels as if her head is about to explode.

- *History of Present Illness:*

   Ellen was in perfect health until 1 week prior to admission, when she discovered a pea-sized lump in her breast during self-examination.

- *Family History:*

   Ellen has been married for 8 years and has a 3-year-old daughter.

25. As the nurse is preparing Ms. Sands for the operating room, she asks the nurse, "Well, do you think I have breast cancer?" Which response is most helpful?

   A. "You need to ask your doctor that question."

   B. "It sounds as if you are worried about what your surgeon will find."

   C. "Breast cancer is more common in older women than in your age group."

D. "Just relax. It won't help if you go to surgery feeling this way."

26. In identifying Ms. Sands's health needs, the nurse is aware that after discovery of a breast lump it is correct to assume that:

   A. Fantasies relating to body mutilation may be set in motion.

   B. If a woman is married, her adjustment to a mastectomy will likely be better.

   C. Depression is usually not an issue when a lump is discovered.

   D. In a sound marriage, husbands have little difficulty in adjusting to the removal of a breast.

27. Ms. Sands's biopsy result was negative and a simple lumpectomy was successfully completed. Which nursing action is indicated?

   A. Remembering her initial anxiety, encourage Ms. Sands to begin psychotherapy.

   B. Encourage Ms. Sands to continue self-examination of her breasts.

   C. Have her schedule a mammography appointment in 3 months.

   D. Inform her that she can expect strong discomfort around her incision for several weeks.

Medical Diagnosis: Sleep disorder.

- *Nursing Problem/Diagnosis:*

   Sleep pattern disturbance.

- *Chief Complaint:*

   Jeremiah Johnson, 35-years-old, is admitted to the skilled care rehabilitation unit following hip replacement.

- *History of Present Illness:*

   While in the rehabilitation unit, Mr. Johnson has been telling the nurses that he is unable to sleep at night. The nurses' notes indicate, however, that he has been asleep every time they make rounds.

28. How does a nurse explain the apparent discrepancy in the report by Mr. Johnson and by the nurses about his sleep?

   A. Mr. Johnson is spending a large portion of his sleep time in Stage II sleep.

   B. Mr. Johnson is spending more of his night in deep sleep—Stage IV.

C. Mr. Johnson is spending a larger portion of the night in REM sleep.

D. Mr. Johnson just happens to be asleep when the nurse makes rounds.

29. The nurse can help the client achieve a restful night's sleep by determining with the client his bedtime habits and also by:

A. Encouraging short naps throughout the day.

B. Eliminating environmental factors that distract him, such as noise.

C. Avoiding all analgesic medications because of their effect of increasing REM sleep.

D. Increasing the client's level of cognitive functioning at bedtime by providing problems to solve.

30. Which nursing measure should be used to relieve initial insomnia for a recently hospitalized client with no history of sleeping difficulty or of taking sleep medications?

A. Increase physical activity immediately prior to bedtime.

B. Increase physical activity during the day and provide monotonous stimulation at night.

C. Give a mild sleeping medication to help the client fall asleep.

D. Encourage the client to take a nap during the day, to provide the rest he is not getting since he cannot sleep at night.

Medical Diagnosis: Suicide attempt.

- *Nursing Problem/Diagnosis:*

Dysfunctional grieving.

- *Chief Complaint:*

Sherman Darby, age 42, was admitted to the psychiatric unit of a general hospital following an unsuccessful suicide attempt. He is considered a successful lawyer, but he repeatedly laments, "I am no good to anyone."

- *History of Present Illness:*

Mr. Darby has lost weight in the past month and has insomnia.

31. The nurse is to work with Mr. Darby. Yesterday the nurse made a contract with him to meet daily, Monday through Friday, for half an hour. When the nurse approaches him at the contracted time, Mr. Darby says, "Just leave me alone. I'm not worth your time." The nurse's most appropriate response is:

A. "Mr. Darby, I can respect your need to be alone sometimes."

B. "I want to stay with you, Mr. Darby. You are worth my time."

C. "O.K., I'll be back tomorrow, but I want you to know I think you're worthy."

D. "Mr. Darby, what makes you say that?"

32. Two weeks later, Mr. Darby states that his depression began when his father died 2 months ago. He also says that his father was very critical and demanding of him. Prior to his death, Mr. Darby's father had been in a nursing home for 2 years due to a stroke. Mr. Darby says, "If only I had taken him out of the rest home so I could have loved him more." The nurse's best response is:

A. "Mr. Darby, I'm sure you did all you could."

B. "Mr. Darby, you had to think of your own family also."

C. "Mr. Darby, you're being too hard on yourself. You were a loving son."

D. "You told me you loved your father. How would taking him out of the rest home have meant that you loved him more?"

33. The defense mechanism implied by Mr. Darby's self-derogation is:

A. Projection.

B. Conversion.

C. Introjection.

D. Regression.

Medical Diagnosis: Bipolar disorder.

■ *Nursing Problems/Diagnosis:*

Hyperactivity.

Altered thought processes.

Altered verbal communication.

■ *Chief Complaint:*

Jonas Craig, age 42, is brought to the hospital by his wife. During the admission process, he is laughing and shouting. He is wearing a bright red shirt and orange pants. He speaks rapidly and readily uses profanity.

■ *History of Present Illness:*

Mr. Craig's wife says he gave away all their artwork and savings bonds.

Mr. Craig's diagnosis is Bipolar disorder. He is started on lithium, 200 mg qid.

---

34. In talking with Mr. Craig, the nurse hears him say: "What a day out. Out is where I want to be. To be or not to be, that is the question. Questions, you are always asking me questions." The nurse assesses that he is using:

    A. Confabulation.

    B. Flight of ideas.

    C. Neologisms.

    D. Rationalization.

35. When planning Mr. Craig's care, the nurse realizes he is prone to using profanity. The nurse is thus prepared to:

    A. Limit his activities to his room.

    B. Ignore him unless he disturbs other clients.

    C. Have him leave the dayroom area.

    D. Tell him that profanity is not allowed in the hospital.

36. Mr. Craig asks the nurse what unit activity he should select. Together they decide the best choice is:

    A. Playing chess.

    B. Group card games.

    C. Walking with the nurse.

    D. Wood carving.

Medical Diagnosis: Depressive disorder.

- ***Nursing Problems/Diagnosis:***

  Self-care deficit: medication administration.

  Suicidal ideation.

  Altered verbal communication.

  Withdrawal/social isolation.

- ***Chief Complaint:***

  Barbara Cullen, age 48, was admitted to the psychiatric unit of the local community hospital and was diagnosed as having an acute depressive reaction.

- ***Family History:***

  Ms. Cullen has been married for 27 years and has three children, all in their early 20s; none live at home. She was an executive secretary for 1 year before she was married and has not worked since.

- ***History of Present Illness:***

  On admission, Ms. Cullen's history revealed a 12-pound weight loss, inability to fall asleep at night, pallor, anorexia, and lack of ability to concentrate.

37. In planning the initial approach for caring for Ms. Cullen, the nurse will include:

    A. Encouraging her to choose all her own menu selections.

    B. Involving her in a group activity on the unit.

    C. Sitting silently at her side when she does not feel like talking.

    D. Providing cheerful activities to uplift her mood.

38. When planning Ms. Cullen's daily care, the most important aspect for the nurse to consider is:

    A. Building her self-image.

    B. Involving her husband in the therapy.

    C. Getting her started in a simple daily routine.

    D. Preventing suicide.

39. Electroconvulsive therapy has been ordered for Ms. Cullen. When the nurse comes to accompany her to the first treatment, Ms. Cullen says, "I'm so dreadfully afraid of these treatments." Which comment by the nurse is most helpful to Ms. Cullen?

    A. "Being frightened is an unpleasant feeling. Try hard not to be so afraid."

    B. "Can you tell me more about your feelings of being afraid?"

    C. "You are not alone in being frightened. Most individuals feel exactly the same way."

    D. "It will be over before you know it, and I will stay with you."

40. In addition to electroconvulsive therapy, amitriptyline (Elavil) has been ordered. What information should the nurse give Ms. Cullen about taking this drug?

    A. It cannot be taken with foods that contain tyramine such as beer and aged cheese.

    B. Blood levels must be monitored regularly.

    C. Hypertension is a common side effect.

    D. It takes 2-3 weeks for the drug to take effect.

Medical Situation: Bereavement related to death of a parent.

- *Nursing Problem/Diagnosis:*

  Altered feeling state: anger related to the loss of a loved one.

- *Situation:*

  Anna King's mother, age 76, has just died on the hospital unit from an acute myocardial infarction. Ms. King was at her mother's bedside when she died.

- *Family History:*

  Ms. King, age 49, is unmarried; her mother lived with her. She has two middle-aged brothers, both of whom are married and have families.

41. Ms. King says to the nurse, "My mother could have lived if she had wanted to. She died because she knew I wanted my own apartment." In assessing how best to help Ms. King deal with her feelings, the nurse realizes that:

    A. Ms. King is displaying normal feelings of anger and hostility toward her deceased mother.

    B. Ms. King is showing strong ambivalence toward her deceased mother.

    C. Ms. King will most likely undergo a severe depression during the next year.

    D. Ms. King blames her mother for the problems in her life.

42. Ms. King says to the nurse, "I just can't believe my mother is gone." What response should the nurse use to better assess Ms. King's needs at this time?

    A. "Do you feel angry about your mother's death?"

    B. "Did you have problems with your mother?"

    C. "I understand how you feel."

    D. "Can you tell me more about how you feel?"

43. Ms. King keeps angrily telling the nurse that now she has no one who cares about her, not even her brothers. The most useful comment by the nurse is:

    A. "I have seen how much your brothers care for you when you are together."

    B. "You are such a nice person. I am sure many people care for you."

    C. "It must be difficult for you to feel that no one cares for you."

    D. "Don't be so hard on yourself. Things will seem different in a very short while."

Medical Diagnosis: Alcohol abuse with delirium.

- *Nursing Problem/Diagnosis:*

  Altered thought processes.

- *Chief Complaint:*

  Marcia Ross, age 50, is hospitalized on a medical ward with a diagnosis of acute gastritis.

- *History of Present Illness:*

  Ms. Ross is dehydrated and has a high fever. She has a history of chronic alcoholism. Toward evening, Ms. Ross becomes restless; as the evening progresses, she becomes more agitated and says that she is afraid that she will miss her bus. Later in the evening, the nurse sees Ms. Ross searching for something. The client states that her clothes have been stolen and that she will be late for work if she does not find them.

---

44. The nurse caring for Ms. Ross understands that she is in a state of delirium. The nurse knows that delirium:

    A. Is irreversible due to the chronic alcoholism.

    B. Develops rapidly due to specific physiologic deficits or increased physiologic demands.

    C. Causes permanent memory lapses.

    D. Does not cause defects in judgment or discrimination.

45. Hallucinations and illusions are common symptoms in delirium. To intervene effectively, the nurse must understand that hallucinations are:

    A. False sensory perceptions without actual stimuli.

    B. False sensory perceptions with actual stimuli.

    C. False fixed beliefs.

    D. Feelings of strangeness and unreality about self.

46. An appropriate response to Ms. Ross's statements about being late for work is:

    A. "You are going to be late for work?"

    B. "It's 11 P.M. and you are in a hospital being treated for a stomach problem."

    C. "Don't worry. Everything will be all right."

    D. "It's 11 o'clock at night. You don't have to go to work until morning."

Medical Diagnosis: Fractured femur; pneumothorax.

- *Nursing Problem/Diagnosis:*

Altered comfort (pain).

- *Chief Complaint:*

George Graflin, a 51-year-old man, was admitted to the hospital from the emergency department following an automobile accident in which he sustained a fractured femur and a pneumothorax.

- *History of Present Illness:*

Mr. Graflin is experiencing a moderate degree of pain in his chest and in his right leg. He is also experiencing pain of undetermined origin in his abdominal area. The pain in his abdomen is intermittent and more intense than his other pain. He has received morphine sulfate, 10 mg IM. The nurse who has been with Mr. Graflin leaves the room to report on his condition. When the nurse returns, Mr. Graflin is moaning loudly and holding his abdomen. There seems to be no other change in his condition.

47. When Mr. Graflin finally appears to be dozing, the nurse starts to leave his room. Mr. Graflin opens his eyes and asks, "Are you leaving?" The nurse should respond by saying:

   A. "Yes. You will be all right. I need to take care of other clients now."

   B. "Yes, but I will be back every 15-20 minutes to see how you are feeling."

   C. "Yes, because the medication I gave you needs time to take effect."

   D. "Yes, but don't worry. Everything will be all right."

48. The "pain is punishment" fantasy is a significant variable for many clients experiencing pain. An example of this response is a client who states:

   A. "I don't want any medication because I want to know what is happening."

   B. "There is no way to relieve this pain."

   C. "What did I do wrong to cause this pain?"

   D. "I don't need any medication. I'll keep busy and forget the pain."

49. The nurse should expect that the 10 mg dose of morphine will:

   A. Relieve severe pain for 2 hours.

   B. Relieve moderate pain for 4-5 hours.

   C. Cause hypotension.

   D. Be ineffective in relieving Mr. Graflin's pain.

Medical Problem: Post-cardiac arrest.

- *Nursing Problem/Diagnosis:*

  Ineffective individual coping.

- *Chief Complaint:*

  Mike Mansfield, a 52-year-old dock worker, was admitted to the coronary care unit of the hospital after experiencing a cardiac arrest.

- *History of Present Illness:*

  Mr. Mansfield was at work when he experienced a cardiac arrest. Paramedics were called to the scene and resuscitated him. He was transported to a local hospital and has been a client on the coronary care unit. His condition is still unstable.

50. When asked if he is worried about the prospect of another cardiac arrest, Mr. Mansfield replies, "Why worry? Besides, my middle name is Lucky." This is an example of:

   A. Undoing.

   B. Fantasy.

   C. Rationalization.

   D. Denial.

51. In planning psychosocial care for Mr. Mansfield, the nurse should understand that:

   A. A strong need for protection may cause a client to hear only what he wishes to hear.

   B. Mr. Mansfield has a realistic perception of his problem and is not troubled by it.

   C. Mr. Mansfield is coping with his illness in a pathologic manner.

   D. Mr. Mansfield's manner of coping is allowing him to experience the full impact of his illness.

52. The nurse's best response to Mr. Mansfield's statement in question 50 is:

   A. "Your middle name is Lucky?"

   B. "You are right not to worry. It doesn't help to worry."

   C. "I can see that you are not worried."

   D. "Sometimes it takes a while before a person can really think about what happened."

Medical Situation: Phase of life problem: adjustment to retirement.

- *Nursing Problem/Diagnosis:*

  Impaired adjustment: reaction to loss.

- *Chief Complaint:*

  Ted Saunders, 64-years-old, has taken voluntary retirement from his job. Mr. Saunders is seen in an outpatient psychiatric clinic due to difficulty adjusting to his retirement.

- *History of Present Illness:*

  Mr. Saunders worked for a large manufacturing concern for 38 years. During that time, he saw many changes in his company and its employees. In recent years he complained bitterly about the caliber of the people being employed and the changing circumstances of his employment. Jane, his wife of 30 years, became used to Mr. Saunders' complaining and was able to tolerate it since he traveled frequently in his job. Jane has many social outlets, but Mr. Saunders did not develop any interests outside his job.

53. Mr. Saunders is experiencing difficulty adjusting to his retirement, even though it was voluntary. One of the reasons could be:

    A. Poor marital adjustment.

    B. Loss of a peer group.

    C. Loss of physical stamina.

    D. Difficulty learning new hobbies at his age.

54. According to Erik Erikson, the developmental task that Mr. Saunders must accomplish is:

    A. Generativity.

    B. Ego integrity.

    C. Industry.

    D. Autonomy.

55. An activity that might be suggested for Mr. Saunders is:

    A. Helping his wife with the housework.

    B. Reading.

    C. Watching television.

    D. Joining a men's political interest group.

Medical Diagnosis: Unresolved grief reaction.

- *Nursing Problems/Diagnosis:*

  Ineffective individual coping: denial.

- *Self-care deficit.*

- *Chief Complaint:*

  Mark Graham, age 64, appears for his appointment at the crisis intervention center. In his initial interview with the nurse, he relates that his problem is not being able to take care of himself anymore. He is unshaven, his clothes are unkempt, and he speaks slowly. During the session, he cries several times.

- *Family History:*

  Mr. Graham's wife died almost 2 years ago; they had no children; and he recently retired from his job as an electrician.

  The health team at the clinic diagnoses his condition as an unresolved grief reaction.

---

56. In planning Mr. Graham's care, it is *most* helpful for the nurse to know:

    A. How he felt about his deceased wife.

    B. Who else he can rely on for support.

    C. His opportunities for employment.

    D. His pattern of communication.

57. Mr. Graham keeps repeating to the nurse that he accepted his wife's death well. He states, "I had to go on. No sense crying over her. I just said to myself, `She's gone and that's it.' I had no problems at all." In assessing these data, the nurse correctly infers that the client is using:

    A. Projection.

    B. Denial.

    C. Undoing.

    D. Displacement.

58. During the therapeutic relationship with Mr. Graham, the nurse realizes, in planning his care, that progress is most likely to be made if:

    A. The nurse can identify Mr. Graham's problems.

    B. The nurse can analyze Mr. Graham's behavior.

    C. Mr. Graham can begin to face his problems with the nurse.

    D. Mr. Graham sets his own pace for the therapy.

Medical Situation: Postoperative care following cataract surgery.

- *Nursing Problem/Diagnosis:*

  Sensory-perceptual alteration.

- *Chief Complaint:*

  Maeve O'Neil, 82-years-old, is admitted to the hospital. She has cataracts in both eyes and is scheduled for surgery for extraction of the cataract in her right eye.

- *Family History:*

  Ms. O'Neil is alert and active. She lives alone and maintains an active social life. Her two adult children are concerned about her upcoming surgery, considering her advanced age.

- *History of Present Illness:*

  On the day after surgery, the night nurse reports to the staff that Ms. O'Neil seems confused and disoriented. When the nurse made rounds during the night, Ms. O'Neil thought that the nurse was her daughter, Mary. Ms. O'Neil is becoming more anxious and withdrawn. The day nurse has not seen any of these behaviors.

59. Ms. O'Neil is most likely showing effects of:

    A. Sensory overload.

    B. Senility.

    C. Acute brain syndrome.

    D. Sensory deprivation.

60. The night nurse will observe more behavioral changes in Ms. O'Neil than the day nurse because:

    A. The intensity of sensory stimuli is increased at night.

    B. The nurse has more frequent contact with Ms. O'Neil at night.

    C. Hypnagogic states cause increased susceptibility to the effects of sensory restriction.

    D. The unit is quieter at night.

61. Which nursing measure will not be effective in assisting Ms. O'Neil?

    A. Placing familiar objects from home at her bedside.

    B. Placing a clock with a large dial at her bedside.

    C. Placing Ms. O'Neil in a private room.

    D. Verbally orienting Ms. O'Neil to time and place.

Medical Diagnosis: Systemic lupus erythematosus (SLE).

- *Nursing Problems/Diagnosis:*

  Disturbance in self-esteem related to illness (i.e., immobility, self-care deficit, altered body image, incontinence) and reinforced by others.

- *Chief Complaint:*

  Mr. Roland, a 19-year-old African-American high school graduate, diagnosed as having SLE, was recently admitted to a university hospital rehabilitation unit to begin a special program of vocational training. He has been unable to find a job because he is confined to a wheelchair.

- *History of Present Illness:*

  Mr. Roland first experienced joint pains, swelling of lower extremities, dizziness, and extreme fatigue 4 years ago. He attributed these symptoms to "overdoing"—playing too much basketball, staying out late, and working after school as a beverage distributor. He was hospitalized once for an episode of mental confusion, sudden memory loss, and behavior changes, and SLE was diagnosed. He was subsequently hospitalized several times for renal involvement and progressive generalized weakness. The disease process is presently stabilized by treatment with steroidal and immunosuppressant drugs on an outpatient basis.

- *Past History:*

  Medical: Usual childhood diseases.

  Allergies: None.

  Social: Lives with mother and three siblings; unemployed.

- *Family History:*

  Sister: Sickle cell anemia.

- *Subjective Data:*

  "I was never happy at home, and now I can't even leave my room. All I do is watch TV. My friends don't come around much any more because they're all working. Sometimes I call them up just to take my mind off my troubles. Last week my girl left to move back with her relatives in the islands. That's probably for the best anyway. She was getting mad because I couldn't take her out any more. Who wants to be with a guy in a wheelchair who's got no job and no money to spend?"

- *Objective Data:*

  Vital signs: Temperature: 98.4°F, BP: 130/84, P: 76, R: 18.

  Ht: 5 feet, 10 inches. Wt: 163 pounds.

  Unable to stand unassisted; unable to raise arms above shoulder level.

Round, "moon" face. Expression is sad and dejected.

Occasionally incontinent of urine.

No dyspnea.

No alopecia noted.

- *Physical Exam:*

Slight swelling of abdomen and lower extremities.

Muscle atrophy of upper and lower extremities.

Good range of motion of all joints.

No joint swelling or arthralgia at this time.

- *Laboratory Data:*

WBC: Leukopenia.

Urinalysis: Moderate proteinuria.

ANA: Positive.

LE cell test: Positive.

---

62. A nurse on the rehab unit recognizes Mr. Roland's problem with disturbance in self-esteem and tries to increase his self-esteem. Which intervention is most likely to serve that goal?

    A. Arrange a date for Mr. Roland with a client who is a young woman on the unit.

    B. Praise Mr. Roland's attractive physical features.

    C. Assign Mr. Roland a task he can learn in a short period of time.

    D. Spend extra time helping Mr. Roland to do his personal self-care.

63. Mr. Roland makes some friends on the unit and becomes very attached to a young woman his age. One day the nurse notices Mr. Roland and his friend embracing warmly and whispering to each other in a corner of the dayroom. Based on Mr. Roland's developmental stage, the nurse assesses Mr. Roland's behavior to be a response to his need for:

    A. Identity.

    B. Attention.

    C. Intercourse.

    D. Intimacy.

Medical Diagnosis: Schizophreniform disorder.

- ■ *Nursing Problems/Diagnosis:*

  Anxiety.

  Impaired individual coping: decisional conflict related to fear of wrong choice.

- ■ *Chief Complaint:*

  Ms. Sola is a 23-year-old graduate student who was admitted to the acute psychiatric unit when she experienced a psychotic episode. She was found wandering the streets of her college town late at night, wearing a bathing suit over her jeans and sweater. Mumbling meaningless sounds, she did not know her name or where she was. She says that she does not know what she wants to do with her life.

- ■ *History of Present Illness:*

  Two weeks before graduation, Ms. Sola stopped going to classes. Friends reported seeing her walking alone on campus, talking animatedly and gesturing as if to another person. Her mother received a phone call during which Ms. Sola alternately cried and laughed, saying that she knew she was failing but that "it was better that way." Because this behavior was so uncharacteristic of Ms. Sola, her mother spoke with her daughter's roommate, who assured her that Ms. Sola was not failing, but that she had been acting strangely for the past month. The mother made arrangements to meet her daughter at school. When she arrived, however, she found that Ms. Sola had been hospitalized the night before for observation.

- ■ *Past History:*

  Medical: No previous hospitalizations. Took part in group therapy as part of a course requirement for 2 semesters.

  Allergies: None.

  Social: Single, dates occasionally; works part-time as a research assistant.

  Only child of parents who are elderly.

- ■ *Family History:*

  No incidence of mental disorders. Parents: Healthy.

- ■ *Subjective Data:*

  "All of a sudden I don't know what to do. So many years of school—I hate to leave but there's a real world out there waiting. What if I can't make it? I have a job offer but I don't know if it's what I want. The money's OK but I'll have to move far from my parents, and they're getting older. ...How I dread the singles scene! But I can't hide behind my books forever. I'm so embarrassed about all this!"

- ■ *Objective Data:*

  Vital signs stable. Ht: 5 feet, 2 inches. Wt: 117 pounds.

Subdued in manner and dress. Speaks in a quiet voice and avoids eye contact. Engages in unit activities but waits to be asked. Pre-fers to spend time reading in bedroom. Visited every day by her mother, who treats her as if she were still a child.

- **Physical Exam:**

Healthy adult woman; no abnormal neurologic findings.

Mental status: Presently oriented to person, place, and time. Memory loss for the day and evening when she was hospitalized; otherwise intact.

No hallucinations or delusions.

Thought content: Preoccupied with decisions about the future and concern for her parents.

Affect: Moderately anxious, worried facial expression.

- **Laboratory Data:**

Chemical urinalysis: No trace of marijuana, barbiturates, morphine, alcohol.

---

64. Ms. Sola is late for breakfast. The nurse finds her in her room trying on one thing after another, clothes strewn about the floor. The nurse's best approach in this situation is to:

   A. Offer a limited set of alternatives to Ms. Sola.

   B. Make a decision for Ms. Sola.

   C. Wait for Ms. Sola to make a decision.

   D. Encourage Ms. Sola to hurry to breakfast.

65. In group Ms. Sola says, "I think I'm ready to go home. I miss my friends, but I'm afraid to tell people about being here." The group leader understands that Ms. Sola is experiencing:

   A. Frustration.

   B. Depression.

   C. Failure

   D. Conflict.

66. In planning for discharge, the nurse and Ms. Sola set goals to prevent relapse and promote a healthy adjustment. Which objective is *most* important?

   A. Move back to the supportive environment of the family home.

   B. Move to a new city to get a fresh start.

   C. Take medication as prescribed and attend therapy sessions.

   D. Discontinue medication as soon as possible but continue therapy sessions indefinitely.

Medical Diagnosis: Spinal cord injury at C–6 level.

- *Nursing Problems/Diagnosis:*

  Body image disturbance.

  Altered feeling state: anger.

  Impaired physical mobility.

  Self-esteem disturbance related to altered self-image regarding sexual dysfunction.

  Altered sexual relations.

- *Chief Complaint:*

  Mr. Frankel is a 28-year-old accountant who sustained a compression fracture of the sixth cervical vertebra in a diving accident 9 months ago. As a result, he is a quadriplegic and is undergoing rehabilitation at a VA hospital. Mr. Frankel does not want to participate in the rehab program and unit activities.

- *History of Present Illness:*

  Emergency procedures and a cervical laminectomy were performed to stabilize the injured spine, but the severed cord could not be repaired. After 3 months, Mr. Frankel had recovered to the extent that he could be transferred to a unit to begin a more active phase of rehabilitation. He had incurred few medical complications but remained depressed, withdrawn, and uncommunicative toward his family members, fiancée, and the staff.

- *Past History:*

  Medical: Smoked 2 packs of cigarettes a day. Social drinking.

  Allergies: None.

  Social: Lives alone; employed by large accounting firm; engaged to be married.

- *Family History:*

  Father: Myocardial infarction 3 years ago; recovered.

- *Subjective Data:*

  "I don't feel up to going to physical therapy today. What's the point? I'd rather read.... (Shouts) I said I'm not going today! Don't you understand English?! Stop standing there gawking at me. Get the hell out of here!"

- *Objective Data:*

  Vital signs within normal limits. Ht: 5 feet, 11½ inches. Wt: 162 pounds.

  Positioned on his stomach on Stryker frame, reading a business magazine.

  Indwelling Foley catheter draining clear, yellow urine.

  Skin dry and intact.

Angry facial expression; voice is loud and emotion-laden.

Engaged to be married in 6 months.

- *Physical Exam:*

No sensation or voluntary movement below the level of a C-6 injury.

Occasional spasms of the lower extremities.

Loss of bowel and bladder control.

Infrequent reflexive erections noted.

Other systems essentially healthy and strong.

- *Laboratory Data:*

Within normal limits.

---

67. Mr. Frankel's outburst when the nurse told him she would help him get ready to go to physical therapy is best interpreted as:

    A. Mr. Frankel hates the nurse and is trying to attack her personally.

    B. Mr. Frankel feels misunderstood and is trying to clarify his feelings.

    C. Mr. Frankel wants to be alone and is trying to get what he needs.

    D. Mr. Frankel is angry and is trying to gain some control over his situation.

68. The nurse notices that Mr. Frankel makes lewd remarks and seems to delight in telling her dirty jokes, particularly during his morning bath routine. In planning for his care, the nurse should:

    A. See that someone else is assigned to do his bath.

    B. Have a ready supply of conversation topics that do not have a sexual context.

    C. Confront his behavior to give feedback about her reactions.

    D. Refer him to a sex therapist for counseling.

69. Mr. Frankel's fiancée visits him less frequently because of the distance she must travel to the VA hospital. Mr. Frankel tells the nurse that he wants to break his engagement because "it isn't fair" to his fiancée to plan marriage. The nurse's *best* response in this situation is:

    A. "What are some of the reasons for considering this now?"

    B. "You'd better discuss this with your doctor first."

    C. "Have you considered the impact of this on your fiancée?"

    D. "You're not in any condition to make such decisions now."

Medical Diagnosis: Phobia (agoraphobia).

- **Nursing Problem/Diagnosis:**

  Impaired adjustment (fear).

- **Chief Complaint:**

  Ms. Uma is a 32-year-old wife and the mother of a 7-month-old boy. When checking the records, the community health nurse discovered that after the first two visits, Ms. Uma had not returned to the well baby clinic for her baby's regular monthly checkup. The nurse decided to make a home visit. During the visit, Ms. Uma tells the nurse that she is afraid to leave the house by herself.

- **History of Present Illness:**

  Ms. Uma was an anxious "new" mother who had had no experience handling and caring for infants prior to her son's birth. When she brought him home from the hospital, she expressed her fears of hurting him and of not providing adequate care. When the infant caught a cold, her fears were confirmed, and she vowed to remain at home where she could keep him safe. The infant quickly recovered, but Ms. Uma found that she was unable to leave the house without experiencing a terrifying feeling of panic. She did make one attempt to go to the store by herself but was unable to complete her errand because of overwhelming feelings of panic.

- **Past History:**

  Medical: Normal vaginal birth, 7 months ago.

  Allergies: None.

  Social: Married 7 years; works as an insurance broker in a small firm, but is presently on maternity leave.

- **Family History:**

  No history of mental disorders.

- **Subjective Data:**

  "I know this is crazy. Every day I wake up and say that today's the day I'm going to go out. But I just can't force myself to do it. My heart starts pounding, I get the cold sweats, and I start shaking like a leaf. I think I'm going to faint. If I were carrying the baby, I might drop him. I can't understand it. How am I going to go back to work? I've got to get control of myself."

- **Objective Data:**

  Vital signs: BP: 110/72, P: 96, R: 18; Ht: 5 feet, 6 inches. Wt: 130 pounds.

  Infant shows normal growth and development for his age; adequate bonding behavior with the baby. Household neat and clean. Husband states that Ms. Uma has not left the house since the baby was 3 months old. Says that he and wife's mother do all the shopping and errands. They entertain at home. Ms. Uma is attractive, well dressed, and verbal but moderately anxious in tone and facial expression. Relationship with husband seems mutually open and supportive.

- *Physical Exam:*

Healthy, well-nourished adult woman.

Mental status: Oriented to person, place, and time. Short- and long-term memory intact. No delusions or hallucinations. Above-average intelligence.

Thought content: Expresses fears openly but lacks insight about their origin. States that she knows her fears are irrational but cannot make herself leave the house.

Affect: Moderately anxious. Does not appear depressed.

---

70. Based on Ms. Uma's history, the nurse makes the assessment that she has an irrational fear that is interfering with her lifestyle. The psychodynamic mechanism that is operating here is:

    A. Sublimation of one source of gratification for another.

    B. Displacement of anxious feelings from the real source to a symbolic one.

    C. Suppression of anxiety from conscious awareness into the unconscious.

    D. Rationalization of anxiety as a consequence of realistic fear.

71. Mr. Uma expresses frustration that his wife cannot go to a movie or out to dinner. The nurse's most helpful response is:

    A. "I hear you, but that sounds like a big step. How about going some place nearer to home the first time out?"

    B. "Your wife cannot go out right now. Why don't you go alone or with friends?"

    C. "Many new mothers are afraid to leave the baby. It's not unusual for them to stay home during these months."

    D. "I understand your point. You've shown remarkable patience, but you must be going stir crazy."

72. Ms.Uma starts to cry. "I knew I couldn't do it—be superwoman, wife, mother, and have a career! Never in my life have I felt such a failure." (Cries) At this point the focus of intervention is to assist Ms. Uma to:

    A. Review her early childhood experiences.

    B. Explore her anxious feelings.

    C. Prepare for behavior modification therapy.

    D. Regain her composure.

Medical Diagnosis: Adjustment reaction to situational crisis.

- *Nursing Problems/Diagnosis:*

    Impaired family coping related to family reorganization due to divorce.

    Psychological factors affecting medical condition.

- *Chief Complaint:*

    The Kelleher family consists of Ms. Kelleher and her four children, who live in a seven-room house in the suburbs. Six months ago, Mr. Kelleher moved into a studio apartment in the city nearby. Ms. Kelleher is considering starting no-fault divorce proceedings because of long-standing marital problems, which have gotten worse during the period of separation. She is also looking for a part-time job to supplement the financial support Mr. Kelleher provides. Son Rob, 9-years-old, has frequent sore throats and stomach aches, and is doing poorly in school.

- *History of Present Illness:*

    Rob's symptoms have required a trip to the pediatrician's office about once a month for the past year. Despite his reports of pain, diagnostic tests and physical exam reveal no significant pathology. His symptoms subside after he remains indoors at home for 2–3 days.

- *Past History:*

    Medical: Chickenpox, age 6. Other family members essentially healthy.

    Allergies: None.

    Social: Rob lives with his mother, older sisters, ages 14 and 12, and younger brother, age 6. He's in the fourth grade at a Catholic parochial school.

- *Family History:*

    Mr. and Ms. Kelleher have been married for 17 years. They met at a local college when he was a student and she was working as an administrative assistant in the registrar's office. After Mr. Kelleher's graduation, they married, and Mr. Kelleher took a job as a salesperson, which required frequent trips to the coast. Family life was organized according to the traditional sex roles. Their Catholic religion was the focus of Ms. Kelleher's social as well as spiritual life. Disagreements about money, life-style, socializing, and sex occurred throughout their married life, but culminated in separation when Ms. Kelleher discovered that Mr. Kelleher was having an affair. With her parents' encouragement, she insisted that Mr. Kelleher move out and refused to let him see the children.

- *Subjective Data:*

  Ms. Kelleher: "The school nurse called and said that I should come get Rob because he was feeling sick again. When I got to the school, I was shocked to hear from his teacher that Rob is failing three subjects! I don't know where to turn."

- *Objective Data:*

  Rob is afebrile; vital signs are normal. He has a worried expression on his face and is clutching his stomach. He starts to cry when his mother walks into the nurse's office. Last year his grades were above average.

- *Physical Exam:*

  Abdomen: Normal bowel sounds; no distention; no rebound tenderness.

- *Laboratory Data:*

  Not available.

---

73. Which may not be a sign that a school-age child is having difficulty adapting to the family reorganization resulting from divorce?

    A. Loss of inner control.

    B. Drop in scholastic grades.

    C. Disturbance in peer relations.

    D. Rivalry with siblings.

74. In planning care for Rob, which suggestion made by the nurse to Ms. Kelleher is likely to have the most favorable impact in the long term?

    A. Spend time on a regular basis with him on an activity they both enjoy.

    B. Enroll him in an after-school program to keep him busy while she is at work.

    C. Take him to the medical center for a complete diagnostic workup.

    D. Hire a tutor to improve his grades so that he will not be left behind.

75. Ms. Kelleher will have made a satisfactory adjustment to the family reorganization when:

    A. Mr. and Ms. Kelleher sign the divorce papers.

    B. Ms. Kelleher establishes a close, meaningful attachment to another person.

    C. Ms. Kelleher finds employment to support the family's life-style.

    D. Mr. Kelleher makes regular visits to see the children.

Medical Diagnosis: Rheumatoid arthritis.

- *Nursing Problem/Diagnosis:*

  Impaired adjustment: difficult adaptation to dependency during illness.

- *Chief Complaint:*

  Ms. Parisi, a 41-year-old homemaker, has had rheumatoid arthritis for 12 years. During this time she has experienced periods of flare-ups and remissions, but there has been progressive deterioration in joint mobility and functional capacity. Accompanied by her 17-year-old daughter, she has come to the arthritis clinic for her regular monthly checkup. Ms. Parisi complains of pain, swelling, and stiffness in hands, wrists, knees, and feet.

- *History of Present Illness:*

  Ms. Parisi was in remission for 14 months until the disease process flared 6 weeks ago. No stressful events, periods of unusual activity, or other illness were noted at the time. She was continuing to take medication as prescribed.

- *Past History:*

  Medical: Tubal ligation, 8 years ago.

  Allergies: None.

  Social: Lives with husband and three children; worked for 10 years as a high school teacher.

- *Family History:*

  Mother: Osteoarthritis.

- *Subjective Data.*

  "The pain's been terrible this week. And the stiffness—I have to wake up at 5:00 A.M. just so that I can finally be up and moving by 9 A.M. What with the holidays coming, I don't know how I'm going to do the shopping and baking—to say nothing about all the cleaning that needs to be done. The children are great, but they're busy with school and their friends. Besides, I can't expect them to take care of me, and the house is my job."

- *Objective Data:*

  Vital signs: Temperature: 99.2°F, BP: 110/72, P: 92, R: 20, Ht: 5 feet, 5 inches. Wt: 118 pounds.

  Walks slowly, assisted by two canes; can only walk short distances. Requires frequent rest periods.

  Facial expression is tired and drawn.

  Functional class: II.

- *Physical Exam:*

  Extremities: Pain, tenderness, and moderate swelling of PIP and MCP joints of both hands. Effusion in right wrist, right elbow, and both knees. Pain, tenderness and moderate swelling of both ankles, PIP and MTP of left foot, and IP of right foot. Range of motion limited in all affected joints but more restricted in wrists, right elbow, right knee, and both ankles. Muscle atrophy of right forearm and muscles of lower extremities.

  No nodules noted.

- *Laboratory and X-ray Data:*

  Rheumatoid factor: Positive.

  Sedimentation rate: Moderate elevation.

  CBC: Slight elevation of WBC.

  X-rays of hands: Subchondral erosions at margins of MCP joints; narrowing of joint spaces.

---

76. Chronic conditions that are characterized by exacerbations and remissions require the client to be flexible in adapting to the dependency of the "sick role." Which statement made by Ms. Parisi most likely reflects that she is having difficulty adapting to the "sick role"?

    A. "The pain has been terrible this week."

    B. "I haven't been able to shop or cook at all."

    C. "I had to get up early to get to the clinic."

    D. "I can't expect the children to take care of me and the house."

77. In analyzing Ms. Parisi's situation of the past week as she described it, the nurse should consider whether:

    A. Ms. Parisi is exaggerating her situation to gain sympathy and attention.

    B. Ms. Parisi is projecting the blame for her illness onto her children.

    C. Ms. Parisi is having difficulty asking for the help that she needs.

    D. Ms. Parisi is minimizing the symptoms of her illness to avoid the need for further therapy.

78. Ms. Parisi tells the nurse that she does not think she can cope with the pain and still manage her household chores. The most appropriate intervention by the nurse is to:

    A. Get the doctor to write a new prescription for pain.

    B. Tell the client's daughter to do the household chores.

    C. Support the client's solution to the problem.

    D. Make a referral to social service for a home health aide.

Medical Diagnosis: Schizophrenia, paranoid type.

- *Nursing Problems/Diagnosis:*

  Altered feeling state: hostility and anger related to sense of inadequacy, powerlessness, and distrust.

  Altered thought processes (distrust).

- *Chief Complaint:*

  Mr. Lasalle is a 45-year-old bricklayer who has spent most of his adult life in and out of mental hospitals. He was recently discharged to a halfway house that has vocational and social programs. However, Mr. Lasalle refuses to share his room with a roommate.

- *History of Present Illness:*

  First psychotic episode occurred when Mr. Lasalle was 22. He was hospitalized when he attacked shoppers in a shopping mall because he thought they were following him and trying to steal his money. At that time, his delusional system was not well formulated. He responded well to medication and was discharged to his home. Subsequent episodes of violent behavior toward strangers, bizarre mannerisms, and the formation of a fixed delusion that "Communists were taking control of America by programming shoppers to buy foreign goods, and were stealing his thoughts" occurred whenever Mr. Lasalle stopped taking his medication. His longest stay outside the hospital was for 26 months, when he was in an after-care program where he received individual therapy and injections of a long-acting major tranquilizer.

- *Past History:*

  Medical: No surgery or major illness.

  Allergies: None.

  Social: Prefers to live alone; unmarried; receives Social Security disability and works part-time on construction jobs "off the books."

- *Family History:*

  Mother: Hospitalized for depression for 2 years when Mr. Lasalle was a child.

  Father: Deceased, natural causes (?).

- *Subjective Data:*

  "I won't share a room with that guy. I caught him looking in my drawers. And now my Sears catalog is missing. You know, he could be an agent sent to spy on me. He can read my mind. He has that shifty look about him—sneaky and secretive! See his shoes? They have rubber soles so that I can't hear him coming up behind me."

- *Objective Data:*

  Vital signs stable. Ht: 6 feet, 0 inches. Wt: 195 pounds.

  Dressed appropriately, in a neat but shabby manner.

Usually sits alone in a corner of the living room. Does not initiate conversation or socialize spontaneously with other residents. Prefers to remain in his room, where he reads sales catalogs and cuts out newspaper advertisements for department store sales. Tries to lock roommate out of the room.

Was fired from his last job because he got into an argument with the boss.

- *Physical Exam:*

Slightly obese; dry mucous membranes; calluses on both hands.

Mental status: Oriented to person, place, and time. Short- and long-term memory intact. No hallucinations.

Thought content: Delusions of persecution and conspiracy, relatively consistent and fixed.

Affect: Hostile, argumentative, angry.

- *Laboratory Data:*

Within normal limits.

---

79. To build a trusting relationship with Mr. Lasalle, the nurse should behave in a manner that is:

    A. Friendly, warm, and caring.

    B. Cool, correct, and distant.

    C. Direct, open, and matter-of-fact.

    D. Firm, decisive, and in control.

80. Mr. Lasalle frequently brings up the disagreement he had with his former boss. He says, "The problem is that he couldn't build a straight wall if his life depended on it! The only reason the steps I built weren't level was because he gave me inferior materials to work with." Mr. Lasalle is using which defense mechanism?

    A. Projection.

    B. Reaction-formation.

    C. Denial.

    D. Repression.

81. The nurse came upon Mr. Lasalle and his new roommate, who were shouting and cursing at each other. As she tried to intervene, Mr. Lasalle took a step toward her and shook his fist menacingly. The best course of action for the nurse to take next is to:

    A. Leave the scene immediately.

    B. Subdue Mr. Lasalle through the use of physical force.

    C. Appeal to Mr. Lasalle's sense of fair play.

    D. Talk to Mr. Lasalle in a calm voice, giving him space.

Medical Diagnosis: Narcissistic personality disorder.

- *Nursing Problem/Diagnosis:*

  Impaired social interaction (manipulative behavior).

- *Chief Complaint:*

  Mr. Dempsey is a 57-year-old bank teller who is admitted to the surgical unit for repair of an inguinal hernia. He feels he deserves special attention that he is not getting.

- *History of Present Illness:*

  Mr. Dempsey first felt a lump in the left groin 1 month ago when he attempted to lift a bushel basket of clams he had dug at the beach. He was able to push the lump in easily and continued his activities until he strained himself playing a game of singles tennis. When the lump could not be reduced, his private physician referred him to a surgeon, who recommended immediate surgical treatment.

- *Past History:*

  Medical: Hair transplants, 2 years ago.

  Allergies: None.

  Social: Divorced twice; father of two grown sons. Works as a bank teller but lists his occupation as "financial consultant"; changes job frequently.

- *Family History:*

  Parents deceased, causes unknown.

- *Subjective Data:*

  "Nurse, I'd like to speak with you a moment. I'm expecting some very important visitors from the diplomatic community, and I'd appreciate it if you could help me make them comfortable. We could use a few chairs, a bucket of ice, some decent glasses—not these plastic things—and perhaps some bread and cheese. Believe me, I'll make it worth your while. As a matter of fact, how would you like to share some of this vintage wine with me right now? I can see that you're a person of quality who appreciates the finer things in life, just as I do. It must be difficult for you to have to deal with the usual riffraff around here. Why not take a break? You look like you could use one."

- *Objective Data:*

  Vital signs: Temperature: 98.6°F, BP: 128/80, P: 72, R: 18, Ht: 6 feet, 1 inch. Wt: 172 pounds.

  Third day postop. Dressing dry and intact. Minimal complaints of incisional pain. Does coughing and deep-breathing exercises as instructed. Voiding every shift. Calls the nurse every 20 minutes to request services and special favors. Had a dozen red roses delivered to the nurse's station. Has had only two visitors during his hospital stay; one, a coworker, brings liquor and wine every day. Watches TV until 1:00 A.M. Refuses medication when it is offered but requests it ½ hour later.

- *Physical Exam:*

Physically fit adult man.

Small incision in left lower quadrant, which is healing.

Lungs clear.

- *Laboratory Data:*

Within normal limits.

---

82. The nurse who answers Mr. Dempsey's call light comes to his room prepared to offer medication for pain. She listens to his "invitation" to take a break and join him in a glass of wine. The best response in this situation is to:

    A. Assess his pain and offer the medication if necessary.

    B. Leave to get chairs, ice, and glasses but not to return.

    C. Decline his invitation and set limits on spending time with him.

    D. Confiscate the wine and report his behavior to the supervisor.

83. With a personality like Mr. Dempsey's, the characteristic that the nurse may find most difficult to deal with is:

    A. His lack of empathy for others.

    B. His sense of self-importance.

    C. His fantasies with unrealistic goals.

    D. His fragile self-esteem.

84. The staff complain to the head nurse that they cannot stand Mr. Dempsey's insincere flattery and cajoling behavior any longer. At team conference they decide that approaching him in a firm, unambivalent manner is best. The key to success for their plan is:

    A. Primary nursing to facilitate continuity.

    B. Clear communication to promote consistency.

    C. Supervisory support to ensure enforcement.

    D. Medical approval to foster cooperation.

Medical Diagnosis: Hypochondriasis.

- *Nursing Problems/Diagnosis :*

  Anxiety.

  Dysfunctional grieving related to father's death.

  Need gratification through fantasized illness.

  Self-care deficit.

  Altered thought processes (preoccupation with somatic distress, flight of ideas).

- *Chief Complaint:*

  Ms. West is a 63-year-old single woman who spent most of her adult years taking care of her aging parents. She was hospitalized in a county medical hospital last month when her uncle discovered that she had been living in the house with her deceased father's badly decomposed body for several weeks. Ms. West has difficulty swallowing and eating; she is worried that she has a stomach ulcer or a tumor.

- *History of Present Illness:*

  Ms. West has had a weight loss of 12 pounds over the past 4 months. She went to her private physician with complaints of dysphagia, indigestion, constipation, severe stomach pain, and headaches. GI series and fluoroscopy done in an ambulatory clinic were essentially normal. Diazepam (Valium), 5 mg tid, and Maalox were prescribed. Ms. West states that her symptoms were unrelieved by the treatment after 2 days.

- *Past History:*

  Medical: Exploratory laparotomy 19 years ago, negative. Severe dysmenorrhea and migraine headaches until menopause at age 51. Several hospitalizations for treatment of chronic low back pain during the past 10 years. Suggestive history of dependence on barbiturates and other minor tranquilizers.

  Allergies: Dust, pollen, strawberries, chocolate, shellfish, aspirin, and meperidine.

  Social: Always lived with her parents; worked as an LPN/LVN until placed on disability retirement because of back injury.

- *Family History:*

  Mother: Died 6 years ago, stroke.

  Father: Died several weeks ago, pneumonia.

- *Subjective Data:*

  "I don't like to complain but—nobody listens to me. I didn't get a wink of sleep last night, what with getting up to go to the bathroom

  … I had the `runs' …then my back was killing me. You know, they undermedicate the clients here. It's criminal… They're starving me to death. How do they expect me to eat that junk they call food? They know I can't swallow meat; it just sticks in my throat (grimaces as if in great pain)."

- **Objective Data:**

  Vital signs are stable. Ht: 5 feet, 4 inches. Wt: 110 pounds.

  Slightly disheveled appearance; hair messy. Many scratches and sores on her forearms and face. Moving restlessly in the chair and swinging her leg rapidly. Punctuates her remarks with facial grim-aces and tics. Tense, worried expression.

- **Physical Exam:**

  Skin: Dry and flaky, poor turgor, lips cracked. Self-inflicted sores and scratches in various stages of healing on upper extremities and face. Healed scar on lower right quadrant of abdomen.

  Neurologic: No abnormalities noted; can do straight leg-raising to 80-degree angle without pain. Facial grimaces appear to be under voluntary control. No cranial nerve damage.

  Mental status: Oriented to person, place, and time. Short- and long-term memory intact except for circumstances surrounding father's death. No delusions or hallucinations.

  Affect: Very anxious; unable to relax.

  Thought content: Preoccupied with somatic complaints and fears of serious illness. Willing to accept reassurance about her health for short periods but reverts back to seeking constant reassurance.

- **Laboratory and X-ray Data:**

  CBC: Anemia.

  X-rays: All negative.

---

85. Ms. West wanders around the ward sighing and moaning, clutching her abdomen, and picking at the sores on her arms. She approaches each staff member to give a detailed account of her aches and pains. She asks repeatedly, "Can't you help me? What's wrong with me? I'm in such pain!" Managing her care presents a problem for the nursing staff *primarily* because:

    A. Her pain is imaginary.

    B. Her complaints evoke feelings of helplessness.

    C. Her physical appearance scares the other clients.

    D. Her condition cannot be cured.

86. The head nurse calls a team conference to discuss Ms. West's case. Several suggestions are made for dealing with her incessant talk about her symptoms. Which is the best approach?

    A. Ask her to leave the room whenever she starts to talk about her symptoms.

B. Walk away as soon as she mentions her symptoms.

C. Tell her to stop talking about her symptoms.

D. Respond with interest when she talks about subjects other than her symptoms.

87. Clients with hypochondriasis often develop "real" pathology, which is ignored because health care personnel focus on the extensive history of fantasized illnesses. Fantasized illnesses are characterized by:

A. Functional disability without organicity.

B. Involvement of the voluntary nervous system and the special senses.

C. Visceral changes, which eventually produce structural changes.

D. Somatic delusions without functional impairment.

Medical Diagnosis: Metastatic cancer of the breast—terminal illness.

- *Nursing Problems/Diagnosis:*

Altered feeling state: guilt related to burden of illness on others. Anticipatory grief.

Hopelessness.

Powerlessness.

Situational low self-esteem.

- *Chief Complaint:*

Ms. Tully is a 71-year-old client in the community hospice program. She lives in a senior citizen housing project with her 75-year-old husband, who has heart failure. Yesterday her doctor told her she might have as much as 6 months to live. Ms. Tully says that she does not want to live because she feels she is a burden.

- *History of Present Illness:*

Ms. Tully had a radical mastectomy of her left breast 9 years ago. She received two series of cobalt treatments. Had a recurrence of cancer in the spine and was treated with cobalt and chemotherapy, which slowed the progression of the disease. Metastasis to her lungs required hospitalization for further treatment, but she was discharged (at her insistence) with her condition unimproved, to be followed by the hospice nurses at home.

- *Past History:*

Medical: No major illness prior to cancer.

Allergies: Codeine.

Social: Married 51 years, lives with retired husband; has two children, three grandchildren.

- *Family History:*

Husband: Heart disease; recently hospitalized for an episode of left-sided heart failure with pulmonary edema. Discharged when condition was stabilized with medication and diet.

- *Subjective Data:*

"I've lived a good life. Why can't I die now? I'm ready—I've suffered enough, but not as much as my poor Joe. My illness is killing him, too. He's the one who needs help now. I wish I could take care of him as he has me."

- *Objective Data:*

Vital signs: Temperature: 97.8°F, BP: 106/70, P: 88, R: 22, Ht: 5 feet, 3 inches. Wt: 106 pounds.

Poor appetite, but able to eat soft foods.

Sits in chair for short periods but is most comfortable lying down.

Shortness of breath only on exertion.

Pale; worried expression.

Affect: Moderately depressed and tense.

- *Physical Exam:*

Lungs: Diminished lung sounds; crackles at the base of lungs.

Extremities: Limited range of motion; muscle atrophy.

Skin: Pale, dry, and flaky; mastectomy scar on the left breast; toughened, slightly discolored area of skin over lower spine.

- *Laboratory and X-ray Data:*

RBC: Low.

WBC: Low.

X-ray: Bone scan—metastasis to spine, ribs, and shoulder.

---

88. Ms. Tully refuses to take her medication. She says, "What's the use? It's only throwing good money after bad. I'm going to die and that's the way it should be." The nurse's best response is:

   A. "You may be right, but we'll miss you."

   B. "The doctor says you must take your medication."

   C. "We care and we're here to help you and your husband."

   D. "You know your husband can't live without you."

89. Ms. Tully continues to berate herself and begs to die. Her husband, Joe, asks the nurse what he should do for his wife. The nurse should consider:

   A. Calling a psychiatric consult for the two of them.

   B. Telling Joe to ignore his wife's pleas.

   C. Telling Ms. Tully of the effect of her pleadings on Joe.

    D. Discussing their feelings in a joint session with both of them.

90. Mr. Tully says that he could never forgive himself if he did not try all medical measures to save Ms. Tully, despite her wishes that he use no heroic means to prolong her life. The nurse is at the deathbed with Mr. Tully when his wife lapses into a coma. At this time the nurse should:

    A. Call an ambulance immediately.

    B. Ask Mr. Tully to decide what he wants to do.

    C. Try to arouse Ms. Tully to consciousness.

    D. Remain quietly at the bedside with the couple.

Answers and Rationale

1. ***A. Support Mrs. Banner's feelings and encourage open communication.***

   A is the correct choice; Mrs. Banner is entitled to handle her child's death in her own way. The nurse should supply support and encourage open communication at all times. *B* ignores Mrs. Banner's feelings. *C* switches the focus to the husband; and *D* could be a totally incorrect assumption on the part of the nurse.

2. ***B. Leave Betsy alone as much as possible so that she can get adequate rest.***

   B is the best answer; a child who is dying should not be left alone, but rather should be supported and comforted. *A*, *C*, and *D* are all correct nursing principles in dealing with a child who is dying.

3. ***D. Denial of reality.***

   D is the correct choice; denial is the first stage of the normal grieving process. The anger, guilt, and emptiness in choices *A*, *B*, and *C* are usually experienced later.

4. ***A. Encourage verbalization about body functions and feelings concerning body functions.***

   The correct answer is *A*. The nurse should discuss thoughts and feelings about body functions—specifically body image, menstruation, and female sex characteristics—with Angela. It is felt that the underlying conflict in anorexia problems is the fact that the girls do not wish to grow up and be women. *B* is incorrect because the nurse should not *force* the client to eat. To insist would be ineffective because at this time the client is unable to eat or to retain food. *C* is incorrect because Angela is in a life-threatening situation due to low body weight; the nurse *cannot* ignore the fact that Angela is not eating. *D* is a threatening response, which is not therapeutic.

5. *A. Discuss with Angela her wish to remain slim and the reasons growing up is painful.*

The correct answer is *A*. Ambivalence is frequently expressed by the client. The nurse can be most helpful by addressing the underlying factors in the communication—that is, the client's wish to remain slim and the reasons growing up is painful. *B*, *C*, and *D* are incorrect because they confront the content of Angela's communications, not the underlying factors. These responses also do not address how Angela is feeling.

6. *B. Behavior modification therapy.*

The correct answer is *B*. Behavior therapy is the most popular treatment for eating disorders. This approach includes the establishment of specific operant consequences—positive reinforcement or punishment—depending on weight gain or weight loss. *A*, individual therapy, is difficult because in anorexic problems the client finds it difficult to trust. Gestalt therapy and reality therapy, *C* and *D*, are not as effective as behavior therapy.

7. *D. Be rewarded for eating.*

The correct choice is *D*. The goal in caring for a teenager with anorexia nervosa is to reestablish good eating habits. Rewarding eating is a fine beginning. *A* is incorrect because it has been found that teenagers with this disorder do best when they are removed from the home environment. *B* is incorrect because there is no reason necessarily to restrict her to the unit. *C* is a poor choice because Carol may choose poorly in deciding when to eat.

8. *D. "I don't know why, but I will try to help you find an answer."*

The correct choice is *D*, because it is an honest, direct response to Carol's question. *A* and *C* avoid Carol's question, and *B* is false reassurance.

9. *C. Not allowing involvement in decision making.*

C is the best answer because it is the nursing approach not warranted in a therapeutic environment for Carol. She *should* be encouraged to participate in decision making. *A*, *B*, and *D* are all appropriate actions.

10. *C. Clear, simple language.*

C is the correct answer; speaking in clear, simple language is of the utmost importance when communicating with someone in an acute withdrawn state. *A* is incorrect because Charles will most likely be unable to make meaningful decisions at this time. Both *B* and *D* are contraindicated. *B* reinforces the isolation, and Charles is not ready to interact with more than one person at a time, *D*.

11. *D. Increase interest in the everyday activities of life.*

   D is the correct answer, as this is the primary focus of remotivation therapy. *A*, *B*, and *C* are not the major areas of concern for this therapy.

12. *C. "You are bleeding in several places. I will help you."*

   C is correct; an immediate medical intervention is indicated. *A* and *B* ignore the seriousness of the situation; and *D* offers a choice, when there can be none.

13. *D. Flight of ideas.*

   The correct answer is *D*. Flight of ideas is a thought sequence, manifested through speech, that is characterized by sudden shifts in topic but that tends to be comprehensible to the listener. Neologism, *A*, is a newly coined word or the act of coining such a word. Delirium, *B*, is an altered level of awareness manifested by disorientation and confusion. Clang association, *C*, is that in which one word recalls another word because of their similarity in sound.

14. *C. Interrupt occasionally to clarify what he is talking about.*

   The correct answer is *C*. The nurse needs to interrupt the flow of words when she or he is unclear about what the client is saying. To not interrupt the client, *A*, implies that the nurse understands the communication, and this is not a corrective experience for the client. The client is unable to stop the flow of words, *B*, and it is impossible at this time for him to keep to one topic, *D*. To attempt to assist him with this at this time only adds to the client's frustration.

15. *A. Develop slowly, as it will take John time to trust.*

   The correct answer is *A*. Development of a therapeutic relationship with a client who is schizophrenic is a slow process, as it is difficult for the client to trust. Choices *B*, *C*, and *D* are not compatible with this principle.

16. *C. Sunbathing.*

   The correct choice is *C*; sunbathing is contraindicated, as chlorpromazine (Thorazine) increases photosensitivity. All the other choices, *A*, *B* and *D*, are permissible; gardening can be done in the shade.

17. *B. A subsequent hearing must be scheduled if Marlene's problems necessitate additional hospitalization time.*

   B is the correct choice; all states have laws governing *temporary*, involuntary admissions. When a client needs to be hospitalized for a longer period, an additional court hearing is scheduled. *A* is incorrect because Marlene's behavior may be a problem long after the right to detain her on an involuntary basis has elapsed. *C* and *D* are in error because they both infringe on Marlene's inherent rights.

18. C. *"I don't hear any music on the unit now. Perhaps we can talk together about how you are feeling."*

The correct answer is *C*; the nurse realizes that Marlene is hallucinating and this answer establishes reality, as well as acknowledges Marlene's feelings. *A* and *B* reinforce the hallucination and are counterproductive to the nursing goal of establishing reality. *D* avoids the issue at hand and also conveys false reassurance.

19. *B. Symbolic in nature.*

The correct choice is *B*. A conversion reaction is symbolic in nature and offers a strong nonverbal message. In this situation the message is that Sara has unconscious rebellious feelings, as well as extreme anxiety about finishing medical school and having to enter her father's surgical practice. *A* and *C* ignore the emotional message of the conversion reaction, which must be recognized to ensure maximum understanding of Sara's anxiety. *D*, anger could be just one aspect causing this reaction.

20. *D. Decrease opportunities for secondary gain.*

The correct choice is *D*. With a conversion reaction, the secondary gains of attention and concern in relation to the physical problems can reinforce the symptomatology and delay improvement. *A* is incorrect because Sara's activity need not be limited. *B* is incorrect because limit setting is not indicated in this type of anxiety reaction. *C* supports dependency, which would be counterproductive for Sara.

21. *D. Encourage Sara to discuss her symptoms freely.*

The best answer is *D*. In a conversion reaction, the focus of nursing care should be *away* from the physical symptoms that are exhibited. *A*, *B*, and *C* are all *correct* approaches the nurse *could* utilize.

22. *B. Linda is testing how others will react to her altered body image.*

B is the correct answer. How others react influences how the client feels about the altered part. This case situation does not provide sufficient data to assume that *A*, *C*, or *D* is true.

23. *A. "Maybe you'd like to look at your incision tomorrow when we change the dressing."*

A is correct; the nurse should gently encourage the client to begin the adaptation to the altered body image. *B* is not a realistic appraisal of how the client would look at the incision. *C* acknowledges a feeling, but the nurse is assuming that Linda will find it difficult to view her incision, and is therefore stating an expectation. *D* is a cliché that is not effective in assisting a client.

24. *C. "You sound angry. Would you like to talk about it?"*

C is the correct answer. Linda is expressing displaced anger about her altered body image; the nurse should help her explore those feelings. *A* does not let the client express her anger. *B* is a defensive statement and is not helpful. *D* does not acknowledge the feelings of the client.

25. **B. "It sounds as if you are worried about what your surgeon will find."**

B is the correct answer. It acknowledges how the client is feeling and encourages her to express her concerns further. *A* ignores the nurse's responsibility to utilize therapeutic communication skills. *C* and *D* disregard the client's feelings and concerns and offer non-therapeutic, trite expressions.

26. **A. Fantasies relating to body mutilation may be set in motion.**

A is the correct choice. After discovery of a lump, clients are consumed with fears relating to alteration of body image. *B* is incorrect; married women, as well as single women, often have tremendous adjustment problems. *C* is incorrect because when a lump is discovered, the occurrence of depression is common. *D* is not totally correct, as many husbands have problems adjusting to their wife's changed body image

27. **B. Encourage Ms. Sands to continue self-examination of her breasts.**

The correct answer is *B*; another lump could occur, and breast self-examination is an accepted preventive health measure. *A* is not indicated; it is natural that Ms. Sands be extremely anxious when dealing with a possible malignancy. *C* is a controversial preventive approach. *D* is unlikely in this type of minor surgery.

28. **A. Mr. Johnson is spending a large portion of his sleep time in Stage II sleep.**

The correct answer is *A*. Clients who are observed to be asleep but who state that they have not slept during the night usually have spent a larger portion of the night in Stage II sleep. In Stage II sleep, the client wakens easily and does not experience the restorative rest that occurs in Stage IV sleep. *B* is incorrect because in Stage IV sleep the client is difficult to awaken and experiences restful sleep. Most dreaming, which is necessary for psychological well-being, occurs in REM sleep. Most clients experience "good" sleep in this stage, so *C* is incorrect. *D* is a frequent explanation given by nurses, but it is not the best choice.

29. **B. Eliminating environmental factors that distract him, such as noise.**

The correct answer is *B*. In the hospital the environment is strange and can affect the client's sleep pattern. Eliminating as many environmental factors as possible and allowing the client as normal a bedtime routine as possible will enhance his sleep pattern. Encouraging naps during the day, *A*, will be a *detriment* to a good night's sleep unless this is part of the client's usual routine. Analgesic medications *reduce* REM sleep, *C*. *D* is incorrect because increasing the client's level of cognitive functioning at bedtime will stimulate him, and therefore is not conducive to sleep.

30. **B. Increase physical activity during the day and provide monotonous stimulation at night.**

The correct answer is *B*. Increasing physical activity during the day and providing monotonous stimulation at night is an effective treatment for *initial* insomnia. Initial insomnia is difficulty falling asleep. Increasing physical activity immediately prior to bedtime, *A*, has the effect of stimulation and decreases the possibility of the client's falling asleep easily. Sleeping medications, *C*, should not be routinely used for initial insomnia for recently hospitalized clients. Other nursing measures, such as manipulation of the environment, should be attempted first. Napping during the day, *D*, will add to the problem of initial insomnia, in that it will be more difficult for the client to fall asleep at night if he rests during the day.

31. **B. "I want to stay with you, Mr. Darby. You are worth my time."**

The correct answer is *B*. This response recognizes that the time is contracted for and it also conveys the nurse's concern and feeling of Mr. Darby's worth. *A* responds to what he says without investigating his feeling tone. *C* gives no indication of why the nurse thinks tomorrow will be different; if Mr. Darby is worthy, why leave? *D* is a challenging statement and does not respond to the client's feeling tone.

32. **D. "You told me you loved your father. How would taking him out of the rest home have meant that you loved him more?"**

The correct answer is *D*. This states what the nurse heard and makes the connection between love and taking the father out of the rest home. *A* denies his statement and gives false reassurance. *B* and *C* are moralizing and also deny his statement.

33. **C. Introjection.**

C is correct because by definition, introjection means incorporating into one's own personality the ideas and attitudes of someone else—in this case, the son is incorporating the father's negative comments about him. *A* is incorrect because it means blaming someone else for one's own behavior. *B* is incorrect because it means translation of psychological difficulties into physical symptoms. *D* is incorrect because it refers to going back to behaviors that were successful as modes of gratification at an earlier stage of development.

34. **B. Flight of ideas.**

   B is the correct choice; flight of ideas is commonly used by individuals in a manic phase of bipolar disorder. **A** is incorrect, as confabulation is a filling in of memory gaps and is usually seen in organic psychiatric conditions. **C**, neologism, is the coining of new words and is common in schizophrenic reactions. **D**, rationalization, is a defense mechanism used to explain a thought or action.

35. **B. Ignore him unless he disturbs other clients.**

   B is the correct choice. Use of profanity is natural in this illness; as the client improves, so will his language. Unless he is disturbing the other clients, it is best just to ignore him. **A**, **C**, and **D** are all punitive in nature and are not justified as nursing measures at this time.

36. **C. Walking with the nurse.**

   C is the best answer; walking involves using large muscles and releasing pent-up energy, both indicated in planning activities for clients having manic symptoms. **A**, chess, requires much concentration. **B** is incorrect because Mr. Craig is not a candidate for a group game that involves competition or requires co-operation and concentration. **D**, wood carving, could be extremely dangerous, as his judgment is impaired at this time.

37. **C. Sitting silently at her side when she does not feel like talking.**

   The correct answer is **C**. When a client is severely depressed, she or he is often unable to talk. Sitting quietly at Ms. Cullen's side offers valuable nonverbal support. It is saying, "I care for you whether you talk to me or not." **A** is incorrect because clients who are severely depressed are unable to make even the smallest decisions and initially need to have their dependency needs met by the nursing staff. **B** is incorrect because an individual who is severely depressed is not a good candidate for a group activity. **D** is a poor choice because a cheerful activity is counterproductive in depression.

38. **D. Preventing suicide.**

   The correct choice is **D**. When a client is severely depressed, the danger of suicide must be considered at all times. In providing daily care, this must be taken into consideration over the entire 24-hour period. Choices **A**, **B**, and **C**, although not incorrect, are of lesser concern at the crisis period of severe depression.

39. **B. "Can you tell me more about your feelings of being afraid?"**

   The correct choice is **B** because it encourages the client to describe her feelings and offers the nurse the opportunity to learn additional specific details about the fear expressed. **A** and **C** serve to reinforce denial of the client's feelings. **D** is incorrect because the focus is moved away from the individual.

40. **D. It takes 2-3 weeks for the drug to take effect.**

    The correct choice is **D**; amitriptyline (Elavil), a popular tricyclic drug, takes several weeks to build to an effective level in the bloodstream. Changes in behavior are unlikely until that time. **A** is indicated when clients are on MAO drugs; **B** is necessary with lithium carbonate. **C** is incorrect; *hypotension* is a possibility. Hypertensive crisis is a problem with the MAO drugs, not the tricyclic group.

41. **A. Ms. King is displaying normal feelings of anger and hostility toward her deceased mother.**

    The correct answer is **A**; anger and hostility are normal feelings when one loses a dearly loved person. There is no indication that Ms. King had deep feelings of ambivalence, **B**, or blamed her mother for problems, **D**. **C** is incorrect because it is difficult, with so little information, to predict a depression.

42. **D. "Can you tell me more about how you feel?"**

    The best answer is **D**; this encourages open communication and will lead to discovery of more pertinent information in assessing Ms. King's needs. **A** and **B** are questions that could be answered "yes" or "no" and are therefore inappropriate. **C** is premature; the nurse does *not* yet understand how Ms. King is actually feeling.

43. **C. "It must be difficult for you to feel that no one cares for you."**

    C is the correct answer; it directly acknowledges Ms. King's feelings and uses the therapeutic communication approach of restating. **A** is incorrect because the nurse cannot know how much caring others are capable of giving. **B** and **D** are both stereotyped expressions that are moralizing in tone.

44. **B. Develops rapidly due to specific physiologic deficits or increased physiologic demands.**

    B is correct; delirium is an altered state of consciousness, often acute and in most cases reversible, manifested by disorientation and confusion and induced by an interference with the metabolic processes of the neurons of the brain. The disturbed metabolism may involve a decreased supply of oxygen and other nutrients, an increased demand for nutrients and oxygen, or an interference with the enzyme processes on which the neurons depend. Neither **A** nor **C** is true in this situation. **D** is incorrect because delirium does affect judgment and discrimination.

45. **A. False sensory perceptions without actual stimuli.**

    The correct answer is **A**. False sensory perceptions with actual stimuli, **B**, are illusions. Fixed false beliefs, **C**, are delusions. Feelings of strangeness and unreality about self, **D**, is a definition for depersonalization.

46. **B. "It's 11 P.M. and you are in a hospital being treated for a stomach problem."**

    B is correct because this response helps to orient a client who is confused and disoriented to time and place. **A** does not point out the reality of the situation, but involves the nurse in the client's confused thought processes. **C** is false reassurance. **D** does orient the client to time but does not assist the client with reality testing.

47. **B. "Yes, but I will be back every 15–20 minutes to see how you are feeling."**

    B is the correct response. Mr. Graflin is anxious and wants the reassuring presence of the nurse. It is not possible to remain with Mr. Graflin constantly, but the nurse can let him know at what time intervals she or he will be with him. **A** is a brusque response and does not provide the client with support. **C** does not confront the client's anxiety, and **D** gives false reassurance and does not allow the client to express his feelings.

48. **C. "What did I do wrong to cause this pain?"**

    C is correct; clients often consider intense pain a punishment for real or perceived faults. Responses **A**, **B**, and **D** do not contain the element of self-blame.

49. **B. Relieve moderate pain for 4–5 hours.**

    B is correct; morphine sulfate is effective in relieving moderate to severe pain for 4–5 hours. **A** is incorrect because morphine sulfate is active for a longer period. **C** is incorrect because the major side effect of morphine sulfate is respiratory depression, not hypotension. **D** is incorrect; since Mr. Graflin is experiencing moderate to severe pain, morphine *will* be effective in relieving his pain.

50. **D. Denial.**

    D is the correct answer. Denial is a psychological defense mechanism that temporarily protects the client from the full impact of the illness. Undoing, **A**, is the performance of a specific action that is the opposite of a previous, unacceptable action or that is felt by the person to neutralize or undo the original action. Fantasy, **B**, is an image formed by recombining one's memories and interpretations of them. Rationalization, **C**, is finding "good reasons" to substitute for the real reasons for one's behavior.

51. **A. A strong need for protection may cause a client to hear only what he wishes to hear.**

    The correct answer is **A**. The experience of cardiac arrest is overwhelming; the client needs some "protection" for his ego so that he can incorporate the experience in a way that his psychological self can handle. Denial assists in this process and is adaptive at this point. **B** is incorrect because at this time Mr. Mansfield does not have a realistic perception of his problem. *C* is incorrect because Mr. Mansfield's manner of coping is not at this time pathologic, but adaptive. *D* is incorrect because denial does not allow a person to experience the full impact of his illness.

52. *D. "Sometimes it takes a while before a person can really think about what has happened."*

D is correct because this response talks about the denial process and attempts to communicate with the client at his level. *A* is incorrect; although it is a reflective statement, it responds to the content of the communication, not to the underlying meaning. *B* and *C* talk about feelings but do not confront the reality the client is experiencing. He is worried but is unable to express the worry at this time.

53. *B. Loss of a peer group.*

B is the correct choice; Mr. Saunders lost the peer group with which he associated daily for 38 years. The data in the case situation are insufficient to verify *A* and *C* as reasons for poor adjustment. *D* is incorrect because at the age of 64, a person is indeed capable of new learning.

54. *B. Ego integrity.*

B is correct. The developmental task for the older age group is ego integrity, the ability to look at one's life and be satisfied with one's accomplishments. The task of generativity, *A*, occurs in the middle adult years. The task of industry, *C*, is accomplished during the school-age years. The task of autonomy, *D*, occurs during the early toddler years.

55. *D. Joining a men's political interest group.*

D is correct; the men's political interest group can begin to replace the lost occupational peer group. Helping his wife with the housework, *A*, will not widen Mr. Saunders's social world. Reading and watching television, *B* and *C*, are solitary activities that will not aid in Mr. Saunders's resocialization.

56. *B. Who else he can rely on for support.*

B is the correct choice; in providing crisis intervention, it is imperative to know what other individuals or resources are available to provide support to the client. Information about *A*, *C*, and *D* can be useful, but is not *initially* important.

57. *B. Denial.*

The correct choice is *B*; the client is denying his real feelings relating to his wife's death. *A*, *C*, and *D* are also defense mechanisms, but do not describe the dynamics of this situation.

58. *C. Mr. Graham can begin to face his problems with the nurse.*

C is the correct answer; the client's ability to begin developing awareness of his problems is an integral step in the success of a therapeutic relationship. Choices *A* and *B* are incorrect because they focus on the nurse; in addition, *B* suggests that the nurse analyze behavior, which is *not* a nursing function. *D* is not a good choice because the client may set a totally unrealistic pace for his therapy at this time.

59. *D. Sensory deprivation.*

D is correct. Ms. O'Neil is experiencing the effects of sensory deprivation brought on by the surgery for removal of a cataract, cataracts in her unoperated eye, and reduced ability to interpret environmental cues due to the night hour. *A* is incorrect; sensory overload is the opposite experience, and Ms. O'Neil is definitely not being overstimulated. *B*, senility, is a chronic brain syndrome with slow onset; since Ms. O'Neil was active and alert before her hospitalization, this choice is incorrect. There are no data in the case situation to support the diagnosis of acute brain syndrome, *C*.

60. *C. Hypnagogic states cause increased susceptibility to the effects of sensory restriction.*

C is correct. The reason more clients exhibit behavioral changes due to sensory restriction at night is the difficulty in interpreting environmental cues in dimmer light and the factors of fatigue and early sleep stages. *A* is incorrect because the intensity of sensory stimuli is usually *decreased* at night. *B* is incorrect because nurses usually have more direct contacts with clients during the day than at night. *D* is only partially true; the quietness of the unit at night increases the problem of sensory restriction, but it does not totally account for the differences in Ms. O'Neil's daytime and nighttime behavior.

61. *C. Placing Ms. O'Neil in a private room.*

C is the ineffective nursing measure and therefore the best answer. Isolating Ms. O'Neil in a private room will only add to the effects of sensory restriction. *A*, *B*, and *D* all provide meaningful stimuli for Ms. O'Neil.

62. *C. Assign Mr. Roland a task he can learn in a short period of time.*

Self-esteem comes from achieving mastery of self and the environment. *C* helps him to achieve mastery by providing a task in which he must do something to achieve success, preferably something easily learned in a short period to provide immediate gratification. *A* takes away his initiative and reinforces the notion that he cannot do things for himself. *B* has no long-standing effect because he did nothing to achieve these physical attributes. *D* is inappropriate because it tends to infantilize him and reinforce his feelings of helplessness.

63. *D. Intimacy.*

According to Erikson's Eight Stages of Man, Mr. Roland is facing the task of establishing intimacy with the opposite sex. *A* is incorrect because given his history (having a previous girlfriend), he has already achieved his sex-role identity. *B* and *C* are unwarranted assumptions given the data and the scene observed by the nurse.

64. **A. Offer a limited set of alternatives to Ms. Sola.**

Ms. Sola is afraid to make a decision for fear of making the wrong choice. Limiting the number of choices enhances decision-making ability. *B*, *C*, and *D* do not facilitate decision making but only increase Ms. Sola's anxiety about what to do.

65. **D. Conflict.**

Ms. Sola is in an approach-avoidance conflict. As she moves toward being discharged, her fear of rejection by her friends becomes heightened. The more she wants to leave, the more she wants to stay—two mutually exclusive goals. *A* is experienced when a person is blocked from reaching one goal. *B* is a state in which no positive goals can be envisioned for the future. *C* is the inability to achieve a desired goal through one's own efforts.

66. **C. Take medication as prescribed and attend therapy sessions.**

The most common cause of recidivism in mental disorders is that clients stop taking their medication after discharge as soon as they begin to feel "better" or "more like themselves." Medication without supportive therapy, however, is rarely sufficient to promote optimal health. *A* is inappropriate and unnecessary for Ms. Sola's developmental stage and situation. *B* may cause too many stresses initially without available support systems, but it is an alternative she might consider in a few months. *D* is incorrect. Medication should be discontinued only under medical supervision, most often gradually. Also, therapy sessions, while open-ended, may be needed for no more than a few months or years—not indefinitely.

67. **D. Mr. Frankel is angry and is trying to gain some control over his situation.**

In *D*, Mr. Frankel, feeling powerless, is venting his anger onto the nurse in an effort to influence her actions and to gain some control over himself and his environment. *A* is incorrect; his anger is *displaced*, not personal—he is angry at his helplessness, not directly at the person who is helping him. *B* is partially correct; he feels misunderstood, but his outburst is meant not to clarify but to express his feelings. *C* is partially correct; he is trying to get what he needs—inner and outer control—but he does not really want to be left alone and helpless. This is testing behavior.

68. **C. Confront his behavior to give feedback about her reactions.**

Clients with Mr. Frankel's condition often use verbal means to express their sexuality when they are incapable of acting out their sexual needs. *C* is correct because Mr. Frankel may be testing his masculinity and sexual appeal to a woman, without being aware of his effect on the woman. This is especially true if the nurse attempts to conceal her adverse reactions or feelings of anger and disgust. Giving honest feedback can clarify feelings and reactions without rejecting the client. *A* and *D* avoid taking responsibility and reject the *client*, rather than the *behavior*. *B* is an ineffective means of avoiding the issue.

69. **A. "What are some of the reasons for considering this now?"**

A opens communication—to explore feelings and thoughts and to get and give information—without making judgments. *B* closes off communication and avoids responsibility. *C* induces guilt and shifts the focus away from Mr. Frankel's thoughts and feelings. *D* also closes off communication and assumes decision-making power that rightfully belongs to Mr. Frankel and his fiancée.

70. **B. Displacement of anxious feelings from the real source to a symbolic one.**

Ms. Uma has displaced her unconscious fears (of failing in her roles), which she cannot control, onto a situation that she can control—leaving the house. Remaining at home may symbolize safety to Ms. Uma. *A*, *C*, and *D* are other coping mechanisms. *A* is replacing one activity with another that is more socially accepted or esteemed, for example, philanthropy rather than business deals. *C* is consciously pushing disturbing or anxious thoughts into the subconscious, from which they may be recalled with relative ease. *D* is the use of logic and reason to explain thoughts and actions in a more socially acceptable way. Also note that Ms. Uma's fears have some basis in reality but are totally out of proportion to that reality.

71. **A. "I hear you, but that sounds like a big step. How about going some place nearer to home the first time out?"**

A acknowledges Mr. Uma's feelings and makes a practical suggestion. The most successful techniques for dealing with phobias involve gradual desensitization to the fearful stimuli, in small steps. *B* is likely to cause Ms. Uma to feel rejected and more isolated by her spouse (principal support). *C* is false; this is *not* a typical reaction to motherhood, although the feelings to a lesser degree may be common among mothers. *D* acknowledges the husband's feelings but aligns the nurse with the husband against the wife.

72. **B. Explore her anxious feelings.**

Ms. Uma's fear is related to her anxiety about how she performs her roles and how her performance affects her self-esteem. Exploring when she feels anxious and what she does to relieve her anxiety may give clues to the unconscious cause of her phobia. *A* may be helpful in the long run but does not deal with the painful feelings of the *present*, or her need for some relief. *C* may be appropriate in the future but *ignores* the present situation. *D* encourages Ms. Uma to deny her feelings, further represses her anxiety, and closes off communication.

73. ***D. Rivalry with siblings.***

D is a normal family dynamic. Sibling rivalry existed before the divorce and will continue until all the children learn to cooperate as well as compete with each other. Initially it should be anticipated that there may even be an increase in bids for the parents' attention until new patterns of relating become familiar and offer security. *A* suggests that the child is acting out because of the stress and cannot sustain acceptable behavior at home or school. *B* is a sign that the child may be depressed over the loss of the noncustodial parent and the "normal" family life. *C* indicates that the child is distancing from friends, perhaps because of shame, guilt, or depression.

74. ***A. Spend time on a regular basis with him on an activity they both enjoy.***

Rob's illnesses may be a reaction to the stress of his family situation, but they also may be an unconscious mechanism to get attention from his mother. *A* gives him the attention he needs in a positive way that does not reinforce his use of symptoms. *B* may be helpful in the short term but does not solve the problem of having time with his mother. *C* is not necessary; he has been followed by his pediatrician. *D* may not be economically feasible; his older sisters could help him with his schoolwork. His grades may improve when his other needs are met at home.

75. ***B. Ms. Kelleher establishes a close, meaningful attachment to another person.***

An attachment bond exists between spouses despite the quality of the marital relationship. However, unless a new attachment is formed, strong emotional bonds to the former spouse interfere with reorganization of a new life for the parent, which filters down to the next generation. With *A*, the couple achieves a legal divorce but not necessarily an emotional divorce. *C* is unrealistic because Ms. Kelleher has a short work history and few marketable skills for a managerial position. *D* will help to reestablish relations with the children but may cause difficulties for Ms. Kelleher until she invests in someone else.

76. ***D. "I can't expect the children to take care of me and the house."***

With chronic illness, clients must learn to accept their dependency on others during bouts of illness and to reassert their independence during remissions. *D* suggests that she cannot relinquish her role responsibilities to others despite the serious functional limitations of her legitimate illness. *A* and *B* give appropriate acknowledgement of her symptoms, that she sees herself as being sick. *C* is appropriate sick role behavior, to seek medical help. *A*, *B*, and *C* are behaviors representative of the components of Parson's Sick Role Theory.

77. *C. Ms. Parisi is having difficulty asking for the help that she needs.*

In an effort to maintain control and to avoid potential helplessness, many clients who are chronically ill try to normalize their life-style so that others will not reject them. They learn to do things differently, or to do different things, rather than depend on others for help. Other ways to cope with chronic illness are *A*, seeking secondary gains from others by exaggerating; *B*, refusing to accept responsibility for one's health status by projecting; and *D*, denying the efficacy of treatment by minimizing symptoms.

78. *C. Support the client's solution to the problem.*

With chronic illness, pain and other distressful symptoms are not strangers to the client. Clients develop many effective means of managing their symptoms and life-style, but often seek the nurse's support or approval of what they are doing or plan to do. To prevent unnecessary dependence, the nurse should encourage problem-solving and decision-making by the client. *A* and *D* avoid responsibility by the nurse and may be unnecessary. *B* takes decision-making power and control away from the client.

79. *C. Direct, open, and matter-of-fact.*

With all clients, but especially with clients who are suspicious\, it is important that nurses present themselves in an authentic manner, conveying interest, disclosing their motives, and stating facts in an unambiguous way. *A* conveys an attitude that some clients may find threatening and overwhelmingly close. *B* may give the client the impression that the nurse is afraid, unwilling to get involved, or disapproving. *D* is likely to engender battles for control between the client and the nurse.

80. *A. Projection.*

A is placing the blame on someone else or assigning unacceptable personal characteristics that one finds particularly objectionable in oneself to someone else. Thus, Mr. Lasalle criticizes his superior for being too critical of him. *B*, *C*, and *D* are also coping mechanisms. *B* is acting excessively in a manner that is the opposite of one's true, unconscious feelings—for example, the mother who is overprotective who really fears that she may harm her child. *C* is disowning an intolerable thought, wish, need, or reality. *D* is involuntary exclusion of painful and unacceptable thoughts and impulses from awareness (forgetting).

81. **D. Talk to Mr. Lasalle in a calm voice, giving him space.**

Mr. Lasalle is in a situation in which he has lost control. It is important for the nurse to convey confidence that she can exert control over the situation without rejecting the client. Her presence and calm manner may help to deescalate tension. *A* may allow Mr. Lasalle to become more out of control and to harm himself or his roommate. *B* may not be a viable alternative unless the nurse has additional help; the principle is to use the minimum amount of restraint necessary to control the situation effectively. *C* is not effective; clients who are angry, in emotional turmoil, and acting out of control can rarely respond to reason and logic. Simple, direct commands are more effective—for example, "Stop shouting, Mr. Lasalle. Listen to me."

82. **C. Decline his invitation and set limits on spending time with him.**

C recognizes that Mr. Dempsey is trying to manipulate the nurse into meeting his needs for attention and special favors at the expense of the nurse's integrity. Setting limits deals with the testing behavior by asserting control without rejecting the client. *A* ignores the behavior, which will provoke more limit testing by Mr. Dempsey. *B* is dishonest and avoids the problem, rather than working to resolve it. *D* is punitive and rejects the client without taking responsibility for setting limits.

83. **A. His lack of empathy for others.**

A, *B*, *C*, and *D* are all characteristics of the narcissistic personality. *A* is the most difficult to deal with because this makes mutually satisfying relationships impossible. Without the ability to recognize and experience how others feel, the person who is narcissistic alienates all with whom he or she comes in contact; relationships are disturbed or cannot be sustained.

84. **B. Clear communication to promote consistency.**

B is the key to success because Mr. Dempsey's strategy will most likely be to "divide and conquer"—to attempt to play one staff member against another to get his way. *A*, *C*, and *D* may also contribute to the success of the plan but are not sufficient in themselves to set and enforce necessary limits on manipulative behavior.

85. **B. Her complaints evoke feelings of helplessness.**

B is correct because Ms. West's needs are insatiable. No amount of reassurance and attention is enough to satisfy her needs for security and love, no matter what the staff say or do. This causes feelings of helplessness in the staff that affect their self-esteem and need to be competent. *A* is false; pain is subjective and is *always* real to the client. *C* may be true, but this is not a primary problem for delivering nursing care. *D* is false; given the right care and treatment, Ms. West's hypochondriacal reaction can be cured and she can learn to gratify her needs in other ways.

86. **D. Respond with interest when she talks about subjects other than her symptoms.**

    Clients like Ms. West use their illness as a means of getting attention, a secondary gain of illness. *D* is the best approach because it gives positive reinforcement to a desirable behavior that will get her the attention she wants and deserves. *A*, *B*, and *C* are rejecting of the client and will probably cause her to increase her symptomatic behavior—to try harder to get more attention by having more symptoms.

87. **A. Functional disability without organicity.**

    A is correct because the client continues to have an unrealistic fear that disease persists despite medical reassurance, and the preoccupation with symptoms causes impairment in social and occupational functioning in the absence of organic pathology. *B* is characteristic of dissociative reaction, in which the disorder in physical functioning symbolizes a psychological conflict or need. *C* is characterized by psychophysiologic diseases, in which a chronic state of expression of emotion produces physiologic damage, for example, ulcers, asthma. *D* is characteristic of some types of schizophrenia, where the false, fixed belief in the presence of disease cannot be corrected by logic.

88. **C. "We care and we're here to help you and your husband."**

    This responds to the underlying message that Ms. Tully perceives herself to be a worthless burden and tries to acknowledge her feelings but also offers help and hope. *A* also conveys caring but accepts the client's assessment and does *not* offer hope. *B* ignores the process or latent content and applies authoritarian pressure to behave differently. *D* has the effect of *increasing* Ms. Tully's guilt feelings.

89. **D. Discussing their feelings in a joint session with both of them.**

    D provides the opportunity for Mr. and Mrs. Tully to open communication and share feelings with the support of a caring person who will not take sides. *A* and *B* evade responsibility and avoid the issue. *C* is a violation of confidentiality, perpetuates the breakdown in communication between Mr. and Ms. Tully, and places the nurse in a triangle coalition against Ms. Tully.

90. **D. Remain quietly at the bedside with the couple.**

It is most important to offer support and consolation to Mr. Tully at this time, preferably in a way that does not violate Ms. Tully's rights. It is also necessary to continue to observe Ms. Tully's condition. *A* and *C* are unnecessary actions and they ignore the wishes of Ms. Tully. *B* encourages Mr. Tully to make decisions at a time when he may not be ready or capable.

III. Coding Tables and Summary Grids

Introduction

The coding tables and summary grids on the following pages are useful study aids. The coding tables identify which areas of expertise each critical-thinking exercise in each chapter tests. Each question is coded for:

- Nursing process

- Client need

- Cognitive level

- Human function

- Client subneed

After you complete the critical-thinking exercises in each chapter and identify any you missed, circle their numbers on the coding table for the appropriate chapter. Then use the summary grids to tally the number of questions you missed in each coding category.

For example, you will find the codes for the chapter on Children and Adolescents on page 429. If you missed question 1, circle its number in the coding table. You will see that the codes for question 1 are PL, IV, AP, HF-7, Health promotion and maintenance. Turn to the summary grid for the chapter on Children and Adolescents on page 450 and put a tick mark in the "planning" box for Nursing Process; put a tick mark in the "IV" box for Client Need; put a tick mark in the "application" box in the Cognitive Level grid; and put a tick mark in the "HF-7" box in the fourth grid; and put a tick mark in the Health Promotion and Maintenance box for Client "Subneed" in the fifth grid.

When you have finished filling in the grids for all the questions you answered incorrectly in a chapter, **you will be able to see at a glance whether there are patterns to the kinds of questions you missed.** Perhaps you missed a number of questions coded HF-8. This tells you that you should spend some time reviewing information on elimination (HF-8) in your textbooks.

See "Typical Test Designs" (pp. 39–49) for an explanation of nursing process (five steps of the nursing process) (pp. 44-46), client need (pp. 43-44), cognitive level (p. 42), categories of human function (pp. 46-49), and client needs and client subneeds (pp. 43-44).

The abbreviations on pages 427–428 are used in the coding tables and summary grids.

Reference Code Abbreviations

- **Nursing Process** (see pp. 14–16, 44–46 for further details):

    Assessment (AS)

    Analysis (AN)

    Planning (PL)

    Implementation (IM)

    Evaluation (EV)

- **Client Needs** (see below also for Client Subneeds and pp. 43–44 for futher details):

    Safe, effective care environment (I):
      Management of care; Safety and infection control

    Physiological integrity (II):
      Basic care and comfort, Reduction of risk potential,
      Pharmacological and parenteral therapies, Physiological
      adaptation

    Psychosocial integrity (III)

    Health promotion and maintenance (IV)

- **Cognitive Level** (see p. 42 for further details):

    Application (AP)

    Analysis (AN)

    Recall/Knowledge (RE)

    Comprehension (COM)

    Synthesis (SYN)

    Evaluation (EV)

- **Human Function** (see pp. 46–49 for further details):

    HF-1: Protective functions

    HF-2: Sensory-perceptual functions

    HF-3: Comfort, rest, activity, and mobility

    HF-4: Nutrition

    HF-5: Growth and development

    HF-6: Fluid-gas transport

    HF-7: Psychosocial-cultural functions

    HF-8: Elimination

- **Client Subneeds** (see pp. 43–44 for further details):

    1: Management of care

    2: Safety and infection control

    3: Basic care and comfort

    4: Pharmacological and parenteral therapies

    5: Reduction of risk potential

    6: Physiological adaptation

12. Coding Tables

Children and Adolescents

Question Number	Nursing Process	Client Need	Cognitive Level	Human Function	Client Subneed
1	PL	IV	AP	7	Health promotion and maintenance
2	IM	I	AP	4	Health promotion and maintenance
3	IM	IV	RE	1	Health promotion and maintenance
4	IM	II	AP	1	Physiological adaptation
5	IM	IV	AP	1	Health promotion and maintenance
6	AS	IV	COM	5	Health promotion and maintenance
7	IM	II	AN	1	Safety and infection control
8	IM	II	AP	3	Health promotion and maintenance
9	IM	IV	AP	5	Health promotion and maintenance
10	IM	II	AP	1	Pharmacological and parenteral therapies
11	AN	III	AN	7	Psychosocial integrity
12	AN	I	AN	1	Management of care
13	PL	I	AP	2	Safety and infection control
14	AN	IV	COM	2	Health promotion and maintenance
15	AS	II	COM	2	Physiological adaptation
16	PL	I	AP	4	Management of care
17	IM	IV	AP	5	Health promotion and maintenance
18	IM	III	COM	1	Reduction of risk potential
19	PL	II	AP	1	Physiological adaptation
20	AS	IV	COM	5	Health promotion and maintenance
21	PL	II	AP	1	Reduction of risk potential
22	IM	IV	AP	1	Health promotion and maintenance
23	IM	IV	AP	1	Health promotion and maintenance
24	AN	II	COM	1	Reduction of risk potential
25	IM	III	AP	7	Psychosocial integrity
26	AN	IV	AP	1	Health promotion and maintenance
27	AS	II	AP	8	Basic care and comfort
28	AN	I	AN	6	Physiological adaptation
29	IM	II	AP	6	Pharmacological and parenteral therapies

Children and Adolescents

Question Number	Nursing Process	Client Need	Cognitive Level	Human Function	Client Subneed
30	IM	I	AP	3	Safety and infection control
31	IM	IV	AP	8	Basic care and comfort
32	IM	II	COM	4	Basic care and comfort
33	IM	IV	AP	5	Health, promotion and maintenance
34	IM	I	AP	2	Safety and infection control
35	IM	III	AP	7	Psychosocial integrity
36	AS	IV	COM	5	Health promotion and maintenance
37	IM	III	AP	7	Psychosocial integrity
38	IM	II	RE	1	Physiological adaptation
39	AN	II	RE	1	Physiological adaptation
40	AS	IV	AP	1	Health promotion and maintenance
41	AS	II	COM	1	Physiological adaptation
42	IM	IV	COM	1	Health promotion and maintenance
43	IM	II	AP	1	Pharmacological and parenteral therapies
44	PL	II	AP	1	Physiological adaptation
45	IM	II	AP	6	Reduction of risk potential
46	PL	II	AN	6	Pharmacological and parenteral therapies
47	IM	II	AN	6	Pharmacological and parenteral therapies
48	IM	II	AN	6	Pharmacological and parenteral therapies
49	AN	II	COM	6	Reduction of risk potential
50	EV	II	AN	6	Physiological adaptation
51	IM	III	AP	7	Psychosocial integrity
52	EV	I	AP	6	Pharmacological and parenteral therapies
53	EV	II	AP	6	Pharmacological and parenteral therapies
54	PL	I	AP	5	Management of care
55	PL	I	AP	4	Management of care
56	EV	I	EV	4	Management of care
57	IM	II	AP	7	Pharmacological and parenteral therapies
58	AN	IV	AP	5	Health promotion and maintenance
59	AN	II	RE	6	Reduction of risk potential
60	EV	II	AN	1	Reduction of risk potential
61	IM	II	COM	1	Pharmacological and parenteral therapies
62	AN	II	AP	6	Physiological adaptation
63	AN	II	AN	6	Reduction of risk potential
64	AN	II	SYN	6	Pharmacological and parenteral therapies
65	AN	II	AN	6	Physiological adaptation
66	IM	II	SYN	4	Basic care and comfort
67	AN	II	COM	6	Physiological adaptation
68	AN	II	AN	6	Physiological adaptation
69	PL	IV	EV	5	Health promotion and maintenance

Children and Adolescents

Question Number	Nursing Process	Client Need	Cognitive Level	Human Function	Client Subneed
70	AN	IV	AN	5	Health promotion and maintenance
71	PL	IV	AP	5	Health promotion and maintenance
72	PL	II	AP	1	Reduction of risk potential
73	AN	III	RE	1	Psychosocial integrity
74	EV	III	EV	7	Psychosocial integrity
75	IM	I	AP	7	Management of care
76	PL	I	AP	7	Management of care
77	IM	I	COM	7	Management of care
78	PL	I	COM	7	Management of care
79	PL	IV	AP	5	Health promotion and maintenance
80	IM	II	AP	6	Pharmacological and parenteral therapies
81	PL	I	AP	7	Management of care
82	EV	III	EV	7	Psychosocial integrity
83	AS	I	AP	1	Safety and infection control
84	AN	I	RE	1	Safety and infection control
85	PL	I	AP	8	Safety and infection control
86	AN	II	AN	6	Reduction of risk potential
87	AS	II	COM	8	Reduction of risk potential
88	AN	II	COM	2	Physiological adaptation
89	AN	II	AN	2	Physiological adaptation
90	PL	II	AP	1	Pharmacological and parenteral therapies
91	AS	II	AP	8	Reduction of risk potential
92	AS	IV	COM	5	Health promotion and maintenance
93	IM	IV	AP	5	Health promotion and maintenance
94	AS	IV	RE	5	Health promotion and maintenance
95	IM	IV	AP	5	Health promotion and maintenance
96	AN	II	RE	6	Physiological adaptation
97	EV	II	EV	6	Reduction of risk potential
98	AS	II	COM	1	Physiological adaptation
99	IM	III	AP	7	Psychosocial integrity
100	IM	III	AP	5	Psychosocial integrity
101	AS	II	AP	1	Reduction of risk potential
102	AS	II	AN	1	Reduction of risk potential
103	IM	III	AP	5	Psychosocial integrity
104	IM	II	RE	1	Pharmacological and parenteral therapies
105	AS	II	AP	1	Physiological adaptation
106	PL	II	AP	1	Reduction of risk potential
107	IM	II	AP	4	Basic care and comfort
108	AN	II	AP	1	Pharmacological and parenteral therapies
109	IM	III	AP	7	Psychosocial integrity

Children and Adolescents

Question Number	Nursing Process	Client Need	Cognitive Level	Human Function	Client Subneed
110	IM	III	AP	5	Psychosocial integrity
111	EV	IV	EV	1	Health promotion and maintenance
112	AS	I	AN	7	Management of care
113	PL	III	AN	5	Psychosocial integrity
114	IM	III	AP	1	Psychosocial integrity
115	IM	II	RE	3	Basic care and comfort
116	AN	II	AN	1	Physiological adaptation
117	IM	II	AN	1	Reduction of risk potential
118	PL	II	AP	3	Pharmacological and parenteral therapies
119	AS	II	AP	6	Reduction of risk potential
120	IM	II	AP	4	Basic care and comfort
121	PL	III	AP	5	Psychosocial integrity
122	AN	I	AN	1	Management of care
123	IM	III	AP	5	Psychosocial integrity
124	IM	III	AP	7	Psychosocial integrity
125	AN	III	SYN	7	Psychosocial integrity
126	IM	IV	AP	7	Health promotion and maintenance
127	IM	II	AP	6	Physiological adaptation
128	PL	II	AP	6	Physiological adaptation
129	IM	I	SYN	5	Management of care
130	AS	II	COM	6	Physiological adaptation
131	AN	II	AN	6	Physiological adaptation
132	IM	II	AN	1	Pharmacological and parenteral therapies
133	IM	IV	AP	5	Health promotion and maintenance
134	IM	II	AN	6	Physiological adaptation
135	AN	IV	AP	6	Health promotion and maintenance
136	AN	II	AN	6	Physiological adaptation
137	AN	I	AN	6	Management of care
138	AN	II	AN	1	Physiological adaptation
139	IM	II	COM	3	Physiological adaptation
140	PL	IV	SYN	5	Health promotion and maintenance
141	IM	II	AP	7	Pharmacological and parenteral therapies
142	PL	II	AP	3	Basic care and comfort
143	AN	IV	AN	5	Health promotion and maintenance
144	PL	II	SYN	4	Reduction of risk potential
145	EV	II	EV	1	Pharmacological and parenteral therapies
146	EV	II	EV	6	Physiological adaptation
147	PL	II	AP	1	Pharmacological and parenteral therapies
148	PL	II	AN	6	Pharmacological and parenteral therapies
149	PL	II	AP	6	Pharmacological and parenteral therapies

Children and Adolescents

Question Number	Nursing Process	Client Need	Cognitive Level	Human Function	Client Subneed
150	IM	II	SYN	5	Basic care and comfort
151	IM	I	AP	1	Management of care
152	AN	II	SYN	6	Reduction of risk potential
153	AS	II	AP	6	Pharmacological and parenteral therapies
154	IM	II	AP	3	Basic care and comfort
155	IM	I	AP	7	Management of care
156	AN	II	AN	6	Reduction of risk potential
157	IM	II	AP	1	Pharmacological and parenteral therapies
158	AN	III	COM	7	Psychosocial integrity
159	EV	II	EV	1	Pharmacological and parenteral therapies
160	EV	III	EV	7	Psychosocial integrity
161	AS	II	COM	3	Physiological adaptation
162	AS	II	EV	3	Reduction of risk potential
163	IM	IV	AP	3	Health promotion and maintenance
164	AN	IV	AP	5	Health promotion and maintenance
165	EV	IV	AP	3	Health promotion and maintenance
166	IM	II	AP	3	Physiological adaptation
167	IM	III	AP	7	Psychosocial integrity
168	IM	IV	AP	1	Health promotion and maintenance
169	IM	IV	AP	7	Health promotion and maintenance
170	EV	IV	EV	7	Health promotion and maintenance
171	AN	II	COM	4	Physiological adaptation
172	EV	II	EV	4	Physiological adaptation
173	AN	II	AN	1	Physiological adaptation
174	AS	II	AN	4	Physiological adaptation
175	AN	II	AN	4	Physiological adaptation
176	EV	II	EV	4	Basic care and comfort
177	IM	IV	AP	7	Health promotion and maintenance
178	IM	III	AP	7	Psychosocial integrity
179	PL	IV	AN	1	Health promotion and maintenance
180	IM	II	SYN	4	Reduction of risk potential

Young Adults and Reproductive Years

Question Number	Nursing Process	Client Need	Cognitive Level	Human Function	Client Subneed
1	PL	IV	AP	5	Health promotion and maintenance
2	AS	IV	RE	5	Health promotion and maintenance
3	AN	IV	RE	5	Health promotion and maintenance
4	AN	IV	AP	5	Health promotion and maintenance
5	AS	IV	RE	5	Health promotion and maintenance
6	AN	II	RE	6	Pharmacological and parenteral therapies
7	AS	I	AP	1	Safety and infection control
8	AN	I	RE	1	Safety and infection control
9	AN	II	RE	1	Physiological adaptation
10	AN	I	AP	1	Safety and infection control
11	IM	III	AP	7	Psychosocial integrity
12	PL	IV	AP	1	Health promotion and maintenance
13	EV	III	AP	5	Health promotion and maintenance
14	EV	IV	EV	5	Health promotion and maintenance
15	EV	IV	EV	5	Health promotion and maintenance
16	IM	IV	AP	3	Health promotion and maintenance
17	EV	IV	EV	7	Health promotion and maintenance
18	AN	IV	AN	5	Health promotion and maintenance
19	IM	II	AP	4	Basic care and comfort
20	IM	II	AP	4	Basic care and comfort
21	IM	II	AP	4	Basic care and comfort
22	PL	II	RE	4	Basic care and comfort
23	AN	IV	AN	5	Health promotion and maintenance
24	AN	IV	AP	4	Health promotion and maintenance
25	IM	II	AP	4	Basic care and comfort
26	EV	IV	EV	5	Health promotion and maintenance
27	IM	II	AP	4	Basic care and comfort
28	IM	II	AP	4	Pharmacological and parenteral therapies
29	PL	IV	COM	7	Health promotion and maintenance
30	AN	II	COM	3	Basic care and comfort
31	AN	III	AN	7	Psychosocial integrity
32	IM	II	AP	5	Reduction of risk potential
33	AS	II	AN	1	Reduction of risk potential
34	IM	III	AP	7	Psychosocial integrity
35	PL	III	RE	5	Health promotion and maintenance
36	AN	I	AN	7	Management of care
37	IM	II	AP	1	Basic care and comfort
38	AN	II	COM	6	Physiological adaptation
39	AS	III	AP	7	Psychosocial integrity
40	EV	IV	EV	5	Health promotion and maintenance

Young Adults and Reproductive Years

Question Number	Nursing Process	Client Need	Cognitive Level	Human Function	Client Subneed
41	AS	III	COM	5	Psychosocial integrity
42	AN	II	AN	3	Basic care and comfort
43	AN	IV	COM	5	Health promotion and maintenance
44	AS	IV	RE	5	Health promotion and maintenance
45	IM	II	COM	5	Reduction of risk potential
46	PL	IV	AP	5	Health promotion and maintenance
47	AN	IV	AP	5	Health promotion and maintenance
48	PL	II	RE	5	Physiological adaptation
49	PL	II	AP	3	Basic care and comfort
50	AN	II	AN	4	Physiological adaptation
51	IM	III	COM	5	Health promotion and maintenance
52	AN	IV	AN	5	Health promotion and maintenance
53	AN	IV	AN	4	Health promotion and maintenance
54	AN	IV	COM	8	Health promotion and maintenance
55	AS	III	COM	5	Psychosocial integrity
56	AN	II	AN	6	Physiological adaptation
57	IM	II	AP	8	Pharmacological and parenteral therapies
58	IM	II	AP	8	Basic care and comfort
59	IM	II	AP	4	Basic care and comfort
60	IM	II	AP	4	Basic care and comfort
61	PL	IV	RE	5	Health promotion and maintenance
62	AN	II	AN	4	Physiological adaptation
63	IM	III	AP	7	Psychosocial integrity
64	PL	III	AP	5	Health promotion and maintenance
65	IM	IV	AP	8	Health promotion and maintenance
66	AN	I	AN	4	Management of care
67	AN	II	AP	4	Reduction of risk potential
68	AN	II	AN	6	Physiological adaptation
69	AN	II	AN	5	Physiological adaptation
70	AN	II	AN	5	Physiological adaptation
71	AN	IV	AN	4	Health promotion and maintenance
72	AN	IV	AN	4	Health promotion and maintenance
73	PL	IV	AP	4	Health promotion and maintenance
74	AN	II	AN	4	Reduction of risk potential
75	PL	II	AP	4	Basic care and comfort
76	IM	II	AP	4	Basic care and comfort
77	AN	II	AN	6	Physiological adaptation
78	IM	IV	AN	4	Health promotion and maintenance
79	PL	I	AP	7	Management of care
80	AN	I	AN	7	Management of care

Young Adults and Reproductive Years

Question Number	Nursing Process	Client Need	Cognitive Level	Human Function	Client Subneed
81	AN	II	AN	5	Physiological adaptation
82	AS	II	AP	6	Physiological adaptation
83	PL	I	AP	2	Safety and infection control
84	IM	I	AP	2	Management of care
85	AS	II	COM	2	Pharmacological and parenteral therapies
86	IM	II	COM	1	Pharmacological and parenteral therapies
87	IM	II	AP	6	Pharmacological and parenteral therapies
88	AN	II	AN	6	Reduction of risk potential
89	AS	II	COM	3	Reduction of risk potential
90	AN	I	AP	1	Management of care
91	AN	IV	COM	5	Health promotion and maintenance
92	AN	II	COM	4	Basic care and comfort
93	PL	IV	AP	3	Health promotion and maintenance
94	IM	III	AP	7	Psychosocial integrity
95	EV	IV	EV	7	Health promotion and maintenance
96	AN	IV	COM	5	Health promotion and maintenance
97	IM	IV	COM	5	Health promotion and maintenance
98	IM	IV	COM	5	Health promotion and maintenance
99	IM	IV	COM	5	Health promotion and maintenance
100	PL	IV	AP	5	Health promotion and maintenance
101	AS	IV	AN	5	Health promotion and maintenance
102	AN	II	AN	5	Reduction of risk potential
103	IM	IV	AP	5	Health promotion and maintenance
104	AN	IV	AN	7	Health promotion and maintenance
105	AN	IV	AN	5	Health promotion and maintenance
106	AN	IV	AN	5	Health promotion and maintenance
107	AS	IV	AN	5	Health promotion and maintenance
108	IM	III	AP	7	Psychosocial integrity
109	IM	IV	AP	5	Health promotion and maintenance
110	IM	II	AP	5	Reduction of risk potential
111	EV	II	EV	5	Reduction of risk potential
112	AN	IV	AP	5	Health promotion and maintenance
113	AN	IV	AN	5	Health promotion and maintenance
114	AS	II	AP	6	Physiological adaptation
115	AS	II	AN	6	Reduction of risk potential
116	IM	I	AP	7	Management of care
117	IM	I	COM	1	Management of care
118	EV	II	EV	6	Reduction of risk potential
119	EV	I	EV	7	Management of care
120	AN	IV	AP	5	Health promotion and maintenance

Young Adults and Reproductive Years

Question Number	Nursing Process	Client Need	Cognitive Level	Human Function	Client Subneed
121	PL	II	AP	3	Basic care and comfort
122	EV	II	AN	5	Reduction of risk potential
123	EV	II	SYN	6	Physiological adaptation
124	AN	II	AN	6	Physiological adaptation
125	IM	II	AP	6	Pharmacological and parenteral therapies
126	PL	IV	AP	4	Health promotion and maintenance
127	AN	II	COM	4	Pharmacological and parenteral therapies
128	AN	IV	COM	6	Health promotion and maintenance
129	AS	III	RE	7	Psychosocial integrity
130	IM	III	AP	7	Psychosocial integrity
131	AN	II	AN	6	Physiological adaptation
132	AS	II	RE	6	Physiological adaptation
133	AS	II	AP	6	Physiological adaptation
134	AS	II	AP	6	Physiological adaptation
135	IM	II	AP	3	Basic care and comfort
136	IM	II	SYN	5	Reduction of risk potential
137	AN	II	COM	5	Physiological adaptation
138	IM	IV	RE	5	Health promotion and maintenance
139	IM	IV	COM	5	Health promotion and maintenance
140	AN	IV	RE	5	Health promotion and maintenance
141	PL	IV	RE	3	Health promotion and maintenance
142	AN	IV	AN	5	Health promotion and maintenance
143	IM	IV	AP	7	Health promotion and maintenance
144	AS	IV	RE	5	Health promotion and maintenance
145	IM	II	RE	5	Reduction of risk potential
146	EV	II	SYN	5	Reduction of risk potential
147	EV	II	AP	5	Physiological adaptation
148	AN	IV	AN	5	Health promotion and maintenance
149	AN	III	AN	7	Psychosocial integrity
150	AS	II	RE	6	Physiological adaptation
151	IM	I	AP	1	Management of care
152	IM	III	AP	7	Psychosocial integrity
153	EV	II	SYN	6	Reduction of risk potential
154	AN	I	AN	1	Management of care
155	EV	II	EV	6	Physiological adaptation
156	AS	IV	AP	5	Health promotion and maintenance
157	IM	II	AN	5	Reduction of risk potential
158	IM	II	AN	8	Reduction of risk potential
159	IM	I	AP	7	Management of care
160	IM	IV	AP	7	Health promotion and maintenance

Young Adults and Reproductive Years

Question Number	Nursing Process	Client Need	Cognitive Level	Human Function	Client Subneed
161	IM	II	AP	3	Basic care and comfort
162	EV	IV	EV	5	Health promotion and maintenance
163	IM	IV	AP	3	Health promotion and maintenance
164	PL	II	AP	3	Reduction of risk potential
165	PL	III	AP	7	Psychosocial integrity
166	PL	IV	AP	7	Health promotion and maintenance
167	IM	III	AP	7	Psychosocial integrity
168	IM	III	AP	7	Psychosocial integrity
169	IM	III	AP	7	Psychosocial integrity
170	IM	IV	AP	7	Health promotion and maintenance
171	IM	II	RE	4	Basic care and comfort
172	IM	IV	RE	4	Health promotion and maintenance
173	PL	IV	AP	4	Health promotion and maintenance
174	AN	II	COM	4	Basic care and comfort
175	AN	II	AP	4	Basic care and comfort
176	AN	II	AN	1	Pharmacological and parenteral therapies
177	EV	I	EV	7	Management of care
178	AN	II	AN	1	Pharmacological and parenteral therapies
179	IM	II	AP	1	Reduction of risk potential
180	IM	IV	COM	5	Health promotion and maintenance
181	EV	IV	EV	5	Health promotion and maintenance
182	EV	IV	AN	5	Health promotion and maintenance
183	AN	IV	AN	4	Health promotion and maintenance
184	AN	IV	AN	4	Health promotion and maintenance
185	AS	IV	RE	5	Health promotion and maintenance
186	AN	IV	AP	4	Health promotion and maintenance
187	AN	IV	AP	4	Health promotion and maintenance
188	IM	II	AN	1	Reduction of risk potential
189	IM	IV	AP	4	Health promotion and maintenance
190	IM	IV	AP	4	Health promotion and maintenance
191	EV	IV	EV	4	Health promotion and maintenance
192	AN	II	RE	1	Reduction of risk potential
193	EV	IV	EV	1	Health promotion and maintenance
194	AN	II	AN	4	Basic care and comfort
195	AN	II	COM	4	Basic care and comfort
196	AN	II	RE	1	Physiological adaptation
197	EV	I	EV	7	Management of care

Adult Health Problems

Question Number	Nursing Process	Client Need	Cognitive Level	Human Function	Client Subneed
1	AN	II	COM	6	Physiological adaptation
2	AN	II	COM	4	Physiological adaptation
3	AS	II	COM	4	Physiological adaptation
4	AN	II	COM	4	Physiological adaptation
5	IM	II	AP	4	Basic care and comfort
6	IM	II	AP	4	Reduction of risk potential
7	AS	II	COM	4	Reduction of risk potential
8	PL	IV	AP	4	Health promotion and maintenance
9	EV	IV	EV	3	Health promotion and maintenance
10	EV	II	EV	1	Reduction of risk potential
11	EV	II	RE	6	Physiological adaptation
12	AN	II	AN	3	Physiological adaptation
13	PL	II	COM	3	Basic care and comfort
14	AN	II	AP	3	Basic care and comfort
15	IM	II	AP	2	Physiological adaptation
16	AS	II	RE	3	Physiological adaptation
17	AN	II	AN	1	Physiological adaptation
18	IM	II	AP	3	Basic care and comfort
19	IM	IV	AP	1	Health promotion and maintenance
20	EV	II	EV	3	Physiological adaptation
21	AN	II	RE	4	Basic care and comfort
22	AS	II	RE	1	Physiological adaptation
23	EV	II	EV	1	Management of care
24	IM	II	RE	1	Physiological adaptation
25	PL	II	RE	1	Pharmacological and parenteral therapies
26	EV	II	AN	6	Physiological adaptation
27	EV	II	EV	4	Basic care and comfort
28	AN	II	COM	4	Physiological adaptation
29	AS	II	COM	1	Physiological adaptation
30	AN	III	AN	7	Psychosocial integrity
31	AS	II	AN	1	Reduction of risk potential
32	AN	II	COM	8	Physiological adaptation
33	AN	I	AP	1	Safety and infection control
34	IM	II	RE	1	Pharmacological and parenteral therapies
35	AS	II	EV	3	Physiological adaptation
36	IM	II	AP	2	Physiological adaptation
37	PL	II	COM	2	Pharmacological and parenteral therapies
38	EV	II	AP	8	Physiological adaptation
39	AN	II	SYN	3	Physiological adaptation
40	IM	II	AP	1	Reduction of risk potential

Adult Health Problems

Question Number	Nursing Process	Client Need	Cognitive Level	Human Function	Client Subneed
41	IM	II	AP	1	Physiological adaptation
42	PL	II	AN	4	Basic care and comfort
43	IM	II	AP	3	Basic care and comfort
44	EV	II	EV	3	Pharmacological and parenteral therapies
45	PL	II	AP	1	Pharmacological and parenteral therapies
46	PL	II	AP	1	Basic care and comfort
47	AS	II	EV	6	Physiological adaptation
48	IM	II	AP	1	Physiological adaptation
49	EV	II	EV	3	Pharmacological and parenteral therapies
50	AN	II	AN	6	Physiological adaptation
51	IM	II	AP	1	Reduction of risk potential
52	AN	II	AN	1	Physiological adaptation
53	IM	II	AP	1	Physiological adaptation
54	AN	II	AP	1	Pharmacological and parenteral therapies
55	EV	II	EV	1	Physiological adaptation
56	PL	II	AP	6	Physiological adaptation
57	EV	II	EV	1	Physiological adaptation
58	PL	II	AP	4	Basic care and comfort
59	AS	II	AN	6	Physiological adaptation
60	IM	II	AP	1	Pharmacological and parenteral therapies
61	IM	II	AP	1	Pharmacological and parenteral therapies
62	AN	II	COM	6	Pharmacological and parenteral therapies
63	AS	II	AP	6	Physiological adaptation
64	EV	II	EV	4	Physiological adaptation
65	IM	II	AP	1	Physiological adaptation
66	AN	II	COM	4	Physiological adaptation
67	IM	II	AP	4	Physiological adaptation
68	IM	II	AP	4	Basic care and comfort
69	EV	III	EV	7	Psychosocial integrity
70	PL	II	COM	3	Reduction of risk potential
71	AS	II	RE	3	Physiological adaptation
72	IM	II	AP	1	Reduction of risk potential
73	AS	II	AN	6	Physiological adaptation
74	IM	I	AN	1	Management of care
75	IM	IV	RE	5	Health promotion and maintenance
76	IM	IV	COM	1	Health promotion and maintenance
77	IM	IV	COM	1	Health promotion and maintenance
78	IM	IV	AP	1	Health promotion and maintenance
79	IM	IV	COM	1	Health promotion and maintenance
80	IM	II	COM	1	Physiological adaptation

Adult Health Problems

Question Number	Nursing Process	Client Need	Cognitive Level	Human Function	Client Subneed
81	EV	III	EV	7	Psychosocial integrity
82	IM	II	AP	1	Physiological adaptation
83	EV	II	EV	1	Physiological adaptation
84	PL	II	RE	1	Pharmacological and parenteral therapies
85	AS	II	RE	1	Pharmacological and parenteral therapies
86	AN	II	RE	1	Pharmacological and parenteral therapies
87	AS	II	RE	1	Pharmacological and parenteral therapies
88	AN	III	AP	7	Psychosocial integrity
89	IM	III	AP	7	Psychosocial integrity
90	IM	IV	RE	1	Health promotion and maintenance
91	IM	III	AP	7	Psychosocial integrity
92	IM	II	AP	1	Pharmacological and parenteral therapies
93	PL	II	COM	1	Pharmacological and parenteral therapies
94	PL	II	AP	3	Basic care and comfort
95	AS	II	AP	1	Pharmacological and parenteral therapies
96	IM	II	AN	1	Physiological adaptation
97	IM	II	AP	6	Physiological adaptation
98	AS	I	AN	1	Safety and infection control
99	IM	II	AP	1	Pharmacological and parenteraltherapies
100	AS	II	COM	1	Reduction of risk potential
101	AS	II	AP	1	Physiological adaptation
102	AN	II	COM	6	Physiological adaptation
103	IM	II	AP	4	Basic care and comfort
104	PL	III	AP	2	Psychosocial integrity
105	AS	II	COM	8	Reduction of risk potential
106	IM	III	AP	7	Psychosocial integrity
107	AS	II	AP	6	Physiological adaptation
108	EV	II	EV	1	Physiological adaptation
109	PL	III	AP	7	Psychosocial integrity
110	IM	II	RE	4	Pharmacological and parenteral therapies
111	PL	II	RE	4	Pharmacological and parenteral therapies
112	AS	II	AP	6	Physiological adaptation
113	IM	II	AP	8	Physiological adaptation
114	AN	I	AP	1	Management of care
115	AS	II	COM	8	Physiological adaptation
116	IM	II	AP	3	Pharmacological and parenteral therapies
117	EV	II	EV	4	Basic care and comfort
118	AN	II	COM	3	Pharmacological and parenteral therapies
119	IM	II	AP	8	Reduction of risk potential
120	EV	II	EV	4	Basic care and comfort

Adult Health Problems

Question Number	Nursing Process	Client Need	Cognitive Level	Human Function	Client Subneed
121	IM	I	AP	1	Management of care
122	PL	II	AN	1	Physiological adaptation
123	IM	II	AN	6	Pharmacological and parenteral therapies
124	AN	II	AN	6	Pharmacological and parenteral therapies
125	AN	II	AN	6	Physiological adaptation
126	PL	II	AN	1	Reduction of risk potential
127	AN	I	AN	1	Management of care
128	AN	II	AP	1	Physiological adaptation
129	PL	I	AN	6	Basic care and comfort
130	IM	II	AP	6	Pharmacological and parenteral therapies
131	IM	II	AN	8	Pharmacological and parenteral therapies
132	IM	II	COM	3	Pharmacological and parenteral therapies
133	EV	II	EV	6	Reduction of risk potential
134	IM	III	AP	7	Psychosocial integrity
135	PL	II	AP	1	Pharmacological and parenteral therapies
136	IM	II	AP	4	Basic care and comfort
137	AN	II	AN	1	Pharmacological and parenteral therapies
138	IM	II	COM	4	Basic care and comfort
139	AS	II	AP	3	Physiological adaptation
140	PL	II	COM	6	Pharmacological and parenteral therapies
141	AN	IV	COM	1	Health promotion and maintenance
142	IM	II	AP	6	Physiological adaptation
143	IM	II	AP	3	Basic care and comfort
144	AN	II	AN	6	Physiological adaptation
145	IM	II	AP	4	Basic care and comfort
146	EV	II	EV	6	Basic care and comfort
147	IM	III	AP	3	Health promotion and maintenance
148	AS	II	COM	1	Reduction of risk potential
149	PL	II	AP	8	Reduction of risk potential
150	IM	II	RE	8	Pharmacological and parenteral therapies
151	EV	II	EV	8	Physiological adaptation
152	AS	II	RE	8	Reduction of risk potential
153	AN	II	AN	6	Physiological adaptation
154	PL	II	COM	1	Pharmacological and parenteral therapies
155	IM	III	AP	7	Psychosocial integrity
156	AS	II	AP	2	Reduction of risk potential
157	AS	II	COM	2	Physiological adaptation
158	IM	II	RE	2	Reduction of risk potential
159	AN	II	AN	6	Physiological adaptation
160	PL	I	AN	1	Management of care

Adult Health Problems

Question Number	Nursing Process	Client Need	Cognitive Level	Human Function	Client Subneed
161	AS	II	RE	2	Physiological adaptation
162	PL	II	AP	8	Basic care and comfort
163	EV	II	EV	4	Reduction of risk potential
164	EV	II	EV	4	Reduction of risk potential
165	EV	III	EV	7	Psychosocial integrity
166	AN	II	AN	6	Reduction of risk potential
167	EV	II	AN	6	Reduction of risk potential
168	IM	II	AN	6	Reduction of risk potential
169	AN	II	AP	3	Basic care and comfort
170	AN	II	AP	6	Pharmacological and parenteral therapies
171	PL	II	AP	6	Pharmacological and parenteral therapies
172	PL	II	AP	6	Reduction of risk potential
173	IM	II	AP	1	Pharmacological and parenteral therapies
174	AS	II	AN	1	Pharmacological and parenteral therapies
175	EV	II	EV	6	Pharmacological and parenteral therapies
176	AN	II	AN	6	Physiological adaptation
177	IM	II	AP	6	Pharmacological and parenteral therapies
178	EV	II	EV	6	Pharmacological and parenteral therapies
179	IM	II	AP	1	Pharmacological and parenteral therapies
180	EV	II	EV	4	Basic care and comfort
181	AN	II	AN	8	Reduction of risk potential
182	PL	II	COM	8	Pharmacological and parenteral therapies
183	AS	II	AP	6	Reduction of risk potential
184	IM	II	AP	4	Basic care and comfort
185	PL	II	AP	4	Basic care and comfort
186	AS	II	AP	6	Physiological adaptation
187	EV	II	EV	6	Reduction of risk potential
188	IM	II	AP	8	Pharmacological and parenteral therapies
189	EV	II	AP	3	Reduction of risk potential

Older Adults and Geriatrics

Question Number	Nursing Process	Client Need	Cognitive Level	Human Function	Client Subneed
1	AS	II	AN	6	Physiological adaptation
2	AS	II	AN	6	Reduction of risk potential
3	PL	II	AP	6	Reduction of risk potential
4	EV	II	EV	6	Pharmacological and parenteral therapies
5	AN	III	AP	7	Psychosocial integrity
6	AN	II	AN	6	Physiological adaptation
7	IM	IV	COM	6	Health promotion and maintenance
8	EV	IV	COM	6	Health promotion and maintenance
9	EV	II	EV	6	Physiological adaptation
10	IM	II	AP	8	Reduction of risk potential
11	AS	II	RE	8	Physiological adaptation
12	PL	II	COM	8	Pharmacological and parenteral therapies
13	EV	II	EV	8	Basic care and comfort
14	IM	II	AP	4	Basic care and comfort
15	AS	II	COM	4	Physiological adaptation
16	IM	II	AP	6	Reduction of risk potential
17	PL	IV	AP	7	Health promotion and maintenance
18	AN	II	COM	8	Physiological adaptation
19	EV	II	COM	8	Physiological adaptation
20	EV	IV	EV	7	Health promotion and maintenance
21	EV	II	EV	6	Reduction of risk potential
22	IM	III	AP	2	Psychosocial integrity
23	IM	II	AP	1	Basic care and comfort
24	AS	II	COM	6	Reduction of risk potential
25	IM	II	AP	2	Basic care and comfort
26	IM	II	AP	4	Basic care and comfort
27	AN	II	COM	8	Basic care and comfort
28	IM	II	AP	6	Reduction of risk potential
29	PL	II	AP	3	Reduction of risk potential
30	PL	II	AP	3	Reduction of risk potential
31	IM	II	AP	3	Reduction of risk potential
32	EV	II	EV	6	Pharmacological and parenteral therapies
33	AS	II	RE	6	Reduction of risk potential
34	AN	II	RE	6	Physiological adaptation
35	AS	II	COM	6	Reduction of risk potential
36	AS	II	COM	6	Reduction of risk potential
37	AS	II	COM	6	Physiological adaptation
38	AS	II	COM	6	Physiological adaptation
39	AS	IV	AP	3	Health promotion and maintenance
40	EV	II	AP	3	Physiological adaptation

Older Adults and Geriatrics

Question Number	Nursing Process	Client Need	Cognitive Level	Human Function	Client Subneed
41	PL	II	COM	1	Reduction of risk potential
42	PL	IV	RE	1	Health promotion and maintenance
43	IM	II	AN	6	Pharmacological and parenteral therapies
44	AN	II	AP	6	Physiological adaptation
45	IM	II	AP	1	Reduction of risk potential
46	EV	IV	EV	3	Health promotion and maintenance
47	IM	IV	AP	3	Health promotion and maintenance
48	AS	II	COM	2	Physiological adaptation
49	IM	III	AP	7	Psychosocial integrity
50	EV	IV	EV	2	Health promotion and maintenance
51	IM	IV	AP	2	Health promotion and maintenance
52	AS	II	COM	2	Physiological adaptation

Behavioral and Emotional Problems

Question Number	Nursing Process	Client Need	Cognitive Level	Human Function	Client Subneed
1	IM	III	AP	7	Psychosocial integrity
2	PL	III	AP	7	Psychosocial integrity
3	EV	III	COM	7	Psychosocial integrity
4	PL	III	AP	7	Psychosocial integrity
5	IM	III	AP	7	Psychosocial integrity
6	PL	III	RE	7	Psychosocial integrity
7	PL	IV	AP	7	Health promotion and maintenance
8	IM	III	AP	7	Psychosocial integrity
9	PL	III	AP	7	Psychosocial integrity
10	PL	III	AP	7	Psychosocial integrity
11	PL	III	RE	7	Psychosocial integrity
12	IM	III	AN	1	Psychosocial integrity
13	AS	III	RE	7	Psychosocial integrity
14	PL	III	AP	7	Psychosocial integrity
15	EV	III	AP	7	Psychosocial integrity
16	PL	II	AP	7	Pharmacological and parenteral therapies
17	PL	I	COM	7	Management of care
18	IM	III	AP	7	Psychosocial integrity
19	AN	III	AN	7	Psychosocial integrity
20	PL	III	AP	7	Psychosocial integrity
21	PL	III	AN	7	Psychosocial integrity
22	AN	III	COM	7	Psychosocial integrity
23	IM	III	AP	7	Psychosocial integrity
24	IM	III	AP	7	Psychosocial integrity
25	IM	III	AP	7	Psychosocial integrity
26	AN	III	COM	7	Psychosocial integrity
27	PL	IV	AP	7	Health promotion and maintenance
28	AN	II	AP	3	Basic care and comfort
29	PL	II	AP	3	Basic care and comfort
30	IM	II	AP	3	Basic care and comfort
31	IM	III	AP	7	Psychosocial integrity
32	IM	III	AP	7	Psychosocial integrity
33	AS	III	COM	7	Psychosocial integrity
34	AS	III	COM	7	Psychosocial integrity
35	PL	III	AP	7	Psychosocial integrity
36	IM	III	AP	7	Psychosocial integrity
37	PL	III	AP	7	Psychosocial integrity
38	PL	III	AN	7	Psychosocial integrity
39	IM	III	AP	1	Psychosocial integrity
40	IM	II	RE	7	Pharmacological and parenteral therapies

Behavioral and Emotional Problems

Question Number	Nursing Process	Client Need	Cognitive Level	Human Function	Client Subneed
41	AN	III	COM	7	Psychosocial integrity
42	AS	III	AP	7	Psychosocial integrity
43	IM	III	AP	7	Psychosocial integrity
44	AN	II	RE	2	Physiological adaptation
45	AN	III	RE	2	Psychosocial integrity
46	IM	III	AP	7	Psychosocial integrity
47	IM	III	AP	7	Psychosocial integrity
48	AN	III	COM	3	Psychosocial integrity
49	EV	II	RE	3	Pharmacological and parenteral therapies
50	AN	III	COM	7	Psychosocial integrity
51	AN	III	COM	7	Psychosocial integrity
52	IM	III	AP	7	Psychosocial integrity
53	AN	IV	AP	5	Health promotion and maintenance
54	AN	IV	RE	5	Health promotion and maintenance
55	IM	IV	AP	5	Health promotion and maintenance
56	AS	IV	AP	7	Health promotion and maintenance
57	AN	III	COM	7	Psychosocial integrity
58	EV	III	EV	7	Psychosocial integrity
59	AN	II	AP	2	Physiological adaptation
60	AN	II	AP	2	Physiological adaptation
61	IM	I	AP	2	Management of care
62	IM	III	AP	7	Psychosocial integrity
63	AN	IV	AP	5	Health promotion and maintenance
64	PL	III	AP	7	Psychosocial integrity
65	AN	III	AP	7	Psychosocial integrity
66	PL	I	EV	7	Psychosocial integrity
67	EV	III	COM	7	Psychosocial integrity
68	PL	III	AP	7	Psychosocial integrity
69	IM	III	AP	7	Psychosocial integrity
70	AN	III	COM	7	Psychosocial integrity
71	IM	III	AP	7	Psychosocial integrity
72	PL	III	AP	7	Psychosocial integrity
73	AS	IV	AN	7	Health promotion and maintenance
74	IM	IV	EV	7	Health promotion and maintenance
75	EV	III	EV	7	Psychosocial integrity
76	AS	III	EV	7	Psychosocial integrity
77	AN	III	AN	7	Psychosocial integrity
78	PL	III	AP	7	Psychosocial integrity
79	PL	III	AP	7	Psychosocial integrity
80	AN	III	COM	7	Psychosocial integrity

Behavioral and Emotional Problems

Question Number	Nursing Process	Client Need	Cognitive Level	Human Function	Client Subneed
81	PL	III	AP	7	Psychosocial integrity
82	IM	III	AP	7	Psychosocial integrity
83	AN	III	COM	7	Psychosocial integrity
84	PL	III	EV	7	Psychosocial integrity
85	AN	III	AN	7	Psychosocial integrity
86	PL	III	AP	7	Psychosocial integrity
87	AN	III	COM	7	Psychosocial integrity
88	IM	III	AP	7	Psychosocial integrity
89	PL	III	AP	7	Psychosocial integrity
90	IM	III	AP	7	Psychosocial integrity

Summary Grids

Nursing Process: Children and Adolescents

AS	AN	PL	IM	EV

Client Needs: Children and Adolescents

I	II	III	IV

Cognitive Level: Children and Adolescents

AP	AN	RE	COM	EV

See pages 427–428 for an explanation of the abbreviations used in these grids.

Human Functions: Children and Adolescents

HF-1	HF-2	HF-3	HF-4	HF-5	HF-6	HF-7	HF-8

Client Subneed: Children and Adolescents

Manage-ment of care	Safety and infection control	Basic care and comfort	Pharma-cological and parenteral therapies	Reduction of risk potential	Physio-logical adaptation

Nursing Process: Young Adult and Reproductive Years

AS	AN	PL	IM	EV

Client Needs: Young Adult and Reproductive Years

I	II	III	IV

Cognitive Level: Young Adult and Reproductive Years

AP	AN	RE	COM	EV

See pages 427–428 for an explanation of the abbreviations used in these grids.

Human Functions: Young Adult and Reproductive Years

HF-1	HF-2	HF-3	HF-4	HF-5	HF-6	HF-7	HF-8

Client Subneed: Young Adult and Reproductive Years

Manage-ment of care	Safety and infection control	Basic care and comfort	Pharma-cological and parenteral therapies	Reduction of risk potential	Physio-logical adaptation

Nursing Process: Adult Health Problems

AS	AN	PL	IM	EV

Client Needs: Adult Health Problems

I	II	III	IV

Cognitive Level: Adult Health Problems

AP	AN	RE	COM	EV

See pages 427–428 for an explanation of the abbreviations used in these grids.

Human Functions: Adult Health Problems

HF-1	HF-2	HF-3	HF-4	HF-5	HF-6	HF-7	HF-8

Client Subneed: Adult Health Problems

Manage-ment of care	Safety and infection control	Basic care and comfort	Pharma-cological and parenteral therapies	Reduction of risk potential	Physio-logical adaptation

Nursing Process: Older Adults and Geriatrics

AS	AN	PL	IM	EV

Client Needs: Older Adults and Geriatrics

I	II	III	IV

Cognitive Level: Older Adults and Geriatrics

AP	AN	RE	COM	EV

See pages 427–428 for an explanation of the abbreviations used in these grids.

Human Functions: Older Adults and Geriatrics

HF-1	HF-2	HF-3	HF-4	HF-5	HF-6	HF-7	HF-8

Client Subneed: Older Adults and Geriatrics

Management of care	Safety and infection control	Basic care and comfort	Pharmacological and parenteral therapies	Reduction of risk potential	Physiological adaptation

Nursing Process: Behavioral and Emotional Problems

AS	AN	PL	IM	EV

Client Needs: Behavioral and Emotional Problems

I	II	III	IV

Cognitive Level: Behavioral and Emotional Problems

AP	AN	RE	COM	EV

See pages 427–428 for an explanation of the abbreviations used in these grids.

Human Functions: Behavioral and Emotional Problems

HF-1	HF-2	HF-3	HF-4	HF-5	HF-6	HF-7	HF-8

Client Subneed: Behavioral and Emotional Problems

Management of care	Safety and infection control	Basic care and comfort	Pharmacological and parenteral therapies	Reduction of risk potential	Physiological adaptation

References

Children and Adolescents

Brunner L, Suddarth D. *Textbook of Medical-Surgical Nursing* (10th ed). Philadelphia: Lippincott, 2003.

Hockenberry MJ, Wilson DW, Winkelstein ML, Kline NE. *Wong's Nursing Care of Infants and Children* (7th ed). St. Louis: Mosby, 2003.

McKenry L, et al. *Pharmacology in Nursing* (21st ed). St. Louis: Mosby, 2003.

Phipps W, Monahan FD, Sands J, Marek JF, Neighbors M. *Medical-Surgical Nursing: Health and Illness Perspectives* (7th ed). St. Louis: Mosby, 2003.

Young Adult and Reproductive Years

Lowdermilk DL, Perry SE. *Maternity Nursing* (6th ed). St. Louis: Mosby, 2003.

Reeder S, Martin L, Koniak-Griffin D. *Maternity Nursing: Family, Newborn and Women's Health Care* (18th ed). Philadelphia: Lippincott.

Adults and Older Adults

Bickley LS. *Bates' Guide to Physical Examination and History-Taking* (8th ed). Philadelphia: Lippincott, 2004.

Brunner L, Suddarth D. *Textbook of Medical-Surgical Nursing* (10th ed). Philadelphia: Lippincott, 2003.

Facts and Comparisons. Drug Facts and Comparisons 2005 (59th ed) Philadelphia: Lippincott, 2004.

Fischbach F. *A Manual of Laboratory and Diagnostic Tests* (7th ed). Philadelphia: Lippincott, 2003.

McKenry L, et al. *Pharmacology in Nursing* (21st ed). St. Louis: Mosby, 2003.

Nettina, Sandra. *The Lippincott Manual of Nursing Practice* (7th ed). Philadelphia: Lippincott, 2000.

Phipps W, Monahan FD, Sands JF, Marenk, J.F., *Neighbors M. Medical-Surgical Nursing: Health and Illness Perspectives* (7th ed). St. Louis: Mosby, 2003.

Thibodeau GA., Patton KT. *Structure and Function of the Body* (12th ed). St. Louis: Mosby, 2004.

Behavioral and Emotional Problems

Aguilera DC. *Crisis Intervention* (8th ed). St. Louis: Mosby, 1998 (a *classic*).

American Psychiatric Association. *Diagnostic and Statistical Manual of Mental Disorders* (DSM-IV-TR). Washington, DC: 2000.

Stuart GW, Laraia MT. *Principles and Practice of Psychiatric Nursing* (7th ed). St. Louis: Mosby, 2001.

Wilson H, Kneisl C, Trigoboff, Eileen. *Contemporary Psychiatric-Mental Health Nursing*, Prentice Hall, 2004.

General Review of Nursing for All Age Groups

Lagerquist, Sally, et al. *Davis's NCLEX-RN® Success (2nd ed)*. Philadelphia: F.A. Davis, 2006.

Lagerquist, Sally (editor) ATI's *NurseNotes Series: 4 books + 4 CDs: Medical-Surgical, Pediatrics, Maternal-Newborn, Psychiatric-Mental Health*

Nursing Review Aids

Client Care: Reduction of Risk Potential (videocassette)
by Karen Johnson-Brennan, RN, EdD
 Three-part set: diagnostic procedures and positioning; clients with tubes; lab values.

CONTENT LECTURE TAPES
 This series includes complete review of content with sample questions and answers, with an emphasis on application of the nursing process. Available on DVD/CD-ROM, audiocassettes or videocassettes:

 Care of the Adult (6½ hours audiocassette/6 hours videocassette and 7 hours DVD/CD-ROM.)

 Behavioral and Emotional (5¼ hours audiocassette, 2½ hours videocassette and 6 hours DVD/CD-ROM).

 Childhood and Adolescence (5½ hours audiocassette, 3½ hours videocassette and 6 hours DVD/CD-ROM).

 Young Adult and Reproductive (5 hours audiocassette, 2½ hours videocassette and 6 hours DVD/CD-ROM).

Effective Test-Taking Techniques (audiocassette)
by Sally Lagerquist, RN, MS
 Causes of test-taking anxiety and what you can do about them.

ATI's How to Pass Nursing Exams: Study Skills and Test-Taking Techniques and 250 Alternate Item Questions (book) by Sally Lagerquist, RN, MS
 Includes checklist of 28 common test-taking errors (companion to *Study Skills for Nursing Students* videocassette, below).

P.A.S.S.™: Online Test
> Assess yourself with more than 1,500 questions that are directly related to the NCLEX-RN® test plan; identify your problem areas and get additional help. Answers give complete rationale. Go to *reviewfornurses.com* to assess yourself in specific areas or all subjects combined.

Relaxation Techniques (audiocassette)
by George Fuller von Bozzay, PhD
> Four classic relaxation exercises, including progressive relaxation and autogenic training.

Review of Diets for NCLEX-RN® (1 hour CD and booklet)

Review of Pharmacology for NCLEX-RN® (4½ hours CD and booklet)

Stress Management for Nurses (audiocassette) by George Fuller Von Bozzay, PhD
> Sixteen techniques for reducing stress and test-taking anxiety: Progressive Relaxation, Alternate Tension Relaxation, Breathing, Body Scan/Stress Scan, the Meadow, Use of Colors, Water Ripple, Magic Carpet, Space, Visualizing an Orange, the Elevator, Preparatory Coping Exercise, Imagining Success, Refuting Your Irrational Belief, and Thought Stopping.

Stress Management While Studying (videocassette)
by Sally Lagerquist, RN, MS
> Exercises to increase one's ability to concentrate, memorize, retain, recall information.

Study Skills for Nursing Students (videocassette)
by Sally Lagerquist, RN, MS
> How to take effective lecture notes, read text outline, and master a textbook.

Successful Test-Taking Techniques (videocassette)
by Sally Lagerquist, RN, MS
> Seven causes of test-taking anxiety with stress reduction techniques, test-taking approaches, and confidence building.

Focus on Frequent NCLEX-RN® Topics (videocassette)
by Sally Lagerquist, RN, MS
> Sample content and test questions with answers: Diet, Drugs, Toys, Positions, Tubes, Lab and Diagnostic Procedures, Communicable Diseases.

Key Concepts to Know for NCLEX-RN® (audiocassette or videocassette)
by Sally Lagerquist, RN, MS
> More sample content areas and test questions with answers in conditions affecting Fluid/Gas, Elimination, Nutrition, Growth and Development, Sensory-Perceptual, Mobility, and Psychosocial.

For information, contact:
Review for Nurses Tapes Co.
PO Box 16347
San Francisco, CA 94116
Toll Free:
800/345-PASS
In California, call:
415/731-0833

Website: reviewfornurses.com

Indexes

Index to Nursing Problems/Diagnosis

This index classifies all the case management scenarios in **Part II** by the nursing problems/diagnosis they represent. To help you find the scenarios easily, we have given both the page number on which each scenario begins and the patient's name. Use this index as a study aid, in the manner described on pages 427–428 for the reference codes.

Index to Medical Diagnosis/ Case Management Scenarios

Adult Health Problems

Older Adults and Geriatrics

Behavioral and Emotional Problems